DEVELOPMENTAL EVALUATION EXEMPLARS

Also Available

Developmental Evaluation:
Applying Complexity Concepts to Enhance Innovation and Use
Michael Quinn Patton

Developmental Evaluation Exemplars

Principles in Practice

edited by

Michael Quinn Patton
Kate McKegg
Nan Wehipeihana

THE GUILFORD PRESS
New York   London

In memory of

Brenda Zimmerman (1956–2014)

Pioneer in applying complexity science to social innovation,
coauthor of *Getting to Maybe: How the World Is Changed*,
and champion of developmental evaluation

© 2016 The Guilford Press
A Division of Guilford Publications, Inc.
370 Seventh Avenue, Suite 1200, New York, NY 10001
www.guilford.com

Printed in the United States of America

This book is printed on acid-free paper.

Last digit is print number: 9   8   7   6   5   4   3   2   1

Library of Congress Cataloging-in-Publication Data
Developmental evaluation exemplars : principles in practice / edited by
Michael Quinn Patton, Kate McKegg, Nan Wehipeihana.
   pages cm
 Includes bibliographical references and index.
 ISBN 978-1-4625-2296-5 (paperback) — ISBN 978-1-4625-2297-2 (hardcover)
 1. Evaluation research (Social action programs) 2. Social service—Research.
I. Patton, Michael Quinn, editor. II. McKegg, Kate, editor. III. Wehipeihana, Nan,
editor.
 H62.D49524 2016
 001.4—dc23
                      2015010961

About the Cover: The blue, swirling imagery of the Paua shell (New Zealand abalone)
symbolizes the dynamic complexity and nonlinearity of developmental evaluation. The
tough and resilient outer shell conceals the highly iridescent mother of pearl inner layer
that is revered by the Māori for its beauty, intrigue, and artistry.

Preface

Developmental evaluation provides *evaluative* information and feedback to social innovators, and their funders and supporters, to inform adaptive *development* of change initiatives in complex dynamic environments. Developmental evaluation brings to innovation and adaptation the processes of asking evaluative questions, applying evaluation logic, and gathering and reporting evaluative data, to inform and support the development of innovative projects, programs, initiatives, products, organizations, and/or systems change efforts with timely feedback. This book presents the current state of the art and practice of developmental evaluation through 12 case exemplars. The book also answers common questions about developmental evaluation; presents a synthesis of patterns, themes, insights, and lessons drawn from the case studies; and, for the first time, identifies and explains the essential guiding principles of developmental evaluation.

The Developmental Evaluation Niche

The developmental evaluation niche focuses on evaluating innovations in complex dynamic environments because these are the types of environments in which social innovators are working. *Innovation* as used here is a broad framing that includes creating new approaches to intractable problems, adapting programs to changing conditions, applying effective principles to new contexts (scaling innovation), catalyzing systems change, and improvising rapid responses in crisis conditions. Because social innovation unfolds in social systems that are inherently dynamic and complex, and often turbulent, social innovators typically find themselves having to adapt their interventions in the face of these system characteristics. Funders of social innovation also need to be flexible and adaptive in alignment with these characteristics. Developmental evaluators track, document, and help interpret the nature and implications of innovations and adaptations as they unfold, and help extract lessons and insights from both processes and outcomes to inform the ongoing adaptive innovation process. At the same time, the evaluators' work provides accountability for funders and supporters of social innovations, and helps them understand and refine their contributions to solutions as they evolve. Social innovators often find themselves dealing with problems, trying out strategies, and striving to achieve goals that emerge from their engagement in the change process, but that could not have been identified before this engagement, and that continue to evolve as a result of what they learn. Developmental evaluators help identify and make sense of these emergent problems, strategies, and goals as social innovations *develop*. The emergent/creative/adaptive interventions generated by social innovators for complex problems are significant enough to constitute *developments*, not just improvements; thus the need for *developmental* evaluation.

Traditional evaluation approaches advocate clear, specific, and measurable outcomes that are to be achieved through processes detailed in a linear logic model. Such traditional evaluation demands for upfront, preordained specificity don't work under conditions of high innovation, exploration, uncertainty, turbulence, and emergence. In fact, premature specificity can do harm and generate resistance from social innovators—as, indeed, it has—by constraining exploration; limiting adaptation; reducing experimental options; and forcing premature adoption of a rigid model not because such a model is appropriate, but because evaluators, funders, or other stakeholders demand it in order to comply with what they understand to be good evaluation. Developmental evaluation emerged as a response to social innovators' criticisms of traditional evaluation and their expressed need for an alternative way to evaluate their work.

Developmental evaluation involves evaluative thinking throughout. Judgments of merit, worth, significance, meaningfulness, innovativeness, and effectiveness (or such other criteria as are negotiated) inform ongoing adaptive innovation. Such evaluative judgments don't just come at the end of some fixed period (e.g., a 3-year grant); rather, they are ongoing and timely. Nor are evaluation conclusions reached and rendered by the evaluators independently. Developmental evaluation is a collaborative, interactive process. Because this process is utilization-focused, and because it unfolds in complex dynamic systems where the particular meaning and significance of information may be difficult to predetermine, making sense together of emergent findings involves the developmental evaluators' interpreting patterns in the data *collaboratively* with social innovators, funders, advocates, change agents, and systems change supporters. Through this empirically focused interaction, developmental evaluation becomes an integral part of the innovative process.

History of Developmental Evaluation

The first article describing developmental evaluation as a distinct approach was written by a coeditor of the present volume, Michael Quinn Patton, and published in *New Directions for Program Evaluation* (Patton, 1992); it described a developmental evaluation of an experimental educational diversity initiative. In 1994, the predecessor journal to the *American Journal of Evaluation*, then called *Evaluation Practice*, featured 20 evaluation theorists and practitioners speculating on the future of evaluation. Patton's contribution to this group of articles (Patton, 1994) focused on developmental evaluation and predicted that in an increasingly complex world, it would become an important evaluation option.

In 2006, Patton had the opportunity to coach a group of Canadian evaluators on developmental evaluation in a series of workshops and consulting sessions sponsored by the J. W. McConnell Family Foundation, based in Montréal. Two of the participants in that coaching experience are contributors to this book, Mark Cabaj and Jamie Gamble. Based on that experience, Gamble wrote *A Developmental Evaluation Primer* (published in 2008 by the McConnell Family Foundation, and still available for free download on its website).

The first full-day workshop ever conducted on developmental evaluation took place in New Zealand in March 2009; it was organized, sponsored, and cofacilitated with Patton by another coeditor of this book, Kate McKegg. The first developmental evaluation workshop in the United States was conducted for The Evaluators' Institute in San Francisco in 2010.

The first book-length description and explanation of this topic was *Developmental Evaluation: Applying Complexity Concepts to Enhance Innovation and Use* (Patton, 2011). In the short time since, developmental evaluation has become recognized and established as a distinct and useful approach. At the annual conference of the American Evaluation Association in 2013, there were over 40 presentations on developmental evaluations. The increasing attention garnered by developmental evaluation has raised questions about its essential elements and practical questions about how to do it, which this book has been written to answer. But by far the most common question is this: "Where can I find good examples of developmental evaluations?" Until now, there has been no such collection of exemplars. Using our knowledge of and relationships with skilled practitioners, we set out to solicit and bring together in one place a diverse set of high-quality, insight-generating developmental evaluation case studies. These case studies constitute the core of this book.

How We Selected the Developmental Evaluation Exemplars

Global Relevance

This book is being completed during the International Year of Evaluation (2015) as declared by the United Nations, the International Organization for Cooperation in Evaluation, the EvalPartners international network, and national evaluation associations around the world. The 12 case exemplars include examples from Australia, Canada, New Zealand, the Pacific Islands, and the United States. They also include an international agricultural initiative working in Africa and South America; a People-to-People Reconciliation Fund Program with projects in Bosnia–Herzegovina, Burundi, and Israel/the West Bank/Gaza; and the Global Partnership for the Prevention of Armed Conflict working worldwide.

Diversity

The innovations evaluated include programs in sustainable agricultural development, poverty reduction, education, community-based arts, supports to homeless youth, health care provision, early childhood systems change, access to college, preventing conflict, and reconciliation among people in areas of conflict. There are local community-based initiatives, programs in Indigenous communities, national efforts at systems change, and a global network. The cases include innovations undertaken by philanthropic foundations, nonprofit agencies, international organizations, universities, community-based organizations, and government reform initiatives. One developmental evaluation has been going on for over a decade and is still developing. Another decade-long national initiative has recently been completed, with the developmental evaluation providing the documentation for what happened and what was achieved. Other examples are in midstream and still evolving, having been in development and operating for a few years. Some examples have been completed that involved years of engagement. One has just completed its first year.

Balance

The cases provide examples of extraordinary success, modest success, rollercoaster-like ups and downs, and some failures.

Reflective Practitioners

The value of case studies ultimately depends on a combination of description of what happened; analysis of major developments and turning points; and deep, honest reflection to generate and share insights and lessons. Reflective practice is a special competence, not to be taken for granted. Of particular importance is the integrity to present "the good, the bad, and the ugly." You'll find all of these qualities and more in the chapters of this book. Our contributors are skilled reflective practitioners.

Authorial Partnerships

Developmental evaluation is a collaborative process between social innovators and evaluators. Honoring the principle of co-creation is essential: The innovation and evaluation develop together—interwoven, interdependent, iterative, and co-created—so that the developmental evaluation becomes part of the change process. Therefore, the case examples in this book are jointly authored by those implementing the innovations and the developmental evaluators who worked with them. Indeed, such joint authorship is a major part of what makes these cases exemplars. This made the writing process more time-consuming, more laborious, more negotiated, and more multiperspectival. It also made the resulting cases more balanced and indicative of the value of co-creation.

The Ongoing Development of Developmental Evaluation

Developmental evaluation is still developing—and will continue to do so. This book is a milestone in the field's own development, or so we hope, but it is by no means the final story. Daily we hear about new applications, new initiatives, and new insights being generated by developmental evaluators as reflective practitioners. Developmental evaluation has truly become a global community of practice.

Acknowledgments

We want to thank all of our contributors. They were responsive to our editorial feedback and suggestions. They worked hard to produce faithful reports of complex, multifaceted initiatives and multidimensional, mixed-methods developmental evaluations in the incredibly confining space of book chapters. Then they graciously acquiesced to our final cuts when, on occasion, their contributions exceeded in length what we could include. Each chapter could become a book. We are delighted and honored to have the opportunity to present readers with at least a glimpse of how to engage real-world complexities within the limitations of a chapter. Although no chapter constitutes the "whole story" (as if that can ever be known or told) of the initiative it describes, we think you'll find a lot to engage you in your own reflective practice.

We want to express special appreciation to Senior Editor and Publisher C. Deborah Laughton of The Guilford Press. She is a consummate, hands-on, meaning-focused, clarity-of-message-oriented *editor*. Yes, an actual *editor*—someone who improves chapter titles, enhances the quality and clarity of writing, and helps separate the wheat from the chaff *in the service of readers*. Editing is becoming a lost art in academic publishing. We're talking about editing that makes a book better—that supports book editors in deciding what to keep, what to discard, and how best to present what is kept. C. Deborah Laughton has a keen editorial eye, an astute editorial mind, and a willingness to spend time applying both. She also has a diplomatic editorial tone in offering suggestions and an irrefutable rationale for those suggestions she offers: to improve the experience for readers. She did her best for you, dear readers. Any failures in this regard are our own.

Dedication

As the manuscript of this book was being prepared for the publisher (December 2014), Brenda Zimmerman was killed in a tragic automobile accident in Toronto. She pioneered the conceptualization and application of the *simple–complicated–complex* distinctions that are the bedrock of identifying the niche of developmental evaluation as complexity-centered. Distinguishing the complicated from the complex was central to *Getting to Maybe: How the World Is Changed*, which Brenda coauthored (Westley, Zimmerman, & Patton, 2006). Brenda's work on complexity and her contributions to *Developmental Evaluation* were featured in Chapter 4 of the book of that name (Patton, 2011). Michael Patton reflects that without Brenda there would have been no *Getting to Maybe,* and *Developmental Evaluation* (Patton, 2011), had it been written at all, would have been a very different book. In her extensive keynote speaking, training, teaching, writing, and consulting, she promoted developmental evaluation as particularly appropriate for complex social innovations. We dedicate this book to her contributions, and in doing so we acknowledge life's uncertainties, which are brought deeply home to us all at times of much-too-soon loss of those we've come to care about.

MICHAEL QUINN PATTON
KATE MCKEGG
NAN WEHIPEIHANA

REFERENCES

Gamble, J. (2008). *A developmental evaluation primer.* Montréal: J. W. McConnell Family Foundation.

Patton, M. Q. (1992). Developmental evaluation: An approach for empowerment-oriented and multicultural programs. *New Directions for Program Evaluation, 53,* 17–33.

Patton, M. Q. (1994). Developmental evaluation. *Evaluation Practice, 15*(3), 311–320.

Patton, M. Q. (2011). *Developmental evaluation: Applying complexity concepts to enhance innovation and use.* New York: Guilford Press.

Westley, F., Zimmerman, B., & Patton, M. Q. (2006). *Getting to maybe: How the world is changed.* Toronto: Random House Canada.

Contents

CHAPTER 1

State of the Art and Practice of Developmental Evaluation

Answers to Common and Recurring Questions

Michael Quinn Patton

*M**ake the world a better place through innovation and systems change.* That is the vision and commitment of social innovators and their funders. They are passionate about making major differences on significant issues. They are strategic about changing systems. As developmental evaluators, we also want to make the world a better place. We are passionate about using evaluation to inform innovation. This means adapting evaluation to the particular needs and challenges of social innovation and systems change. This book provides case exemplars of evaluators doing just that. You will get an inside look at variations in developmental evaluation, as well as illumination of guiding principles that make it distinct as an evaluation approach.

The Preface describes the basics of what developmental evaluation is, how it has evolved, and its niche as evaluating innovations in complex dynamic environments. I won't repeat that explanation here. Instead, I'll "cut to the chase" and go right to the developmental evaluation value proposition.

The Developmental Evaluation Value Proposition

As developmental evaluation has become more widely practiced (as evidenced by the case exemplars in this book), a value proposition has emerged. Colleague James Radner of the University of Toronto, one of the contributors to this book, has a breadth of experience working with many different organizations in many different capacities on a variety of initiatives, including doing developmental evaluation. He is thus especially well positioned to identify developmental evaluation's value proposition, which he articulates as follows:

1

"The discipline of *evaluation* has something to offer social innovators that can really help them succeed. Developmental evaluation is based on the insight that evaluative thinking, techniques, practice, and discipline can be a boon to social innovation—that data systematically collected and appropriately tied to users' goals and strategies can make a difference, even in open-ended, highly complex settings where the goals and strategies are themselves evolving. Developmental evaluation has something distinctive to offer through the way it marries empirical inquiry focused on the innova*tion* to direct engagement with the innova*tor*. What developmental evaluators do helps innovators advance social change, *but* it only works when customized to the very special context of each social innovation."

Q&A about Developmental Evaluation: 10 Questions, 10 Responses

Developmental evaluation has become widely recognized and established as a distinct and useful evaluation approach (Dickson & Saunders, 2014; FSG, 2014; Lam & Shulha, 2014; Preskill & Beer, 2012). As new practitioners hear about and try implementing this approach, questions naturally arise. This chapter answers the 10 most common questions I get about developmental evaluation. The emergence of these questions provides one window into the state of the art and practice of developmental evaluation, for these questions, even without answers, reveal what practitioners are encountering, grappling with, and developing responses to in their own contexts. Below, then, are the questions I respond to as one contribution to the continuing evolution of developmental evaluation. The answers also set the stage for the case studies in the following chapters.

1. What are the essential elements of developmental evaluation?
2. How is developmental evaluation different from other approaches: ongoing formative evaluation, action research, monitoring, and organizational development?
3. What is the relationship between developmental evaluation and development evaluation?
4. How do systems thinking and complexity theory inform the practice of developmental evaluation?
5. What methods are used in developmental evaluation?
6. What conditions are necessary for developmental evaluation to succeed?
7. What does it take to become an effective developmental evaluation practitioner? That is, what particular developmental evaluator skills and competencies are essential?
8. How can developmental evaluation serve accountability needs and demands?

9. Why is developmental evaluation attracting so much attention and spreading so quickly?

10. What has been the most significant development in developmental evaluation since publication of the Patton (2011) book?

Now, on to the answers.

1. What Are the Essential Elements of Developmental Evaluation?

The first question represents the *fidelity challenge*. An experienced practitioner recently told me, "More often than not, I find, people say they are doing developmental evaluation, but they are not."

The fidelity challenge concerns the extent to which a specific evaluation sufficiently incorporates the core characteristics of the overall approach to justify labeling that evaluation by its designated name. Just as fidelity is a central issue in efforts to replicate effective programs in new places (are the replications faithful to the original model on which they are based?), evaluation fidelity concerns whether an evaluator following a particular model is faithful in implementing all the core steps, elements, and processes of that model. What must be included in a theory-driven evaluation to justify its designation as *theory-driven* (Coryn, Noakes, Westine, & Schröter, 2011)? What must occur in a participatory evaluation for it to be deemed genuinely *participatory* (Cousins, Whitmore, & Shulha, 2014; Daigneault & Jacob, 2009)? What must be included in an empowerment evaluation to justify the label *empowerment* (Fetterman, Kaftarian, & Wandersman, 2014)?

Miller and Campbell (2006) systematically examined 47 evaluations labeled *empowerment evaluation*. They found wide variation among practitioners in adherence to empowerment evaluation principles, as well as weak emphasis on the attainment of empowered outcomes for program beneficiaries. Cousins and Chouinard (2012) reviewed 121 pieces of empirical research on participatory evaluation and also found great variation in approaches conducted under the *participatory* umbrella. I've seen a great many evaluations labeled *utilization-focused* that provided no evidence that primary intended users had been identified and engaged to focus the evaluation on those users' priorities. What, then, are the essential elements of *developmental evaluation*?

The answer is that there are eight essential principles:

1. *Developmental purpose*
2. *Evaluation rigor*
3. *Utilization focus*
4. *Innovation niche*
5. *Complexity perspective*
6. *Systems thinking*
7. *Co-creation*
8. *Timely feedback*

Each of these is defined, described, and discussed in Chapter 15. From my perspective, these principles must be explicitly addressed in any developmental evaluation, but how and the extent to which they are addressed depend on situation and context. The principles serve the role of sensitizing concepts. This is a significant departure from the usual approach to *fidelity*, which has traditionally meant to implement an approach operationally in exactly the same way each time. Fidelity has meant adherence to a recipe or highly prescriptive set of steps and procedures. The principles of developmental evaluation, in contrast, involve sensitizing elements that must be interpreted and applied contextually—*but must be applied in some way and to some extent if the evaluation is to be considered genuinely and fully developmental*. This means that when I read a developmental evaluation report, or talk with those involved in a developmental evaluation, or listen to a developmental evaluation presentation at a conference, I should be able to see/detect/understand how these eight essential principles informed what was done and what resulted.

The authors of the case chapters in this book did not have the principles before them when they wrote about their developmental evaluation experiences. Rather, I developed the list of principles after reading the cases and interacting with developmental evaluator colleagues. So, as you read the cases, see if you can detect the principles in practice. Coeditors Nan Wehipeihana and Kate McKegg provide a synthesis of the cases in Chapter 14, identifying major cross-case themes and incorporating the principles in their synthesis. Then, in Chapter 15, the book ends with an in-depth elaboration of each principle.

2. How Is Developmental Evaluation Different from Other Approaches?

Because developmental evaluation claims a specific purpose and niche, questions about how it differs from other approaches are common. Examples include how (or even if) developmental evaluation is different from ongoing formative evaluation, organizational development, monitoring, and action research. So let me try to clarify.

Developmental Evaluation in Contrast to Formative Evaluation

Developmental evaluation offers an alternative to formative and summative evaluation, the classic distinctions that have dominated evaluation for four decades. In the original conceptualization, a formative evaluation served to prepare a program for summative evaluation by identifying and correcting implementation problems, making adjustments based on feedback, providing an early assessment of whether desired outcomes were being achieved (or were likely to be achieved), and getting the program stabilized and standardized for summative assessment. It is not uncommon for a new program to go through 2–3 years of formative evaluation, working out startup difficulties and getting the program model stabilized, before a summative evaluation is conducted. Over time, formative evaluation has come to designate any evaluative efforts to *improve* a program. Improvement means making it better. In contrast, developmental evaluation focuses on *adaptive development*, which means making the program different because, for example, (1) the context has changed (which comes with the territory in a complex dynamic environment); (2) the clientele have changed significantly; (3) learning leads to a significant change; or (4) a creative, innovative alternative to a persistent issue or challenge has emerged. Here are three examples of such adaptive developments.

- A program serving one population (white, low-income high school dropouts) adapts to demands to serve a different population (e.g., immigrants, people coming out of prison, or people with particular disabilities). This kind of adaptation goes beyond improvement. It requires developmental adaptation.
- A workshop or course moves online from the classroom. Teaching effectively online requires major adaptation of both content and process, as well as criteria for interpreting success. Again, this goes well beyond ongoing improvement.
- Public health authorities must adapt to a new disease like Ebola. Innovation and adaptation become the order of the day, not just improving existing procedures.

Keep in mind here that supporting ongoing adaptive development of programs is only one of the five purposes of developmental evaluation. Developmental evaluation also supports development of completely new innovations. Kate McKegg has offered these innovative examples from New Zealand:

- Development of low-cost, environmentally friendly housing for marginalized people in rural areas.
- Development of child care options for low-income parents that can accommodate children from birth to age 16.
- Development of a local food service that uses local food sources as a response to the failure of multinational food distribution to solve hunger and nutrition.

Developmental Evaluation in Contrast to Action Research

Action research takes many forms. The methods of action research and developmental evaluation (e.g., use of reflective practice) can be the same. The difference is purpose. Action research is typically used to understand and solve problems: Why aren't patients keeping follow-up appointments? Why aren't databases being kept up to date? Why is there so much negativity about staff meetings? Action research is typically undertaken to solve these kinds of problems. Developmental evaluation, in contrast, focuses on innovation and systems change.

Developmental Evaluation in Contrast to Monitoring

Ongoing monitoring (the M in M&E, where E is evaluation) typically involves tracking progress on predetermined indicators. Monitoring is used to comply with accountability requirements and to watch for important changes in key output indicators. Because indicators are predetermined and standardized, and focus on quarter-to-quarter and year-to-year comparisons to report progress against prede-termined targets, they are fairly useless for picking up unintended consequences and emergent developments. Data from a monitoring system can provide useful devel-opmental evaluation information for documenting changes in key indicators, but additional fieldwork and inquiry will be needed to understand why the monitoring indicators are moving as they are. Moreover, monitoring data are typically collected at an output level rather than at a system, strategic, or outcome level, which is the arena for major innovative developments. Monitoring serves best to track prog-ress against implementation plans when a detailed implementation plan has been funded for a model-based project. Innovations lack detailed implementation plans and predetermined monitoring indicators precisely because they are occurring in complex dynamic systems, where both the work and the indicators are emergent, developmental, and changing.

Developmental Evaluation in Contrast to Organizational Development

Organizational development supports increased organizational effectiveness, usu-ally by analyzing processes of communication, staff interactions, work flow, power dynamics, personnel competencies, capacity needs, and related functions to help make things run more smoothly. Organizational development, like formative evalu-ation for programs, helps improve organizations, often by identifying problems and taking people through a process of problem solving. Developmental evaluation, in contrast, when working with an organization as the unit of analysis, focuses on innovation to support the organization's becoming more adaptable to the uncertain and unpredictable dynamics of complexity.

Developmental Evaluation as Dynamic Reframing

In elaborating the preceding distinctions, I've drawn on the experiences and insights of many developmental evaluation practitioners. Nathaniel Foote—managing director of the TruePoint Center for Higher Ambition Leadership, as well as a dis-tinguished organizational effectiveness and leadership scholar, experienced man-agement consultant, and coauthor of Chapter 6—has insightfully identified the role of developmental evaluation as *dynamic reframing* and has positioned it along a spectrum from traditional evaluation at one end and organizational consulting at the other end. Exhibit 1.1 presents this role and positioning, which I think is partic-ularly useful in delineating the niche of developmental evaluation. Foote explains:

> I see developmental evaluation occupying a midpoint on a spectrum. At one end is evaluation to serve the interests of a third-party (typically a funder or policy-maker) seeking to assess a well-defined intervention, and understand whether it will work, independent of the specific actor who has implemented it. At the other end is a con-sulting intervention that is focused solely on the interests of a client to achieve more effective action. The focus is entirely on the actor and what s/he should do next, inde-pendent of any broader assessment of the intervention and its validity in other contexts or as undertaken by other actors.

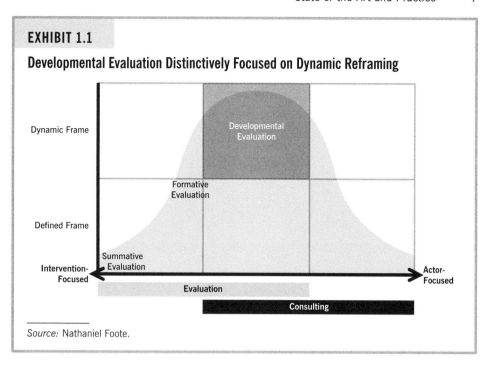

EXHIBIT 1.1

Developmental Evaluation Distinctively Focused on Dynamic Reframing

Source: Nathaniel Foote.

Developmental evaluation is needed where "actors" are embedded in and seeking to change a complex system. Actors and intervention are intertwined and cannot be separated. The intervention is inevitably shaped by characteristics of the actors, and observations and insights about the intervention can only fully be appreciated and acted on by actors in the system. Because it is a complex system, actions always lead to unintended consequences (whether good or bad), which in turn offer the potential to learn more about the dynamics of the system and how the "actors" can better achieve their intent. At its essence, developmental evaluation is about ***dynamic reframing***, seeking to articulate, test, inform, and reframe the mental models of the "actors" for the system they are operating in and the ways they have been and could be influencing it, so as to realize their intent. This explicit focus on the overall frame as dynamic, rather than defined, is, to me, the most significant aspect that differentiates developmental evaluation from more conventional evaluations (summative and formative) on the one hand and from more conventional consulting interventions on the other. (personal communication, January 4, 2015)

3. What Is the Relationship between Developmental Evaluation and Development Evaluation?

Ah, adding that pesky little *-al* at the end of the word *development* transforms one meaning into another. Development*al* evaluation is easily and often confused with development evaluation. They are not the same, though developmental evaluation can be used in development evaluations. *Development evaluation* is a generic term for evaluations conducted in developing countries, usually focused on the effectiveness of international aid programs and initiatives. An evaluation focused on development assistance in developing countries could use a developmental evaluation approach, especially if such developmental assistance is viewed as occurring under conditions of complexity with a focus on adaptation to local context. But developmental evaluation is by no means limited to projects in developing countries.

The *-al* in *developmental* is easily missed, but it is critical in distinguishing development evaluation from developmental evaluation. Moreover, languages other than English don't have a grammatical way of distinguishing *development* from *developmental*. So translation is a problem, as I've found in doing international and cross-cultural training. For example, international developmental evaluator Ricardo Wilson-Grau, a contributor to Chapter 10, says, "I translate 'developmental evaluation' into Spanish and Portuguese as 'evaluation for the development of an innovation.'"

Another way to mitigate the confusion is to use labels other than *developmental evaluation*, as some are doing, preferring to call it one of the following:

- Real-time evaluation
- Emergent evaluation
- Action evaluation
- Adaptive evaluation

4. How Do Systems Thinking and Complexity Theory Inform the Practice of Developmental Evaluation?

Thinking systemically is fundamental to developmental evaluation. This means, at a minimum, understanding interrelationships, engaging with multiple perspectives, and reflecting deeply on the practical and ethical consequences of boundary choices. The shift in thinking required is from focusing on discrete components of a program to thinking in terms of relationships. In delineating the dimensions of "being systemic," Bob Williams, the 2014 recipient of the American Evaluation Association (AEA) Lazarsfeld Theory Award for his contribution to systems approaches in evaluation, explained: "Every endeavour is bounded. We cannot do or see everything. Every viewpoint is partial. Therefore, holism is not about trying to deal with everything, but being methodical, informed, pragmatic and ethical about what to leave out. And, it's about taking responsibility for those decisions" (2014, p. 1).

Innovation involves changing an existing system at some level and in some way. If you examine findings from the last 50 years of program evaluation, you'll find that projects and programs rarely lead to major change. Effective projects and programs are often isolated from larger systems, which allows them the autonomy to operate effectively, but limit their larger impact. On the other hand, projects and programs often fail because they operate in dysfunctional systems. Thus social innovators are interested in and motivated by changing systems—health care systems, educational systems, food systems, criminal justice systems. In so doing, they engage in efforts and thinking that supersede traditional project and program logic models. To evaluate systems change, developmental evaluators need to be able to engage in systems thinking and to treat the system or systems targeted for change as the *evaluand* (the thing being evaluated). This means inquiring into, tracking, documenting, and reporting on the development of interrelationships, changing boundaries, and emerging perspectives that provide windows into the processes, effects, and implications of systems change (Williams, 2005, 2008; Williams & van 't Hof, 2014).

Thinking systemically comes into play even in small pilot projects. Systems and complexity concepts are helpful for understanding what makes a project innovative. Moreover, even small innovations eventually face the issue of what it will mean to expand the innovation if it is successful—which directly and inevitably will involve systems change. The cases in this book all involve systemic thinking and systems change. Here are five diverse examples:

- Changing the youth homelessness system (Chapter 4)
- Changing the early childhood system (Chapter 6)
- Changing indigenous food systems in Africa and in the Andes (Chapter 8)
- Changing community systems where people are mired in poverty (Chapter 9)
- Changing Ontario's school system (Chapter 13)

These cases illustrate and illuminate how developmental evaluation is attuned to both linear and nonlinear relationships, both intended and unintended interactions and outcomes, and both hypothesized and unpredicted results. Fundamental systems-oriented developmental evaluation questions include these: In what ways and how effectively does the system function for whose interests? Why so? How are the system's boundaries perceived? With what implications? To what extent and in what ways do the boundaries, interrelationships, and perspectives affect the way the innovative change process has been conceptualized and implemented? How has social innovation changed the system, through what processes, with what results and implications?

The Complexity Perspective

Viewing innovation through the lens of complexity adds another way of framing, studying, and evaluating social innovations. Innovations involve uncertain outcomes and unfold in situations where stakeholders typically disagree about the nature of the problem and what should be done to address it. These two dimensions, degree of uncertainty and degree of disagreement, define the zone of complexity (Patton, 2011, Ch. 5). In essence, complexity theory directs our attention to characteristics and dimensions of dynamic systems change—which is precisely where innovation unfolds. Core developmental evaluation questions driven by complexity theory include these: In what ways and how can the dynamics of complex systems be captured, illuminated, and understood as social innovation emerges?

How Developmental Evaluation Can Enhance Innovation under Conditions of Complexity

Chi Yan Lam and Lyn M. Shulha (2014) conducted a case study on "the cocreation of an innovative program." The case study describes the pre-formative development of an educational program (from conceptualization to pilot implementation) and analyzes the processes of innovation within a developmental evaluation framework. Lam and Shulha concluded:

> Developmental evaluation enhanced innovation by (a) identifying and infusing data primarily within an informing process toward resolving the uncertainty associated with innovation and (b) facilitating program cocreation between the clients and the developmental evaluator. Analysis into the demands of innovation revealed the pervasiveness of uncertainty throughout development and how the rendering of evaluative data helped resolve uncertainty and propelled development forward. Developmental evaluation enabled a nonlinear, coevolutionary program development process that centered on six foci—definition, delineation, collaboration, prototyping, illumination, and reality testing. (p. 1)

To what extent do the dynamics of uncertainty and disagreement shift and change during the unfolding of the innovation? How is innovation's development captured and understood, revealing new learning and knowledge that can be extrapolated or applied elsewhere?

Complexity theory is sometimes viewed as a subset of systems theory. In other framings, complexity theory and systems theory are sufficiently distinct to constitute separate and unique but overlapping approaches to understanding the world, like seeing and hearing. Seeing someone speak can enhance hearing and deepen understanding about what the person is saying. Listening to someone is given additional meaning by watching that person's expressions. Both are senses. They operate separately, but can overlap to reinforce what we take in and make sense of in an interaction. I find it useful to conceptualize systems thinking and complexity theory as distinct but overlapping frameworks (Patton, 2015, p. 151), as shown in Exhibit 1.2. Both perspectives are essential to developmental evaluation.

5. What Methods Are Used in Developmental Evaluation?

My response to this question has five parts.

- *Developmental evaluation does not rely on or advocate any particular evaluation method, design, tool, or inquiry framework.* A developmental evaluation can include any kind of data (quantitative, qualitative, mixed), any kind of design (e.g., naturalistic, experimental), and any kind of focus (processes, outcomes, impacts, costs, and cost–benefit, among many possibilities)—depending on the nature and stage of an innovation, and on the priority questions that will support development

EXHIBIT 1.2

Systems Theory and Complexity Theory as Distinct but Overlapping Inquiry Frameworks

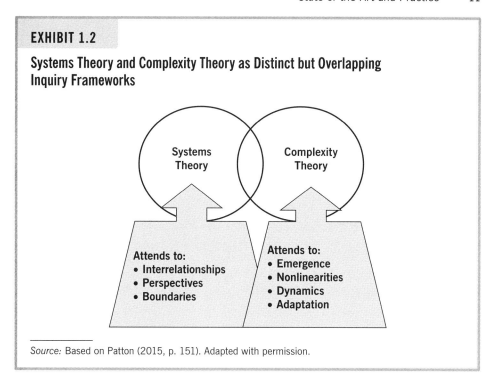

Source: Based on Patton (2015, p. 151). Adapted with permission.

of and decision making about the innovation. Methods and tools can include rapid turnaround randomized controlled trials, surveys, focus groups, interviews, observations, performance data, community indicators, network analysis—whatever sheds light on key questions.

Moreover, developmental evaluation can use any of a number of inquiry frameworks. For example, the *Developmental Evaluation* book (Patton, 2011) presents and discusses a number of different inquiry frameworks that can be useful for different situations, including triangulated learning, the adaptive cycle, appreciative inquiry, reflective practice, values-driven inquiry, wicked questions, outcome mapping, systematic risk management, force field analysis, actual–ideal comparisons, and principles-focused evaluation, among others. The trick is to use a framework that is appropriate for the particular situation and resonates with the social innovators engaged collaboratively in the particular developmental evaluation. Chapter 10 demonstrates the use of *outcome harvesting* as both an inquiry framework and a developmental evaluation tool. (See also Wilson-Grau & Britt, 2012.)

• *The process and quality of engagement between the primary intended users (social innovators) and the developmental evaluators is as much the method of developmental evaluation as any particular design, methods, and data collection tools are.* Asking evaluation questions, examining and tracking the implications of adaptations, and providing timely feedback on an ongoing basis—these are the methods of developmental evaluation.

Cartoon by Christopher P. Lysy. Used with permission.

• *Whatever methods are used or data are collected, rapid feedback is essential.* Speed matters. Dynamic complexities don't slow down or wait for evaluators to write their reports, get them carefully edited, and then have them approved by higher authorities. Any method can be used, but it will have to be adapted to the necessities of speed, timely reporting, and just-in-time, in-the-moment decision making. This is a major reason why the developmental evaluators should be part of the innovation team: to be present in real time as issues arise and decisions have to be made.

• *Methods can be emergent and flexible; designs can be dynamic.* Contrary to the usual practice in evaluation of fixed designs that are implemented as planned, developmental evaluation designs can change as an innovation unfolds and changes. If surveys and interviews are used, the evaluators may change questions from one administration to the next, discarding items that have revealed little of value or are no longer relevant, and adding items that address new issues. The sample can be emergent (Patton, 2015, Ch. 5) as new participants or sites emerge, and others are abandoned. Both baselines and benchmarks can be revised and updated as new information emerges.

• *Developmental evaluators need to be agile, open, interactive, flexible, observant, and highly tolerant of ambiguity.* A developmental evaluator is, in part, an instrument. Because the evaluation is co-created and the developmental evaluator is part of the innovation team, bringing an evaluation perspective and evaluative thinking to the team, an evaluator's capacity to be part of the team and facilitate the evaluation elements of the innovative process involves both essential "people skills" and is part of the method for developmental evaluation. The advice from experienced developmental evaluators offered throughout this book, as well as other research with practitioners (Cabaj, 2011), affirms and reinforces this point.

6. What Conditions Are Necessary for Developmental Evaluation to Succeed?

Readiness is important for any evaluation. Utilization-focused evaluators work with intended evaluation users to help them understand the value of reality testing and buy into the process, thereby reducing the threat of resistance (conscious or unconscious) to evaluation use. A common error made by novice evaluators is believing that because someone has requested an evaluation or some group has been assembled to design an evaluation, the commitment to reality testing and use is already there. Quite the contrary: These commitments must be engendered (or revitalized if once they were present) and then reinforced throughout the evaluation process. Utilization-focused evaluation makes this a priority (Patton, 2012, pp. 15–36).

Developmental evaluation adds to general readiness the following 10 readiness characteristics:

1. Commitment to innovation, the niche of developmental evaluation.
2. Readiness to take risks—not just talk about risk taking, but actually take risks.
3. Tolerance for ambiguity. Uncertainty, unpredictability, and turbulence come with the territory of systems change, innovation, and therefore developmental evaluation.
4. Some basic understanding of systems thinking and complexity. This will increase through engagement with developmental evaluation, but some baseline understanding and comfort with the ideas are needed to begin the design process.
5. Contextual and cultural sensitivity centered on innovation and adaptation. Those searching for standardized so-called "best practices" are not good candidates for developmental evaluation, where contextual customization rules.
6. Commitment to adaptive learning and action.
7. Flexibility. Developmental evaluation involves flexible designs, flexible relationships, flexible budgeting, and flexible reporting.
8. Leadership's understanding of and commitment to developmental evaluation. Ignore leadership at your peril.
9. A funder or funding stream that understands developmental evaluation.
10. Preparation to stay the course. Developmental evaluation is not about flirting with change. Authentic engagement is long-term engagement.

What these readiness factors mean will vary by context. This is merely a suggestive list to highlight the importance of raising the readiness question and doing a joint assessment of readiness with the primary intended users who need to be engaged in the process. Exhibit 1.3 highlights additional dimensions of readiness to engage in developmental evaluation.

EXHIBIT 1.3

Where and When Is Developmental Evaluation Appropriate?

Appropriate contexts	Inappropriate contexts
• Highly emergent and volatile situations (e.g., the environment is dynamic) • Situations that are difficult to plan or predict because the variables and factors are interdependent and nonlinear • Situations where there are no known solutions to issues, new issues entirely, and/or no certain ways forward • Situations where multiple pathways forward are possible, and thus there is a need for innovation and exploration • Socially complex situations, requiring collaboration among stakeholders from different organizations, systems, and/or sectors • Innovative situations, requiring timely learning and ongoing development • Situations with unknown outcomes, so vision and values drive processes	• Situations where people are not able or willing to commit the time to participate actively in the evaluation and to build and sustain relational trust • Situations where key stakeholders require high levels of certainty • Situations where there is a lack of openness to experimentation and reflection • Situations where organizations lack adaptive capacity • Situations where key people are unwilling to "fail" or hear "bad news" • Situations where there are poor relationships among management, staff, and evaluators

Source: Kate McKegg and Michael Quinn Patton, Developmental Evaluation Workshop, African Evaluation Association, Yaounde, Cameroon, March 2014.

7. What Does It Take to Become an Effective Developmental Evaluation Practitioner?

The AEA's Guiding Principles for Evaluators emphasize that "Evaluators should possess (or ensure that the evaluation team possesses) the education, abilities, skills and experience appropriate to undertake the tasks proposed in the evaluation" (AEA, 2004, B1). The *basic competencies* for developmental evaluation are the same as those for any evaluation based on the profession's standards and guiding principles. What developmental evaluation adds is a greater emphasis on direct engagement with primary intended users of the evaluation (social innovators and funders) and therefore increased attention to interpersonal and group facilitation skills. As Exhibit 1.4 shows, developmental evaluation poses particular challenges in applying general evaluator competencies.

Research on evaluation use consistently shows that findings are more likely to be used if they are credible—and *evaluator credibility* is a central factor in the overall credibility of the findings. Yes, the methods and measures themselves need to be credible so that the resulting data are credible. But methods and measures derive their credibility from appropriate and competent application by the person(s)

EXHIBIT 1.4

General Evaluator Competencies and Specialized Developmental Evaluator Competencies

Six essential competency areas*	General evaluator competencies	Specialized developmental evaluator competencies
1. *Professional practice*	Knowing and observing professional norms and values, including evaluation standards and principles.	The importance of the ongoing relationship between social innovators and developmental evaluators increases the need for professional boundary management as an essential competency.
2. *Systematic inquiry*	Expertise in the technical aspects of evaluations, such as design, measurement, data analysis, interpretation, and sharing results.	Developmental evaluator Mark Cabaj has observed, "The competencies demanded are greater because you need a larger methods toolbox and capability to come up with creative approaches."
3. *Situational analysis*	Understanding and attending to the contextual and political issues of an evaluation, including determining evaluability, addressing conflicts, and attending to issues of evaluation use.	Being able to distinguish the simple, complicated, and complex is essential. So is understanding how to use complexity concepts as part of situation analysis: emergence, nonlinearity, dynamical, uncertainty, adaptability.
4. *Project management*	The nuts and bolts of managing an evaluation from beginning to end, including negotiating contracts, budgeting, identifying and coordinating needed resources, and conducting the evaluation in a timely manner.	Special project management challenges in developmental evaluation include managing and adapting the emergent design, timely data collection and feedback, handling the sheer volume of data that emerges as the project unfolds, and flexible budgeting.
5. *Reflective practice*	An awareness of one's program evaluation expertise, as well as the needs for professional growth.	Reflective practice is a data collection approach in developmental evaluation, as is a commitment to assess and further develop one's developmental evaluation competencies. This practice includes reflexivity—reflecting on one's contribution and role in relation to particular contexts and processes.
6. *Interpersonal competence*	The "people skills" needed to work with diverse groups of stakeholders to conduct program evaluations, including written and oral communication, negotiation, and cross-cultural skills.	A developmental evaluation is co-created with primary intended users (social innovators, funders, and implementation staff). The approach is heavily relationship-focused, so interpersonal relationships are parallel to methods in determining the evaluation's relevance and credibility.

*Ghere, King, Stevahn, and Minnema (2006).

conducting the evaluation. Methods don't just happen. Someone, namely an evaluator, has to employ methods. So the evaluator's competence in selecting and applying
appropriate methods and measures, and appropriately and competently analyzing
and presenting the findings, are the fundamental source of an evaluation's credibility. Developmental evaluator Mark Cabaj adds:

> "In fast-moving, complex contexts, the traditional challenges of evaluation
> design and getting valid and reliable data are amplified, requiring evaluators
> to use their best *bricoleur* [creating customized solutions for unique problems]
> skills to come up with real-time methods and data. Moreover, the signals from
> that data are often weak and ambiguous, [so] the challenge of helping social
> innovators—who, like any of us, are eager to find patterns and meaning in data
> even when they don't exist—properly interpret and use that data [becomes]
> more challenging than normal.
>
> "In my thesis research [on early adopters of developmental evaluation;
> Cabaj, 2011], several people pointed out that they thought the methodological
> challenges in a developmental evaluation situation may sometimes outstrip the
> capacity of any one evaluator—and in those situations, developmental evalu-
> ation might be offered by a lead evaluator who can draw upon a network of
> evaluators with different expertise and skills."

Earlier, I have noted the importance of leadership buy-in as part of organizational readiness. Developmental evaluators also play a leadership role in providing
leadership for the direction of the developmental evaluation, which also affects the
direction of innovation and intervention adaptations.

> An element of leadership is involved in developmental evaluation because the develop-
> mental evaluator is actively helping to shape the initiative. *How* that's done makes a
> world of difference to the effectiveness of their work. (Dozois, Langlois, & Blanchet-
> Cohen, 2010, p. 23)

The traditional emphasis on methodological competencies assumes that methodological rigor is the primary determinant of evaluation credibility. But the evidence from studies of developmental evaluation use shows that evaluator characteristics interact with methodological criteria and facilitation skill in determining an
evaluation's credibility and utility. In essence, how the evaluation is facilitated with
meaningful involvement of primary intended users and skilled engagement of the
developmental evaluators affects the users' judgments about the evaluation's credibility and utility—and thus their willingness to act on feedback. The active and
engaged role of the developmental evaluator has been called "the art of the nudge"
(Langlois, Blanchet-Cohen, & Beer, 2012, p. 39):

> [F]ive practices [have been] found central to the *art of the nudge*: (1) practicing servant
> leadership; (2) sensing program energy; (3) supporting common spaces; (4) untying

---

EXHIBIT 1.5

The Developmental Evaluation Context and the Developmental Evaluator

Context/Context: Organization	Evaluator: The pragmatic *bricoleur*
High levels of awareness of context and changes in the wider environment	Vigilance in tracking internal and external emergence
Willing to balance development and innovation with a commitment to testing reality	High tolerance for ambiguity, as well as the ability to facilitate values-based sense making, interpretations, and decision making
Willingness to explore, dig deeper, interpret whatever emerges, and provide timely feedback as the innovation develops	Methodological agility and creativity, combined with a willingness and ability to change and respond with adapted design, framework, program theory, methods, and processes
Courage to keep going and adapt in the face of uncertainty	Courage to take on messy journey of ups and downs, sidetracks, and the unexpected, all the while retaining a tolerant and critical open-mindedness and commitment to truth telling
Readiness to co-create the future, collaborate, and trust	Readiness to develop long-term relationships of trust—to be "in it for the long haul"

Source: Kate McKegg and Michael Quinn Patton, Developmental Evaluation Workshop, African Evaluation Association, Yaounde, Cameroon, March 2014.

---

knots iteratively; and (5) paying attention to structure. These practices can help developmental evaluators detect and support opportunities for learning and adaptation leading to right-timed feedback.

Question 6 in this chapter has asked about organizational readiness. This question has examined evaluator readiness to conduct a developmental evaluation. Exhibit 1.5 puts these two questions together.

8. How Can Developmental Evaluation Serve Accountability Needs and Demands?

Accountability is traditionally associated with spending funds in accordance with contractual requirements to achieve set targets. But the developmental evaluation approach to accountability includes *accountability for learning and adaptation*. This was the conclusion the senior staff of the Minnesota-based Blandin Foundation reached while engaged in developmental evaluation focused on the foundation's strategic framework. The result was a report titled *Mountain of Accountability* (Blandin Foundation, 2014). I urge readers to examine the report online for the graphic depiction and full explanation of the Mountain of Accountability concept. It's a resource I use regularly to explain how developmental evaluation addresses accountability concerns. Here I can only provide a brief overview.

The *Mountain of Accountability* graphic depicts three levels of accountability and the interconnections among them.

- *Level 1: Basic accountability.* The first level of accountability assesses the extent to which resources are well managed, the quality of personnel management practices, the implementation of programs with due diligence and professionalism, and basic accountability-oriented reporting. The data for basic accountability should be embedded in fundamental management processes.

- *Level 2: Accountability for impact and effectiveness.* The second, more advanced level of accountability involves assessing intervention (program) outcomes and impacts. This is the arena of traditional program evaluation.

- *Level 3: Accountability for learning, development, and adaptation.* The third level approaches accountability through the lenses of complexity concepts and systems change. At this level, developmental evaluation is used to support learning, adaptation, systems change, mission fulfillment, principles-focused evaluation, and "walking the talk" of values. Whereas traditional evaluations focus on improving and making decisions about projects and programs, developmental evaluation addresses strategy implementation and effectiveness at the overall organization and mission fulfillment levels.

Developmental evaluation integrates accountability with *ongoing development* by paying particular attention to changes in the organization's environment (e.g., economic, social, demographic, policy, and technological changes) that affect strategic adjustments. *Accountability for learning and development* involves identifying lessons learned through deep reflective practice that can be applied to innovative systems change initiatives, adaptation, and making a difference in complex dynamic systems.

The Blandin Foundation's *Mountain of Accountability* report describes one creative approach to incorporating accountability concerns into developmental evaluation. The point is not to replicate the Mountain of Accountability concept. The point is to negotiate and clarify what *accountability* means within the context and arena of innovative and systems change action where developmental evaluation is being undertaken.

9. Why Is Developmental Evaluation Attracting So Much Attention and Spreading So Quickly?

As documented in the Preface, since the publication of *Developmental Evaluation* (Patton, 2011), the idea has taken off. Weekly I receive examples of developmental evaluations either underway or completed. In a short time, developmental evaluation has become recognized and established as a distinct and useful approach. So the question is "Why?"

I would point to four intersecting social change trends, with developmental evaluation sitting at the point where these trends converge. First is the worldwide demand for *innovation*. The private sector, public sector, and nonprofit sector are all experiencing pressure to innovate. As the world's population grows, climate change threatens, and technology innovations expand horizons and possibilities exponentially (to mention just three forces for change), social innovation is recognized as essential to address global problems. A good way to see how developmental evaluation has intersected with the more general innovation trajectory over the last decade is to look at the *Stanford Social Innovation Review,* which began publishing in 2003. A recent archival search turned up a number of references to developmental evaluation, including "next generation evaluation" and "a game-changing approach" (FSG, 2014).

The second trend consists of *systems change.* Evaluation "grew up" in the projects and has been dominated by a project- and model-testing mentality. I would say that the field has mastered how to evaluate projects. But projects, we've learned, don't change systems—and major social problems require action at the systems level. Project-level evaluation doesn't translate directly into systems change evaluation. Treating a system as a unit of analysis—that is, as the evaluand (thing evaluated)—requires systems understandings and systems thinking. Developmental evaluation brings a systems orientation to evaluating systems change.

The third trend is *complexity.* Innovation and systems thinking point to complexity theory as the relevant framework for making sense of how the world is changed. Question 4, earlier in this chapter, has addressed how systems thinking and complexity theory inform developmental evaluation practice.

The fourth trend is the acknowledgment of developmental evaluation as a *legitimate evaluation approach.* I've heard from evaluators and social innovators all over the world who were already engaged in developmental evaluation thinking and practices, but didn't have a recognizable name for what they were doing and expressed appreciation for identifying the approach as a rigorous option. I've heard from evaluators that the publication of the 2011 book gave developmental evaluation legitimacy, brought it into sharper focus for people allowing them to better do what they were already intuitively led to do, created a common language that allows people to talk with each other about taking a developmental approach to evaluation, and demonstrated that developmental evaluation can be done with validity and credibility. Exhibit 1.6 displays these four intersecting forces propelling developmental evaluation.

As a matter of balance, it is only appropriate to acknowledge that the rapid spread of developmental evaluation has also generated problems with fidelity (see Question 1 in this chapter); confusion about what developmental evaluation is and how to do it; and, unfortunately, misinterpretations and misuses of developmental evaluation. Exhibit 1.7 provides examples of some common issues that have emerged and my advice for dealing with them.

EXHIBIT 1.6

Global Societal Forces Propelling Developmental Evaluation

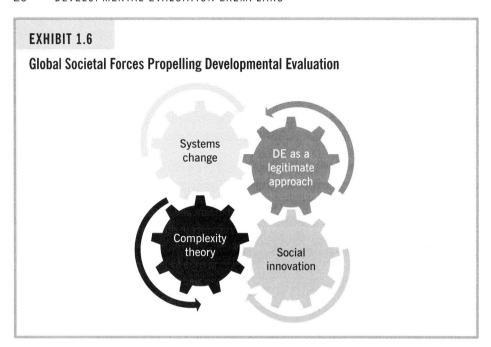

EXHIBIT 1.7

Developmental Evaluation Issues and Challenges

Issue	Developmental evaluation approach	Potential problem or misuse of developmental evaluation	Advice
1. **Understanding emergence:** Learning and adapting through engagement, not detailed advance planning. The innovation unfolds through active engagement in change processes, fostering learning and adaptation.	Letting the evaluation evolve naturally: As the nature of the intervention emerges, so do the developmental evaluation design, data collection, and feedback.	Staff members' using developmental evaluation as an excuse for not planning: "We'll just make it up as we go along" becomes a convenient way to resist logic models, theories of change, or other upfront evaluation design work that may be appropriate.	Distinguish between situations where enough is known to engage in traditional planning and evaluation, and situations where the complex nature of the problem necessitates emergent, innovative engagement and use of developmental evaluation as the appropriately aligned approach.

(continued)

Issue	Developmental evaluation approach	Potential problem or misuse of developmental evaluation	Advice
2. **Hybrid approaches:** Combining developmental evaluation with other evaluation approaches (e.g., outcome mapping, feminist evaluation) and purposes (formative, summative).	Aligning the evaluation approaches with the situation and context.	Confusion and lack of focus by dabbling with multiple approaches: starting with developmental evaluation, throwing in some theory-driven evaluation and a dash of empowerment evaluation, adding formative and summative evaluation to offer familiarity, then a heavy infusion of accountability . . .	Employ *bricolage* (creative design and integration of multiple approaches, drawing on available resources) and pragmatism: Do what makes sense for a given situation and context, and be explicit and transparent about why what was done was done. Know the strengths and weaknesses of various approaches.
3. **Treating developmental evaluation as just initial exploration and experimentation.**	Emphasis on ongoing development and adaptation. Understanding that the purpose and nature of developmental evaluation are different from those of formative and summative evaluation.	Engaging in "bait and switch" or failing to stay the course: Funders ask for developmental evaluation without knowing what it entails. They start with it, then halfway through start demanding traditional deliverable products (e.g., logframes, formative reports) and expect a traditional summative report to be produced.	Become adept at explaining the purpose and niche of developmental evaluation— and reiterate the commitment to it on an ongoing basis. Don't expect an initial commitment to developmental evaluation to endure without reinforcement. The initial commitment needs nurturing and deepened reinforcement as the evaluation unfolds.
4. **Responding to requests for proposals or tender solicitations.**	Understanding that the developmental evaluation design emerges as the innovative process emerges, so a fully specified design is not possible at the request-for-proposals or terms-of-reference stage.	Rejecting a developmental evaluation response to a request as indicating lack of design specificity.	Work to switch solicitations and tenders from requesting design details to requesting qualifications and competences. Demonstrate design and methods competence, then show why and how the developmental evaluation design will emerge.

(continued)

Issue	Developmental evaluation approach	Potential problem or misuse of developmental evaluation	Advice
5. **Budgeting for developmental evaluation.**	Understanding that as the developmental evaluation design emerges, the budget emerges. Budget options are presented to offer alternative inquiry paths to support emergent information and decision-making needs.	Rigid upfront budgeting requirements, which reduce flexibility, adaptability, and emergent responsiveness.	Do the developmental evaluation budget in stages, rather than for the whole initiative all at once and at the beginning. Be prepared to do a series of budgets as the innovation unfolds in stages over time.

10. What Has Been the Most Significant Development in Developmental Evaluation since Publication of the Patton (2011) Book?

Principles-focused evaluation has emerged as a major inquiry framework and focus for developmental evaluation. For example, in their insightful volume titled *Evaluating Complexity*, Preskill and Gopal (2014) advise: "Look for effective principles of practice in action, rather than assessing adherence to a predetermined set of activities" (p. 16). Treating principles as the focus of evaluation requires principles-focused sampling (Patton, 2015, p. 270). This involves identifying and studying cases that illuminate the nature, implementation, outcomes, and implications of principles. Studying the implementation and outcomes of effective, evidence-based principles is a major new direction in developmental evaluation (Patton, 2011, pp. 167–168, 194–195; Patton, 2015, p. 292).

A principles-based approach is appropriate when a group of diverse programs are all adhering to the same principles, but each is adapting those principles to its own particular target population within its own context. A *principle* is defined as a fundamental proposition that serves as the foundation for a system of belief or behavior or for a chain of reasoning. An approach grounded in evidence-based, effective principles assumes that while the principles remain the same, implementing them will necessarily and appropriately require adaptation within and across contexts. Evidence for the effectiveness of principles is derived from in-depth case studies of their implementations and implications. The results of the case studies are then synthesized across the diverse programs, all adhering to the same principles, but each adapting those principles to its own particular target population within its own context.

The ideal is that the principles guiding the innovation and those informing the evaluation are aligned. This is a distinguishing feature of Chapter 2, in which the innovative program and the developmental evaluation are based on a holistic set of Māori cultural principles that guide ways of knowing and being in tribal and Māori contexts. This seamless blending of cultural and evaluation principles exemplifies principles-focused developmental evaluation. Chapter 4 also presents a principles-focused evaluation exemplar.

Developmental Evaluation Case Exemplars

This opening chapter has offered responses to the 10 most common questions I get about developmental evaluation. We turn now to the heart of this book: case exemplars of actual developmental evaluations. As I do keynote speeches, conduct training, and consult on developmental evaluations, the most common request I get is for real-world applications and case examples. This book responds to that demand. As you read these examples of different kinds of developmental evaluation in a variety of settings, focused on quite diverse innovations, I invite you to look for patterns, themes, and principles in practice. In Chapter 14, coeditors Kate McKegg and Nan Wehipeihana present a synthesis of the patterns and themes they have observed, drawing on both the cases and their own extensive experiences as developmental evaluators. Chapter 15 completes the book with a detailed discussion of the eight essential developmental evaluation principles.

REFERENCES

American Evaluation Association (AEA), Task Force on Guiding Principles for Evaluators. (2004). *Guiding principles for evaluators* (rev. ed.). Washington, DC: Author. Retrieved from *www.eval.org/p/cm/ld/fid=51*.

Blandin Foundation. (2014). Mountain of accountability. Grand Rapids, MN: Author. Retrieved from *http://blandinfoundation.org/resources/reports/mountain-of-accountability*.

Cabaj, M. (2011). *Developmental evaluation: Experiences and reflections of 18 early adopters*. Unpublished master's thesis, University of Waterloo, Waterloo, Ontario, Canada.

Coryn, C. L. S., Noakes, L. A., Westine, C. D., & Schröter, D. C. (2011). A systematic review of theory-driven evaluation practice from 1990 to 2009. *American Journal of Evaluation, 32*(2), 199–226.

Cousins, J. B., & Chouinard, J. A. (2012). *Participatory evaluation up close: An integration of research-based knowledge*. Charlotte, NC: Information Age.

Cousins, J. B., Whitmore, E., & Shulha, L. (2014). Arguments for a common set of principles for collaborative inquiry in evaluation. *American Journal of Evaluation, 34*(1), 7–22.

Daigneault, P. M., & Jacob, S. (2009). Toward accurate measurement of participation: Rethinking the conceptualization and operationalization of participatory evaluation. *American Journal of Evaluation, 30*(3), 330–348.

Dickson, R., & Saunders, M. (2014). Developmental evaluation: Lessons for evaluative practice from the SEARCH program. *Evaluation, 20*(2), 176–194.

Dozois, E., Langlois, M., & Blanchet-Cohen, N. (2010). *DE 201: A practitioner's guide to developmental evaluation.* Montreal: J. W. McConnell Family Foundation. Retrieved from *www.mcconnellfoundation.ca/en/resources/publication/de-201-a-practitioners-guide-to-developmental-evaluation.*

Fetterman, D., Kaftarian, S. J., & Wandersman, A. H. (Eds.). (2014). *Empowerment evaluation: Knowledge and tools for self-assessment, evaluation capacity building, and accountability.* Thousand Oaks, CA: Sage.

FSG. (2014). Next generation evaluation: Embracing complexity, connectivity, and change. *Stanford Social Innovation Review.* Retrieved from *www.ssireview.org/nextgenevaluation.*

Ghere, G., King, J., Stevahn, L., & Minnema, J. (2006). A professional development unit for reflecting on program evaluation competencies. *American Journal of Evaluation, 27*(1), 108–123.

Lam, C. Y., & Shulha, L. M. (2014). Insights on using developmental evaluation for innovating: A case study on the cocreation of an innovative program. *American Journal of Evaluation* [published online before print]. Retrieved from *http://aje.sagepub.com/content/early/2014/08/08/1098214014542100.*

Langlois, M., Blanchet-Cohen, N., & Beer, T. (2012). The art of the nudge: Five practices for developmental evaluators. *Canadian Journal of Program Evaluation, 27*(2), 39–59.

Miller, R. L., & Campbell, R. (2006). Taking stock of empowerment evaluation: An empirical review. *American Journal of Evaluation, 27*(3), 296–319.

Patton, M. Q. (2011). *Developmental evaluation: Applying complexity concepts to enhance innovation and use.* New York: Guilford Press.

Patton, M. Q. (2012). *Essentials of utilization-focused evaluation.* Thousand Oaks, CA: Sage.

Patton, M. Q. (2015). *Qualitative research and evaluation methods* (4th ed.). Thousand Oaks, CA: Sage.

Preskill, H., & Beer, T. (2012). Evaluating social innovation. Retrieved from *www.fsg.org/tabid/191/ArticleId/708/Default.aspx?srpush=true.*

Preskill, H., & Gopal, S. (2014). Evaluating complexity: Propositions for improving practice. Retrieved from *www.fsg.org/tabid/191/ArticleId/1204/Default.aspx?srpush=true.*

Williams, B. (2005). Systems and systems thinking. In S. Mathison (Ed.), *Encyclopedia of evaluation* (pp. 405–412). Thousand Oaks, CA: Sage.

Williams, B. (2008). Systemic inquiry. In L. M. Given (Ed.), *The Sage encyclopedia of qualitative research methods* (Vol. 2, pp. 854–859). Thousand Oaks, CA: Sage.

Williams, B. (2014, November 16). A systems practitioner's journey [Post to AEA365 blog]. Retrieved from *https://us-mg204.mail.yahoo.com/neo/launch?.partner=sbc&.rand=3sva69d24c9fe#.*

Williams, B., & van 't Hof, S. (2014*). Wicked solutions: A systems approach to complex problems.* Wellington, New Zealand: Bob Williams. Retrieved from *www.bobwilliams.co.nz/wicked.pdf.*

Wilson-Grau, R., & Britt, H. (2012). *Outcome harvesting.* Cairo, Egypt: Ford Foundation Middle East and North Africa Office. Retrieved from *www.outcomemapping.ca/resource/resource.php?id=374.*

CHAPTER 2

Cultural Responsiveness through Developmental Evaluation

Indigenous Innovations in Sport and Traditional Māori Recreation

Nan Wehipeihana, Kate McKegg, Veronica Thompson, and Kataraina Pipi

Whaia te pae tawhiti kia mau, whaia te pae tata whakamaua kia tina.
(Pursue the vision of the distant horizon, by achieving the goals at hand.)

EDITOR'S INTRODUCTION (BY MICHAEL QUINN PATTON)

This book's first developmental evaluation case study was conducted in New Zealand. It highlights the crucial importance of culture in human life, and it illuminates how developmental evaluation can be aligned with and sensitive to cultural meanings and dynamics when grounded in and attentive to essential principles. In Chapter 1, I have discussed the emergence of principles-focused evaluation as an important approach to developmental evaluation. The sport and recreation innovation in this example was built on Māori principles—*as was the evaluation*. Kaupapa Tuku Iho is a holistic set of Māori cultural principles that guide ways of knowing and being in tribal and Māori contexts. The case study showcases the rich array of cultural, community, facilitation, and methodological knowledge and expertise needed for this kind of evaluation, together with *the seamless blending of cultural and evaluation principles*. Honoring cultural principles undergirded by developmental evaluation principles is at the heart of this collaboration—an exemplar of *principles-focused developmental evaluation*.

The innovation started as a vision, became an idea, and took shape as a cultural transformation realized through specific ways of engaging in sport and recreation. Program design, implementation, and evaluation were interwoven together through this emergent process. The case study speaks to the relational nature of developmental evaluation; to the importance of developmental evaluators' being embedded deep within the innovation; and to the emergence of a "developmental team" combining evaluators, the program manager, and program delivery personnel who were actively involved in simultaneously developing the innovation and implementing the evaluation. The star-shaped, culturally expressive conceptual framework that guided both program development and the developmental evaluation is as elegant, evocative, and engaging—not to mention information-packed—as any visual depiction of systems change and complexity dynamics I've ever seen. Spend some time with Exhibit 2.7. Savor it. It's almost like one of those Magic Eye pictures that draw you in, and as you stare at it, you see things not at first visible. There are starry heights and ocean depths in that diagram.

I want to suggest one other thing to look for in this case and savor. I'm not sure how much of this you can detect in the writing, for even the kind of deep reflective practice you'll see demonstrated in this chapter cannot do justice to the affective dimension. Nan, Kate, and Kataraina genuinely enjoy doing evaluation. They laugh together a lot and display passion for the work and the systems changes their work supports. At the annual American Evaluation Association conference, Kataraina with her guitar is the quasi-official minstrel of the global evaluation community, ready with new lyrics to fit whatever may be the occasion. Kate and Nan, in addition to being Kataraina's chorus, champion Indigenous and culturally sensitive evaluation, not just in New Zealand but worldwide.

One *wee* thing to add (*wee* being an old English/New Zealand form of understatement): This evaluation was given the Best Evaluation Policy and Systems Award by the Australasian Evaluation Society in 2013. It is the first developmental evaluation in the world that has received such official recognition from a professional association, and I am honored to present it here as the first of the 12 case exemplars in this book.

He Oranga Poutama (HOP) is a Sport New Zealand (Sport NZ) initiative that supports Māori well-being through sport and recreation. In 2009, there was a significant change in the strategic direction of HOP from increasing "participation by Māori in sport" to increasing "participation and leadership as Māori in sport and traditional physical recreation, at a community level." This shift from "participation *by Māori*" to "participation and leadership *as Māori*" was a bold step by Sport NZ, as there was little to no practical application of the latter concept from which to draw lessons for program design and implementation.

Developmental evaluation was used to develop a practical, grounded, community-up understanding of what participation *as Māori* looks like in sport and recreation contexts. What developed—Te Whetu Rēhua (the framework)—was not a "model" that would be replicated across the program; rather, a set of core principles and concepts emerged that could be adapted by Sport NZ and HOP partners in their various local settings.

This case study illustrates the role of developmental evaluation in supporting Indigenous innovation—taking an innovative concept through to program design implementation and evaluation. Māori cultural principles were and are at the heart of this evaluation, and cultural practices are utilized and adapted to guide engagement, data collection, collaborative sense making, and capacity development. This chapter showcases the cultural, facilitation, evaluation, and community knowledge and expertise needed for this evaluation, as well as the seamless blending of cultural and evaluation principles. It affirms the responsiveness of developmental evaluation to culture and cultural context, and it concludes with lessons learned and practice-based insights.

He Oranga Poutama

He Oranga Poutama (the name means "a pathway to well-being") began in 1995 as an interagency[1] initiative with a focus on developing "by Māori for Māori" sport and leisure activities, to improve Māori health and employment outcomes through the promotion of healthy lifestyles via such activities.

The program funds kaiwhakahaere (coordinator) positions in selected regions in New Zealand, delivered through Regional Sports Trusts (RSTs) and Iwi (tribal) and Māori providers, to promote health messages and employment opportunities through the medium of sport and physical recreation. In 2003, following the establishment of Sport and Recreation New Zealand (SPARC),[2] responsibility for the HOP program was transferred to SPARC.

SPARC was established as a Crown entity on January 1, 2003, under the Sport and Recreation New Zealand Act 2002 to "promote, encourage and support physical recreation and sport in New Zealand." Its legislative function was to "promote and support the development and implementation of physical recreation and sport in a way that is culturally appropriate to Māori."

In 2009, SPARC undertook an internal review of HOP and in particular its strategic direction. The review noted that HOP had struggled to maintain its links with Māori communities and alignment to SPARC's strategic directions. Program inequities between Iwi and Māori providers and RSTs were evident, as Iwi and Māori providers had access to fewer SPARC resources (expertise, advice, and financial resources) to assist them to grow their capacity and capability. The dual delivery mode of HOP through Iwi and Māori providers and RSTs raised questions about the cultural capacity and capability of RSTs to engage with and deliver to Māori, and the equity of partnership relationships between SPARC and Iwi and Māori HOP providers. Furthermore, the achievement of the HOP strategic goal to "increase physical activity among Māori" was deemed beyond the resourcing levels of SPARC and increasingly out of scope for SPARC. The review highlighted the need to tighten HOP's focus and align the program to demand narrower, but more realistic, goals for the available investment resources. The outcome of the HOP review was the development of a new strategic goal: "to increase participation and leadership *as Māori* in sport and traditional physical recreation, at a community level."

The evaluation team contributed to the review activities, to the development of the new HOP outcome framework, and to communications about the new program goal and its policy and operational implications for the organization. Through this work, the team members developed a good understanding of the rationale for the

---

[1]Members of the interagency group included Te Puni Kōkiri (the Ministry of Māori Development), the Community Employment Group, the Health Sponsorship Council, and the Hillary Commission (the forerunner to Sport NZ).

[2]Sport and Recreation New Zealand (SPARC) was renamed Sport New Zealand on February 1, 2012. In this chapter, we use the organizational name applicable to the period being discussed.

> **Kate:** "At the time I was providing evaluation support to SPARC's research and evaluation team, and when the HOP review was flagged, the evaluation manager asked if I could help the project leader (Ronnie [Veronica Thompson]) develop an evaluation plan for a major programme revision. I took one look at the set of papers and was struck by the boldness of the vision. I also realized that it would require someone who could bring Māori cultural knowledge and evaluation expertise to the work, and recommended Nan immediately."
>
> **Nan:** "I remember meeting with Ronnie and being in awe of the bold vision she had for the program. Her conception of participation as Māori participation in sport and recreation was ground breaking and ahead of its time, and I felt privileged just being around Ronnie and exposed to her thinking, contributing what I could through conversation, reflection, and evaluative inquiry. I was also mindful that we would need a high level of facilitation skills and strong connection to Māori community networks, so I asked Kataraina Pipi to join the team."

new HOP strategic goal; got to meet with some of the HOP managers and kai-whakahaere; and established a strong relationship with Veronica Thompson, the senior adviser responsible for the operational oversight and management of the HOP program.

"As Māori": An Innovative Concept

Māori want to live *as Māori*, actively participate as citizens of the world, and enjoy a high standard of living and good health (Durie, 2001).

When SPARC was established in 2003, the concept of Māori living *as Māori* (Durie, 2001) was a newly emerging policy idea. There were no roadmaps, guidelines, or examples of what Māori participating *as Māori* might look like, or how the concept could be given effect to and applied in 21st-century Aotearoa New Zealand.

The change in HOP's strategic direction was a bold undertaking by Sport NZ, given the dearth of evidence for the practical application of *as Māori*. There were no examples of this concept's implementation in a government policy and operational context, and there were no definitions about what participating *as Māori* in sport consisted of or might look like, let alone how it might be measured or evaluated. It also signaled a more explicit program connection to te ao Māori (the Māori world), the valuing of tikanga Māori (Māori cultural principles and practices), te reo Māori (the Māori language), and tino rangatiratanga (Māori leadership and self-determination).

The Cultural Foundations of HOP

The development of the new HOP strategic goal revisited what "culturally appropriate to Māori" might look like in fulfilment of SPARC's legislative function to "promote and support the development and implementation of physical recreation and sport in a way that is culturally appropriate to Māori." It drew on the Māori Potentials Approach (Te Puni Kōkiri, 2009), Kaupapa Māori (Māori ideology) principles (G. Smith, 1997), and the Māori Development framework (Durie, Fitzgerald, Kingi, McKinley, & Stevenson, 2002) in considering the term *culturally appropriate*.

The Māori Potentials Approach (see Exhibit 2.1) is a public policy framework that aims to realize Māori potential. It is guided by three key principles: the Māori potential principle, the culturally distinct principle, and the Māori capability principle.

Kaupapa Māori (Māori ideology) principles (see Exhibit 2.2) assert and take for granted the validity and legitimacy of being Māori, the importance of ensuring the survival and revival of Māori language and culture, and the centrality of self-determination to Māori cultural well-being. Six key principles underpin Kaupapa Māori.

The Māori Development framework (see Exhibit 2.3) identifies outcomes that are important to Māori, determinants considered important by Māori, and processes that signal adherence to culturally appropriate progress.

The re-visioning of the HOP program and the new strategic goal were thus deeply grounded in Māori principles, values, and aspirations. Given the foundational nature of these cultural aspects, and the unique expression of participation

EXHIBIT 2.1

The Māori Potentials Approach

The *Māori potential principle* recognizes that Māori are diverse, aspirational people with a distinctive Indigenous culture and value system. It affirms all Māori as having positive potential, regardless of age, gender, location, or socioeconomic status. This principle guides government agencies in supporting Māori to identify their strengths and to develop and facilitate opportunities to maximize this potential.

The *culturally distinct principle* recognizes that the Māori community and its Indigenous culture are both parts of, and significant contributors to, the identity, well-being, and enrichment of New Zealand society. It distinguishes Māori as the first people of New Zealand, while acknowledging the positive contributions they make to their communities as an Indigenous people, as cultural beings, and as citizens of New Zealand and the world. This principle guides government agencies in supporting the creation of opportunities for Māori to sustain and leverage off their Indigenous identity and culture.

The *Māori capability principle* affirms the capability, initiative, and aspiration of Māori to make choices for themselves. This principle guides investment in Māori to bring about change in their life circumstances and their environments. This principle advocates strengthening organizational and infrastructural capacity, while at the same time building the capability of people and their sense of choices and power to act. This principle guides government agencies to support opportunities for investment in Māori people that build upon their own capability and initiative to be catalysts for change in their own lives.

EXHIBIT 2.2

Kaupapa Māori Principles

Tino Rangatiratanga (the self-determination principle) is foundational to Kaupapa Māori. It has been discussed in terms of sovereignty, autonomy, self-determination, and independence, as well as seeking more meaningful control over one's own life and cultural well-being.

Taonga Tuku Iho (the cultural aspirations principle) asserts a position that to be Māori is both valid and legitimate, and being Māori is taken for granted. Te reo Māori (the Māori langauge), matauranga Māori (Māori knowledge), and tikanga Māori (Māori culture) are actively validated and legitimated.

Ako Māori (the culturally preferred pedagogy principle) promotes teaching and learning practices that are unique to tikanga Māori (Māori culture). There is an acknowledgment of "borrowed" pedagogies, as well as affirming Māori as able to choose their own preferred and/or culturally based pedagogies.

Kia piki ake i nga raruraru o te kainga (the socioeconomic mediation principle) addresses the issue of Māori socioeconomic disadvantage and the negative impact this has on whānau (extended family). It asserts Kaupapa Māori mediation practices and values as able to intervene successfully for the well-being of whānau.

Whānau (the extended family structure principle) is foundational to Kaupapa Māori. The whānau and the practice of whakawhanaungatanga (establishing relationships, relating well to others) are integral aspects of Māori identity and culture, and the cultural values, customs, and practices are necessary parts of Māori survival and well-being.

Kaupapa (the collective philosophy principle) acknowledges the importance of a "collective" commitment and vision. This vision connects Māori aspirations with political, social, economic, and cultural well-being.

EXHIBIT 2.3

Māori Development Framework

Outcomes that are important to Māori: the Treaty of Waitangi* settlements, kotahitanga (unity), tino rangatiratanga (self-determination), Māori asset base, te reo Māori (the Māori language), tikanga Māori (culture), whakapapa Māori (cultural identity), whānau (extended family), hauora (well-being), and Hauora Māori (Māori well-being).

Determinants considered important by Māori: education and economics, Māori participation in society, political agendas, tino rangatiratanga (self-determination), application of the Treaty of Waitangi, Indigeneity, and globalization.

Processes that signal adherence to culturally appropriate progress: application of Māori values set, recognition of Māori aspirations, Māori-centered analytical frameworks, evidence-based approaches, and integration of multiple data.

*Under the Treaty of Waitangi Act 1975, Māori can make claims to the Waitangi Tribunal relating to actions or omissions of the Crown that breach the promises made in the Treaty of Waitangi. *Treaty settlements* refer to the compensation awarded (e.g., financial payments or land settlement) by the New Zealand Government.

as Māori to be developed within the HOP program context, tikanga Māori would need to be at the center of the development, implementation, and evaluation of HOP.

Operational Implementation Changes

The advent of the new strategic goal was also accompanied by delivery changes, and by the recognition that the context of participating *as Māori* would best be understood and nurtured by partner organizations with strong connections to Māori culture—organizations in which Māori cultural distinctiveness is valued and "normal."

It was not assumed that existing HOP partners would guarantee the best fit for the new program goal and outcomes. On the one hand, it was acknowledged that some of the then-current partners had been involved since the program's inception in 1995 and would bring good sport and cultural knowledge and capacity to the initiative. On the other hand, there were concerns that some of these partners might see the new program as an "upgraded old program" and find it difficult to shift from what they were currently doing; others might not have the energy or commitment needed to drive the new program's vision.

Furthermore, SPARC recognized the significantly changed delivery context (1995 compared to 2008) and the availability of a wider pool of potential providers, particularly Iwi and Māori organizations, able and willing to deliver this program. Under the previous funding program model, there had been a relatively fixed group of RSTs delivering the HOP program. An open and contestable selection process was put in place to select HOP providers, to ensure that they would have the necessary mix of management, sport, and cultural capabilities to deliver the "new" HOP initiative. Twelve providers,[3] five RSTs and seven Iwi and Māori providers, were eventually selected through this open-tender process to deliver the HOP program for the 2009–2012 period.

> **Veronica:** "The underlying principle of an open and contestable process is that we want the best providers possible—people who want to be in the space and are culturally capable of being in the space. When I say culturally competent, I mean providers who have people at every level—governance, management, and delivery—with strong cultural capability, and who managerially have good support and systems."
>
> **Nan:** "Kate and I supported the new contestable process by developing criteria to guide the selection of HOP providers and contributing to the program investment guidelines."

[3]He Oranga Pounamu, Mataatua Sports Trust, Ngāti Hine Health Trust, Sport Northland, Sport Taranaki, Sport Hawkes Bay, Sport Waikato (Tainui and Maniapoto), Sport Waitākere (lead provider for the Auckland region), Te Hauora o Tūranganui-ā-Kiwa, Te Papa Taakaro o Te Arawa, Te Wharekura o Rākaumanga, and Tūwharetoa Sports.

What Kind of Evaluation?

At the same time as the HOP program tender was released, an open-tender process for the evaluation of HOP was also issued. Following a short-listing process, Research Evaluation Consultancy Limited (Nan Wehipeihana's company) was one of two evaluation teams interviewed by the selection panel, and was subsequently awarded the evaluation contract. Veronica Thompson was not part of the evaluation selection panel.

Nan: "Despite our role in aiding the development of the *as Māori* concept and our relationship with Ronnie, we advocated for an open-tender process for the contracting of the evaluation, to ensure that the contracting process for evaluation would be perceived as credible and ethical. In 2009, given that developmental evaluation was almost unknown in New Zealand government and evaluation circles, we needed to take developmental evaluation through the front door, and not slide it under the door because of our organizational and program knowledge and our relationships with Ronnie. When advised that we were one of two companies short-listed for the evaluation, we worried that we might not win the work. What we proposed did not look like a 'typical' evaluation, whereas we were sure that the other evaluators would have proposed something more familiar and recognizable as traditional evaluation."

Kate: "We knew we needed an evaluation approach that would best fit the complexity surrounding the initiative; the significance of the innovation and change process, the uncertainty ahead, as well as the centrality of tikanga Māori [Māori principles and practice]."

The evaluation also needed to be responsive to the Māori cultural context of the program and be sensitive to the uniquely Māori context within which HOP operates at a community level. Cultural concepts, language and values are implicit within evaluation thinking, processes, tools, frameworks, data collection, judgment and reporting, and we needed an evaluation approach—and evaluators—who could provide a genuine and valid evaluation experience in the eyes of Māori providers and communities. (McKegg, Wehipeihana, Pipi, & Thompson, 2013, p. 11)

Nan: "The evaluation had to walk the talk and support the *as Māori* vision. As evaluators, we would not be able to sit outside the program's development process, distant and removed from the messiness of the developmental journey to come. We would need to be intimately involved in HOP's development—achieving the delicate balance between supporting creativity and innovation, while at the same time bringing critical inquiry and evaluative thinking to the program's development, decision making, and the evaluation."

Veronica: "Well, I knew not a lot about evaluation to start with and even less about developmental evaluation, and the way developmental evaluation was articulated to me initially by Kate and Nan, it just felt right. Not particularly objective, but then I went away and read some articles by Michael Quinn Patton. And I thought, yes, it fits even more having read the literature because it allows for creativity. It's still quite heady, you know, but there's a fluidity for things to emerge and for us to affirm or question those things as they emerge."

Kate: "When I proposed developmental evaluation, there was little formal litera-ture (Patton, 2006a, 2006b, 2009) to guide our practice. But we'd had the ben-efit of the social innovation literature (Westley, Zimmerman, & Patton, 2006) and of Michael [Quinn Patton] visiting New Zealand in 2004, 2005, and 2009, running a series of workshops on systems thinking, complexity science, and developmental evalu-ation. On the other hand, it had a feel of familiarity, giving a name—*developmental evaluation*—to much of our evaluation practice."

Nan: "The other critical factor was the extensive skill set and experience of the team. For me, as the person whose company would hold the contract, the breadth of evaluation, facilitation, and cultural expertise within the team provided a strong measure of reassur-ance, given the uncertainty of the journey ahead."

Kataraina: "I wanted to ensure in our developmental evaluation approach that in every contact with HOP providers, we would facilitate Māori processes that supported critical reflection of the naturally Māori ways we do things, affirming and validating Māori ways of being and knowing."

The selection of developmental evaluation was based on a number of factors: Nan Wehipeihana's and Kate McKegg's recommendation of it as an evaluation approach most suited to the program development context and to organizational information and accountability needs; and the perceived flexibility of developmen-tal evaluation for working with uncertainty and emergence, facilitating reflective practice, and weaving evaluative thinking into program development and data deci-sions as the understanding of participation as Māori unfolded. So developmental evaluation made sense on many fronts: methodologically, culturally, and in relation to the emergent program's scope and implementation context. There is no doubt, however, that at the time developmental evaluation was a "leap of faith" for the evaluators as well.

How Was the Developmental Evaluation Implemented?

On the face of it, the data collection methods employed in the evaluation looked fairly typical. They included national and regional 1- and 2-day hui (meetings/work-shops) with HOP providers (two to three per year); field visits to program provid-ers (one to two per provider, per year); telephone and face-to-face interviews with HOP providers, Sport NZ officials, and program personnel; quarterly[4] evaluation team planning meetings; systematic reflective practice by the developmental team members, utilizing a structured reflection template; and an ongoing scan of relevant Māori, sport/recreation, and evaluation literature. In addition, we had access to

---

[4]There was some fluidity in the timing of these meetings, to respond to learning as it emerged and to organizational information needs and reporting requirements.

and input into the design of the program baseline and annual provider monitoring reports,[5] as well as six monthly provider verbal update reports.

However, HOP was a Māori program, and the deep cultural principles and values evident in the program would be foundational to the implementation of the developmental evaluation (see Exhibit 2.4). Kaupapa Māori (Cram, 2009; G. Smith, 1997; L. Smith, 1999) literally means a "Māori way" of doing things, and the concept implies a way of framing and structuring how we think about and do evaluation with Māori. Kaupapa Māori is concerned with both methodology (a process of inquiry that determines the methods used) and methods (the tools that can be used to produce and analyze data). A Kaupapa Māori approach is open to a wide range of methods, but critically signals the interrogation of those methods in relation to tikanga Māori.

As a core principle, we consciously utilized tikanga Māori to underpin all engagement with HOP partners, infusing them throughout the evaluation by observing cultural protocols and privileging cultural ways of knowing and being. For example, the principle of whakapapa is typically defined as "genealogy or kinship connections." In the HOP evaluation, it had a number of dimensions: honoring people and organizations past and present, and their history and contributions to the program; acknowledging the personal kinship and professional relationships among the evaluators, program personnel, and HOP providers; and (in a very pragmatic sense) ensuring that we developed a thorough understanding of the program's history and purpose.

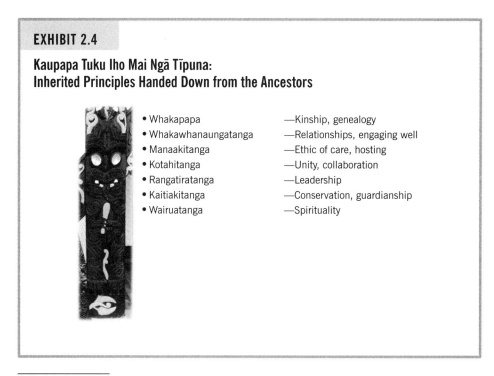

EXHIBIT 2.4

Kaupapa Tuku Iho Mai Ngā Tīpuna:
Inherited Principles Handed Down from the Ancestors

- Whakapapa —Kinship, genealogy
- Whakawhanaungatanga —Relationships, engaging well
- Manaakitanga —Ethic of care, hosting
- Kotahitanga —Unity, collaboration
- Rangatiratanga —Leadership
- Kaitiakitanga —Conservation, guardianship
- Wairuatanga —Spirituality

---

[5]The monitoring reports designed by the evaluation team included both quantitative data on participation *as Māori* and qualitative vignettes on such participation.

Nan: "Kaupapa tuku iho mai ngā tīpuna loosely translates as 'inherited principles, values, and philosophies handed down from ancestors.' Kaupapa tuku iho are a holistic set of life principles that guide ways of knowing and being in tribal and Māori contexts [Wehipeihana, 2014]. Some of these principles include whakapapa (genealogy, kinship, and connectedness to others), whakawhanaungatanga (establishing relationships, relating well to others), manaakitanga (an ethic of care/hosting), and rangatiratanga (leadership)—and as we do (and did), we consciously infused these principles into all aspects of the evaluation."

Katarina: "I think we just took for granted that developmental evaluation would be a good fit with tikanga Māori—weaving cultural principles into all aspects of the evaluation, using culturally based methods and ways of working and locating the evaluation within Kaupapa Māori."

Whakawhanaungatanga, the principle of engaging well and building respectful and trusted relationships, is at the heart of Māori cultural practices in all spheres of life. Relationships matter in Māori communities—as they do in evaluation—and getting the relational aspects right is both the glue and the lubricant for spirited debate, courageous conversations, and ongoing engagement. As a matter of course, we observed cultural engagement practices such as mihimihi (an introduction protocol) and poroporoaki (an acknowledgment, feedback, and farewell protocol); this demonstrated our understanding of the importance of these cultural practices within all engagement forums, and of building and strengthening relationships through these practices.

Manaakitanga is a cultural principle that speaks to a relational ethic of care (Wehipeihana, 2013). We observed this principle in the ways we designed and utilized a range of approaches to facilitate conversations and reflection, responded to kaiwhakahaere who needed evaluation or program support, provided tools and resources for use in contexts other than the HOP program, and maintained a genuine interest in the personal and professional well-being of the HOP community.

We privileged cultural ways of knowing and being. For example, we used specific cultural activities such as waiata (song) and mahi toi (traditional arts and crafts) as facilitation and data generation techniques, and we invited participants to provide feedback through the use of song, poetry, dance, or traditional crafts. We also developed and used culturally relevant examples as part of our evaluation capacity development approach. This made evaluation concepts more relevant and relatable to participants; it also highlighted the practice of evaluation and evaluative judgment as a naturally occurring cultural practice for Māori, and as something that we all do every day.

> It is through language that we give meaning to the world
> It is through language that our values are expressed
> And it is in language that our identity is embedded.
> (Wehipeihana, McKegg, & Pipi, 2010)

We had a deliberate focus on language in the evaluation. Experienced working with and in Māori communities, we knew that if we didn't get our use of language (both evaluation and Māori) right, then we would end up talking past each other. As a result, we would not be truly eliciting and giving voice to the perspectives, values, and experiences of participants (and stakeholders).

To ensure that the language of evaluation was not a barrier to developing shared understanding, learning, and meaningful inclusion of participants, we were deliberate in our use of "plain" language. Furthermore, to aid understanding, we reframed or "translated" evaluation terminology by using Māori concepts, metaphors, or icons that were similar to the ideas being discussed. Embedded in these concepts is cultural "knowing," and the "common" understanding and familiarity associated with this knowledge aided comprehension of the areas being discussed (Kaminsky, 2000).

We were also conscious of the way the language of evaluation (as expressed through our questions, data, analysis, and framing) typically favors the dominant culture, while at the same time devaluing or excluding the perspectives and experiences of minority groups (Hopson, Kenya, & Peterson, 2000). To counter these tendencies, we used and encouraged the use of te reo Māori (the Māori language), and we privileged Māori ideas and values in our questions, data, analysis, and framing, utilizing the language of participants whenever possible.

Cultural concepts, values, and te reo Māori were thus integral within the tools, frameworks, and data collection processes utilized in the evaluation and we were intentional in our approach to ensure that the analysis and collaborative meaning and sense making were guided by Māori cultural values and perspectives. This ensured that implicit values and assumptions underpinning the *as Māori* concept were brought to the surface, and that the things that HOP providers prioritized or saw as important were identifed and acknowledged as being the sources of valuing.

How Did the Evaluation Unfold?

The team developed the principles and *as Māori* framework, which would come to be known as Te Whetu Rēhua, iteratively and collaboratively—initially over a 12-month period, with more nuanced refinements occurring over the following 12 months. In the first year, in a series of 1- and 2-day national and regional hui (three in all), representatives of all the HOP providers, including some managers and program staff, came together to articulate and develop their understanding of participation *as Māori*. We utilized a range of cultural practices to surface and unpack deep cultural knowledge, often subconscious and taken for granted because of its day-to-day lived application and reality. At the same time, we used the workshops to progressively develop and refine data collection tools, to create annual monitoring reporting templates, and to build provider evaluation capacity.

In the second and third years, we had two national hui; undertook one round of field visits to each of the 12 HOP providers, as well as telephone interviews enriching our understanding of the expression and application of participation *as Maori* in traditional (and contemporary) sport and recreation contexts; and analyzed annual provider monitoring data.

After each workshop, the developmental team would come together; reflect on what was emerging in relation to *as Māori* and how well, or not well, the workshops and the activities within the workshops such as evaluation capacity development were working; and then plan for the next round of engagement.

Many of the HOP providers had mixed views about evaluation, influenced by previous evaluation experiences (both positive and negative), and some had no experience of evaluation at all. Over time, as they saw their values and perspectives included in the framework and data collection tools, they committed themselves to the evaluation, some even becoming champions of evaluation in their organizations. Importantly, they could see how developmental evaluation was strengthening their program delivery and their evidence of outcomes.

> "[I] find this such a valuable journey to be a part of and am thankful I have been exposed to it and take everything back to the organization to see how we can adopt it."
>
> —COMMENT FROM A HOP PROVIDER HUI (October 2010)

> "[T]he first time we saw it [developmental evaluation], it was over our head, we had no clue. It has taken us a long time . . . you can see the value of the process as we are going through it . . . and how it helps development of your services. . . . We knew how to do it [deliver the program], but it was that aspect [developmental evaluation] we were weak on. . . . [It] has led to the growth of the service and improvements."
>
> —HOP PROVIDER FEEDBACK (February 2011)

The active participation of HOP providers in the exploration and articulation of *as Maori*, and their buy-in to "learning as we go," were critical to the development of the framework and data collection tools and to the subsequent adaptation of some tools.

Despite our attention to cycles of planning, our structured and documented reflection sessions after each workshop, and the evaluation team meetings, we didn't always get things right—and some of our learning was more serendipitous than intentional. For example, in the first session of a 2-day workshop, where we had planned to explore concepts of excellence and success through "rich descriptions," it was clear from the glazed eyes, puzzled expressions, and lack of engagement that the background information, the language we were using, and the exercises we had prepared weren't working. Trusting our instincts, we stopped the session after less than 40 minutes, and we got the room full of participants to take an early morning tea break while we revised how we would proceed. We changed the nature of the activity, and we later received mixed feedback about the success or otherwise of the session (see Exhibit 2.5).

EXHIBIT 2.5

Participant Workshop Feedback, 2010

Worked well	Didn't work well
• "The opportunity to extract deeper explanation and development of key areas." • "Not being locked into a state or space, but having the ability to move along what we value, forward, learn, and grow." • "The activity template was easy to follow, and the step-by-step guide helped a lot."	• "The process didn't work for me." • "Getting to grips with 'rich description' and 'What does success look like?'" • "Describing excellence in the absence of numbers." • "I'm used to supplying data, not a fancy story."

The serendipitous outcome was a casual conversation between Nan and one of the regionally based program advisers, when they should have been participating in another activity. By chance, they came up with four principles that would become key elements of the framework.

What Was Developed?

A touchstone question that anchored the HOP developmental evaluation was "What is being developed?" It was a question that we returned to time and time again throughout the evaluation. We developed the following:

- An understanding of participation *as Māori* in traditional sport and recreation.
- A framework—Te Whetu Rēhua—to support HOP providers in designing programs aligned to the innovative program goal.
- Program criteria (and a scoring matrix) to support Sport NZ in assessing the alignment and fit of activities proposed by providers to the program goal.
- Development of data collection tools designed to support program management and evaluation.
- The evaluation capacity of the HOP provider and program manager.

The first year of the 3-year evaluation focused on developing an understanding of participation *as Māori* in sport and traditional recreation. The framework—Te Whetu Rēhua—sets out the Maori concepts and principles that collectively define participation *as Māori* in sport and recreation, in the HOP program context. The five key concepts and principles of Te Whetu Rēhua are summarized in Exhibit 2.6.

EXHIBIT 2.6

Key Concepts of the Framework: Te Whetu Rēhua

Dimension	Description
With Māori language and culture	Points to the importance of Māori language and culture as central to the survival and affirmation of what it means to live *as Māori*.
By Māori	Refers to the extent of rangatiratanga (control) by Māori in the governance, management, and delivery of an initiative.
For Māori	Emphasizes the importance of whānau (extended family), hapū (subtribe), and Iwi (tribe), which come together around a common kaupapa (purpose or interest).
Through	Sporting and recreational activities that can be distinguished *as Māori*—typically, but not exclusively, traditional sports and games.
In/On places of cultural significance to Māori	From ancestral marae (traditional places of gathering) and tribal awa (rivers), maunga (mountains), and whenua (land), to more contemporary places founded on Māori principles, such as kōhanga reo (preschool Māori language centers) and kura (schools that teach through the medium of the Māori language).

The framework recognizes the contemporary complexity of living *as Māori*, and therefore each dimension has three levels:

- The outer level reflects mainstream (non-Māori, non-Iwi) provision and participation in which Māori also participate; however this level is more aligned to participation by Māori.
- The middle level moves closer to the aspirational goal of HOP, recognising contemporary realities such as the mixed Te Reo Māori (Maori language) abilities of many Māori whānau.
- The inner level, most closely reflects as Māori participation in the HOP context. That is, the closer an activity maps to the centre of the Rēhua, the more likely it is to contribute to the HOP goal of participation as Māori in sport and recreation. When comparing general sport and recreation experience relative to the five key dimensions, it becomes easier to distinguish the difference between participation in sport and recreation by everyone including Māori and the more culturally distinctive participation as Māori. (McKegg, Wehipeihana, Pipi, & Thompson, 2013, pp. 17–18)

Once developed, Te Whetu Rēhua (see Exhibit 2.7) became the foundation for HOP's program management, delivery, monitoring, and evaluation. It was used by Sport NZ to guide and clarify the types of activities providers might deliver that mapped most closely onto the program's goals. It was used by providers, particularly RSTs, to set clear boundaries about where their efforts should/needed to be focused to meet HOP program goals and outcomes; and it was used by the

EXHIBIT 2.7

Te Whetu Rēhua: A Guide to Deciding Appropriate Activities for He Oranga Poutama

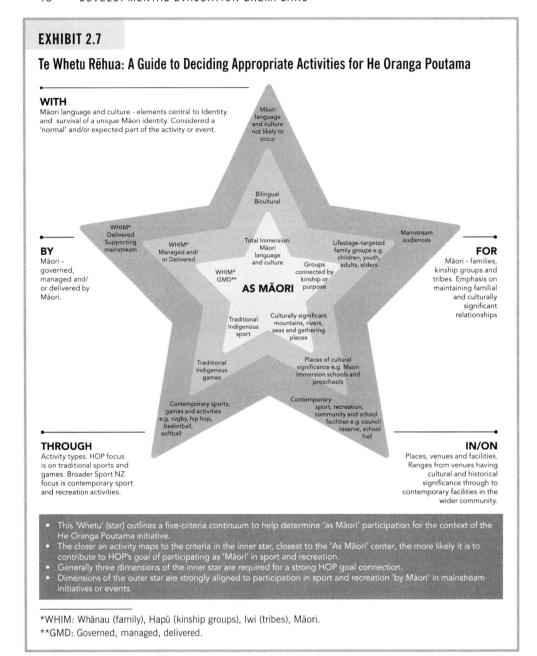

WITH
Māori language and culture - elements central to Identity and survival of a unique Māori identity. Considered a 'normal' and/or expected part of the activity or event.

Māori language and culture not likely to occur

Bilingual Bicultural

WHIM* Delivered Supporting mainstream

WHIM* Managed and/ or Delivered

Total Immersion: Māori language and culture

Lifestage-targeted family groups e.g. children, youth, adults, elders

Mainstream audiences

WHIM* GMD**

Groups connected by kinship or purpose

AS MĀORI

BY
Māori - governed, managed and/ or delivered by Māori.

FOR
Māori - families, kinship groups and tribes. Emphasis on maintaining familial and culturally significant relationships

Traditional Indigenous sport

Culturally significant mountains, rivers, seas and gathering places

Traditional Indigenous games

Places of cultural significance e.g. Maori immersion schools and preschools

Contemporary sports, games and activities e.g. rugby, hip hop, basketball, softball

Contemporary sport, recreation, community and school facilities e.g. council reserve, school hall

THROUGH
Activity types. HOP focus is on traditional sports and games. Broader Sport NZ focus is contemporary sport and recreation activities.

IN/ON
Places, venues and facilities. Ranges from venues having cultural and historical significance through to contemporary facilities in the wider community.

- This 'Whetu' (star) outlines a five-criteria continuum to help determine 'as Māori' participation for the context of the He Oranga Poutama initiative.
- The closer an activity maps to the criteria in the inner star, closest to the 'As Māori' center, the more likely it is to contribute to HOP's goal of participating as 'Māori' in sport and recreation.
- Generally three dimensions of the inner star are required for a strong HOP goal connection.
- Dimensions of the outer star are strongly aligned to participation in sport and recreation 'by Māori' in mainstream initiatives or events.

*WHIM: Whānau (family), Hapū (kinship groups), Iwi (tribes), Māori.
**GMD: Governed, managed, delivered.

evaluators not only to develop data collection tools, but as the framework for monitoring and assessing HOP's performance.

What Was the Value of Developmental Evaluation?

DE has supported an iterative, culturally grounded, collaborative way of working among Sport NZ, HOP providers, and the evaluators, all playing key contributory roles. It has facilitated the development of the Māori concepts and principles—embodied in the Te Whetu Rēhua framework—that collectively define participation *as Māori* in sport and recreation, in the HOP program context. In so doing, it has supported the revitalization of traditional sport and recreation, affirmed traditional ways of knowing and being, and nurtured Māori development aspirations.

> "Yes, there's been lots of value. It's [the evaluation has] enabled definitions of our high-level outcomes to come from community, so it's been very contextualized . . . and it [the evaluation and framework] has been affirming of kaupapa Māori and Māori development, and that's important from my point of view."
>
> —VERONICA THOMPSON, senior adviser,
> HOP (Wehipeihana, McKegg, Te Hurihanganui, & Rangi, 2011)

> "Developmental evaluation processes that we have implemented over the last 2 years have given a greater voice to our Indigenous communities, [given] greater value to our traditional knowledge, validated traditional ways of doing things, and enhanced our strengths-based and inclusive approach."
>
> —PAORA TE HURIHANGANUI, manager,
> Te Papa Takaro o te Arawa (Wehipeihana et al., 2011)

> "The evaluation has affirmed sport as a vehicle for cultural affirmation and revitalization . . . and contributed to the survival and expression of a unique Māori identity. From a provider perspective, it [the framework] has increased the cultural distinctive elements in program focus and delivery, and defined Indigenous values in an evaluation space."
>
> —TE MIRI RANGI, kaiwhakahaere,
> Te Papa Takaro o te Arawa (Wehipeihana et al., 2011)

What Have We Learned about Applying Developmental Evaluation?

The evaluation of HOP was our first foray into using developmental evaluation. It was a new evaluation approach, and we were early adopters entering unchartered waters. Because the end was unpredictable and emergent, we were clear that cultural principles and values, and the processes that give effect to these, would be our compass as we navigated our way forward—and that our relationships with each other and with our client would be the anchor providing balance and reassurance in times of uncertainty. Systematic, evaluative reflection and sense making were important markers in our developmental evaluation journey, providing time to pause and harness the collective knowledge and wisdom of the developmental team to inform decision making, future cycles of engagement, and data collection.

Kia ako tahi tātou, Kia tipu tahi tātou, Kia puawai tahi tātou.
(Let us learn together, grow together, and flourish together.)

Our insights and learnings have been many, and we share some of these below to support the practice of developmental evaluation.

Developmental evaluation is a (relatively) new evaluation approach, and this can give rise to concern and anxiety about whether it is appropriate and will deliver what is needed. We learned that it is vitally important to do the following:

- Articulate the unique value proposition of developmental evaluation.
- Clearly differentiate developmental evaluation from other evaluation approaches.
- Orient funders and project personnel to developmental evaluation at the outset of the evaluation process, and continue to reinforce and "educate" throughout the process.
- Plan for a series (and different types) of reporting deliverable products, to progressively demonstrate what is being learned and developed, and to counter credibility concerns.

Developmental evaluation is characterized by emergence and uncertainty because the journey and its destination are often unknown or not clear. This can result in a desire to have a greater level of prescription and longer-term evaluation planning to allay fears and insecurities. We further recommend the following:

- Maintain a focus on what is being developed.
- Use well-documented, iterative planning cycles to provide a roadmap for navigating and responsively implementing the evaluation, and for adapting to learning and context factors as they emerge.
- Use data-driven engagement and reporting outputs to provide rigor and reassurance throughout the evaluation process.
- Get people "on the same page," and check back on this at each step of the journey; doing so provides a critical point of reference to anchor decisions as the initiative—and therefore the evaluation—unfolds.

It can be daunting to proceed without a predetermined approach or set of methods, and with the knowledge that the context, the innovation, and the evaluation are all likely to change over time. We thus recommend the following:

- Develop a deep methodological toolkit and a rich repertoire of facilitation skills, to support collaborative engagement and the use of methods tailored to context and purpose. Build teams with these skills wherever possible.
- Tap into and utilize the knowledge, wisdom, skills, and experience of the developmental team—funders, program personnel, community, program participants, and evaluators.

When we first began our developmental evaluation journey, we cautioned that it was not for the faint-hearted (Wehipeihana & McKegg, 2009)—given its novelty at that time, as well as a context typically characterized by emergence, ambiguity, and uncertainty. Although developmental evaluation is still a "fringe" approach for some in the evaluation community, the learning and insights that are accruing from our own and many other projects about how to do developmental evaluation, and what it can contribute to innovation and making a difference, should continue to increase the community's understanding of its opportunity and potential for evaluative endeavors.

REFERENCES

Cram, F. (2009). Maintaining Indigenous voices. In D. Mertens & P. E. Ginsberg (Eds.), *The handbook of social research ethics* (pp. 308–322). Thousand Oaks, CA: Sage.

Durie, M. E. (2001). *A framework for considering Māori educational advancement.* Paper presented at the Hui Taumata Matauranga, Taupo, New Zealand.

Durie, M. E., Fitzgerald, E., Kingi, T. K., McKinley, S., & Stevenson, B. (2002). *Māori specific outcomes and indicators: A report prepared for Te Puni Kōkiri, the Ministry for Māori Development.* Palmerston North, New Zealand: Massey University.

Hopson, R. K., Kenya, J. L., & Peterson, J. A. (2000). HIV/AIDS talk: Implications for prevention intervention and evaluation. *New Directions for Evaluation, 86,* 29–42.

Kaminsky, A. (2000). Beyond the literal: Metaphors and why they matter. *New Directions for Evaluation, 86,* 69–80.

McKegg, K., Wehipeihana, N., Pipi, K., & Thompson, V. (2013). *He Oranga Poutama: What we have learned. A report on the developmental evaluation of He Oranga Poutama.* Wellington: Sport New Zealand.

Patton, M. Q. (2006a). *Elaboration of developmental evaluation.* Unpublished manuscript expanded from the book *Getting to maybe: How the world is changed* (Westley, Zimmerman, & Patton, 2006).

Patton, M. Q. (2006b). Evaluation for the way we work. *Nonprofit Quarterly, 13*(1), 28–33.

Patton, M. Q. (2009, September). Connecting evaluation to what people know [Guest editorial]. *Aotearoa New Zealand Evaluation Association Newsletter,* pp. 5–9.

Smith, G. (1997). *The development of Kaupapa Māori: Theory and praxis.* Unpublished doctoral dissertation, University of Auckland, Auckland, New Zealand.

Smith, L. (1999). *Decolonising methodologies: Research and Indigenous peoples.* New York: Zed Books/Dunedin, New Zealand: Otago University Press.

Te Puni Kōkiri. (2009). *Māori potential stocktake.* Wellington, New Zealand: Te Puni Kōkiri.

Wehipeihana, N. (2013, September). *A vision for indigenous evaluation.* Keynote address presented at the annual conference of the Australian Evaluation Society, Brisbane, Australia.

Wehipeihana, N. (2014, October). *Mai Nga Tipuna—From the ancestors: Insights and reflections on generating evidence based principles from developmental and adaptive evaluation practice in innovative and complex settings.* Paper presented at the annual conference of the American Evaluation Association, Denver, CO.

Wehipeihana, N., & McKegg, K. (2009, November). *Developmental evaluation in an Indigenous context: Reflections on the journey to date.* Paper presented at the annual conference of the American Evaluation Association, Orlando, FL.

Wehipeihana, N., McKegg, K., & Pipi, K. (2010, November). *Grappling with uncertainty in innovative and complex settings: Weaving quality in developmental evaluation.* Paper presented at the annual conference of the American Evaluation Association, San Antonio, TX.

Wehipeihana, N., McKegg, K., Te Hurihanganui, P., & Rangi, T. M. (2011, November). *Developmental evaluation on the red carpet.* Paper presented at the annual conference of the American Evaluation Association, Anaheim, CA.

Westley, F., Zimmerman, B., & Patton, M. Q. (2006). *Getting to maybe: How the world is changed.* Toronto: Random House Canada.

CHAPTER 3

Using Developmental Evaluation to Support College Access and Success

Challenge Scholars

Srik Gopal, Katelyn Mack, and Cris Kutzli

EDITORS' INTRODUCTION

Some of the evaluations described in this volume have been completed. Some are in midstream. This case focuses on the crucial startup of a developmental evaluation: It describes the first year of an evaluation designed both to help develop and to assess an experimental educational model. Social innovators attack major problems and aim to change systems. Access to college in the United States is a matter of equity and opportunity. Increasing access means changing significant aspects of the college entrance system. Toward that end, the Challenge Scholars program was created as an innovative experiment and tested in Grand Rapids, Michigan. The innovation revolved around a dynamic partnership among the local community-based philanthropic foundation, the school district, and other community partners. Economic, social, political, and educational dynamics made for a shifting environment and turbulent context. The situation analysis pointed to developmental evaluation as a way of navigating these complexities and uncertainties. The implementers of the Challenge Scholars program worked closely with the evaluators to ensure a commitment to and process for real-time learning. Timely feedback helped shape the program as it evolved. The evaluators implemented an adaptive and flexible design, and co-created meaning and synthesis with program leaders through ongoing and frequent feedback and conversation. This case illustrates and illuminates the importance of building understanding of what developmental evaluation is from the beginning; co-creating and iterating the evaluation's design and implementation; always finding ways to have an "ear to the ground"; and setting expectations for action or inaction, as circumstances dictate. This case shows how expectations, norms, and lessons learned during the first year of a developmental evaluation set the stage for incorporating new methods and insights into the next phase.

Grand Rapids, Michigan, is experiencing a resurgence that sets it apart from many other Midwest cities. Employment rates in the area are consistently among the highest in the state, with persistent job growth in health care and high-tech manufac-turing (W. E. Upjohn Institute, 2014). This vibrancy, however, masks more troubling trends of low educational attainment in neighborhoods of concentrated poverty. Over 80% of the 17,000 students attending the area's largest district, Grand Rapids Public Schools (GRPS), are economically disadvantaged, and 4-year graduation rates hover just below 50%. Of those who do graduate, only half enroll in a postsecond-ary program (Center for Educational Performance and Information, 2013). Recent data show that an average of 19% of GRPS graduates obtained a degree or credential within 6 years of graduation (National Student Clearinghouse, 2013).

For the vast majority of students who don't cross the postsecondary finish line, the outlook is grim. Researchers for the Pew Research Center (Morin, Fry, & Brown, 2014) found that "on virtually every measure of economic well-being and career attainment, . . . young college graduates are outperforming their peers with less education." Based on national U.S. Census and survey data, Morin and col-leagues found that the unemployment rate of young adults with only a high school diploma was three times that of young adults with at least a bachelor's degree, and that nearly 22% of those with only a high school diploma were living in poverty, compared to just under 6% of those with a bachelor's degree.

For the Grand Rapids Community Foundation, statistics like these were a cata-lyst for change. Since its founding in 1922, the Community Foundation has made hundreds of large and small grants to support local teachers, schools, and districts. At the same time, negative trends in GRPS's enrollment, graduation rates, and stan-dardized test scores hinted that those investments were bearing little or no return. In 2008, leaders at the Community Foundation launched an unprecedented assess-ment of their education grant-making process, which found no overall correlation between Community Foundation investments and student achievement. Leaders knew it was time for a new approach: one that was targeted and strategic, was deeply rooted in evidence-based approaches, and offered opportunities for replica-tion. A new approach also called for a clear direction—a defined goal around which the Community Foundation's resources could be organized. The foundation's board of trustees ultimately adopted a single intended outcome to drive its education investments: *First-generation, low-income students successfully complete a degree or high-quality credential.*

Defining and creating the conditions under which students can be successful in achieving this goal has been the work of the Challenge Scholars initiative. In 2009, the Community Foundation entered into a formal partnership with GRPS to design and develop the Challenge Scholars program. What has evolved over time is an "early promise"[1] initiative that not only guarantees a college scholarship, but also

---

[1]The Kalamazoo Promise was the nation's first place-based scholarship program. Since it was announced in 2005, over 30 communities and several states have developed some form of "promise" program. Whereas all of these programs offer financial support to students pursuing postsecondary studies, and are place-based and long-term, they vary widely in their scope, scale, and design. Most seek to improve educational outcomes for students, to support economic revitalization efforts, or both. For information on promise programs across the country, see the W. E. Upjohn Institute collection of data and research on the Kalamazoo Promise and other promise programs (*www.upjohn.org/research/ education/kalamazoo-promise-place-based-scholarships*), and Miller-Adams's (2013) *Introduction to Promise Scholarship Programs* presentation.

provides students (and their families) with the early supports needed to ensure that they graduate from high school and college.

The Challenge Scholars initiative is similar to other "promise" programs in that it guarantees a scholarship for a defined group of students. It is a place-based initiative targeting the West Side neighborhoods of Grand Rapids, where 25% of adults lack a high school diploma and another 53% have no education beyond high school. Enrollment in Challenge Scholars is limited to sixth graders attending the two GRPS middle schools located in the neighborhood. These sixth graders, their parents and teachers, and Community Foundation staff all sign a "Promise Pact," which outlines expectations for each of these stakeholders. To maintain eligibility, students must continue enrollment at their school and graduate from GRPS's Union High School, also located in the neighborhood. In addition, students are expected to maintain a behavioral standard, earn a C average, and have excellent attendance. The scholarship that Challenge Scholars will receive is considered "last dollar," meaning that it will cover college costs after financial aid and other scholarships are received.

The scholarship promise is essential in that it serves to remove one key barrier to college access: the widespread perception, especially among those with lower incomes, that postsecondary education is unaffordable (Perna & Li, 2006). From the moment they sign the Promise Pact in sixth grade, Challenge Scholars and their families know that college is truly possible. With the promise of a free education, a world of opportunities is suddenly available to them—if only they can overcome the other obstacles along the way.

The emphasis on addressing these obstacles is what sets the Challenge Scholars initiative apart from other "promise" programs. By making early investments in students' academic preparation, attendance, and postsecondary aspirations, and by engaging parents throughout, the Challenge Scholars initiative creates the conditions necessary for students to graduate from high school and obtain a degree or credential (Gándara, 2001; Oakes, 2003; Perna & Li, 2006; Tierney, Bailey, Constantine, Finkelstein, & Hurd, 2009; Tierney, Colyar, & Corwin, 2003). The specific strategies that are being used, in addition to scholarship, in order to enable college and career success, are outlined below. A visual depiction is shown in Exhibit 3.1.

1. *Health and human services to improve attendance.* Recognizing that absenteeism is often symptomatic of underlying issues, the Community Foundation supports the Kent School Services Network, a full-service community school initiative, which works alongside other school and district initiatives to increase attendance. Michigan Department of Human Services caseworkers, along with nurses and behavioral health clinicians, are on staff full-time in school buildings. With these wrap-around supports, families can gain self-sufficiency, find health care, and obtain counseling.

2. *Instructional support to accelerate achievement.* To ensure that Challenge Scholars are on track academically, a grant from the Community Foundation provides funding to GRPS for additional instructional support at the three Challenge Scholars schools, using a coaching model to build teacher capacity. Students thus

EXHIBIT 3.1

Key Elements of the Challenge Scholars Initiative

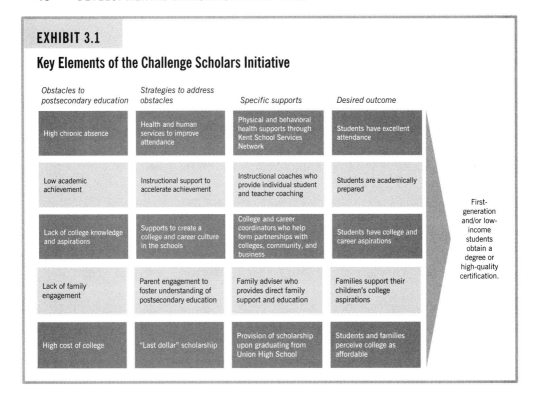

Obstacles to postsecondary education	Strategies to address obstacles	Specific supports	Desired outcome	
High chronic absence	Health and human services to improve attendance	Physical and behavioral health supports through Kent School Services Network	Students have excellent attendance	
Low academic achievement	Instructional support to accelerate achievement	Instructional coaches who provide individual student and teacher coaching	Students are academically prepared	First-generation and/or low-income students obtain a degree or high-quality certification.
Lack of college knowledge and aspirations	Supports to create a college and career culture in the schools	College and career coordinators who help form partnerships with colleges, community, and business	Students have college and career aspirations	
Lack of family engagement	Parent engagement to foster understanding of postsecondary education	Family adviser who provides direct family support and education	Families support their children's college aspirations	
High cost of college	"Last dollar" scholarship	Provision of scholarship upon graduating from Union High School	Students and families perceive college as affordable	

have access to instruction that is high-quality and highly personalized—both of which are correlated with academic outcomes.

3. *Supports to create a college and career culture in the schools.* To surround Challenge Scholars with a college-going culture, a Community Foundation grant supports college/career coordinators at all three Challenge Scholars schools. These individuals work closely with community partners—including local businesses, nonprofits, and especially higher education providers—to facilitate college and career experiences for students and parents. They serve as relationship builders: organizing college visits, bringing in guest speakers and college volunteers, modeling "college talk," and connecting students with out-of-school time experiences.

4. *Parent engagement to foster understanding of postsecondary education.* To inspire and facilitate parents' support of their children's postsecondary aspirations, the Community Foundation's family advisor works closely with community allies and school staff to build trusting relationships with parents. In particular, the advisor helps parents understand the significance of Challenge Scholars and the importance of parental support, provides tools and encouragement, and brings parents along as vital partners on their children's journeys.

Through this multipronged approach, the Challenge Scholars initiative addresses the highly complex social issue of college access and success for disadvantaged students. The initiative involves multiple partners and systems, takes place within the ever-changing context of public education, requires long-term deployment of resources, and represents a significant financial investment by the Grand Rapids Community Foundation. The initiative also has a clear goal to which both the Community Foundation and GRPS are accountable, and therefore a rigorous evaluation was required. As a foundation representative describes, "As we considered the emergent nature of the initiative, we knew intuitively that a traditional evaluation approach would be ineffective at best. The initiative was still in its infancy; the strategies were fluid; the relationships were fragile." This led project leaders to ask themselves: So what would be evaluated, and how?

Inception of the Developmental Evaluation

The complexity of the Challenge Scholars initiative invited an innovative approach to its evaluation—one that was highly rigorous, highly adaptable, and designed to support the long-term success of the program. It required an approach to evaluation that would support and inform the initiative as it matured. This approach would not prematurely indicate success or failure, but rather highlight what was working and what wasn't. It would provide signals that could be used in real time to refine and improve the design. The project leaders could describe what they wanted in this evaluation, but they had no name for it—it was neither summative nor formative. The project leaders also had no notion of who was equipped to serve in this ambiguous role of learning partner/evaluator. Nevertheless, the Community Foundation was fully committed to exploring this approach and was prepared to make a significant investment in support of it.

The path forward remained frustratingly unclear until a colleague at a local university hand-delivered Michael Quinn Patton's (2011) text, *Developmental Evaluation: Applying Complexity Concepts to Enhance Innovation and Use*. It quickly became clear that developmental evaluation was precisely the approach that the project leaders were seeking, and that it was the most appropriate approach for the complex, emergent nature of the Challenge Scholars initiative. As a foundation representative recalls, "It was as if the volume had been written with Challenge Scholars in mind." A national search was soon conducted for a firm that could effectively carry out long-term implementation of the developmental evaluation, and FSG was chosen as the evaluator. The FSG team was composed of two consultants (Srik Gopal and Katelyn Mack) with a breadth of experience in evaluation, as well as experience in the K–12 education sector.

The evaluators' charge was to work closely with the Challenge Scholars project leaders—a program director from the Grand Rapids Community Foundation and an assistant superintendent from the GRPS. These two individuals were chiefly responsible for designing and developing the initiative, and for overseeing implementation and integration of various program elements. The project leaders also met monthly with a "Partners' Group," composed of the three building principals, key district administrators, and the Community Foundation's family advisor. Finally, bringing community voice and support to the initiative was the Challenge Scholars Advisory Council, which included individuals from local business, parent groups, higher education, and philanthropy.

Designing the Developmental Evaluation

The developmental evaluation was officially launched in a 3-hour kickoff meeting with the Partners' Group in January 2013. During the meeting, the FSG team members were introduced and spent significant time educating this critical set of stakeholders about what developmental evaluation is and describing what distinguishes it from other types of evaluation. Planting the seeds early for how this approach to evaluation would be different from what most people had come to expect from an "evaluation study" has been important to developing an atmosphere of trust and creating a shared set of expectations. For example, deliberate conversations informed by credible data and "key findings" would become a primary mechanism for supporting data-informed strategic learning among key decision makers (Coffman & Beer, 2011; Patton, 2011). These conversations, more so than a comprehensive final report, provided the space for reflection and collective sense making around what was taking shape, and the dialogue often led to action planning around implementation.

The first order of business following the kickoff meeting was to design the evaluation. This included developing a set of initial guiding questions, a sound methodology for collecting data, and a timeline of activities and key deliverable products. The evaluators envisioned taking a similar approach to past evaluations, which included interviewing key stakeholders and then developing a draft evaluation plan based on (1) the evaluation request for proposals, (2) key documents related to the initiative, and (3) early conversations with people involved in the design and/or implementation of the initiative. The questions during interviews with key stakeholders were deliberately framed around the landscape and context in which Challenge Scholars was developing, as opposed to what people thought was working well or needed attention. This respected the program partners' desire for the evaluators not to be "evaluating the initiative" at this early stage. The purpose of these conversations was to help the evaluators better understand the context of the work; connections between and among different components of the initiative; and ways in which various organizations, conditions, and systems might accelerate or inhibit its success.

After reviewing the notes from the kickoff meeting, sifting through the literature on Challenge Scholars and other "promise"-type scholarship programs, and reviewing interview notes, the evaluators scheduled a meeting with the Community Foundation and GRPS representatives to discuss and refine the evaluation plan for the first year of Challenge Scholars. The plan was carefully crafted from start to finish. It included everything a complete evaluation plan would have in place:

- Background and context for the work.
- A draft "systems map," in place of a theory of change articulating the various systems players involved in the various facets of the initiative.
- A set of illustrative outcomes based on the literature review and conversations.
- Data collection methods and sources.

- A communications and reporting plan.
- Roles and responsibilities for the implementation team.

Although the evaluation design created was "technically sound," the evaluators realized quickly that it did not pass muster with the group, and had to recalibrate. The plan was too "fully baked," and the program partners—in true developmental evaluation fashion—asked that the plan be redesigned in a more collaborative process. As the program leader from the foundation reported, "the proposal to start from scratch and co-create a new plan was a pretty significant turning point for the developmental evaluation; it deepened the partnership between the foundation and the school district, and created buy-in around the developmental evaluation process."

(Re)Designing the Developmental Evaluation Plan

A 2-day working session was scheduled for a time when all key stakeholders, including the GRPS superintendent and the Community Foundation's president and CEO, could come together to co-create the developmental evauation plan. The goals for the meeting were to do the following:

- Develop an increased understanding of the Challenge Scholars "system" and its component parts.
- Discuss the outcomes of Challenge Scholars and how they would be expected to evolve over time.
- Identify and own a set of "learning questions" that would drive the developmental evaluation.
- Begin to craft a plan for data collection and use.

One of the items in the evaluation plan, a systems map, raised some questions when it was first developed for the program partners. Systems mapping is an iterative, often participatory process of graphically representing a system, including its components and connections. Some systems maps show causal loop connections, as well as patterns of influence, between and among various components, such as those designed for advocacy evaluation (Coffman & Reed, 2009). Yet, when developed collaboratively among stakeholder groups, the systems map became a critical visual tool for illustrating that the Community Foundation, schools, and community partners were and are "all in it together" (see Exhibit 3.2). The systems-mapping exercise underscored the importance of ongoing coordination and collaboration among stakeholders. In addition to developing a systems map for the initiative, the group identified and prioritized outcomes for the initiative over a 10-year time horizon.

The group was tasked with creating learning questions for the first year of the Challenge Scholars initiative. The evaluators used a simple prompt: "What questions, if answered with data, would help us create/strengthen/refine aspects of the Challenge Scholars program in 2013–2014?" The questions created during this

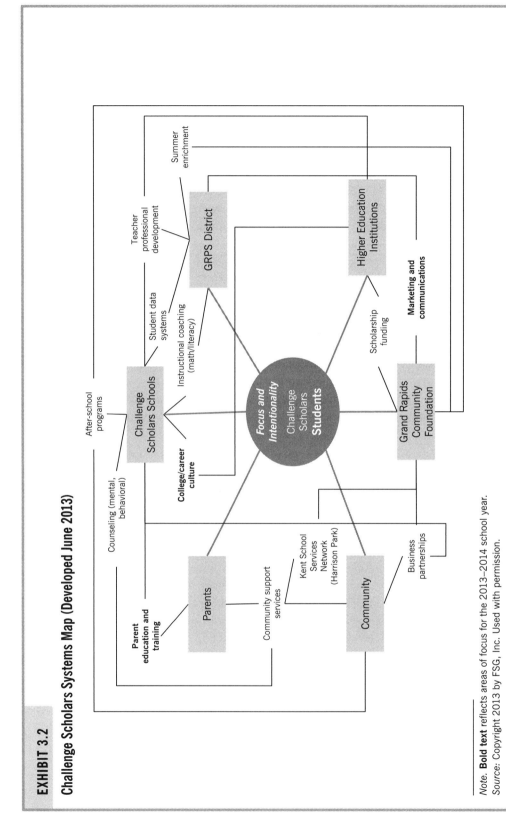

EXHIBIT 3.2

Challenge Scholars Systems Map (Developed June 2013)

Note. **Bold text** reflects areas of focus for the 2013–2014 school year.
Source: Copyright 2013 by FSG, Inc. Used with permission.

2-day working session guided the first year of the evaluation and included the following:

1. How is a college and career culture emerging within the schools and broader West Side community?
2. How are parents and families being engaged as part of Challenge Scholars?
3. How are students becoming more college- and career-ready?
4. What do exemplary teaching and learning look like in a college and career culture?
5. How are the community, businesses, and higher education responding to Challenge Scholars?
6. How is the school district's feeder pattern influencing Challenge Scholars?

As these questions were developed, the evaluators paid attention to the nature and tone of the questions, in order to keep them focused on "what Challenge Scholars is" and "how it is developing." It was important to the evaluators and partners to ensure that the questions did not imply testing a "fully baked" model, which would suggest a more formative evaluation, or assessing the impact or outcomes of the initiative, which would suggest a summative evaluation (Preskill & Beer, 2012).

Data Collection Methods and Deliverables

These questions guided data collection throughout the year. In total, the evaluators collected qualitative data from more than 70 individuals through interviews and focus groups, and conducted three surveys to gather information from parents, school staff at Westwood and Harrison Park Schools, and sixth-grade students at these two schools. A timeline of these activities is shown in Exhibit 3.3.

Over the course of the year, the FSG team planned to share back information from the developmental evaluation with key Community Foundation and school district partners in a variety of ways. By the end of the year, this reporting had been accomplished in a variety of ways:

- *Four learning briefs* after on-the-ground visits, which addressed the learning questions and were used to facilitate discussions among the Partners' Group about what was being learned.
- *Biannual (midyear and year-end) summary reports* highlighting lessons learned over the course of the year and implications for the Challenge Scholars initiative. These reports were also used to facilitate conversations around the "so what" of the findings with the Partners' Group.
- *Three survey decks* synthesizing findings from the surveys with parents, students, and staff.
- *Two additional memos:* one highlighting obstacles to and strategies for further parent engagement in Challenge Scholars, as well as a metareflections

EXHIBIT 3.3

Data Collection Activities Timeline

Data Collection Activities	2013					2014						
	Aug	Sep	Oct	Nov	Dec	Jan	Feb	Mar	Apr	May	Jun	Jul
Document Review	●		●		●		●			●	●	
Interviews		School staff			Business and higher ed.	Parents		Community leaders				
Observation		Schools			Challenge Scholars event	Schools		Schools		Challenge Scholars event		
Focus Groups					Parents	Teachers				Students		
Surveys					Parents				Students / School staff			
Appreciative Inquiry								●				
Email Questionnaires			●		●					Front-line staff		

Half-day learning session (January)

Full-day learning session (June)

Evaluation team on the ground in Grand Rapids for 2–4 days

memo summarizing patterns and themes observed throughout the year that might affect the Challenge Scholars initiative.

Ongoing Learning from the Developmental Evaluation

Implementation of the developmental evaluation began in July 2013. The first round of on-the-ground data collection took place in early September, when the FSG team traveled to Grand Rapids to present the developmental evaluation plan to the advisory council and interview front-line Challenge Scholars staff as the school year got underway. The evaluation plan outlined on-the-ground data collection in Grand Rapids every other month. Yet, in order to accommodate schedule changes and key activities and events, the spacing of the evaluators' visits was flexed.

Right from the start, it was clear to the evaluators that Challenge Scholars would be continually evolving throughout the year. For example, boundaries in the school district had been redrawn due to school closings, which meant that one of the schools, Harrison Park, had an influx of new sixth graders whose families weren't familiar with Challenge Scholars or the college and career culture that had started to develop there. New staff (the Challenge Scholars family advisor) had been hired, and the membership and roles of the advisory council were changing: Students and parents representing the three Challenge Scholars schools were invited to sit on the advisory council for the first time. In addition, there was urgency around defining the various elements for the Promise Pact—a document that all sixth-grade students and their parents/guardians would need to sign in order for the students to officially "enroll" in the Challenge Scholars program and be eligible for the scholarships upon graduating from Union High School.

One of the major lessons from implementing this developmental evaluation has been the importance of pacing and framing information in a way that fits with how the program's decision makers process and share information. For example, at the end of each site visit, the FSG team developed a learning memo that captured the key "take-aways" from the visit, and shared this memo with the Partners' Group. No longer than four pages, these memos initially presented a series of "Strengths," "Challenges," "Wonderings," and "Implications for the Developmental Evaluation" that reflected what had been learned during the visit. During monthly check-ins, usually 2 weeks following a visit, the FSG team members would discuss their insights and questions with the representatives from the Community Foundation and GRPS. However, after the second visit by FSG in December, the project leaders asked the evaluators to change how and how often learnings were being communicated. They wanted to hear in closer to real time what the FSG team was learning, so that action could be taken right away. Two weeks was too long to wait. The memo was restructured explicitly around the six key learning questions, with information about "what's working well" and "what needs attention," as well as a seventh category focused on program implementation. In addition, the FSG team scheduled time with the project leaders immediately following data collection and while still on the ground in Grand Rapids, to share initial thoughts and insights.

Although the developmental evaluation began with six overarching questions, a subset of these questions emerged as particularly important to explore during the ensuing months. Through discussions with representatives from the Community Foundation and GRPS, the three questions that emerged as having the greatest relevance were the ones related to college and career culture, parent engagement, and community partnerships. As a result, in-person working sessions with the Partners' Group in January and June were designed to spend more time on what was being learned in relation to those three questions.

As a fundamental principle, developmental evaluation requires flexibility in approach and focus; knowing if and when to shift focus is paramount (Langlois, Blanchet-Cohen, & Beer, 2013; Patton, 2011). For example, after conducting focus groups with parents in early December, the FSG team shared insights and wonderings that spurred additional questions about how Challenge Scholars could further support parents in being able to prepare their students for college or other postsecondary careers. As a result, the evaluators decided to conduct additional one-on-one interviews with parents, with the aim of talking with parents who were less engaged in Challenge Scholars and who had not attended the focus group. Unfortunately, the evaluators learned quickly that successfully convening parents who were not yet engaged was extremely challenging. The evaluators tried a few strategies to reach a broader population of parents, but ultimately these fell short. This led the evaluators to utilize the totality of other data and information at their disposal—including other field reports, as well as advice from professional experts on successful parent engagement strategies—in order to answer the question that the Community Foundation and GRPS partners had posed. This experience also reinforced the importance of continuing to strengthen the capacity and network of the evaluation team and partners to be able to collect data representing a wide range of potential perspectives and experiences.

The focus on strategic learning (Coffman & Beer, 2011) that is the hallmark of developmental evaluation has been valuable at multiple levels. At a macro level, it allows the project leaders and Partners' Group to understand how the initiative is engaging with other actors and systems. At a micro level, it provides signals about the initiative's direction as it is being implemented. This real-time feedback is useful in several ways: It can validate the impressions of the project team, illuminate topics that were previously unclear, and spotlight issues that were off the radar.

Low parent awareness of Challenge Scholars was an issue that surfaced through the developmental evaluation, and it resulted in a rapid course correction. Several months into data collection, and a month before the initial Challenge Scholars enrollment period was to begin, the FSG team highlighted findings related to parent awareness and understanding of Challenge Scholars in a postvisit learning memo. The learning memo indicated that although highly engaged parents were excited about the opportunity to enroll their children in Challenge Scholars, this enthusiasm dropped off considerably for less engaged parents. Among those parents—who represented the large majority of prospective Challenge Scholar parents—awareness of the initiative was remarkably low. The evaluators voiced concern that this lack of awareness would have a negative impact on enrollment in Challenge Scholars. Since the 4-month enrollment window was rapidly approaching, and enrollment required parents to take action by signing the Promise Pact, this finding was highly significant and called for quick action.

Within days of receiving this learning memo, the Challenge Scholars staff, the Community Foundation's public relations and marketing team, and GRPS's communications staff got to work. Together, they developed an awareness and enrollment strategy, with fully defined tactics, timelines, and enrollment targets. The plan leveraged a network of highly engaged, highly aware parents, teachers, and school staff, who were recruited as "ambassadors." Enrollment events were scheduled for each school, and a direct outreach plan was developed to reach parents who didn't attend a formal event. Recognizing that teachers exercised key leverage in reaching families, the Challenge Scholars family advisor sat with sixth-grade teachers at parent–teacher conferences. Two weeks after the learning memo had been received, a Challenge Scholars "newsletter," in both Spanish and English, was mailed out to every family of a sixth grader, outlining the benefits of Challenge Scholars and listing multiple ways to enroll. The enrollment strategies were successful: By the deadline, 84% of sixth graders had enrolled in Challenge Scholars.

Not all developmental evaluation findings warrant such immediate or urgent action. As the project leader from the foundation explained, "While we have been able to take action in response to data that requires immediate attention, the evaluators' findings have more often helped us zero in on pain points in the initiative's growth." For example, through various focus groups, interviews, and surveys, the evaluators were able to identify a disconnect between stakeholder groups about what it means to have a "college and career culture." Because people were using different definitions of "college and career culture," the concept was being communicated and implemented inconsistently. As the project leader recalled, "Although we were sensing the inconsistencies, it was the broader perspective brought by the FSG team that crystallized the underlying issue and pointed toward a solution." As a result, project leaders are facilitating a process to create a shared definition that reflects the perspectives of different stakeholders.

Developmental evaluation findings that confirmed the impressions of the project leaders were also plentiful and valuable. For example, staff members at all levels had a sense that students' attitudes about postsecondary education were changing, and this was validated by the data collected by the evaluators. Project leaders expected students at the school that had recently brought on a college/career coordinator to show smaller shifts in attitudes, and the data bore this out. The data also validated project leaders' hypotheses concerning parents' fears about high school and their concerns about their ability to support their children in the journey to college. In these ways, the developmental evaluation has served as a highly effective "on-track/off-track" indicator.

Overall Lessons Learned

As the first full year of implementing the developmental evaluation came to an end, the project leaders and the evaluators took a step back and reflected on some of the lessons learned. They carried out a structured "plus–delta" exercise to understand some of the things that had worked well with the implementation, as well as some aspects that needed improvement. A synthesis of these learnings is outlined in Exhibit 3.4.

The key messages arising from the plus–delta exercise have been incorporated into the evaluation plan and design for the 2014–2015 school year.

In addition to the reflections in Exhibit 3.4 on the implementation of this developmental evaluation, a few overall key lessons have emerged that are applicable to other developmental evaluations:

1. *Build understanding of what developmental evaluation is, really.* Although the evaluation was explicitly labeled as a "developmental evaluation" from the start, the evaluators found themselves explaining what developmental evaluation is, and how it's different from other forms of evaluation, at almost every single meeting. Metaphors helped (e.g., one was a comparison to baking a cake from a brand-new, innovative recipe rather than a tried and tested one), but were also limiting (e.g., once the cook has figured out the new recipe, the problem is solved—which was nowhere near the case with the actual initiative; there was a series of new recipes,

---

EXHIBIT 3.4

What Worked Well and What Could Be Improved in Implementing the Developmental Evaluation

"Pluses": What worked well with the implementation of the developmental evaluation?	"Deltas": What could be improved?
• The evaluators showed great understanding of the initiative in all its complexity. • It felt like a true partnership among the evaluators, the Community Foundation, and the school district. • The developmental evaluation surfaced several assumptions in the work that needed to be tested and refined. • The format of the Learning Memos worked well, and should be maintained as the evaluation goes forward. • The evaluators were skilled facilitators and provided the right mix of giving information and facilitating deeper conversations. • The evaluators were open to questioning, feedback, and co-creation. • The evaluation captured voices from different groups.	• The evaluation should provide feedback to participants from whom data was collected (e.g., parents and teachers who participated in focus groups). • As part of the evaluation, benchmarks for progress need to be developed and tested. • A more targeted outreach should be made to involve those who are typically disengaged from the initiative; "outliers" should be included more intentionally in the sample. • The existing calendar of events at the schools should be leveraged more intentionally for evaluation data collection. • The evaluation should leverage data collected by other parties that are partnering with the school district (e.g., the Kent School Services Network).

contextual issues, and complications to deal with). A few times, the evaluators even had to catch themselves from veering off into formative/summative language (which was more familiar to participants), and instead stayed in "developmental evaluation territory" by emphasizing that the central overarching question was about *how the initiative is developing.* By the middle of the first year of implementation, the language and understanding finally started to shift.

2. *Co-create, iterate, rinse, repeat.* The evaluators learned the importance of co-creating early, while creating the evaluation design—and the importance of co-creation only grew as the evaluation proceeded. Synthesis and meaning were created together as the evaluators shared their data and observations with the program leaders during informal debriefs at the end of each visit, as well as through more formal processes such as the learning memos and biannual meetings. In line with lessons learned by other practitioners of developmental evaluation (Langlois et al., 2013), the evaluators found that iteration was the name of the game when it came to implementing the evaluation. The evaluation design was adapted on several occasions based on what was being learned, and communication and reporting mechanisms were often created in real time. For example, as previously mentioned, after receiving feedback that input was needed before the learning memos (which often took several days to be created) were received, the evaluators started scheduling informal debriefings at the end of each visit.

3. *Be there when you are not there.* When the evaluation first got underway, the evaluators found that they were often missing important pieces of contextual and programmatic information because they were only on the ground every other month. Hence they had to improvise several ways to have their "ears to the ground" as the evaluation proceeded. One such way was to send a "check-in" email every 2–3 months to key Challenge Scholars front-line staff, with three simple questions:

- What aspects of your work have been going particularly well over the past month?
- What challenges are you currently facing with respect to your role and responsibilities?
- What have you learned in the past month that you hope to apply to future activities or efforts?

As the year progressed, these check-in emails (which did not take staff members more than 5–10 minutes to respond to) became a critical tool for the evaluators—and, somewhat unexpectedly, core reflection tools for the front-line staff, who commented on how writing such an email allowed them to take a few minutes outside the "busyness" of their days to reflect. In addition to these check-in emails, and monthly check-in calls with the project leaders, the evaluators tapped into social media as a sensing tool. Being subscribed to the Twitter and Facebook feeds of the school district and local media organizations, for instance, helped the evaluators understand some of the contextual issues around the school district's budget cuts and restructuring, and made this possible in a timely manner.

4. *Set expectations for action—and, equally, inaction.* Acting on findings is often where the proverbial "rubber meets the road" for most evaluations. However, given the nature of the developmental evaluation process and data, it is important to clarify in what ways and to what extent there is an explicit expectation for action. In other words, is there an expectation that every single finding (or even the germ of one) will be acted on, every time it was delivered? This question was further complicated in the case of the Challenge Scholars developmental evaluation by the unstated and never-invoked, yet ever-present, power dynamic between the Community Foundation and the school district. Much as they were partners in the Challenge Scholars initiative, GRPS was still technically a "grantee" of the foundation. Hence it was important to clarify early on that the right course of action, in some cases, might be inaction. In other words, some early findings needed time to be borne out, to confirm that the patterns were indeed repeating and not one-off, before the project leaders needed to jump in and "fix" the issue. At the end of the first full year of the evaluation's implementation, this aspect still remained a work in progress. Putting forth evaluation findings, as well as processing them in a way that indicates where to act and where not to, is a skill set that all three groups of partners (the evaluators, the Community Foundation, and the school district) are continuing to work on.

Next Steps

The first 18 months of the developmental evaluation coincided with the most critical—and tumultuous—period of growth for the Challenge Scholars initiative to date. In many ways, Challenge Scholars evolved from concept to reality: The Promise Pact was developed and finalized, and has been signed by 140 students and families; the initiative expanded from one school to three; four new staff members were hired; and the initiative went "public" in every conceivable way.

Fortunately, the "churn" of the startup phase is easing, and the tone of the developmental evaluation will evolve as well. As the initiative has stabilized, the learning offered by developmental evaluation will become more strategic—with learning questions adapted to reflect what project leaders need to know and want to learn over the next several months. The process of identifying these priorities took place at a year-end session with the Partners' Group, led by the evaluators. During the meeting, evaluators reviewed data, surfaced themes and patterns through deliberate lines of questioning, and facilitated reflection and discussion among members of the Partners' Group, out of which emerged a clear direction for both the developmental evaluation and the initiative itself. Over the next year (2014–2015), the Challenge Scholars initiative looked forward to a period of moving to greater coherence and alignment, specifically in four key areas:

• *Creating a shared definition of college and career culture.* The developmental evaluation found that school staff, parents, and other community partners often have differing interpretations of what constitutes a college and career culture.

Clarifying what this culture looks like, and contextualizing this clarification for different stakeholder groups, have become priorities.

• *Authentically engaging parents in support of their children's academic journeys.* As illustrated in a set of developmental evaluation findings related to parent engagement, the obstacles that students and their family face along the journey to postsecondary education are substantial and multidimensional.

• *Continuing to monitor and support students to ensure that they are academically on track.* This could lead to opportunities for collaboration with other community partners who can provide resources and supports for students and families.

• *Developing the notion of a "family of schools" on the West Side.* Greater collaboration among West Side schools could offer a more seamless, supportive environment for parents and students.

Going into Year 2 of implementation, the developmental evaluation was continuing to support the initiative by focusing on these four themes, as well as continuing to reflect on the entire "system" of Challenge Scholars. The systems maps and key learning questions that were initially developed in June 2013 have been updated to capture what has subsequently been learned, and a timeline is being worked out for the evaluation's implementation that aligns with the existing school calendars. Several of the data collection and reporting methods have been retained, while some new ones have been added. The evaluation has broadened the lens in some areas (e.g., understanding what is being done to address affordable housing issues on the west side that have a bearing on Challenge Scholars families) while narrowing around some others (e.g., looking at core academic support for Challenge Scholars students).

Conclusion

A hallmark of an effective evaluation is that it not only accomplishes its primary goals, but also builds capacity among users to think differently. It's still too early to tell what the impact of the Challenge Scholars developmental evaluation will be on the overall initiative. However, there are several early signs that the parties involved in the evaluation have benefited from a "developmental evaluation way of thinking." The project leader from the Community Foundation, while reflecting on the developmental evaluation experience, noted that it "opened our eyes more to the complexity of the problems we are trying to address and how the Community Foundation can approach problems differently even beyond Challenge Scholars." The project leader from the school district articulated that "GRPS found the developmental evaluation a viable means for learning that could be shared by the partners to inform the work and influence strategic thinking, giving us more traction with implementation."

By co-creating the evaluation design, building in rapid feedback processes, and engaging stakeholders in making meaning, the developmental evaluation team was able not only to accomplish its primary goals, but in the process to build trust, partnership, and capacity. However, as illustrated earlier, it wasn't an entirely smooth journey, and lessons are still being learned every day about what can be done differently. As others look to developmental evaluation as a promising approach for systemic interventions in their early stages, they would be well advised to learn not only from its successes, but also from its challenges.

REFERENCES

Center for Educational Performance and Information. (2013). Michigan cohort graduation and dropout reports. Retrieved from *www.michigan.gov/cepi*.

Coffman, J., & Beer, T. (2011). *Evaluation to support strategic learning: Principles and practices*. Washington, DC: Center for Evaluation Innovation.

Coffman, J., & Reed, E. (2009). *Unique methods in advocacy evaluation*. Los Angeles: California Endowment. Retrieved from *www.innonet.org/resources/node/390*.

Gándara, P. (2001). Paving the way to postsecondary education: K–12 intervention programs for underrepresented youth. Report of the National Postsecondary Education Cooperative Working Group on Access to Postsecondary Education. Retrieved from *http://nces.ed.gov/pubs2001/2001205.pdf*.

Langlois, M., Blanchet-Cohen, N., & Beer, T. (2013). The art of the nudge: Five practices for developmental evaluators. *Canadian Journal of Program Evaluation, 27*(2), 39–59.

Miller-Adams, M. (2013, October 11). *An introduction to promise scholarship programs*. Presentation given at Lumina Foundation, Indianapolis, IN.

Morin, R., Fry, R., & Brown, A. (2014). The rising cost of not going to college. *Pew Social Trends*. Retrieved from *www.pewsocialtrends.org/2014/02/11/the-rising-cost-of-not-going-to-college*.

National Student Clearinghouse, Student Tracker for High Schools. (2013). *Aggregate report prepared for Grand Rapids Public School District*. Herndon, VA: Author.

Oakes, J. (2003). Critical conditions for equity and diversity in college access: Informing policy and monitoring results. Retrieved from *http://escholarship.org/uc/item/427737xt*.

Patton, M. Q. (2011). *Developmental evaluation: Applying complexity concepts to enhance innovation and use*. New York: Guilford Press.

Perna, L. W., & Li, C. (2006). College affordability: Implications for college opportunity. *Journal of Student Financial Aid, 36*(1), 7–24.

Preskill, H., & Beer, T. (2012). Evaluating social innovation. FSG and Center for Evaluation Innovation. Retrieved from *www.fsg.org/tabid/191/ArticleId/708/Default.aspx?srpush=true*.

Tierney, W. G., Bailey, T., Constantine, J., Finkelstein, N., & Hurd, N. F. (2009). Helping students navigate the path to college: What high schools can do (IES Practice Guide. NCEE No. 2009-4066). What Works Clearinghouse. Retrieved from *http://ies.ed.gov/ncee/wwc/PracticeGuide.aspx?sid=11*.

Tierney, W. G., Colyar, J. E., & Corwin, Z. B. (2003). *Preparing for college: Building expectations, changing realities*. Los Angeles: Center for Higher Education Policy Analysis.

W. E. Upjohn Institute. (2014, June). Business outlook for west Michigan. *Business Outlook, 30*(2). Retrieved from *http://research.upjohn.org/bus_outlook/vol30/iss2/1/*.

CHAPTER 4

Nine Guiding Principles
to Help Youth Overcome Homelessness

A Principles-Focused Developmental Evaluation

Nora F. Murphy

It was hard, scary, didn't know if I was gonna live. Sometimes I just thought about killing myself. I have this one cousin—my uncle died. She will give me clothes to get up and go to school. Sometimes she'll have to sneak me in her house. And that's how I was living my life—like sneakin' in and wearin' other people's clothes—have nowhere to go—I didn't know what I'm gonna eat. One time—I was young, I sold my body to keep clothes on my back and eat. I didn't wanna go through that life no more.
                    —MARIA (a pseudonym) on being homeless

EDITORS' INTRODUCTION

The last of the 10 questions addressed in Chapter 1 of this volume is "What has been the biggest development in developmental evaluation since publication of the Patton (2011) book?" The answer: *Principles-focused developmental evaluation.* That is the focus of this chapter. Let us set the context for its importance.

Evaluation "grew up" in projects, and the field remains deeply enmeshed in a project/program mentality. As a profession, we know how to do project and program evaluation. But a major lesson of the last 50 years is that projects and programs seldom, if ever, change systems. Social innovators working on systems change have to navigate complexity, deal with turbulence and uncertainty, adapt rapidly to changing conditions, be vigilant about what is emerging as they engage, and watch for nonlinear interactions and consequences. How do they do all that without following the traditional advice to "plan your work and work your plan," which doesn't work very well in the face of complexity? They do it by articulating a vision and identifying the principles they will adhere to in working adaptively toward that vision. *Principles* as a unit of analysis—as the *evaluand*, to use the jargon of the field—poses quite different challenges from evaluating implementation of a logic model and attainment of clear, specific, and measurable goals. Evaluating principles involves a minimum of three challenges: (1) identifying the principles; (2) examining the work to see if the principles are actually guiding action (are they "walking the talk?"); and (3) determining what results from principles-focused engagement—both intended and emergent results.

Principles-driven social innovation and systems change require principles-focused developmental evaluation, an innovative evaluation approach. This chapter describes the pioneering example of principles-focused evaluation. Independent corroboration that this is an exemplar: The developmental evaluator, Nora Murphy, received the 2013 Michael Scriven Dissertation Award for Outstanding Contribution to Evaluation Theory, Methodology, or Practice for this evaluation. You may not have heard of principles-focused evaluation before reading about it here, but we feel confident that you'll be hearing a lot more about it in the future. Prepare to journey to the cutting edge.

Homeless youth are hugely diverse. Some have spent much of their lives in shelters for homeless persons with their families, while others grew up in foster care. Some still have family connections, while others do not. Some have been homeless off and on in a repeating pattern, while others are new to the streets and are experiencing homelessness for the first time. Some are barely teenagers, while others may be in their late teens or early 20s. Some face health and mental health challenges. Some have learning or developmental disabilities. Some are addicted to alcohol or drugs. Homeless youth come from both middle-class and poor families, and include all races and ethnic groups. Homeless youth include straight youth, as well as gay, lesbian, bisexual, and transgender young people (Homeless Youth Collaborative on Developmental Evaluation, 2014; Murphy, 2014).

Of course, those of us looking deeper into youth homelessness will start to recognize patterns. Many homeless youth are people of color. Although many are straight, many others are gay, lesbian, bisexual, or transgender. Few have strong or varied social support systems. Many find that homelessness occurs slowly, over a number of years; such young people have shared that there was not a single event that "caused" homelessness, but rather a series of cumulative events (Kennedy, Agbényiga, Kasiborski, & Gladden, 2010; Murphy, 2014). Most homeless youth have experienced serious trauma at the hands of people they loved and by the society they live in. Once homeless, they are more likely to experience stigmatization, sexual victimization, and negative experiences with people who are in positions to help (Kidd, 2007; Stewart et al., 2004). Despite these experiences, nearly all of them want to love and be loved. Our challenge is to meet and connect with each young person where he or she is, and build a relationship from the ground up.

In this chapter, I describe an evidence-based, principles-focused developmental evaluation that supports collaborative work among a foundation, six agencies serving homeless youth, and two evaluators. I go in depth to explain the nature of the evaluation inquiry, methods, processes, and lessons learned.

Evidence-Based, Principles-Focused Developmental Evaluation

The Otto Bremer Foundation, a private foundation serving the Minneapolis/St. Paul metro area (also known as the Twin Cities), believes that a path for healthy development should be within reach of all young people. At the end of 2011, the foundation provided grants totaling almost $4 million, to be allocated over 3 years to address youth homelessness in the Twin Cities. Six grantees (three emergency shelters, two youth opportunity drop-in centers, and one street outreach organization) received funding to expand their existing services, as well as to support collaboration and improved outcomes at the systems level through collaboration amongst the grantees. The grantees were Avenues for Homeless Youth, Catholic Charities (Hope Street), Face to Face (Safe Zone), Lutheran Social Services (Street-Works Collaborative), The Salvation Army (Booth Brown House), and YouthLink (Youth Opportunity Center).

Each person experiencing homelessness is unique—and organizations that serve homeless youth are also unique. No recipe exists, or can exist, for how a person or an organization ought to engage with a particular homeless young person. Street outreach organizations, drop-in centers, emergency shelters, and housing programs offer youth necessarily different assistance and solutions. And even within a particular type of service, there is tremendous variability—a Catholic Charities shelter, a Salvation Army shelter, and an independent, locally grown shelter all have different supports, resources, and constraints. This is one of the strengths of the system: Variations across service providers allow youth to have options, to find the places and people that will best support them on their journey.

At the onset of this initiative, the Otto Bremer Foundation contracted with Michael Quinn Patton to facilitate an evaluation process that could both honor the unique and diverse needs of youth and agencies, *and* provide increased collaboration and coherence across the system. In the current research and evaluation climate, the tendency is to search for "best practices" and to attempt to implement these with consistency and fidelity across the system. But in this context—where a diversity of approaches is desirable—rigid rules and standardized procedures aren't helpful. In fact, they can cause considerable harm. Guiding principles, by contrast, can provide clarity and shared purposes while allowing for adaptation across time and contexts. Rather than telling people who serve youth exactly what to do and when, principles provide guidance and direction in the face of uncertainty and complexity (Patton, 2011).

The group members decided that an *evidence-based, principles-focused developmental evaluation* would best support their collaborative work. They selected *developmental evaluation* because, although there was intent to collaborate, they didn't have a common understanding about how the collaborative process would unfold or to what end. They agreed upon a *principles-focused* approach because guiding principles would give youth workers, shelter staff members, and those providing services to homeless youth a basis for how to engage and interact; what to watch for; and how to communicate with consistency, compassion, and respect. They wanted to collect *evidence* from the youth they serve, to confirm that the principles they identified were indeed the right principles and/or to identify where there were gaps in their understanding.

When I asked Patton why the group committed to an emerging cutting-edge approach, he replied, "These are savvy, experienced directors; they *got it*" (M. Q. Patton, personal communication, October 24, 2014). With backgrounds in higher education, business, youth development, and policy, the directors of the different agencies followed different paths to their roles as directors. One thing they all shared was the experience of following rules to satisfy funding requirements even when the rules didn't make sense in their particular setting. They had all experienced collecting and reporting standardized data to satisfy funding requirements, despite the fact that the data collected were not always useful, were sometimes burdensome to obtain, and often oversimplified the complexity of the phenomena being evaluated. By contrast, this approach assumes that while the principles remain the same, adaptation is both necessary and appropriate and will occur within and across contexts (Homeless Youth Collaborative on Developmental Evaluation, 2014). The directors were thrilled that this approach created and honored space in the process for ambiguity and emergence, that it offered them a chance to further their own understanding of how to best work with homeless youth, and that it created a safe space for collaboration in a competitive world.

The remainder of this section explains how the evidence-based, principles-focused developmental evaluation unfolded over a span of nearly 2 years.

Nature of Inquiry

We had two main purposes for the developmental evaluation. Our first goal was to create a process by which the six individual agencies could collaborate in a way that would lead to improved outcomes for youth. Once the group decided to adopt a principles-focused approach, the second goal was to identify and empirically validate guiding principles. To meet these goals, we sought to incorporate two overlapping methods: (1) engaging the Otto Bremer Foundation and agency leaders in collaborative evaluation inquiry, and (2) analyzing multiple case studies. Collaborative evaluation inquiry consisted primarily of monthly reflective practice meetings with the foundation and grantee leadership over 2 years. Multiple case analyses—involving a total of 14 youth case studies—were conducted to empirically validate the identified guiding principles. The methods were highly interrelated, with the reflective practice group participating in every aspect of the multiple case analyses. Exhibit 4.1 outlines the evaluation process, divided into three phases, and identifies the key activities in each phase. Below, I describe each of these phases in depth.

EXHIBIT 4.1

The Three Phases of the Evaluation Process for the Homeless Youth Collaborative on Developmental Evaluation

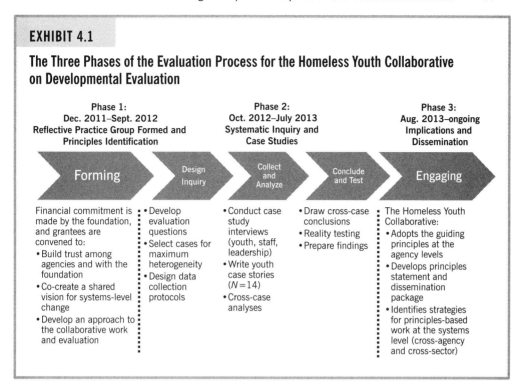

Phase 1: Dec. 2011–Sept. 2012 Reflective Practice Group Formed and Principles Identification	Phase 2: Oct. 2012–July 2013 Systematic Inquiry and Case Studies		Phase 3: Aug. 2013–ongoing Implications and Dissemination
Forming	Design Inquiry → Collect and Analyze	Conclude and Test	Engaging
Financial commitment is made by the foundation, and grantees are convened to: • Build trust among agencies and with the foundation • Co-create a shared vision for systems-level change • Develop an approach to the collaborative work and evaluation	• Develop evaluation questions • Select cases for maximum heterogeneity • Design data collection protocols	• Conduct case study interviews (youth, staff, leadership) • Write youth case stories ($N=14$) • Cross-case analyses	• Draw cross-case conclusions • Reality testing • Prepare findings	The Homeless Youth Collaborative: • Adopts the guiding principles at the agency levels • Develops principles statement and dissemination package • Identifies strategies for principles-based work at the systems level (cross-agency and cross-sector)

Phase 1: Reflective Practice Group Formed and Principles Identified

Forming the Reflective Practice Group

Reflective practice groups can vary in how often they meet, how much time they devote to group reflection, the scope and scale of their experiences, and their reasons for reflection. We formed a reflective practice group early in the process, with the purposes of (1) regularly and consistently sharing and exploring our individual experiences, (2) co-creating a shared vision for the collaborative work, and (3) building trust among members. This group met at least once per month over a period of nearly 2 years to engage in an examination of the ways in which they could improve outcomes for youth experiencing homelessness. The group—whose members eventually named themselves the Homeless Youth Collaborative on Developmental Evaluation—was the heart of the developmental evaluation process. Forming the group was both a commitment to consistent evaluative inquiry and a statement of trust by the foundation that with the right people in the room sharing their combined wisdom, solutions would emerge.

The reflective practice group initially included members of the foundation staff, the directors from each agency, and Michael Quinn Patton. This group first convened in February 2012 and built the foundation for engagement by (1) defining the "we/us" in this work, (2) getting a commitment from each of the agencies to work together, and (3) introducing evaluation as a way the group could identify success (M. Q. Patton, personal communication, 2012). Defining the "we/us" was important because, as is typical in the world of nonprofits, the agencies' personnel were used to seeing each other primarily as competition for limited resources—particularly funding. It was critical to the formation of the collaborative that they begin to see each other as "we," and that they willingly commit to exploring together where they might benefit from supporting each other's work and connecting more systematically. Once established, the evaluation discussion explored what the group would like to say about the work at the end of 1 year and at the end of the 3-year funding commitment.

As is often the case with organizations working alongside each other in the same community, the collaborative's members, who all came from different organizations, had varying degrees of knowledge about each other's range of services and approach to serving youth. So later that spring, the group organized a bus tour attended by 40 community members. The Road to Success tour showcased the recent expansion of services and emergency shelters for homeless youth in the Twin Cities metro area, engaged participants in conversations with staff and young people at each of the sites, and ended with a lunch prepared by youth interns in YouthLink's food service program. At the end of the day, people commented that the tour powerfully conveyed that *collaboration leads to better outcomes for homeless youth.* One piece of feedback received was that "This was a pivotal event in the formation of the group," contributing tremendously to the building of trust, sense of purpose, and mutual positive regard.

Identifying Shared Principles

At the next meeting, grantees were asked to share principles, values, philosophies, theories of change, and other factors and beliefs that were currently informing their approach to working with homeless youth. What agencies shared varied widely, from a published manual (Able-Peterson & Bucy, 1993) to bulleted lists. To identify cross-cutting themes, the collaborative's members laid out the shared documents and reflected on these questions: "What is it that we all believe? What is it that we can all commit to?" Although the language used by each agency was sometimes different, it was clear that there were some commonly held beliefs. Together, the group identified eight shared principles across agencies: harm reduction, trusting relationships, positive youth development, trauma-informed care, nonjudgmental engagement, strengths/assets-based approach, collaborative, and holistic. When asked if there were principles that the group members wished were present but weren't, they added a ninth principle: journey-oriented.

But were these the "right" principles? Given that the collaborative's members were committed to being youth-driven, the obvious questions raised were these: Would homeless young people also identify these principles as important? If so, what do these principles look like in practice? Are there principles that have not been identified or articulated? What is the impact of these principles on a young person's trajectory when homeless? The collaborative's members discussed many options for answering these questions, and decided that they would like to commit to an inquiry process that would allow them to learn from the stories of youth who had achieved success in working toward their goals.

Phase 2: Systematic Inquiry and Case Studies

It was at this point that I met with Patton for the first time. I was a doctoral student in evaluation studies at the University of Minnesota and wanted to learn more about using complexity theory in my work. I walked up to Patton at an evaluation event and asked if he would be willing to talk with me. To my surprise and delight, he said yes! When we met, I shared my experience as a high school teacher at an alternative school in Washington, D.C.; told him about my frustrations with the social science research paradigm; and mentioned that his most recent book had helped me see a future path for myself. I also talked about my journey as a single mother, about my son who had passed away a year earlier, and about my commitment to build my family through foster care and adoption. He listened patiently, and when I was done talking, he described a project that he had been working on with a local foundation and six agencies to address youth homelessness. He then asked if I'd be interested in exploring the possibility of using this project as my dissertation research. Of course I said yes. Sometimes in developmental evaluations it feels as though serendipity intervenes. This was one of those moments.

Developing the Case Study Approach

In September 2012, I attended my first meeting of the collaborative. I walked into a basement room and found 16 smart and passionate individuals who were deeply interested in understanding my values and beliefs regarding youth homelessness. They questioned me at length about my ability to build rapport and "do no harm" when engaging with vulnerable youth, as well as my commitment to supporting the collaborative's work. After an hour of these exploratory questions, we turned to the discussion of a dissertation. What was it? How would they benefit from partnering with a graduate student? What would they lose? What would be my commitment to them versus the institution/university? After I answered their questions, they dismissed me so they could discuss our meeting. I feel lucky that they decided to invite me to join them in their work.

With approval from the Otto Bremer Foundation's trustees and the University of Minnesota's institutional review board, I joined the group for the first time at the November 2012 meeting. The collaborative had decided that case studies would be used to generate empirical support for the principles, but the question of how to proceed with case selection remained. After discussing various possibilities, we decided that we would use the *success case method* (Brinkerhoff, 2003) and seek maximum heterogeneity in the cases, using the following criteria. Each of our participants would (1) be over 18 years of age; (2) be accessible (have current contact information); (3) represent a "success case" (e.g., in housing, school, and/or job); and (4) have been involved in some way with at least three agencies. As a whole, the sample would reflect the racial makeup of youth served by the agency, as well as specific variables of interest (e.g., interactions with the juvenile justice system, engagement with the foster care system, and pregnant or parenting status).

In December 2012, personnel from each agency nominated a few homeless youth that they knew well and shared a brief overview of each youth with the group. We decided collaboratively on the final set of 14 young people asked to participate. We also decided that in order to understand a young person's journey more fully, we would ask each youth to nominate one staff person at the agency who knew the youth's journey well and whom I could interview for additional information about him or her. I would also ask each young participant for permission to review his or her case file. The members of the collaborative felt it was important for the youth interview to be the first step, so that the young person's story set the tone for the remainder of the inquiry process. At the next meeting, the group reviewed the interview protocols I drafted, with attention to the types of data the interview protocol might yield, as well as how the 16 questions might be interpreted by potential interviewees. One question was added, several were removed, and two were modified. Though everything takes longer when decided by committee, I can't overemphasize how important it was that the collaborative members were engaged at every decision point. As Heather Huseby, executive director of YouthLink, said, "The involvement of each member bridged the gap between research and practice in important ways. It increased the credibility of the process and the relevancy of the findings."

Collaborative Inquiry and Shared Meaning Making

Sometimes in developmental evaluations serendipity intervenes, but just as often things fall out of sync. When this happens, it feels as though a rhythm that was once there is gone, leading to unease. The next meeting of the collaborative was one of those moments. While I had already started interviewing young people and felt that I was gaining momentum, other members of the collaborative were losing trust in the process. They wanted to pause to ask: How was this process going to be important to their work? How would the principles be used? Was this really a good use of their time, expertise, and resources? Luckily, I was able to write a draft of the first case study in advance of our next meeting—the story of Thmaris, a young man who shared how his case manager was able to help him earn his welding degree and see a different path for himself, despite the enormous obstacles he was facing. After the collaborative's members read the case, the tone changed and anxieties lessened. Members shared "ah-ha" moments, such as these observations about the journey-oriented principle:

> "I had originally thought that the stages-of-change model [Prochaska & Norcross, 2001] might be the same as 'journey-oriented.' But I am now thinking that this is different and important."

> "[This case] explains why you can't 'rush' young people through services so that they can meet the age requirements. In fact, pushing young people to make changes before they are ready can actually backfire."

It was at this meeting that the principles began to come to life, and the time-consuming but critical work of collaborative meaning making began in earnest.

Several more case studies were written and shared before we met again in April 2013. Teams of three to four people were assigned to read three case studies and instructed to conduct a cross-case analysis. This allowed the group members to deepen their understanding of how the analysis was conducted, and it allowed them to make evidence-based connections among the principles, their work, and the participants' experiences. This was also the first opportunity for the group to hear about the interactions between and among the organizations from a youth perspective. Even though young people's experience with agencies were not always portrayed as positive, group members took a position of openness and learning rather than defensiveness. This was a clear indication that a sense of trust and safety had developed among the collaborative's members. Without it, the process would have developed into posturing, which would have undermined the potential impact of the entire effort.

By the May 2013 meeting, a draft of cross-case analyses of several principles was completed. The cross-case analysis of each principle consisted of (1) a brief review of research, (2) a description of themes that emerged across the cases, and (3) supporting quotes provided as evidence for the themes. For example, the themes in Exhibit 4.2 were identified under the principle of trusting youth–adult relationships (Murphy, 2014). Exhibit 4.3 provides examples of the types of evidence provided for this theme.

Group members were asked to review the written cross-case analysis of the trusting youth–adult relationships principle in small groups. Some reactions shared at the end of the meeting included these: "Reading this was validating. It's what we know and what we do, but this formalizes its importance." And "This reinforces that we need to keep encountering the youth. It may be the second, third, or fourth interaction that makes the difference."

By June 2013, the cross-case analyses of all nine principles were drafted, and the collaborative was asked to read all nine of the principles in advance of the

---

EXHIBIT 4.2

Themes Identified under the Trusting Youth–Adult Relationships Principle

Theme 1: Past experiences make it hard to trust.

Theme 2: Nonjudgmental engagement is an essential first ingredient in developing a relationship.

Theme 3: Learning to open up is important and happens through relationship.

Theme 4: Listening is as important as doing.

Theme 5: Relationships help youth learn to ask for and receive help.

Theme 6: People matter more than programs.

Theme 7: It means a lot when staff convey that they truly care.

Theme 8: Relationships are the critical ingredient for effective programming.

meeting. The focus of this meeting was "Bringing It All Together: Interrelationships between Principles." Group members worked in small teams to create visual representations of how the principles interrelated. Each visual relationship was different, but most were organized around the idea that homeless youth are on a journey and that each of these principles work together to support youth in different ways along their journey. Implications for practice and opportunities for collaborative work across agencies were emerging and are discussed below in connection with Phase 3.

Note: After this meeting, the locus of responsibility for maintaining momentum shifted back to the collaborative, as my dissertation was complete.

EXHIBIT 4.3

Examples of the Types of Evidence Provided from the Case Studies for the Principle of Trusting Youth–Adult Relationships

Alexa, a 23-year-old mother of two young children, has lost several loved ones in her life to homicide and incarceration. She is a long-time victim of domestic abuse. Alexa shared that past experience made it difficult for her to trust people (Theme 1):

> "That's just how I grew up—like don't never let nobody get close to you. [Because] then you lose them. So what is the point of gettin' close to somebody?"

Maria, an 18-year-old woman, had a childhood marked by physical abuse, sexual abuse, and loss. Maria cited her relationships with her case manager, Izzy, as one of the most important positive factors in her life. When Izzy would ask Maria if she needed help, Maria would often tell her that what she really needed was someone to talk to (Theme 4):

> "It's like Izzy will always be there for me. I'll just go talk to her and tell her my problems. She ask me what could she do to help me. I tell her I just need to talk to people every now and then."

Thmaris, a 22-year-old father of a young son, described why his relationship with his case manager, Rahim, was critical to his ability to end his gang involvement, stay out of jail, and earn a degree in welding from a local community college:

> "Out of all the other caseworkers I had, nobody ever really sat me down and tried to work out a resolution for my problems. They always just gave me pamphlets like, "Well, go call these people and see if they can do something for you." Or "You should go to this building because this building has that, what you want." It was like every time I come to him, I don't have to worry about anything. He's not going to send me to the next man, put me onto the next person's caseload. He just always took care [of] me. If I would have never met Rahim, I would have been in a totally different situation, I would have went a totally different route."

Thmaris had worked with two other case managers at the same drop-in center before working with Rahim. He never felt the same sense of caring from them that he did with his new case manager. The relationship he established with Rahim was a critical ingredient to his success (Theme 8).

Source: Murphy (2014).

Phase 3: Implications and Dissemination

Whereas Phase 2 was largely driven by the case study process, Phase 3 became more open-ended as agencies were asked this question: Given what we've learned, what's next? One implication that emerged from our discussion was the realization that a principles-focused approach is different from a rules-focused approach in a very important way: The principles-based approach requires a great deal of judgment and trust. Rather than requiring staff members to follow rules, agencies help staff members understand the principles and then empower them to exercise their professional judgment. This led to these related questions: How does one make a judgment? How do we build a culture that supports trust in people's ability to make good judgments? How do we train for principles-based work? How do we evaluate this?

Agency leaders met the following month to try to answer these questions. Exhibit 4.4 displays some highlights of the thinking that emerged. It was becoming increasingly clear that working in a principles-based way created a pathway for collaboration and systems change by driving changes at the individual, agency, cross-agency, and cross-sector levels.

Dissemination

In order to change organizational culture or cross-sector collaboration to be principles-based, the group needed to develop materials that conveyed what was learned in a clear and concise way. Over the next few months, the agencies worked together to prepare a dissemination package that explained each principle and its research base, and listed some of the practice implications. To start, members of the collaborative had to agree upon the specific wording of individual principles. So at the September 2013 meeting, small groups drafted principles statements to share with the group, using the evidence described in the dissertation as the foundation. The group easily reached consensus on the wording of some principle statements, whereas others, such as the collaboration principle, required a great deal of time and discussion. The group had to decide: Who was collaborating with whom, in what way, and to what end? For example, some working ideas included for collaboration included these:

> "Deliver services in a coordinated manner that creates, and teach youth how to build, an integrated network of support."

> "Establish a seamless network of support for the holistic needs of the youth."

> "Work together intentionally and strategically, across agencies, services, and system barriers, always focused on supporting each youth, while working toward a seamless system of practices, policies, and procedures that is grounded in our shared principles."

Ultimately, none of these were quite right. So as a large group, the collaborative adopted new ideas, finessed the language, and reviewed the draft statements.

EXHIBIT 4.4

Examples of Strategies for Working in a Principles-Based Way at the Agency and Systems Levels

Opportunity	Why this is important	Implications	Possibilities for action
Hiring	Working in a principles-driven way means that there are often not clear or easy answers. Staff members need to be able to work within contexts of ambiguity and to make principles-based contextualized judgments on a case-by-case basis.	Conceptualization of **staff roles**, **position descriptions**, and the **interview process** should attract people who can work with ambiguity, who have good judgment, and who have the capacity to work in a *principles*-based way.	**Share documents and processes** with other organizations (position descriptions, interview process, philosophy of care, staff evaluation, etc.), to demonstrate how a principles-based approach can be embedded in language and expectations.
Organizational culture	In rules-based work, it is easier to know what staff members are doing "right" or "wrong" by examining the degree to which they enforced the rules. In principles-based work, staff members need to reflect continually on what they did, why they did it, and how it worked, and to identify new learning.	The organizational culture should support **self-reflection** and **self-awareness**—enabling people to "be who they are and ask for what they need." It should support **compassion**, allow people to feel **vulnerable**, and build **trust** among staff members so that they trust the judgments of others.	Develop tools and processes for engaging staff with principles and boundaries associated with principles—such as exercises that can be done at staff meetings.
Cross-organization collaboration	While agencies often see each other as discrete and separate entities, youth move between them fluidly. Young people would benefit from staff collaboration across agencies around the principles.	Opportunities need to be created to allow organizations and individuals within those organizations to work together around the principles.	Shared **training and professional development** across organizations, **shared case management** across agencies, and **continued conversation among leaders** to identify needs and opportunities for working collaboratively around principles.

It was a slow process, but the final product is powerful. Each of these final principles has merit on its own. But, together, this set of principles provides a framework for cohesive approaches and solutions. Youth workers, shelter staff, and those providing services to homeless youth can now be given guidance on how to engage and interact, what to watch for, and how to communicate compassion and respect. The final statements of the principles are shown in Exhibit 4.5.

We now had our principles statements, so we could complete our dissemination packet. This packet included the following:

- The principles statements.

- An explanation of principles-based practice.

- Principles flash cards (Patton, 2014) explaining why each principle matters, the research basis for the principle, the implications for practice, and evidence from the case studies prepared as a part of this evaluation.

- An "outcomes snapshot" for each youth, summarizing the youth's journey and making the link between the principles and outcomes.

- A full case study to provide a sense of the depth and quality of the data.

EXHIBIT 4.5

Nine Evidence-Based Guiding Principles to Help Youth Overcome Homelessness

The principles begin with the perspective that youth are on a journey; all of our interactions with youth are filtered through this **journey-oriented** perspective. This means that we must be **trauma-informed** and **nonjudgmental,** and must work to **reduce harm**. By holding these principles, we can build a **trusting relationship** that allows us to focus on **youth's strengths** and opportunities for **positive development**. Through all of this, we approach youth as **whole beings** through a youth-focused **collaborative** system of support.

1. **Journey-Oriented.** Interact with youth to help them understand the interconnectedness of past, present, and future as they decide where they want to go and how to get there.

2. **Trauma-Informed.** Recognize that all homeless youth have experienced trauma; build relationships, responses, and services on that knowledge.

3. **Nonjudgmental.** Interact with youth without labeling or judging them on the basis of background, experiences, choices, or behaviors.

4. **Harm Reduction.** Contain the effects of risky behavior in the short term, and seek to reduce its effects in the long term.

5. **Trusting Youth–Adult Relationships.** Build relationships by interacting with youth in an honest, dependable, authentic, caring, and supportive way.

6. **Strengths-Based.** Start with and build upon the skills, strengths, and positive characteristics of each youth.

7. **Positive Youth Development.** Provide opportunities for youth to build a sense of competency, usefulness, belonging, and power.

8. **Holistic.** Engage youth in a manner that recognizes that mental, physical, spiritual, and social health are interconnected and interrelated.

9. **Collaboration.** Establish a principles-based youth-focused system of support that integrates practices, procedures, and services within and across agencies, systems, and policies.

Source: Principles developed by the Homeless Youth Collaborative on Developmental Evaluation: Avenues for Homeless Youth; Catholic Charities (Hope Street); Face to Face (Safe Zone); Lutheran Social Services (StreetWorks Collaborative); the Salvation Army (Booth Brown House); and YouthLink (Youth Opportunity Center).

This packet[1] was developed to support the organizations' ability both to work in a principles-based way (hiring, professional development, relating to youth, etc.) and to collaborate in a principles-focused way (sharing common expectations, evaluation, applying for funding, etc.). Once the packet was formalized, the next step was to present what was developed to the Otto Bremer Foundation's board of trustees. It was an important time for the collaborative's members to come together publicly to talk about what they had developed together, what it meant for their work personally and collectively, and what their hopes were for future principles-focused work.

In the months since our last meeting together in March 2014, the six organizations have been utilizing the principles, each in its own unique way. One nationally affiliated organization shared that the principles had changed the agency-level conversations, but that "organizational culture change moves very slowly." By contrast, an organization without affiliation to a larger agency has been able to move more quickly, hiring an external consultant to begin working with the staff and board of directors to effect organizational change. Multiple agencies have started using the resources that were developed at staff trainings, and some have applied to provide training at state and national levels. Some agencies report that the work has opened up internal dialogues about different evaluation practices and strategies. At the systems level, the work is being used by a downtown Minneapolis task force focused on youth behavior. My hope is that these documents continue to be adopted, adapted, and used widely and deeply.

What Was Developed?

Clearly, the principles statements and the dissemination packet were developed in the process described above. But other things were developed that are worth describing: (1) a community of practice characterized by evaluative thinking, trust, listening, and learning; (2) an understanding of principles-focused work; and (3) a commitment to change at the systems level. Although these things are less tangible than the dissemination packet, they are equally important. The dissemination packet is virtually worthless if not used.

A Community of Practice

Nonprofit agencies' leaders operate in a world that focuses on individual programmatic or organizational outcomes. In the collaborative, it took regular monthly meetings to build the trust between and among agencies necessary to support this shift—a shift organizational leaders indicated that they would not have achieved without the developmental evaluation process. Our monthly reflective practice sessions shifted the emphasis from individual organizations' outcomes to an emphasis on collaboration that placed homeless youth at the center of the work. Conversations

---

[1]The packet can be viewed online and downloaded (*http://bit.ly/9GuidingPrinciples*).

during these sessions focused on (1) what was being discovered and confirmed, (2) understanding what this meant for youth, and (3) discussing implications for individual and collaborative work. Interviews with agency directors have revealed that going beyond principles-based work at the organizational level to principles-based collaboration at the systems level has been a big and important shift for organizations.

An Understanding of Principles-Focused Work

Understanding principles-focused work requires, at its heart, that people have a high degree of tolerance for ambiguity. For many of the agency leaders in the collaborative, working in this way is not new to them. One member of the collaborative shared: "We call it working in the gray zone. There's nothing black and white. We are working with youth 24/7, and we never know the full story." But they wrestled with the implications for being principles-based at all levels of their organization. Staff members who are comfortable with rules and manuals and uncomfortable with ambiguity may have trouble working in a principles-based environment. Whereas in other contexts they might tell a youth, "You are kicked out because you returned to the shelter high tonight," staff members doing principles-based work must take time to understand the needs of that particular young person, engage with him or her without judgment, and take a harm reduction approach to the undesirable behavior. The ability to do this comes in part through intuition, in part through training, and in part through a collective staff commitment to exploring what the principles look like in practice. When asked recently to provide an update about how this work has impacted each agency, Hanna Getachew-Kreusser, the program director at Avenues for Homeless Youth, shared the following:

> "The developmental evaluation has prompted us in an urgent manner to ensure that our agency fully understands the principles and is clear on their practical day-to-day implications of applications. We are planning on taking one principle per month for our all-staff trainings and dig deeper the next 9 months.
>
> "We are also planning to update all our 'rule books' (i.e., our program manual and resident handbook) according to the applications of the principles.
>
> "We have been making huge headway in intentionally integrating the principles as ways of approaching difficult situations related to youth during our weekly team meetings. During the last few years of our intentional effort to be principles-based in our work, we have been able to lengthen the stay of the youth in our program and reduce the number of discharges.
>
> "As we all know, allowing youth to make mistakes in safe places and learn from them increases their rate of success in their journey of life."

A Commitment to Outcomes at the Systems Level

There was a deep sense of values regarding the importance of this work and its alignment with each agency's vision, mission, and values at play. What developed was an understanding that all six organizations want the same things for the youth they serve, and that they can work better on behalf of young people collectively than they can individually. One program administrator shared: "The conversations that we've had in those meetings have helped me see from a higher systems level than before. . . . I'm seeing things differently." Engaging in a principles-based developmental evaluation has provided staff members with a new way to state their values and to think about solutions they all believe in. As two program leaders shared, "It's about where we want to put the stake in the ground." Another shared:

> "Sitting in a room with colleagues and [understanding] where they come from and what ideas and thoughts and their principles are really has been helpful. . . . I want to work somewhere that tells me we are going to do it this way, in a way that makes sense, that we are principled people, and we are going to stand up for what we believe in. Together we're going to effect change."

And it's happening. Through changed cross-sector conversations, revised principles-based memoranda of understandings, and collaborative grant proposals, there is increasing commitment to systems-level outcomes.

Lessons Learned about Developmental Evaluation

At the same time that we were learning about the work, we were also learning about developmental evaluation. Below are a few of the lessons we learned.

Attention to the "It" Being Developed Is Essential

Often the "it" (evaluand) being developed in a developmental evaluation is an approach, a set of strategies, or a collaboration, rather than a clearly defined program. With rapidly developing innovative approaches, it can be challenging to understand what and where the evaluand's boundaries are. To add to the challenge, once an evaluator has figured these boundaries out, they might change. This process is fundamentally different from that of a formative or summative evaluation. Michael Quinn Patton posted the following explanation about the "it" in this project on EvalTalk (a listserv of the American Evaluation Association):

> What was being developed initially was the collaboration among the six youth-serving agencies. They came together and self-organized around a sense that they had some common ways of working and could learn from each other. They were all grantees of a common foundation initiative. Figuring out what that meant was emergent and led to articulation of shared principles and evaluation of those principles in both implementation and results. That was not on the table when they began and was not even imagined. The development of the principles, which did not exist in any formal, identifiable way at the beginning, supported further development of the collaboration.
>
> The development of the collaboration supported development and evaluation of the principles. Both emerged. They became intertwined and mutually reinforcing. Plans

and commitments emerged month-by-month. There was no blueprint. Still isn't. Issues arose in the larger policy and funding environment that the group took on. Neither the collaboration nor the principles had a predetermined destination or process. Both are still developing. The developmental evaluation is also thus continuing. (EvalTalk, "Re: SWOT analysis vs. needs assessment vs. developmental evaluation," May 6, 2014)

What Patton's response illustrates beautifully is that sometimes what is being developed changes or emerges. I've learned through this project and others that if we don't keep asking ourselves to articulate clearly "what is being developed," we potentially lose focus and miss opportunities.

Working alongside a Foundation Increases Accountability to the Evaluation

The grantee representatives identified continual engagement with the Otto Bremer Foundation as contributing to an emerging shift in the nature of their collaboration. Because there was significant funding attached to the initiative and strong engagement by the foundation staff, there was a high level of accountability that supported the momentum of the principles-focused work. One leader explained that the financial investment made by the foundation held the organizations accountable for working collaboratively:

> "With Bremer it's this force that's holding us accountable to like, 'No, you're going to continue to meet. You're going to continue to talk, and you're going to continue to work together.' And so just being brought to the table consistently to have conversations about how we all work together has been huge."

As a result, there were high rates of participation and engagement in the initiative, differentiating it from other initiatives that start with a great deal of momentum and quickly fizzle out. After a year and a half of meeting together, nearly every member was still in attendance at the reflective practice group meetings.

Developmental Evaluation Builds Adaptive Capacity

Engaging in a principles-focused developmental evaluation allows the staffs of organizations to live in a gray area and be more open-minded when thinking about how to work toward their intended outcomes. One agency administrator described it as allowing staff members to see the unexpected and then ask, "What should we do when we see something we didn't expect? And how will the principles help up decide what to do?" For example, when one agency opened a new space for a new population, they found that some youth were spending their time sleeping, rather than working toward the goals they determined with their case managers. They had to ask themselves, "Why are they sleeping?" And it turned out that these particular youth were typically up all night because they lacked a safe place to sleep. Having a principles-focused foundation allowed the staff to identify the tension between meeting these youth where they were (nonjudgmental) and working toward goals (journey-oriented). It opened up the possibility for meaningful discussion about how they wanted to manage this tension and allowed them to adapt their approach in principles-driven ways.

It Is Important to Conceptualize the Evaluator as an Instrument

It was clear from my first meeting with the collaborative's members that if my values and beliefs had been out of alignment with theirs, I would never have been invited to participate in the project. Technical skills and past experience were not enough. Good sampling procedures and interview protocols were not enough. The collaborative's members also had to perceive me as a credible and trustworthy instrument. I was an instrument in the process—my beliefs, my skills, and my aptitudes. The personnel of each agency were, and are, passionate about their work and protective of and committed to the youth they serve. The trust and rapport I established with the president of a foundation, a world-renowned evaluator, executive directors, case managers, and youth improved my ability to collect quality data and engage people in evaluative activities. One agency's executive director shared the following:

> "I met with Nora when she interviewed me for the project, and I was nervous. But within 1 minute, I felt completely comfortable. Her ability to connect with people and be so genuine is remarkable. It made this process possible. Young people felt comfortable connecting with her. And the feedback I received from staff was all very positive. Her ability to connect with young people helped them be able to tell their story, validate their journey."

Striving to be "objective" or "distant" simply was not appropriate or ethical. I needed to show up in an open and authentic way, knowing that the relationships I built would change the process and influence the outcomes (Bledsoe & Hopson, 2009). Kirkhart (2013) contends that there are five interdependent justifications of multicultural validity: relational, theoretical, methodological, consequential, and experiential. For Kirkhart, "the quality of relationships that surround and infuse the evaluation process" are essential to justifying the validity of findings (p. 135).

Paying Attention to Personal Impacts Is Vital

Working in this way—as a part of the development process rather than as a distant observer—took a personal toll. The stories were so powerful because they are real and true—and sharing these truths meant opening wounds. I felt guilty that I could not help the young people I interviewed more, and I often feared I was exploiting them. At times we would cry together. Sometimes I would email my advisors and just let them know that this was hard. In the midst of this, it helped that the participants glowed when I read them their stories. They would say, "You made connections about me that I didn't realize. No one else in my life knows all of this." Or

"I want to share this with my brother. It will help me explain things to him that I've never been able to say before." I left each interview with the feeling that the youth appreciated being listened to and felt uplifted by the process. Even so, I still feel guilt that I could not do more for each of them, and I continue to carry some of the sadness that I experienced as I sat with these bright, resilient young people while they told me about their lives. I am grateful that I also carry the hope I felt in witness of their wisdom, optimism, and strength.

Conclusion

Developmental evaluation offered the members of the Homeless Youth Collaborative on Developmental Evaluation a new way to think and operate with each other at a systems level. Through this work, we were able to explain the differences between rules-focused and principles-focused work, to shift away from focusing on individual outcomes and toward a systems-level focus, and to understand why making the shift is necessary. Given the potential of collaborative relationships and networks as vehicles for achieving societal goals, it is important that we continue to generate knowledge about the circumstances under which interorganizational collaborations are best formed; what types of collaborative relationships may work best, depending on the purpose and the context; and how best to support the evolution of collaborative networks.

Developmental evaluation also helped us bridge the important connections between young people and their experiences on the one hand, and the organizations that work with them on the other, in ways that improved services and outcomes. Ultimately, that's what this work is about: helping these agencies better support young people who have been marginalized and stigmatized by society. I'll close with a quote from Isaiah, one of the youth I interviewed. He became homeless when his family moved away while he was in his first year of college, leaving no forwarding information. Overnight, his support network disappeared. He wants others to know just how hard it is to try to make it on your own when you are 18 years old, and the importance of principles-based helping organizations:

> "It's hard to go through these things, especially if you've never gone through anything [hard before]. It's hard to become an adult [when] you don't even know how to ask for help. It's hard to be happy when you're going through the situation. It's hard to talk about the situation. It's scary, too. Sometimes I've been scared.
>
> "Having [the drop-in center] means a lot. It's hard to ask for help. To have a place where you can come and ask for help and not feel bad about it is great. There are a lot of people here who care and want to help you, and it's just a safe place to be when you don't have nowhere to go.
>
> "Getting somewhere you want to go [in life] takes time. They know that. I know that. Them just being there throughout the whole process helped me out. They believed in me. They made me feel like I could do anything."

REFERENCES

Able-Peterson, T., & Bucy, J. (1993). *The streetwork outreach training manual.* Washington, DC: U.S. Department of Health and Human Services.

Bledsoe, K. L., & Hopson, R. H. (2009). Conducting ethical research in underserved communities. In D. M. Mertens & P. Ginsberg (Eds.), *Handbook of ethics for research in the social sciences* (pp. 391–406). Thousand Oaks, CA: Sage.

Brinkerhoff, R. (2003). *The success case method: Find out quickly what's working and what's not.* San Francisco: Berrett-Koehler.

Homeless Youth Collaborative on Developmental Evaluation. (2014). 9 evidence-based principles to help youth overcome homelessness. Retrieved from *www.terralunacollaborative.com/wp-content/uploads/2014/03/9-Evidence-Based-Principles-to-Help-Youth-Overcome-Homelessness-Webpublish.pdf.*

Kidd, S. A. (2007). Youth homelessness and social stigma. *Journal of Youth and Adolescence, 36*(3), 291–299.

Kirkhart, K. E. (2013). Advancing considerations of culture and validity: Honoring the key evaluation checklist. In S. I. Donaldson (Ed.), *The future of evaluation in society: A tribute to Michael Scriven* (pp. 129–160). Charlotte, NC: Information Age.

Kennedy, A. C., Agbényiga, D. L., Kasiborski, N., & Gladden, J. (2010). Risk chains over the life course among homeless urban adolescent mothers: Altering their trajectories through formal support. *Children and Youth Services Review, 32*(12), 1740–1749.

Murphy, N. F. (2014). *Developing evidence-based effective principles for working with homeless youth: A developmental evaluation of the Otto Bremer Foundation's support for collaboration among agencies serving homeless youth.* Doctoral dissertation, University of Minnesota. Retrieved from *www.terralunacollaborative.com/wp-content/uploads/2014/03/Murphy-Dissertation-Final.pdf.*

Patton, M. Q. (2011). *Developmental evaluation: Applying complexity concepts to enhance innovation and use.* New York: Guilford Press.

Patton, M. Q. (2014). Evaluation flash cards: Embedding evaluative thinking in organizational culture. Retrieved from *www.ottobremer.org/sites/default/files/fact-sheets/OBF_flashcards_201402.pdf.*

Prochaska, J. O., & Norcross, J. C. (2001). Stages of change. *Psychotherapy: Theory, Research, Practice, Training, 38*(4), 443–448.

Stewart, A. J., Steiman, M., Cauce, A. M., Cochran, B. N., Whitbeck, L. B., & Hoyt, D. R. (2004). Victimization and posttraumatic stress disorder among homeless adolescents. *Journal of the American Academy of Child and Adolescent Psychiatry, 43*(3), 325–331.

CHAPTER 5

Fostering Learning through Developmental Evaluation with a Nontraditional Arts Organization and a Traditional Community Funder

Jamie Gamble, Shawn Van Sluys, and Lisa Watson

EDITORS' INTRODUCTION

This is the only chapter that presents two cases together. Both of these cases were compelling, each in its own way; in the end, rather than choosing one or the other, we trusted Jamie Gamble to compare, contrast, and integrate them, and to draw cross-case lessons. And that's what he and his collaborating authors have done so well. Canadian Jamie Gamble was a trailblazing participant in the world's first developmental evaluation training and coaching collaboration, conducted by coeditor Michael Quinn Patton and sponsored by the Montreal-based J. W. McConnell Family Foundation. Following that experience, Jamie Gamble wrote *A Developmental Evaluation Primer* (2008), which became the first published resource on developmental evaluation and remains available for free download on the McConnell Foundation website.[1] (By the way, it remains the most often downloaded resource on this website, which is a treasure-trove of resources on social innovation.)

The two cases presented here exemplify the 2008 description of how developmental evaluation unfolds. In this chapter, Jamie Gamble models the link between critical thinking and reflective practice. The two programs he evaluated were an innovative arts initiative and a United Way Toronto youth education program. Jamie teams up here with Shawn Van Sluys, executive director of the Musagetes Foundation, and Lisa Watson, former director of strategic initiatives at United Way Toronto. Shawn and Lisa have since woven developmental evaluation into their ongoing professional practice—Shawn into the work of Musagetes to help us understand the transformative power of the arts, and Lisa into her social change consultancy. Despite how different these experimental initiatives were, developmental evaluation, in Jamie Gamble's experienced hands, was flexible enough to be tailored to their different organizational needs and

---

[1] *www.mcconnellfoundation.ca/kh/resources/publication/a-developmental-evaluation-primer.*

styles. This chapter invites you to learn from one of North America's most experienced developmental evaluation practitioners and two astute and committed social innovators.

What happens when developmental evaluation is applied in different circumstances? How does developmental evaluation adapt in response? What features remain the same? This chapter examines two cases in which developmental evaluation has been introduced, and increasingly integrated, into the activities and decision making of two experimental initiatives. One example is in the domain of the arts; the other is in youth education. One organization is relatively new, its approaches dynamic yet nascent. The other is well established, yet ready to challenge some assumptions with a new idea and strategy.

From 2011 to 2014, the Canadian arts foundation Musagetes included developmental evaluation as part of an ongoing initiative in Sudbury, Ontario. And since 2009, developmental evaluation has supported a United Way Toronto initiative to build a community of practice for Toronto's youth education sector. These are two very different kinds of funders, operating in different domains. This chapter explores lessons in developmental evaluation by discussing the contrasts and similarities between the two examples, examined through the perspectives of Shawn Van Sluys, executive director of Musagetes; Lisa Watson, United Way Toronto's former director of strategic initiatives; and Jamie Gamble, developmental evaluation consultant and coach for both projects.

In classical mythology, Musagetes is the name given to the god Apollo in his role as protector and promoter of the Muses. It's an apt name for an organization that strives to make the arts a more central and meaningful reality in our daily lives and in our communities. Musagetes advances the role of art in the pursuit of positive social and economic transformation. Musagetes focuses its work on midsize cities that are in a period of transition; it establishes multiyear relationships with local organizations and change agents in a process of intensive dialogue, research, and artistic projects.

Toronto, one of the world's most diverse cities, is home to the largest United Way in North America. Working in partnership with others, United Way Toronto mobilizes people and resources to support a network of community agencies that help people when they need it most. United Way Toronto also works strategically to create lasting change by addressing the root causes of social problems.

Musagetes's Sudbury Initiative

Musagetes was interested in Sudbury as a place that has sparked the interest of artists for decades. Sudbury has been synonymous with the practice of resource extraction; this mode of production has dominated the city's narratives, its history, and its culture. In more recent years, there has been a new current of discourse—one that looks to new models of design-based production that rely on and propose alternative social, spatial, and organizational systems. This context—unlike any in the world—is enriched further by a blend of communities, nations, and cultures. Greater Sudbury and its environs boast an extensive Aboriginal population (primarily Ojibwe and Métis), a large Francophone minority, and a considerable population of new immigrants.

As Musagetes's team members came to know Sudbury, they were compelled to think about alternatives that question, respectfully, how the production of culture in Sudbury is informed by the history of industry and community. Over a 3-year period, their research, artistic program, and dialogue activities examined the relationships among industry, community, and culture; among the three cultural "solitudes" (Aboriginal, Francophone, and Anglophone communities); and between vulnerable youth populations and the spaces they occupy physically and mentally.

Musagetes's Sudbury program included the following:

- A Café consisting of a series of five conversations with approximately 40 participants, intended to examine the complex understandings of the production of culture in Sudbury. These understandings reflect a set of narratives about Greater Sudbury itself, and were to inform the artistic program in Sudbury, as well as the other cities in which Musagetes is engaged.

- A creative exploration of the city with youth, led by DodoLab—an artist collective (consisting of Lisa Hirmer and Andrew Hunter) that is engaged with provocative, experimental, and creative approaches to research and community actions. DodoLab's program of youth-focused community labs in Sudbury was launched in September 2010 and consisted of an initial introductory lab followed by five youth-led artistic projects. The goal of the work was "to encourage young people to become active, engaged participants in their city."

- An artistic project titled *Between a Rock and a Hard Place*, by Dutch artists Bik Van der Pol (the team of Liesbeth Bik and Jos Van der Pol). This project featured local bands performing on a string of the black rock locations that are so distinctive to Sudbury because of the many decades of nickel mining and smelting, with an audience following the bands as part of a free rock concert bus tour.

- A photographic series by photographer Geoffrey James, who visited Sudbury in June 2012 to document the city—a mining town slowly reclaiming and restoring the region's landscapes after a period of massive, systemic pollution.

- A theatre production titled *Nowhere du Nord*, by Sudbury playwright Miriam Cusson, about a place in northern Ontario where three distinct cultures and their urban mythologies coexist: Anglophone, Francophone, and Aboriginal. Nearly 400 people gathered for this once-in-a-lifetime, multilingual theatre performance, which took place in the public spaces of Chelmsford, a small northern Ontario town.

- A performance for film and installation titled *Private Perimeter*, by artist Rebecca Belmore. In the natural surroundings of Sudbury, Belmore's creation drew a conceptual line through the amalgamated areas of Sudbury, the mining territories bordering the city, and the Whitefish Lake First Nations Reserve.

Toronto's Community of Practice

In 2008, United Way Toronto launched the Community of Practice on Youth Educational Attainment Partnerships (CoP). This citywide initiative engaged a network of practitioners who shared the goal of improving outcomes in youth educational attainment.

Jack Lee, a long-serving former United Way Toronto board member and chair of the board's Community Impact Committee, describes the impetus for the CoP:

> "The motivation for the CoP came from a couple of places. For one, we had conducted research that told us there was fragmentation among the organizations [that] serve the city's youth. We heard that front-line practitioners who work with youth facing multiple barriers to education were having difficulty accessing information, building networks, and learning about resources that support their work. At the same time, we were investing in a number of programs and initiatives aimed at supporting youth to be successful in school, and there was important learning emerging from this work. We believed there was a great opportunity to build stronger relationships and networks of support for young people by creating a space for practitioners to share what they were learning, learn about effective practices in other areas, and take that learning back to their work."

The CoP consists of a variety of network-building and knowledge exchange activities designed to do the following:

- Facilitate learning in the field by developing a network of community-based partners focused on youth success.
- Create peer-learning experiences that enable members to share resources and knowledge.
- Build a body of knowledge on effective practices.
- Develop collaborative relationships to strengthen work in the field as a whole.
- Engage young people in shaping and informing practice.

A *community of practice* (Wenger, McDermott, & Snyder, 2002) is a group of people who regularly convene to learn how to get better at what they do, in order to advance common outcomes. This community facilitates the sharing of discoveries, deepens relationships, and enhances the dissemination of knowledge and experience through the exchange. These features are what distinguish a community of practice from other types of collaborations and networks. The community of practice also supports innovation, as often, in the process of the exchange, new ideas are created and traditional ways of working begin to shift. The premise of a community of practice is that the standard of learning evolves and strengthens over time.

As the convening organization, United Way Toronto provided strategic supports and ongoing evaluation, event planning, and logistical coordination. A generous donation provided financial support for the various network-building and knowledge-sharing activities that made up the CoP. Since its beginning in 2008,

CoP membership has grown to over 450 individuals from over 100 different organizations and institutions.

Why Developmental Evaluation for These Projects?

Musagetes's developmental evaluation addressed two objectives:

- To understand conceptually how socially engaged artistic practices can be transformative in a community; and
- To develop Musagetes' program model which combines practice (experiments and collaboration) and theory (café discussions and publications).

Musagetes's general propositions are that artists who engage with complex issues in cooperation with social actors can create meaningful experiences for individuals, and that this meaningfulness can be translated into greater consciousness of and activist engagement with the world. The Sudbury initiative marked an expansion of effort and a transition in approach for Musagetes's work. Musagetes wanted to examine emerging ideas about its approach, such as identifying and nurturing unconventional leaders, expanding public engagement in the arts, increasing the scope of its artistic program, and experimenting with different forms of research to feed into dialogue and artistic processes. Musagetes's experiences in Rijeka, Croatia, and in Lecce, Italy, had generated some valuable learning about its role as an organization external to a place; ways to approach its relationship with communities; and the design and implementation of the associated research, dialogue, and artistic projects. The Musagetes team members wished to further this learning in the Sudbury effort.

The CoP represented a new and different way of working for United Way Toronto. Utilizing a donor gift to go beyond funding individual programs, the CoP enabled United Way Toronto to contribute to sector-level change through a role as system-level convener amplifying the learning from a wide range of programs across the city. The CoP was not based on a specific model; rather, it was a variation on the idea of a community of practice, in which United Way Toronto balanced a convening and stewarding role while working with an emerging, self-directing learning community.

The evaluation questions guiding the developmental evaluation were these:

- What are the strategies and activities that will most effectively engage practitioners in learning and networking around common interests?
- How do these strategies and activities help to bring about a stronger network of supports and stronger programs and services, and how does this contribute to improved educational attainment?
- How effective is a community of practice in bringing about the conditions and capacity in this sector that will enable young people to have greater opportunity to achieve their education goals?

In both Musagetes and United Way Toronto, the leaders of these projects recognized the iterative nature of these initiatives, as well as the potential of a feedback mechanism that would help them respond to changing circumstances. Continual learning was seen as an important input to their understanding of the change they were influencing as it occurred.

United Way Toronto consistently draws upon evidence and established practice in the design of programs, and while the CoP was based on research about communities of practice and what was needed in the field, the innovative nature of the CoP meant that this initiative was entering uncharted territory. Lisa Watson, United Way Toronto's former director of strategic initiatives, describes what it was like to embark upon such a journey:

> "As we began to build the CoP, we knew the idea was ahead of the evidence. Without manuals or roadmaps, there was very little established practice to guide the design of network-building activities at a citywide scale. The CoP involved a growing number of participants, whose engagement and needs ebbed and flowed over time. We knew it would be a very fluid and unpredictable thing to try to make sense of. We required an evaluation that would enable a deep understanding of what happens when this type of network forms, and as new learning emerges and cross-boundary relationships form within and across a system. Developmental evaluation suited the complexity of an evolving idea for an evolving network."

Reflecting on what developmental evaluation offered to Musagetes as a methodology, Shawn Van Sluys, executive director of Musagetes, had this to say:

> "Developmental evaluation provided a blend of research and direct immersion in learning for Musagetes's staff and collaborators. In an artistic context, the very prospect of evaluation can be alienating to artists, producers, curators, and participants because the inherent value of the arts cannot be evaluated [by] using the mechanistic and quantitative measures that are so frequently used. However, what developmental evaluation can do is invite people to tell the stories of their experiences with art, create new opportunities and contexts for creativity, and give artists a new tool for cultural mediation."

In the case of Musagetes's Sudbury work, developmental evaluation took the form of rigorous sociological research, to give new insights into processes and implications that are far from obvious or simple. Developmental evaluation avoids reductionism and embraces the complexity that shapes the world around us. So do artists.

Both the Musagetes Sudbury project and the United Way Toronto CoP were:

* Made up of a suite of activities that were component parts of an overall initiative. Learning from each activity was needed to help inform subsequent activities, guide improvements to repeated activities, and provide insight into an overall design.
* Involved in an ever-evolving and iterative relationship with a network of people whose interests and actions shaped the overall initiative.

- Evolving a theory of change based on new insight.
- Expected to communicate progress on an emergent initiative to a board of directors and other stakeholders.
- Anticipated to make meaningful differences in their communities.

Both cases are also examples of an internal–external hybrid in which the developmental evaluator functions were shared between an external consultant and staff members/volunteers of the organizations. As a developmental evaluation coach, Jamie Gamble assisted the organizations in the overall evaluation design, advised and in some cases conducted instrument design and data gathering, and played a facilitation role with the sense making and analysis. Staff and volunteers from each organization also conducted some tracking, data gathering, systematic observation, and critical thinking, and participated in the sense-making and analysis sessions. According to Lisa Watson,

> "As a result of this hybrid approach, the internal team developed a practice of inquiry that led us to new strategic questions and evaluation activities to help us answer them. We made sense of things together as a team, with our developmental evaluator's guidance and probing questions. At times the process caused some tensions in the team, as this was a new way of working. This approach forced us to hold our ideas about the initiative lightly, to be willing to allow it [to] change and form on its own, and to support one another through that process. This helped to build our skills and to develop a more adaptive team culture of evaluation and learning that affected all our work."

The Developmental Evaluation Design and Implementation of Musagetes's Sudbury Project

The developmental evaluation for Musagetes's Sudbury Project began with a series of workshops with Musagetes's staff and some board members. This took the form of a series of interviews and discussions that surfaced the primary intentions of the work, the underlying theory of change, and the uncertainties and assumptions attached to these. As the initiative moved forward, specific activities would have an evaluation component, sometimes to improve the design of that activity, and other times to explore some aspect of the larger experiment.

Evaluating the Café

Prior to Sudbury, Musagetes had convened three major Cafés (in London, Barcelona, and Rijeka, Croatia), each with a distinct emphasis and approach. In Sudbury, the Café evolved from a stand-alone, "think-tank"-style event, to a vital part of a multiyear relationship and effort. For the Sudbury Café, Musagetes intended to experiment with different forms of research that could give Musagetes and visiting Café participants a deeper understanding of the locality; feed the overall research for the artistic program; cultivate more partners and work toward more local collaboration; and experiment with having artists work before, during, and after the Café, to see how this would shape their work and the overall initiative.

The evaluation included activity in advance of, during, and following the Café. The advance work involved discussion with Musagetes's staff members about their thinking and some of the design choices that they were making as they prepared for the experience. During the Café, the project's developmental evaluator, Jamie Gamble, was on site as a participant-observer. He, along with two assistants, conducted brief, informal interviews with participants during the experience. These interviews explored the design of the Café, as well as new ideas and relationships stimulated by the experience. Approximately 1 month following the Café, all participants were invited to complete a survey of three questions with open-ended responses. Three months after the Café, 20 telephone interviews were conducted with a cross-section of Café participants. The follow-up work examined the extent to which new relationships had formed, and the ways that ideas from the Café had influenced people's work.

Evaluating DodoLab

DodoLab's approach to its work is highly self-reflective. The collective's members naturally embed critical thinking into their process; as such, they consistently revisit their approaches, learn from them, and apply this learning going forward. The Sudbury Action Centre for Youth (SACY) became DodoLab's primary partner throughout the tenure of the Sudbury program. The focused partnership with SACY was a change in strategy from what was originally intended. This was beneficial, as it allowed DodoLab to "[establish] strong connections and a presence in the community and gain support from local media, community organizations, public services (transit and police for example) and educators" (Hunter, 2012). In July 2012, SACY representatives traveled to Hamilton, Ontario, DodoLab's home base, to participate in an exchange of ideas and experiences. The purpose of this session was to better understand effective collaboration, and how this could be supported in the context of Musagetes's work.

Evaluating *Between a Rock and a Hard Place*

The developmental evaluation of *Between a Rock and a Hard Place* (see Exhibit 5.1) focused on the concert phase of the project. The intention was to embed the evaluation components into the art experience. Jamie Gamble, as evaluator, was situated as a collaborator with Bik Van der Pol to help layer evaluation into what was happening in a way that would enrich the program experience for participants. The evaluation also intensively documented the entire process: Liesbeth Bik and Jos Van der Pol were interviewed at various times; Jamie was a participant-observer in an earlier artistic research activity, rock washing; and during the concert tour, Jamie interacted with the participants on the bus, interviewed them on camera, and asked them to answer questions, draw maps, and write stories. A few months after

***Between a Rock and a Hard Place*, an Artistic Project by Bik Van der Pol**

Source: Photo by Jamie Gamble. Courtesy of Musagetes.

the concert, participants were invited to share further reflections. The purpose of the developmental evaluation in *Between a Rock and a Hard Place* was to examine the ways in which participants in these artistic activities articulated or described those experiences, in order to gain a better understanding of how the arts can be meaningful for people.

Evaluating *Nowhere du Nord*

For the developmental evaluation of *Nowhere du Nord* (see Exhibit 5.2), Musagetes had several objectives:

- To document the collaborative creative process as a way of understanding its features, so that this could inform future artistic initiatives.
- To experiment with an evaluation activity that would allow for a deeper exploration of themes and ideas relating to an artistic project.
- To see what could be achieved in the evaluation with a smaller scale of effort than that needed for *Between a Rock and a Hard Place.*

EXHIBIT 5.2

Nowhere du Nord, a Theatre Production by Miriam Cusson

Source: Photo by Tenille Heinonen. Courtesy of Musagetes.

To accomplish these objectives, two specific evaluation activities occurred. First, Miriam Cusson was asked to track her observations and reflections during the creative process. She kept a journal and then provided summary reflections in an interview with Jamie Gamble a few weeks after the performance. Second, a half-day discussion with a small group of people was held approximately 1 month after the performance of *Nowhere du Nord*. This session explored the themes of intercultural interaction and collaboration that emerged in *Nowhere du Nord*. The aim for this session was to draw inspiration from the theatre intervention, as well as from colleagues' experiences, to explore questions of cross-cultural work as it relates to their organizations.

Evaluating *Private Perimeter*

The day after the exhibition opened, Rebecca Belmore and Shawn Van Sluys discussed Musagetes's experience of Sudbury, the creation of the work, and her engagement with the world. Musagetes wanted to experiment with a small-scale evaluation activity for Rebecca's project. The focus was entirely on the contemplative experience of creation for the artist.

These component parts of Musagetes's developmental evaluation stood alone, and lessons were routinely brought back to an ongoing conversation about the overall concept and approach. The uniqueness of each artistic project was a purposeful decision. Musagetes wanted to be able to integrate developmental evaluation beyond Sudbury; having a diverse set of experiences would provide a bigger set of options and ideas.

The Developmental Evaluation Design and Implementation of United Way Toronto's CoP

The developmental evaluation of the CoP began in much the same way as that of Musagetes. There was a period of intense discussion and dialogue intended to surface the fundamental ideas about how this initiative was to work. Staff members at United Way Toronto had invested significant time in developing a theory of change and identifying the expected stages of development for the CoP.

Through internal discussions with evaluation staff members who were learning about developmental and utilization-focused evaluation, and a staff leader who had worked with Jamie Gamble on a developmental evaluation, developmental evaluation was deemed the most appropriate evaluation approach for something that was expected to continue to evolve. Lisa Watson recalls the decision to use developmental evaluation:

> "We had a very short time frame in which to launch the CoP and, because this was a new role for United Way Toronto to take on, we knew we would need to steward it thoughtfully and demonstrate progress to our donor, our board, and the sector in short order and at regular intervals. We needed real-time evaluation. We weren't sure how to do that, and worried that our traditional evaluation approach wasn't going to give us the information we needed in time. We had been reading about developmental evaluation; in a session with Michael Quinn Patton, we learned more about this approach. Because we needed to get going quickly, and adapt as we went along, we thought that developmental evaluation would be suitable to this unknown future we were stepping into."

United Way Toronto assigned a portion of an internal evaluator's time to support this work in an advisory capacity with the program staff, and retained Jamie Gamble as an external consultant with expertise in developmental evaluation to act as a coach. Developmental evaluation was new to many in the organization, so efforts were made to share the theory of change and introduce developmental evaluation to senior leaders, both at the start and at key points throughout the initiative. These discussions provided opportunities to describe the activities underway, to show how they fit into the theory of change, and to share learning gleaned from evaluation activities. Senior leaders heard about the initiative as it was unfolding, including what worked and what didn't, and what adjustments and improvements were made. Lisa Watson describes an example of how they engaged leaders in the developmental evaluation:

"A significant challenge in the early days was how to demonstrate that the CoP would lead to improved graduation rates. By taking a developmental approach, and engaging thought leaders from different sectors, we began to understand that the CoP could tell a contribution [story] rather than an attribution story. The theory of change helped us to show that the CoP was aiming toward, and eventually achieving, an important new set of conditions in the sector, and that these were part of that contribution story. This helped us to assure decision makers that we were stewarding the initiative cautiously, carving out the path one step at a time, using the data and knowledge available to us. And that enabled leaders and governors to make strategic, informed decisions along the way."

The ultimate outcome for the CoP was defined as improving educational attainment for youth. This outcome was based on the assumption that progress in the following outcome areas would contribute to a stronger system for supporting youth:

- *Strengthened CoP*—establishing a network to facilitate knowledge transfer, shared learning, and peer support. (See Exhibit 5.3.)
- *Knowledgeable practitioners*—increasing youth education practitioners' understanding of relevant issues and promising or effective practices.
- *Supportive learning environments*—creating conditions to support effective learning, as well as the orientation of community organizations toward a learning culture.

EXHIBIT 5.3

The Community of Practice (CoP)

Source: Photo by Tamara Eberle. Courtesy of United Way Toronto.

- *Stronger network of supports*—improving connectivity among CoP members to facilitate information exchange, peer support, and the creation of new resources available to the system in support of youth.
- *Stronger programs and interventions*—improving use of evidence-based practice in youth education programs and initiatives.

The premise of the CoP was, and is, that relationships and behaviors that facilitate learning can be strategically enhanced through activities such as network building, convening actors in a field, and documenting and sharing research and good practice. The dynamic nature of a network means that patterns of interaction will emerge. United Way Toronto sought early feedback on how the five CoP outcomes were taking shape within this dynamic, and the ways in which network-supporting activities contributed to the process. United Way Toronto staff reviewed data, analyzed emerging patterns in the CoP, and considered the implications of what they were learning as part of their regular planning and supervision meetings. They also met with their developmental evaluation coach three to four times a year to review the initiative's progress relative to the five outcome areas, and to consider the implications of what was being learned for their strategy for moving forward. These meetings were organized around the following questions:

- How is the CoP evolving, given recent activity, who is involved, and what is happening in the youth education landscape that could affect this initiative?
- To what degree are the outcomes we are expecting occurring? Are there signs that show positive movement toward them?
- Are there things happening that were not anticipated, and if so, are they positive or negative?
- What changes should we make going forward, given the evolution in the CoP and/or what we are learning?

The initiative drew upon multiple perspectives, data sources, and evaluation activities. Many evaluation activities were conducted directly by United Way Toronto with contributions and support from a variety of external advisors and researchers, as well as CoP participants. Data were gathered through surveys; questions posed at CoP events; group discussions; interactions with CoP members; strategy and planning sessions with CoP members; tracking of participation; and key informant interviews. The developmental evaluation for United Way Toronto required investment in both internal and external dedicated resources and expertise to implement and sustain the developmental evaluation. This meant that sometimes internal staff members were directly involved in evaluation activities for the first time—doing the hands-on work of developing and analyzing surveys, as well as procuring and overseeing external experts to conduct activities such as focus groups.

At the outset of the initiative, critical questions about the outcomes of the CoP, and what these really should be, were challenging for United Way Toronto. There was a keen desire to demonstrate progress on the stated goals quickly, but the initiative was evolving and adapting in unpredictable ways. What was anticipated to be a focused community of up to 40 front-line practitioners working in United Way Toronto member agencies quickly grew to hundreds of practitioners at all levels from front-line staff to executive directors, representing an expansive range of organizations and institutions. Initial ideas about how to structure learning events and support member engagement had to be quickly adapted to respond to the unexpected expansion. The assumption was that the initiative would contribute to improved graduation rates, and United Way Toronto recognized that the CoP's contribution to this change would be indirect and long-term. Starting in the fall of 2010, an expert panel of four independent experts, from disciplines that included community development, economics, research, and communities of practice, assisted United Way Toronto staff and CoP members in making an independent assessment of the CoP's value and benefit toward achieving this larger outcome. This group helped United Way Toronto to develop a more nuanced understanding that the CoP was one of numerous efforts by many players contributing to this broader, population-level goal.

Another challenge was getting sufficient perspective on the final two outcome areas listed previously: a stronger network of supports, and stronger programs and interventions. One of the expert panel's members led a group of postdoctoral fellows at St. Michael's Centre for Research on Inner City Health. The 2011–2013 cohort of this postdoctoral program partnered with United Way Toronto to conduct research on the CoP's effects on building networks and strengthening programs. The fellows provided technical expertise to a difficult component of the evaluation through case studies focused on these two outcomes.

The CoP members were consistent and vital reference points for the developmental evaluation, and they made ongoing contributions to planning and adjustments in strategy. Throughout this initiative, members were engaged to provide their perspectives on the data and to help make sense of what was happening. For example, a workshop with a group of active CoP members helped interpret data on network activity, which gave increased understanding of and confidence in the benefits of spontaneous interactions that were happening outside of formal events. The process of engaging CoP participants and experts alike in conversations that helped make sense of what was emerging in the initiative, and shape what needed to happen next, created a sense of shared ownership.

Developmental Evaluation's Contributions to These Initiatives

Musagetes

In exploring how art can facilitate improvements in people's lives and in communities, the developmental evaluation of the Sudbury initiative gave Musagetes insight into how people make sense of the art they encounter. The research led to the creation of a new program, SenseLabs, a pedagogical and artistic experiment to better understand how people make sense of their encounters with art and their participation in artistic creativity. Musagetes interprets *sense making* as the process by which individuals perceive the world around them and make meaning from those perceptions.

The Sudbury developmental evaluation embedded sense-making exercises particularly intensively into *Between a Rock and a Hard Place*. The evaluator, Jamie Gamble, spent the day of the rock concerts with the participants, talking to them about their experience and asking them to think deeply about the significance of art in their lives and in their communities. The insightful responses that we received inspired Musagetes staff members to ponder the importance of sense making and pedagogy in their mandate of making the arts more central and meaningful. At the core of this research is the question of how the arts make individuals more resilient to changing conditions in the world around them.

The developmental evaluation in Sudbury helped to establish the following values that are guiding Musagetes's pedagogical and artistic work moving forward:

- A belief that encounters with art can ignite shifts in perception, inspiring and moving individuals to action.
- Confirmation that art instills in people the possibility of change, of hope; specifically, it sparks in people the possibilities of living with uncertainty, imagining something beyond present conditions, transforming, and starting again.
- An emphasis on dialogue—articulating perception and determining meanings through conversation.
- An approach that enriches individuals and builds community, creating a sense of belonging and acknowledging the role of love in our humanity.
- An open exploration of concepts, ideas, identities, and representations that the participants choose and define by themselves; the facilitator of the pedagogy is not the sole proprietor of knowledge.
- An acceptance of all the diversity of our humanity.
- A recognition of the unequal distribution, mutual dependency, and multiple uses of various forms of knowledge, such as traditional, academic, social, and practical knowledge.
- A mélange of everything the participants and facilitators bring to a group that makes the pedagogy useful in many contexts (all of the senses, physical abilities, and learning modalities).

The process of engaging in a developmental evaluation over several years has been a valuable support to the evolution of Musagetes and its programs. The critical thinking, engagement, and careful observation of its activities during the developmental evaluation helped evolve how Musagetes approaches its work, as well as how it articulates what it does. Annual retreats for the board, staff, and advisors are intense moments of collective reflection in which learning, such as the developmental evaluation, feeds into a critical consideration of the programs, communications, and ways of thinking about the arts as transformative agents in society.

United Way Toronto

Developmental evaluation supported United Way Toronto's CoP team to make informed, data-based decisions, and it enabled effective responses to unanticipated challenges. Working methodically, the team members did not rush into implementation; rather, they continually related their learning to the theory of change in ways that encouraged the team members to consider emerging ideas and share what they were learning (Exhibit 5.4). In making this a central element of the initiative, the developmental evaluation provided a safe space to measure their experiences against assumptions and expectations. Data were utilized to inform implementation and decision making, in order to respond continually to needs and improve the project. For example, when questions emerged about the best way to facilitate

EXHIBIT 5.4

The Community of Practice (CoP)

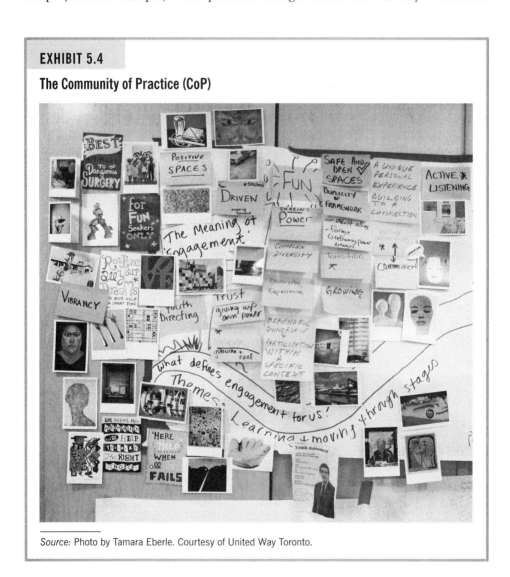

Source: Photo by Tamara Eberle. Courtesy of United Way Toronto.

the participation of front-line youth workers, as it became evident that it was more challenging for them than for managers to attend learning events, several ideas were generated through discussion with some front-line CoP members. Over the course of subsequent CoP events and activities, several ideas were tested in small proto-types. Observing these in action, and engaging with front-line workers to learn from their experience in these activities, helped United Way Toronto to understand the efficacy of these ideas; in turn, this led to improvements in the overall design of the CoP to accommodate front-line worker participation.

The developmental evaluation enabled the CoP team—and United Way Toronto as a whole—to tell the story of the CoP at every stage of the process, including how it was developing and what progress was being made. This reinforced the legiti-macy of the approach being taken, and helped to communicate this to stakehold-ers both inside and outside the organization. Developmental evaluation gave the initiative a mechanism by which to manage risks related to an adaptive initiative, helping to meet internal and external accountability requirements in a way that did not constrain the adaptation. This was crucial to the team's ability to demonstrate progress and impact to decision makers, donors, CoP participants, and others in the sector who became inspired by the learning and network-building opportunity and decided to join. In being actively observant in a systematic way, the team could construct a narrative to explain what was happening, as well as how and why, in a grounded and credible way.

Reporting on progress with transparency and credibility was enhanced because the theory of change was being tested with many small prototypes and regular data gathering, which enabled a deeper understanding of what was changing and how, as the story was unfolding.

Ultimately, the developmental evaluation helped United Way Toronto in mak-ing decisions about the continuation of the CoP. In 2011, the initial mandate was extended from 3 years to 4, and in 2013 to a second phase with an additional 2 years of support.

Lessons in Developmental Evaluation

The ambiguity of the arts, the dynamic and evolving nature of a community of practice, and the innovative nature of these initiatives meant that each of the proj-ects described in this chapter was grappling with strategies for change that did not translate into straightforward cause-and-effect approaches. Both projects were initiated with gaps in their theory of change—a typical characteristic of projects in development. Valuable products of the developmental evaluation in both exam-ples included an improved conceptual understanding and an increasingly clarified change model. In more linear situations, evaluation helps by testing predictions and validating well-constructed theories of change. With greater complexity, how change happens only becomes clear in retrospect. In a developmental situation, doing is a part of theory making, and the continual efforts of Musagetes and United

Way Toronto to observe and critically examine what was taking place resulted in ongoing improvements and upgrades to the theory of change for each initiative. Developmental evaluation is interventionist, in that the evaluation is tasked with accelerating the learning curve in critical initiatives that are fully in action even while many underlying ideas are still in the fledgling stage. Rather than expectations of performance on a well-defined outcome, the expectation is for further development on something innovative. The stakes are lower, thus creating space for experimentation and adaptation for implementers and decision makers alike.

In the efforts to introduce evaluative thinking into each initiative, the developmental evaluation sought to integrate evidence and critical perspective in a way that was unobtrusive to activities and participants. In this way, developmental evaluation does a delicate dance—weaving evaluative thinking into what is happening in a way that does not distract from it, but firmly asserting a critical and constructive voice throughout. In becoming an integrated part of the initiatives, developmental evaluation can contribute insight into the fundamental questions of an organization or initiative, and to the incremental design choices that recur throughout a developmental process.

The multicomponent, community-integrated nature of Musagetes's Sudbury program and United Way Toronto's CoP helped each organization to work effectively with the multiple collaborators and partners involved at various stages. Developmental evaluation can be highly participatory, but it is important to note that developmental evaluation is not synonymous with participatory evaluation. *Developmental evaluation* is a purpose distinction; *participatory evaluation* is a methods distinction. When developmental evaluation is participatory, it helps accelerate feedback loops. The highly participatory nature of the evaluation constructively facilitated the network-building purposes of these two initiatives. The act of engaging in the evaluative process when something is in development is in itself supportive of building relationships.

Understanding the nature of change and progress in a complex system is essential for developmental evaluation. In helping people (both inside and outside the organizations) to engage with the developmental evaluation, the evaluator has an ongoing role in helping people to understand the nature of innovation and complex situations, and the implications of these for evaluation. People often have expectations of evaluation based on experiences in more firmly established programs. Developmental evaluators play a role in helping people engage with the evaluation by supporting their understanding of concepts of complexity and innovation, and reminding stakeholders of this framing as they work with findings and develop new strategies.

From the outset, each initiative considered messages and interactions that would facilitate legitimacy and familiarity for the evaluation. Because United Way Toronto is a very large organization, with many layers of decision making and accountability, there was a need in the CoP project for a senior champion to navigate the developmental evaluation internally. As that champion, Lisa Watson helped senior managers, board members, and the project's donor understand and support what was emerging, and managed expectations relating to the nature of innovation in an emerging initiative. As a smaller organization, Musagetes was able to accommodate this process more naturally, as the whole organization was often involved in critical discussions.

The contrasting situations of Musagetes and United Way Toronto underline the value of a utilization focus within developmental evaluation. Despite how different these organizations are, developmental evaluation was flexible enough to be tailored to their different organizational needs and styles. For example, different modes of communication about evaluation findings were more suitable for each initiative. For United Way Toronto, there was a high need for engagement with the CoP members, so findings were often shared in presentations and exchanges with members. Visual diagrams helped communicate the theory of change internally with simplicity and efficiency. For Musagetes, a written narrative was preferred to describe the theory of change because visual diagrams failed to capture the nuances of the organization's thinking and experiences.

Developmental evaluation was resource-intensive in these two examples. These organizations were making investments in new areas, and the developmental evaluation was seen as an essential accompaniment to navigate, and on some level mitigate, risks by allowing for rapid learning and adjustment. This can raise concerns about how to sustain developmental evaluation over time, or how to do it when resources are tight.

In the second phase of the CoP, developmental evaluation remains part of the initiative, but at a much smaller scale. There is increased confidence in what is understood about most of the outcome areas, and in the design of the activities that support the network. In this next phase, developmental evaluation is specifically focused on outcome areas where gaps in understanding remain, and in the ongoing support of a meaningful engagement with CoP members. As a result, the budget is much more modest. Musagetes has internalized developmental evaluation, and as it launches new initiatives, developmental evaluation is a core function, supported by staff, artists, and other collaborators. For example, Musagetes now embeds writers in artistic projects such as its Guelph (Ontario) Improviser-in-Residence project and the Free Home University (Italy) to tell the story of the project's emergence. The lesson from the experience of these two organizations is that there may be moments when a more intense mode of developmental evaluation is a vital part of designing and implementing something new, and that it can also function at a more modest scale.

These new phases of developmental evaluation for United Way Toronto and Musagetes signal that organizations can easily and inexpensively apply aspects of developmental evaluation to their everyday work. Is there someone connected to your organization who is a good interviewer, can listen to what is being done, and can connect this into broader conversations of strategy? Can you creatively link evaluative questions into engagement tools and processes that you are already using? Can you create time and space for those closest to a new initiative to come together and critically examine what is emerging and why?

Such questions are reflective of a culture of inquiry and curiosity, and a willingness to be systematic in using the critical perspective of evaluation to instruct the often difficult journey through ideas and initiatives that are highly adaptive. This is what Musagetes and United Way Toronto did, in their different ways. Perhaps they are not that different after all?

REFERENCES

Gamble, J. (2008). *A developmental evaluation primer.* Montreal: J. W. McConnell Family Foundation.

Hunter, Andrew. (2012). *DodoLab-Sudbury Final Report to the Ontario Trillium Foundation.* Guelph, Ontario, Canada: Musagetes.

Wenger, E., McDermott, R., & Snyder, W. (2002). *Cultivating communities of practice.* Boston: Harvard Business School Press.

CHAPTER 6

Science and How We Care for Needy Young Children

The Frontiers of Innovation Initiative

Julie Asher, Nathaniel Foote, James Radner, and Tassy Warren

EDITORS' INTRODUCTION

This chapter features the developmental evaluation of a still emergent nationwide innovation initiative during the first 3 years of at least a 10-year time horizon. Every aspect of the initiative is being developed: who is involved; what each will contribute and what they will do together; the theory of change; the separate projects that make up the initiative; research in support of innovation; the network of participants and projects; how to manage and integrate them; and, of course, the developmental evaluation. This chapter also highlights the important use of high-quality visual aids in developmental evaluation. Space constraints have prevented the chapter authors from explaining the graphics in detail in the text, but each is rich in information and conveys visually what has been developed; we urge readers to study them closely, especially given the increasing importance of visualization in evaluation. Exhibits 6.1, 6.2, and 6.7 show developments in the theory of change. Exhibit 6.3 presents a developmental evaluation scorecard. Exhibits 6.4, 6.5, and 6.6 depict how the adaptive and iterative cycle of interaction, feedback, and interpretation worked to enhance use. Exhibits 6.8, 6.9, and 6.10 show developments in the initiative's organizational architecture. The full annual developmental evaluation reports have many more visual representations that cannot be included here because of space limitations, but those that are included point to an important direction and competency in developmental evaluation.

This chapter examines the role of developmental evaluation in the Frontiers of Innovation Initiative, which aims to apply advances in science to provide better services to vulnerable young children. We focus on how developmental evaluation supported paradigm shifts in the initiative—that is, how it helped people arrive at

103

big "ahas" as they worked on specific, on-the-ground projects, as well as how it contributed to the evolving nationwide strategy in which those projects are embedded. We begin by describing the initiative as a whole. Then we provide a narrative of the developmental evaluation, including methods and tools developed, followed by key developmental evaluation findings. Finally, we highlight some emergent lessons with a look to the future.

Building a Research and Development Platform for Early Childhood Services: The Launch and First Years of the Frontiers of Innovation Initiative

Origins: A Problem and a Proposal

In May 2011, the Center on the Developing Child at Harvard University (HCDC) brought together 65 leaders in the early childhood field. While the largest stakeholder group at the event was researchers, participants also included state and federal policy makers, practitioners, agency leaders, and philanthropists. In advance of the convening, HCDC and its partners[1] had conducted roughly 100 interviews to assess people's perceptions of the state of the early childhood field. The consensus from those interviews, reinforced by attendees at the convening, was that the field had a problem: Despite decades of investment in services for vulnerable young children, and despite increasing awareness of the importance of the early years for life-long health, learning, and productivity, millions of children are still growing up in North America with their life prospects threatened by the biological effects of early adversity. Programs to serve young children are making a valuable contribution, but too many children do not benefit sufficiently. Moreover, the field seemed stuck: The structure, content, and (all too often) results of our programs have changed little in the past half-century.

The May 2011 convening dubbed this concern *constructive dissatisfaction*. Forming a nucleus for what was later named the Frontiers of Innovation (FOI) community, the group set a goal of helping the field progress faster toward ways to achieve better life outcomes for children whose needs (or the needs of their caregivers) are not being met by existing investments.

Countless individual ideas emerged from the May 2011 meeting, but the group's thinking also coalesced around a broader proposal to apply results from the biology of adversity in a way that might accelerate progress in the field. The proposal (see Exhibit 6.1) called for a shift from a service model emphasizing cognitive and other forms of enrichment for disadvantaged young children to one that balances such enrichment with protection against the harmful effects of toxic stress and other forms of adversity. As the convening came to a close, subgroups began to form to work out different ways to put this broad proposal into action.

---

[1]The founding partners of the initiative, in addition to HCDC, were the National Conference of State Legislatures, the National Governors Association, and the TruePoint Center for Higher Ambition Leadership.

EXHIBIT 6.1

Diagramming a Proposed New Theory of Change

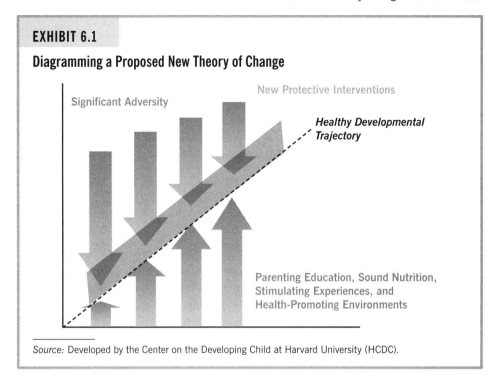

Source: Developed by the Center on the Developing Child at Harvard University (HCDC).

The Growth and Development of FOI

From the 2011 launch meeting described above through 2014 (when this chapter was written), a wide variety of projects and partners joined FOI, each contributing to and further developing the initiative. We discuss below the role of the developmental evaluation in both tracking and stimulating this growth and development, and in facilitating reflections and judgments about the implications and significance of what was developing. To set the stage for the developmental evaluation, we first provide some examples of FOI's expansion, as it attracted new innovators who in turn contributed to shaping the whole. After illustrating FOI's growth in this way, we highlight a few early results from the work before turning to the design and execution of the evaluation itself.

Summer and Fall 2011: Postlaunch Working Groups

Although the discussions at the launch meeting were largely exploratory, two quite specific initiatives emerged directly from those explorations. First, a working group of seven scientists from different fields coalesced around the theme of *building caregiver capacities*. The group began with the idea that to better protect young children from toxic stress, adult caregivers would need opportunities for active skill building, rather than simply passive information sharing. By September 2011, the group had developed a key additional hypothesis that undergirds much of FOI's work to this day: that a series of adult capacities within the domain of self-regulation and executive functioning could be critical *both* to buffering children from toxic stress *and* to achieving family economic stability. These ideas in turn became part of FOI's broader theory of change, so that Exhibit 6.2 can be viewed as a supplement to Exhibit 6.1.

In a second initiative that grew directly out of the FOI launch meeting, leaders from both the executive and legislative branches of the Washington State government who had attended the meeting asked FOI to join them in using science-based approaches to improve child outcomes in the state. So FOI and Washington State established a charter to set goals and working methods for their partnership, and FOI began advising the state's interagency "One Science" working group on policy applications of advances in the science of self-regulation and executive functioning.

2012: Convergence—Research Meets Practice

The work of the Building Caregiver Capacity and One Science groups converged in the fall of 2011, when the Washington State Department of Early Learning decided to begin field-testing the ideas under discussion. The Department convened a group of top-quality, community-based service providers, and FOI invited West

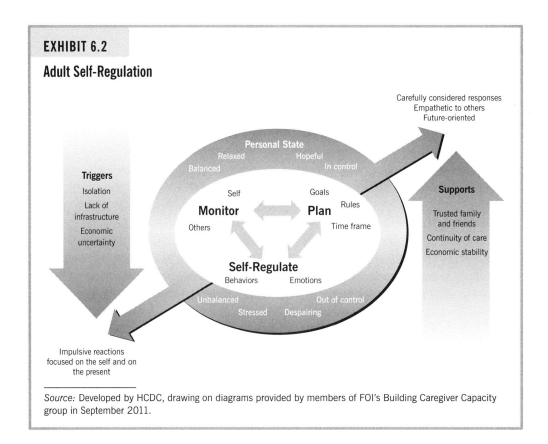

EXHIBIT 6.2

Adult Self-Regulation

Source: Developed by HCDC, drawing on diagrams provided by members of FOI's Building Caregiver Capacity group in September 2011.

Coast researchers from the Building Caregiver Capacity group to meet with them. Researchers and practitioners formed "co-creation" groups to work together, as equals, in the search for ways to help the neediest cases: families that were hardest to reach and retain, parents who were facing extreme adversity, and children who were receiving services but not benefiting from them sufficiently. Families identified included those in the child protection system, those enrolled in Early Head Start, and those with a history of trauma; suggested interventions ranged from professional psychotherapy to "lighter-touch" ideas such as game playing and mindfulness training. Here is one example of the (at last count) nine researcher–practitioner collaborations that emerged from these beginnings:

To help Early Head Start families facing significant adversity, Children's Home Society of Washington worked with researchers at the University of Oregon to deliver a video coaching intervention called Filming Interactions to Nurture Development (FIND).[2] FIND is designed to help mothers and children develop supportive interactions that, in accordance with the theory of change described above, can protect children from toxic stress. FIND uses the concept of *serve and return* as a key to such interactions: A *serve* occurs when a child initiates an interaction by using words or gestures, or by focusing attention on something or someone; the serve is *returned* when the caregiver notices and responds. In Washington, home visitors are now using FIND with families they see regularly under the Early Head Start program. They begin by taking a video of a mother with her child at home. That video goes to an editing room, where short clips are extracted to show key moments of successful mother–child connection, within the serve-and-return framework. These clips form the basis of a series of coaching sessions for the mother, organized to build parenting skills.

A key ingredient of the co-creation work in Washington State was the focus on unmet needs. As one staff member put it, "The big 'aha' for us was to start thinking about people we're not reaching, kids most in need—working out a range of different services with different doses."

2012–2013: New Partners—A Community Focus

In 2012, Building Caregiver Capacity researchers on the East Coast teamed with a community-based, multineighborhood initiative in New Haven, Connecticut— the Mental Health Outreach for MotherS (MOMS) Partnership[3]—for a similar

---

[2]FIND was developed by Philip Fisher and colleagues at the Oregon Social Learning Center and Oregon Social Learning Center Developments, Inc. The approach has roots in the tradition of microsocial interaction research at this center and in an intervention called Marte Meo, which has been widely implemented in Europe and elsewhere. The serve-and-return framework used by FIND was developed by HCDC.

[3]For a fuller description of the MOMS Partnership, see its website (*http://newhavenmomspartnership. org*). The research team at MOMS is led by Megan Smith and colleagues at Yale University. The mobility mentoring model mentioned on page 108 was developed by Elizabeth Babcock and the Crittenton Women's Union.

collaborative effort. MOMS was already established as an active partnership including social service groups, government agencies, local businesses, and the Yale University School of Medicine, with unusual on-the-ground reach through *community mental health ambassadors*. Community mental health ambassadors are neighborhood mothers, peers of those being served. They identify families' needs, participate in service delivery, suggest new strategies, and provide feedback to modify existing ones. With this foundation, MOMS proved particularly adept at drawing in researchers from the FOI network to jointly create local solutions. For example, MOMS's work with the Building Caregiver Capacity group has led not only to an ongoing group-based adaptation of the FIND video coaching model, but also to the introduction of a *mobility mentoring* model aimed at helping improve mothers' parenting and employability.

The combination of the theoretical framework developed by the Building Caregiver Capacity researchers, which identified a common core of capacities important to both parenting and employability, and local demand in New Haven brought family economic stability to the fore within FOI. This became a central theme of FOI's third annual convening, in April 2013, where participants from both the early childhood and workforce development fields came together to explore "hybrid" service models. The convening spawned a series of cross-disciplinary collaborations, which FOI supported through small planning grants. Such hybrid models are now being tested in communities ranging from Washington State to Boston, Massachusetts.

Examples of additional partnerships within FOI's growing network include the following:

• In 2012, the Center for the Study of Social Policy joined FOI as a partner, with a focus on family and community resources. This center has worked with FOI on projects ranging from innovations in New Haven to a new initiative to develop reforms in child welfare programming.

• A nationwide search in 2012 to recruit leaders from innovative community-based agencies led to a new round of researcher–practitioner collaborations, including the formation, in April 2013, of a working group of researchers and agency leaders to develop and test new programming to support parents in such family routines as mealtime and bedtime.

• In early 2013, FOI formed a partnership with the province of Alberta, Canada. The Alberta Family Wellness Initiative had laid a remarkable foundation by making current scientific knowledge and best treatment practices accessible to policy makers and practitioners across the province. The province began work with four local communities to build innovative programming on this foundation.

• Hard on Alberta's heels, in mid-2013 Georgia became the second U.S. state to partner formally with FOI. The Georgia Early Education Alliance for Ready Students spearheaded the partnership in collaboration with the governor's office, the Department of Early Care and Learning, and the Department of Public Health.

Early Results: Two Examples of Iterative Learning

Childhaven, a therapeutic day care program for highest-risk children in Washington, is working with researchers from the University of California–Berkeley[4] on experimental games for 4- and 5-year-old children, with the aim of building executive functioning. After an initial 10-week randomized microtrial, about half the children receiving the program showed major gains in cognitive flexibility, a core executive function. But surprisingly—since the game design targeted executive functioning in general—those children showed no gain in a second executive function, selective attention. By analyzing detailed data on the different groups of children, the team produced hypotheses on why the second group of children showed no benefits, and why the first benefited on only one skill. They are now running a second microtrial, which mixes in a mindfulness intervention already being tried in Washington by a different scientist–agency team in the state.

A second example is the parent–child attachment intervention, which began as a collaboration between the Children's Home Society of Washington's Early Head Start home visiting team and a group of researchers and clinicians at the University of California–San Francisco who had developed the child–parent psychotherapy (CPP) intervention.[5] Though the home visitors saw CPP as a valuable intervention strategy, they needed a less intensive model that they could deliver to a larger number of clients with existing resources. So the team developed a nine-session parent education program, Attachment Vitamins, that home visitors can bring directly to parents. Feedback from an initial trial suggested that while home visitors found the insights from the prototype curriculum valuable, it did not work for them as a teaching module in the home. So the team revised the program for delivery in group settings; early feedback from this second round has been promising.

These examples illustrate a larger point highlighted by the developmental evaluation: Researchers and community members had found a way of working that enabled constant reconfiguring of the interventions to discover new solutions. Here are some quotations from different front-line staffers from a meeting with a member of the developmental evaluation team in 2013:

> "Now we're not just delivering services; we're part of an effort to figure out a better way."

> "There's a wonder in what we're doing. We're able to feed new findings in right away as part of our work. This is so different from normal research."

> "I can't believe my luck that I've been given permission to do this."

---

[4]This research team is led by Silvia Bunge.

[5]CPP is a relationship-based treatment model developed by Alicia F. Lieberman and Patricia van Horn. The Attachment Vitamins program discussed in this example was developed by Lieberman and colleagues at the University of California–San Francisco, in collaboration with Jason Gortney and colleagues at the Children's Home Society of Washington.

The Developmental Evaluation Process

Creating an Evaluation Design

In December 2010, HCDC commissioned the TruePoint Center to facilitate the developmental evaluation process for FOI. The TruePoint–HCDC team selected developmental evaluation because it saw a fit with the initiative's emergent quality, its goal of catalyzing innovation, and its complex, multistakeholder structure. In keeping with the developmental evaluation approach, TruePoint and HCDC formed a working partnership for the entire evaluation, both at the staff level and, critically, at the senior management level: HCDC's director remained personally engaged throughout, and the partnership with HCDC's leadership turned out to be a central source of value in the process overall.

The TruePoint evaluation team included people who had been engaged all along in developing FOI, as well as people brought on exclusively for the evaluation project. This dual composition turned out to embody in very practical ways the "inside–outside" principle of developmental evaluation: External team members, who conducted the stakeholder interviews throughout the evaluation process, consistently introduced fresh perspectives; at the same time, given the complexity of the initiative itself, it proved important to have the internal team members available to help make sense of the diverse results coming in. The FOI team designated an HCDC staff person as responsible for ensuring that the evaluation process was inclusive and on track. The senior management of HCDC and the staff leadership of FOI took deep interest in the evaluation process and its results throughout.

To create an evaluation design, the TruePoint–HCDC team reached out to two senior consultants in the evaluation field, Michael Quinn Patton and Hallie Preskill. These discussions culminated in a March 2011 design workshop involving the senior consultants, TruePoint, HCDC leadership and staff, and FOI partners. The May 2011 launch event was then just 2 months away, so the workshop had a dual focus: (1) for the near term, preparing to harvest feedback and learning from the launch; and (2) for the longer term, structuring an ongoing, reflective evaluation and learning process to cover the first 3 years of the initiative. Major evaluation design features arising from the workshop included a focus on continually bringing in information from the field, enabling the creativity of external participants to emerge, and using the evaluation as a vehicle for learning.

Harvesting Early Feedback and Creating an Evolving Scorecard

To gather feedback during and immediately after the May 2011 convening, the developmental evaluation team used the following methods:

- A networking survey and interactive map set out on computer terminals at the May 2011 meeting itself.
- Notes taken at the sessions, immediately fed into on-site graphic displays (e.g., word clouds), and then assembled for later review by the evaluation team.

- Audience polling at both the opening and closing plenaries.
- Video recording of sessions and of interviews with participants.
- Evaluation forms collected at the end of the meeting.
- Telephone interviews with attendees during the weeks that followed.
- Reflective interviews with leadership and staff of HCDC and the initiative's launch partners.

This abundance of raw information was at first daunting to the evaluation team, but the effort to make sense of it set a pattern that proved vital to the entire evaluation process. First, the evaluation team reviewed the material and presented a very rough summary to the leadership and staff of HCDC. At a series of meetings and conference calls with TruePoint and HCDC in June and July 2011, the evaluation team posed a sequence of core questions to the group:

- What had actually happened so far?
- What does it mean—how can we assess its significance?
- How should we then view the initiative going forward?

In short: What, so what, and now what?[6]

Combining the results of these meetings with the stated goals and theory of change of the initiative itself, the evaluation team then created a scorecard to assess progress on key dimensions of the initiative. These included, for example: level of engagement of key community members around a common theory of change; degree of cross-sector connection for shared learning (innovation by influence); development of field-tested "accelerated" innovation projects on the ground (innovation by design); and results emerging from these field tests for the life prospects of young children. When the evaluation team developed progress criteria along each of these dimensions, they discovered a pattern: The criteria could be sorted naturally into three stages.

- Stage 1: Creating a context, an architecture for innovation and change.
- Stage 2: Putting the elements of the architecture into motion: concerted action to initiate and carry out demonstration projects.
- Stage 3: Achieving better life prospects for vulnerable young children.

Organizing the scorecard in this way enabled the team to assess even the initial round of feedback with the initiative's long-term goals in mind. But because the theory of change for the initiative itself was evolving, based on work on the ground and on the results of the developmental evaluation, the scorecard was designed to evolve as well. Each year, the evaluators documented modifications to the initiative's

---

[6] At a more granular level, the team organized preliminary feedback around a more detailed series of questions, following the same basic sequence. These questions were elaborated for this evaluation by Patton and Preskill as one of the key outcomes of the design consultation.

theory of change and resultant changes to the scorecard for application in future years, as well as progress against the scorecard itself during the past year. Thus was born the *evolving* scorecard (see Exhibit 6.3).

Reporting, Reflecting, Reframing: The Ongoing Developmental Evaluation

The evolving scorecard appeared for the first time, along with the results of the first round of feedback, in the initial developmental evaluation report submitted in August 2011. At this writing, the evaluation team has produced two subsequent

---

EXHIBIT 6.3

Evolving Scorecard

Stage 2	Practitioners	Policymakers	Researchers	Philanthropists
a. A revised theory of change that builds upon earlier versions and achieves broader resonance with and commitment from leaders in relevant fields.				
b. "Innovation by design" groups in areas of research, policy, and practice progressing along a "gradient" of commitment and activity, leading to piloting of promising new ideas; creation of a "measurement and evaluation group" to support shared, fast-cycle learning in the FOI community and enable cumulative testing of FOI's evolving theories of change.				**NA**

Comment on 2b above: "Innovation by design" groups have moved to piloting in exciting fashion, but primarily through collaborations among practitioners and researchers, with links to policymakers; however, innovation by design at the policy level has not moved as rapidly.

▪   ▪   ▪   ▪

Targeted Objectives for 2013

Comment: The FOI New Haven cluster, the MOMS partnership, is an example of where FOI needs to go more generally on both dimensions below.

a. Fuller engagement at the community level	
b. Cultural and racial diversity across FOI	

Key:

Good progress	
Moderate progress	
Some progress	
No activity or not applicable	**NA**

Note. This graphic displays two short extracts from the scorecard as it appeared in a report on progress achieved by mid-2013. Here specific aspects of Stage 2 are being assessed. The text in the left column represents preset objectives; the assessments (see the key at bottom right) are supplemented by written comments in boxes that run all the way across the table. Note that the second extract ("Targeted Objectives for 2013") scores progress against goals set as part of the 2012 developmental evaluation process, reflecting the evolution of the scorecard from its original 2011 version.

annual reports, and the process is ongoing. Core elements of the developmental evaluation work since the first round have included the following:

- Ongoing data gathering similar to what was done in the first phase, from sources such as these:
  - Key informant interviews done by an external member of the evaluation team, chosen in significant part because of his skill in reflective practice interviewing.
  - Reviews of conference evaluation results, meeting notes, strategic concept papers (prepared by HCDC senior management), and other documentation.
  - Video interviews.
  - Written surveys of core stakeholders.
  - Evolving network maps of the FOI community.
  - Site visits.
  - Reports from the field on results of early trials.
- Case studies. For the third year of the developmental evaluation, where the team reviewed not just a 1-year period but a full 3-year period, the data included both the empirics from the FOI community at large as well as three "deep-dive" cases, researched by the outside evaluation team. The case reports, which became part of the developmental evaluation, covered Washington State, New Haven, and the community partnerships that led to the "family routines" initiative.
- Strategic dialogue and reflection within the evaluation team, with the management and staff of the initiative at HCDC, and with the larger FOI community. This process developed its own distinctive rhythm, involving these elements in sequence:
  - Regular data reviews and presentations to the TruePoint–HCDC leadership team.
  - Reflections on those reviews, based on the evaluation questions prepared by Patton and Preskill (under the broader headings "What?", "So What?", and "Now What?").
  - Annual interim evaluation reports prepared by the TruePoint evaluators.
  - Annual strategy papers prepared by HCDC's senior leadership, which built upon observations and recommendations from the preceding evaluation report.
  - Communitywide consultations based on the strategy papers.

At the heart of the evaluation process were the reflective meetings of the evaluation team, the FOI staff, and the senior management of HCDC. The meetings were held in roughly three rounds each year, each round consisting of a series of presentations and structured discussions. The two midyear rounds did this in compressed format, but the year-end round generally involved several in-person sessions and conference calls, leading up to the preparation of the annual report.

Each reflective round opened with the evaluators presenting new data (e.g., from interviews or surveys) in a form that was responsive to a set of detailed evaluation questions, but that did not attempt to provide a full synthesis. The discussion then went around the table, and each participant was asked a simpler, more general question: "What?" (see Exhibit 6.4). More specifically, "What, from your perspective, is actually happening in FOI now, and what has been accomplished to date?" When all the contributions had been heard, the group attempted a synthesis on the "What?" question—a substantial task, since the complexity of FOI meant that listening to the individual answers often felt like hearing the proverbial descriptions of an elephant from multiple viewpoints.

After at least a trial close on the "What?" question, the group went around the table again, this time to answer the next question: "So What?" (see Exhibit 6.5). This normally took at least two cycles of individual contributions, group discussion, and offline synthesis by the internal and external evaluation teams. The first time through the cycle, the goal was to create a basic list of key themes from the reported results—for example, on the significance of work in each of a series of states and communities. Then the group moved to a strategic assessment one level up, reviewing common implications of the work at all those locations taken together.

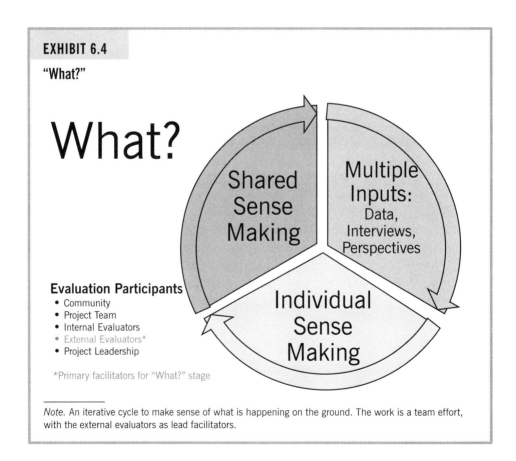

EXHIBIT 6.4

"What?"

What?

Shared Sense Making

Multiple Inputs: Data, Interviews, Perspectives

Individual Sense Making

Evaluation Participants
• Community
• Project Team
• Internal Evaluators
• External Evaluators*
• Project Leadership

*Primary facilitators for "What?" stage

Note. An iterative cycle to make sense of what is happening on the ground. The work is a team effort, with the external evaluators as lead facilitators.

EXHIBIT 6.5

"So What?"

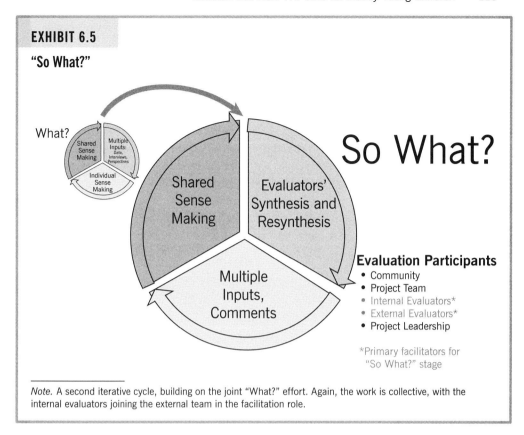

Note. A second iterative cycle, building on the joint "What?" effort. Again, the work is collective, with the internal evaluators joining the external team in the facilitation role.

For the larger, annual review rounds, the process continued after the in-person meeting, through an additional series of conference calls and often a final in-person session. These follow-up sessions always began with a *trial synthesis* presented in advance by the evaluators. It was here—annually, but not during the midyear reviews—that the evaluators put ideas about the third major question, "Now What?", on the table for discussion.

Findings: What Was Developed and How Was It Used?

A striking result of this process was that each year the team ended up spotting new patterns and viewing the initiative through a new frame. For example, the idea of aligning local and community work to policy-level work in a state or province was a product of the second annual report; the team labeled this concept *vertical alignment*. The idea of the *innovation cluster* as the fundamental building block of FOI's work emerged from the third annual evaluation. Each of these became an organizing and priority-setting principle for FOI as its members worked through how best to stimulate and accelerate progress within the innovation community.

Each annual report included recommendations building on the synthesis achieved in the "So What?" phase. For example, the evaluators and project participants spotted the significance of what they named innovation clusters, and the report that followed recommended steps to strengthen the clusters' collective work. (For a definition of innovation clusters, see the section "The Emergence of the Cluster Model.")

At this stage, the evaluators' recommendations remained *trial syntheses*. That is, although they drew upon the participative process, they did not represent decisions by the management of the initiative. Thus, *after* each annual developmental evaluation report was filed, the leadership team prepared a new strategy paper, dubbed the Green Paper. (Green because the strategy was always evolving, never final.) This additional step afforded the leadership an opportunity to process the evaluators' recommendations, consult with the broader community, work through the needed decisions, and write up the results. The Green Papers detailed the initiative's evolving theory of change for critical review and discussion among the members of the FOI community as a whole.

The results of that discussion then fed into the following year's developmental evaluation, so the entire annual cycle supported a learning partnership among the initiative's leadership, its membership, and the developmental evaluators. Although the evaluation did not define strategy, it did enable management to respond effectively to the emergent nature of the initiative—to evolving facts on the ground—and to select or adapt *stretch recommendations* offered by the outside evaluators.

Al Race, deputy director of HCDC, contrasted this approach to what he called "a static evaluation method." For him, using the more dynamic developmental evaluation model helped the leadership:

> "sharpen, refine, and refresh our thinking based on what we learned from the previous year's work and informed by the input of the evaluators as well as those whom they interviewed. It is also an opportunity to then communicate the refined strategy to the growing FOI community in order to plant seeds for new ideas and connections that will ultimately feed back into the strategy in a virtuous loop."

Exhibit 6.6 illustrates the full cycle culminating in the "Now What?" phase.

Contributing to an Evolving Theory of Change

At the center of this cycle of planning, action, reflection, and reframing was the initiative's overall theory of change, which retained two basic components:

1. A science-based *causal model*, including testable hypotheses regarding ways the field could move to substantially better outcomes for children.

2. An *innovation architecture*—ways of organizing the growing FOI community and of stimulating iterative, outcomes-driven learning.

EXHIBIT 6.6

"Now What?"

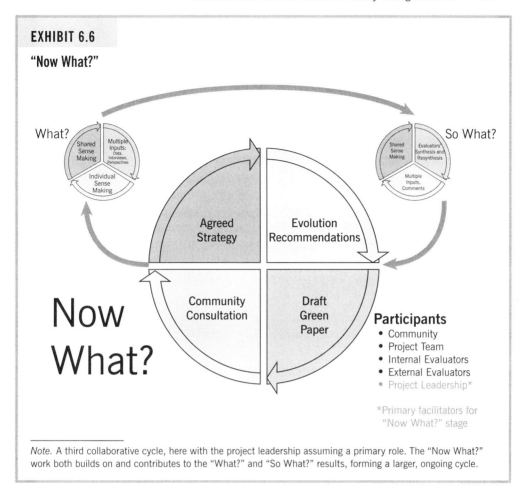

Note. A third collaborative cycle, here with the project leadership assuming a primary role. The "Now What?" work both builds on and contributes to the "What?" and "So What?" results, forming a larger, ongoing cycle.

Each year saw a reframing of strategy and a new understanding of what FOI was doing based on the results of the developmental evaluation. Exhibits 6.7 through 6.10 track the reframing of the two components of FOI's theory of change: (1) the science-based causal model (Exhibit 6.7) and (2) innovation architecture (Exhibits 6.8, 6.9, and 6.10).

Learning from the Developmental Evaluation: The Emergence of the Cluster Model

In its early stages, FOI focused largely on the research and policy levels rather than on community-level engagement with service providers. The Building Caregiver Capacity and Washington One Science working groups began just this way. However, FOI's policy-level initiatives, particularly those focusing purely on interagency coordination, yielded limited results. The developmental evaluation in the first 2 years drew out a vital lesson: FOI innovation work, even if its impetus is at a state

EXHIBIT 6.7

Evolution of the Science-Based Causal Model

Topic	Pre-2011	2013
Objective for vulnerable, young children	Ready to learn	Ready to learn + Foundations of lifelong health in place
Focal "entry point"	Children's executive functioning and self-regulation	Children's executive functioning and self-regulation + Adult (caregiver) executive functioning and self-regulation
Objective for adults	Build caregiving capacities	Build caregiving capacities + Employability
Parental education	Provide information	Provide information + Build skills and capacities
Preventing and buffering toxic stress	At the family level	At the family level + At the community level

Note. The model changed through interaction with innovators in the field, in an iterative process supported and tracked by the developmental evaluation. This chart summarizes evolution from the initial model developed from the prelaunch consultation process ("Pre-2011") to the model described in the 2013 developmental evaluation report.

policy or systems level, needs a direct connection at the practice level to families being served. This insight changed both how the initiative was structured (the shifts reflected in Exhibits 6.8 and 6.9) and how FOI allocated its resources, leading to a new emphasis on community-level work.

By the third year, that emphasis had enabled a new pattern to emerge: the innovation cluster, epitomized by the FOI partners working in Washington State and in New Haven, Connecticut, as described in the opening section of this chapter. The developmental evaluation team suggested the term *innovation cluster* to capture what was organically developing there, with key features including these:

- Partnerships between researchers and community agencies to develop or adapt interventions aimed at addressing unmet needs identified at the community level. The partnerships are based on mutual learning: All participants both teach and learn.

- A diversity of pilots emerging from each such partnership, with each pilot starting small enough to enable fast, low-cost implementation, and ongoing modification based on early feedback and results.

EXHIBIT 6.8

FOI's Architecture as Planned in 2011

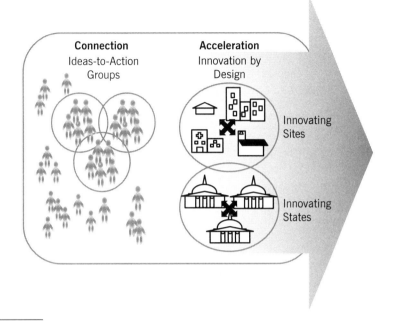

Note. This model envisioned two complementary functions: *connection* through thematic ideas-to-action groups across diverse disciplines, and *acceleration* through investments in specific innovation-by-design states and sites. The Building Caregiver Capacity group was the first ideas-to-action team, and Washington became the first innovating state.

- Thematic links across the pilots—in the Washington State example, these were based on executive functioning and self-regulation—enabling comparisons and shared learning across the cluster.
- Institutional links to enable both sustainable funding and scalability.

Once these features were identified, evaluators recommended a strategic focus on building and sustaining them, including the following:

- *Leadership development.* At a basic level, the innovation cluster's strength is the strength of its local leaders. FOI learned that a cluster needs leadership at a community hub and a research hub, as well as state-level links. Thus FOI has been supporting individual leaders playing such roles in its clusters, and is now creating programming aimed at discovering and developing the resources, skills, and capacities these leaders need to succeed.

- *Vertical alignment.* Here the recommendation was to link the cluster from the outset to the policy level, so its innovations could be built with scalability in view. This includes assuring that new strategies can be feasibly and cost-effectively delivered by existing systems, and that policy reforms go hand in hand with what's being learned on the ground.

  • *Horizontal networking.* The observation that different clusters face common challenges and common sources of opportunity led to the recommendations that FOI support shared learning around specific themes across its clusters, and that it recruit thematic leaders from the wider innovation community accordingly. Examples of potential themes include identifying key adult capacities, using video technology, and leveraging home visiting as a platform for new interventions.

  • *Sustainability and portfolio management.* A sustainable funding model for an innovation cluster remains a challenge, in that traditional public and private funding typically requires fuller specification of plans and activities than is possible in the model offered here. At this writing, HCDC and the evaluation team are discussing a portfolio management model as a way to frame FOI's role: FOI as the steward of a portfolio of interventions (developed and implemented through innovation clusters) and a portfolio of capacities (developed through vertical alignment

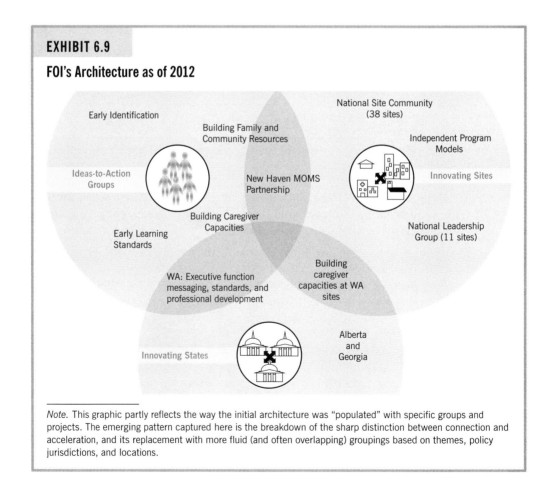

EXHIBIT 6.9

FOI's Architecture as of 2012

Note. This graphic partly reflects the way the initial architecture was "populated" with specific groups and projects. The emerging pattern captured here is the breakdown of the sharp distinction between connection and acceleration, and its replacement with more fluid (and often overlapping) groupings based on themes, policy jurisdictions, and locations.

EXHIBIT 6.10

Innovation Architecture 2013: A Model of an Innovation Cluster

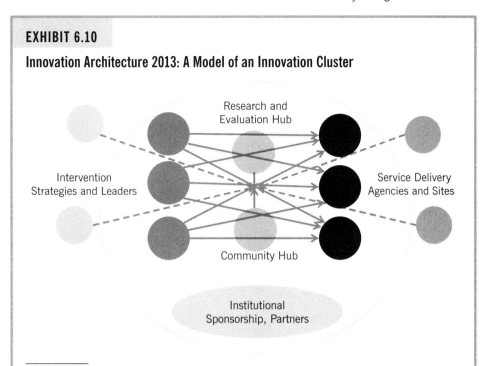

Note. Here elements from Exhibits 6.8 and 6.9 coalesce around a community hub. For the Washington State cluster, the Children's Home Society of Washington serves as the community hub; the Washington State Department of Early Learning serves as institutional sponsor; and the University of Washington serves as the research and evaluation hub. Intervention strategy developers and delivery agencies within the large oval—the cluster boundary—collaborate closely, as the solid arrows suggest. In Washington, cluster members currently include researchers at four universities and staff members at five community agencies. The dashed arrows represent connections to innovators within the nationwide FOI community, but outside the innovation cluster being illustrated. For example, the FIND intervention, a significant project within the Washington State cluster (via individual home visits in Early Head Start), is also being adapted (to group settings where neighborhood mothers support each other) in the New Haven cluster through the MOMS Partnership.

and horizontal networking). The team hopes that such a model will help the cluster work achieve sustainable funding.

Within a Cluster: Developmental Evaluation at the Community Level

> "This changes the way I look at my work. I have a chance to focus on the forest, not just the trees."

This quotation came from a meeting of the Washington State innovation cluster, attended by a member of the developmental evaluation team. Observations from that meeting informed the overall evaluation report through the process discussed above. But something more was happening at that meeting—another consequence of the evaluation work itself. Becky Jaques, who facilitated the meeting as Senior Project Manager for FOI, described what happened:

"Throughout the innovation process with the practitioners and researchers to develop, test, and evaluate new, science-based strategies, we used the developmental evaluation approach to bring a critical eye to what worked [and] what didn't work, and challenge community organizations to look at why, and what could be done differently. This process allowed us to focus on short-cycle feedback, rapid interpretation of results, and continuous adaptation of strategies over time. This has helped the members of the innovation cluster, individually and jointly, to adopt a more reflective perspective on the work, stimulating the kind of ongoing, critical review that can be seen as an adoption in microcosm of a developmental evaluation approach to innovation."

In short, developmental evaluation is becoming part of the work with communities and families on the ground. As another staff member put it, "This is a paradigm shift—we are all much more reflective about our work. We have the space to do that, to make it better."

Sample Lessons from This Developmental Evaluation

One way of understanding this developmental evaluation is as a learning partnership. The learning partnership in this case operates first and foremost between the evaluators and the senior leadership of HCDC and FOI, but it also encompasses a wider set of internal and external stakeholders. Members of the larger FOI innovation community are engaged throughout the process and animate the constant "bringing in" of both fresh empirical data and challenging outside perspectives.

Senior leadership time is always a scarce resource, and the commitment of the HCDC leadership team to the evaluation work shouldn't be underestimated as a key to what was achieved here. At the same time, the developmental evaluation approach proved an effective way to leverage available time and make the learning partnership productive. Ingredients of that approach that proved valuable in this evaluation included the following:

• *The separation of evaluation space from decision space.* The evaluation meetings engaged the leadership actively, but in the spirit of discovery and reflection, with no requirement to reach decisions or closure. This enabled a different kind of conversation from what happens in a typical strategy or management meeting—a conversation that could explore ambiguity and push for new insights. Similarly, the annual strategy cycle included two separate documents: the developmental evaluation reports and the strategic Green Papers. This separation gave the teams working on each document space to develop their thinking; meanwhile, each team could draw productively on the other's efforts.

• *Inside–outside collaboration.* As the evaluator–implementer partnership model suggests, the evaluation was carried out through dialogue between insiders and outsiders. This actually involved a spectrum running from a core inside team (i.e., the leadership and staff of the initiative itself) though to external stakeholders in the FOI community and on the TruePoint evaluation team, which itself comprised both participants in FOI's ongoing work and external evaluators involved only in the inquiry and assessment process. Every portion of the spectrum proved critical; insiders alone could not have seen what outsiders saw, and outsiders alone could not have interpreted it.

• *Rich feedback.* From the opening design workshop onward, the evaluation team was voracious in seeking data in a wide variety of forms, ranging from meeting evaluations to stakeholder interviews to intervention data to audience polling. FOI is a complex, multiple-stakeholder initiative that is all about catalyzing innovation across disciplines and geographies and encouraging independent creativity. The flow of outside data and feedback from the field, in flexible and varied formats, provided managers a way to keep their fingers "on the pulse" of what was happening on the ground—with the families FOI sought to serve—and stimulated the constant reframing that was a hallmark of this developmental evaluation.

• *Reflection and reframing.* The evaluation's most important work occurred in regular rounds of reflective sessions, fed by fresh data and external perspectives and structured to systematically assess the "What?", "So What?", and "Now What?" questions. This structure enabled the HCDC–TruePoint partnership to spot emerging patterns and use them to reframe FOI's theory of change and reset its priorities, goals, and strategies. Meanwhile, interviewees have told us that their reflective discussions with the outside developmental evaluator helped them see their own work differently, and that they themselves are now asking, as part of that work, the core questions "What?", "So What?", and "Now What?"

• *The evolving scorecard.* The reflective process gained essential discipline from the use of an evaluation scorecard that enabled the evaluators to assess progress and highlight not only patterns of success, but also trouble spots and failures. The developmental framework in turn enabled rapid adjustment based on these results. For example, the shift of priorities in Washington State emerged from scorecard reporting, as did the insight that innovation clusters represented a key opportunity. Reframing strategic goals did not mean abandonment of standards of assessment; rather, those standards evolved along with the theory of change, in an explicit way.

• *The urgent versus the important.* It is difficult for anyone to carve out time for the kind of reflection that formed the core of this evaluation, and even more so for senior executives of dynamic organizations. The evaluation process itself, including the need to produce regular reports and thus to conduct periodic review sessions, had the helpful effect of "forcing" those involved to set aside special time. In this way, the important task of long-term, evaluative thinking managed, just often enough, to trump the urgent press of daily events.

Developmental evaluation as employed here should be seen as an integral part of the underlying initiative, rather than as an activity that happens after, or separately from, an on-the-ground project or intervention. When the objectives explicitly include innovation and the context is as highly complex as early child development, the process for collective learning becomes as important as the process for collective action. Developmental evaluation has provided a systematic and repeatable framework for that collective learning.

The FOI Initiative began when a small group of individuals with aspirations for systemwide change reached out to the larger early childhood development field to build a learning community. Together, they embarked on a process that required progressive elaboration of both the strategy for achieving their shared objectives and the architecture through which to enlist, mobilize, and align participants to enact the strategy. Developmental evaluation has enabled an ongoing iteration between strategy and design, so they can inform each other and effectively coevolve. By encouraging openness to new sources of data and perspective, developmental evaluation has also provided a way for an ever-widening circle to reflect on the overall progress of the initiative and shape its further evolution; in this way developmental evaluation has laid the groundwork for expansion of the initiative's leadership group.

FOI comprises an array of activities—some grouped in geographical clusters like those in Washington State and New Haven, others emerging from initiatives by innovators elsewhere. Already, we have seen the reflective practice at the heart of developmental evaluation take shape not only at the level of the initiative as a whole, but also within clusters. Thus far, this has been an informal process, going hand in hand with the informal expansion of the leadership group. But as the initiative continues to grow in scale and scope, and to engage an increasingly broad array of actors, it will be important to institutionalize this practice. Sustaining an effective ongoing process for developmental evaluation, both at the level of the overall initiative and within each core area of activity, will be essential if the initiative is to achieve its ultimate goal of catalyzing changes that improve the life prospects of large numbers of needy children.

CHAPTER 7

Developmental Evaluation's Role in Supporting Community-Led Solutions for Māori and Pacific Young People's Educational Success

*The Foundation North Māori
and Pacific Education Initiative*

Kate McKegg, Nan Wehipeihana, Moi Becroft, and Jennifer Gill

He ira
He puawaitanga
He ponanatanga
He matauranga
He maramatanga

(A dot
A blossoming
Uncertainty
Knowledge
Enlightenment)
—WHAKATAUKI (a Māori proverb)

EDITORS' INTRODUCTION

This case study tells the story of a large, multiyear developmental evaluation of the Māori and Pacific Educational Initiative (MPEI)—an innovative philanthropic approach to investing in community-led solutions. The alignment of developmental evaluation with the nonlinear and emergent trajectory of innovation and development is a feature of this case study, demonstrating the need for contextually grounded evaluation practice. It highlights and affirms the relational nature of developmental evaluation, together with the importance of relationships for the evaluation's credibility, quality, and effectiveness and for the development of innovation. It focuses attention on the use of contextually appropriate cultural principles within an evaluation and innovation process, and on the challenges and learning that emerge in embedding these authentically. Importantly, it draws our gaze to the importance of acknowledging and paying attention to multiple perspectives and relationships when undertaking developmental evaluation in a complex innovation—in particular, the need for collaborative, participative values-based engagement in regard both to expectations and to key evaluative practices/processes.

125

Also of note, this was a high-stakes evaluation. A prestigious philanthropic foundation decided to finance this innovative education approach, which was completely new and untested. For the first time ever, the foundation was investing in a vision—funding multiple innovative initiatives over 5 years in different communities, with a diverse range of starting places, skills, and capacities. The investment was understood to be high-risk, and the potential benefits were highly uncertain. Not only was the initiative high-stakes, then, but so was the evaluation. The developmental evaluation would be highly visible, closely scrutinized, and potentially controversial—qualities that come with the territory in high-stakes evaluations. The traditional approach to managing high uncertainty and high risk is to maximize control, but the initiative's development from the outset was highly organic and emergent. Nothing was predetermined except the focus on lifting educational achievement for Māori and Pacific young people. The complexity of what lay ahead in order to realize the far-reaching vision was acknowledged, as was the inevitability of a journey that would be full of ups and downs. It's now time to mount the rollercoaster, the difference from an actual rollercoaster being that this ride doesn't end where it started. Read on to find out where these ups and downs—*the normal experience of developmental evaluation*—end up. Spoiler alert: It's wisdom articulated by a 12-year-old Pacific Islander.

In 2006, Foundation North (formerly ASB Community Trust), in the face of overwhelming evidence of long-term, systemic educational failure for Māori and Pacific young people, set out to explore a new, transformational approach to philanthropy in the hope that it could go some way toward overcoming educational underachievement in Māori and Pacific communities in Auckland and Northland. The cold, hard reality was that if the existing situation was left to continue, the well-being and prosperity of Māori and Pacific communities was at serious risk; worse still, New Zealand's economic progress, social cohesion, and national identity could be argued to be on the line (Hancock, 2009).

> "Let's do something big and bold." (Pat Sneddon, Deputy Chair, ASB Community Trust, 2006, quoted in Hancock & MPEI Contributors, 2013)

Trustees set aside substantial funds and committed themselves to a long-term, innovative investment approach—one that they knew would be risky and challenging, but necessary, if community-led solutions to seemingly intractable problems were to be found. In the context of philanthropy in New Zealand, the amount of funding set aside was extraordinary: An amount equal to half the annual grants budget of the largest philanthropic grant maker in Australasia was set aside for one initiative. The Māori and Pacific Education Initiative (MPEI) vision, "Ma tātou ano tātou e kōrero" ("We speak for ourselves"), captures the essence of the initiative—namely, "that communities know what is good for them, and must be able to speak for themselves and make their own decisions" (Kevin Prime, Chair of ASB Community Trust, 2003–2009, quoted in Hancock, 2009).

A number of projects (nine in total) were chosen, and were funded for 5 years. Each project was inspired from within a Māori or Pacific community, received community backing, and focused on lifting the educational achievement of Māori and/or Pacific young people. The aspirations of these communities were clear:

"We want what others have: university enrollments; high paying jobs; people who are successful in their life careers whatever their field and confident about themselves and their culture. How come the state education system works for most people in the population but not for our peoples?" (Māori and Pacific reference group, MPEI, quoted in Hancock, 2009)

The projects selected offered a diverse range of solutions to the problem of educational underachievement, from early childhood to the tertiary level. They thus demonstrated the ability of Māori and Pacific communities to generate compelling answers to the challenges they face (Hancock & MPEI Contributors, 2012).

Along with long-term funding for a diverse range of projects, Foundation North committed itself to evaluating the MPEI initiative, so that the trustees might build an evidence base about the value of their investment (from which they could also learn important lessons for future philanthropic efforts).

This chapter tells the story of a large, multiyear developmental evaluation of the MPEI—an innovative philanthropic approach to investing in community-led solutions. The chapter is written largely from the perspective of the evaluators, although many of the insights and learnings include those of Foundation North. Our reflections and learnings are very much a collaboration, so although at times the "we" in the chapter refers to the evaluators only, at other times, the "we" very definitely includes the foundation.

The MPEI evaluation team was a network of evaluation colleagues called the Kinnect Group, based in New Zealand. The evaluation team was made up of Māori, Pacific, and Pākehā[1] evaluators. In collaboration with the trust, the MPEI evaluation design and approach evolved and adapted throughout the life of the initiative.

The MPEI was a courageous, innovative step for Foundation North and for philanthropy in New Zealand generally. The trustees recognized that the bold, long-term vision they had committed themselves to was at the high-risk end of the investment spectrum; there was a lot at stake. The challenge that lay ahead in 2006 was turning the vision into a reality, on the ground, in the Māori and Pacific communities of Auckland.

From the outset, embedded within the initiative's design and development were principles of collaboration, co-design, and community development. Community and project leaders and staff were to become more than just partners in a "high-trust" journey toward the realization of vision: They were recognized by Foundation North as the "hosts" of the vision (i.e., the solutions were to be developed and determined by them). By providing a meaningful resource, the foundation hoped to create an opening for Māori and Pacific communities to realize their aspirations and be the agents of the changes they wanted.

The MPEI approach was completely new and untested. For the first time ever, the foundation was investing in a vision—funding multiple innovative initiatives over 5 years in different communities, with a diverse range of starting places, skills, and capacities.

---

[1]Pākehā is a term used in New Zealand to refer to New Zealanders of English, Scottish, Irish, or European descent.

"We were working within the frame of uncertainty that inevitably marks any quest for social transformation. Community development initiatives often require enormous leaps at the front end. To find a way forward you must put your faith and trust in people, and expect to shape the journey with them as you go along together." (Pat Sneddon, Deputy Chair, ASB Community Trust, quoted in Hancock & MPEI Contributors, 2013)

As Pat Sneddon's statement quoted above indicates, the approach underpinning the MPEI was a relational one: Trust and faith in people were foundational premises. Rather than following the well-worn path of having trustees consider the evidence and make decisions about priorities and funding, the foundation opted for an approach that put the decision-making power over funding priorities into the hands of knowledgeable, well-respected Māori and Pacific educational and community leaders. A partnership was established early between the trustees and two reference groups whose members were focused on Māori and Pacific educational aspirations.

"The Trust sought from the outset to establish a working partnership with members of the reference groups that would enable them to shape the development of the MPEI and their role in it." (Kirsten Kohere-Soutar, ASB Community Trust Māori Trustee, quoted in Hancock & MPEI Contributors, 2013)

A deep commitment to the dynamics of relationships was modeled by the foundation's leaders, who actively invited deep discussion, participation, and engagement on the issues of importance, both within and across cultural lines. Together, the reference groups determined that MPEI projects were to advance Māori and Pacific Islander engagement in citizenship through educational achievement.

The initiative's development from the outset was highly organic and emergent. Nothing was predetermined except the focus on lifting educational achievement for Māori and Pacific young people. The complexity of what lay ahead, in order to realize the far-reaching vision was acknowledged, as was the inevitability of a journey that would be full of ups and downs.

In spite of this uncertainty, the foundation was committed to evaluation:

"We resolved to undertake an organic process, even if it led us into a cul-de-sac with nothing to show for our enterprise. We were determined to evaluate each step of the journey and put ourselves on the line." (Jennifer Gill, CEO, ASB Community Trust, quoted in Hancock & MPEI Contributors, 2013)

The foundation made it clear that it needed an evaluation approach aligned with the far-reaching vision and the complexity of the initiative; with the emergent and organic process of development that was to occur; with the commitment to collaboration and capacity development; and with the importance it placed on trusting people and building relationships. It also valued an approach that would "harness critical enquiry, count what's countable and situate MPEI projects in relevant literatures to distinguish their contributions" (Hancock & MPEI Contributors, 2012). The foundation eventually settled on a developmental evaluation approach.

"The overall purpose is to develop an appropriate and flexible evaluation framework that will support the developmental journey of successful applicant groups, determine and assess measurable outcomes and deliver a credible evidence base for MPEI." (ASB Community Trust, quoted in Hancock & MPEI Contributors, 2012).

Setting the Scene for Developmental Evaluation

The trustees knew they wanted an evaluation approach that was responsive and flexible, and that was aligned with the initiative's underpinning principles and vision. In spite of this, they hadn't had a great deal of luck finding evaluators who could implement such an approach. The first year of evaluation hadn't gone as well as they had hoped. Although the evaluators came with good credentials and were highly respected in educational circles, they hadn't "gelled" with all the Māori and Pacific projects and communities. The evaluation approach that was initially implemented was more traditional, operating at quite a distance from the providers and the foundation. At the end of 1 year, the trustees didn't feel they had what they needed from an evaluation, and they didn't feel part of it; the fit just wasn't right.

So Foundation North came to the Kinnect Group, asking if we would work with them on a developmental evaluation. They had heard about developmental evaluation by the time they came to engage us. Frances Westley, Brenda Zimmerman, and Michael Quinn Patton's book *Getting to Maybe* (2006) had made it onto the reading list of a growing group of social entrepreneurs in New Zealand; Frances and Michael had also visited New Zealand, and so a number of people had been exposed to the concept of developmental evaluation. Developmental evaluation sounded to the trustees like the kind of approach they needed.

By the time the Kinnect Group was engaged, the MPEI was in full swing, and things were changing and developing at a rapid pace. Programs were experimenting with new ideas, systems, and structures, and continually responding and adapting to new and emerging situations and information. The staff members of the various projects were also a bit "evaluation-shy" after their first experience. The trustees realized that what they needed was evaluation that could be:

- Dynamic and emergent (i.e., able to flexibly fit the changing circumstances, skills, knowledge, and capacity of projects).

- Responsive to context (i.e., cognizant of the historical and cultural contexts of programs, as well as of the fast-paced developmental context in which the projects were operating).

- Operational at different levels of the system (i.e., the evaluation approach needed to build evaluation capacity within the projects, as well as to be able to say something about the worth and value of the overall MPEI).

- Participative (i.e., the projects and Foundation North staff and trustees wanted to feel part of the evaluation process; this was a high-stakes initiative for all of them, and they didn't want to be at arm's length from the evaluation).

- Transparent, relational, and use-oriented (i.e., just as the MPEI was founded on relational premises, so too should the evaluation approach be; a no-surprises, high-trust approach was what all participants wanted).

This sounded like developmental evaluation (Patton, 2011), and after a short period of familiarizing ourselves with the project and conducting contractual due diligence, we agreed to become partners with the foundation and join the developmental journey that is the MPEI.

Our Developmental Evaluation Practice: Founded on a Relational Ethic of Care

Much like the foundational premise of the MPEI, our developmental evaluation practice begins from a cultural and relational ethic of first taking care of relationships. This approach recognizes that it is within relationships that change happens. That is, relationships are the pivotal philosophical and practical change makers (Anae, 2010)—or, as evaluator and chapter coauthor Nan Wehipeihana says, "relationships are the business" (Wehipeihana, 2011).

We recognize that underpinning our developmental evaluation practice are the relationships we form with the people we work with. Caring and respect, reciprocity and collaboration, and the creation of opportunities for mutual learning and growth—all these are aspects of the relationships that become interwoven during a developmental evaluation. As such, these become integral to the quality and effectiveness of the evaluation, as well as of the projects we are working to support.

In our view, the program theory, logic models, evaluation design, and data analysis are not the only things that matter for evaluation quality and effectiveness; just as important is the relational quality between people in the contexts in which the evaluation is implemented (Abma & Widdershoven, 2008). In evaluation generally, our methods are often put up as our cloak of expertise, but we believe that they can also be something to hide behind. We are not rejecting methods, and we acknowledge the need for skilled and careful execution of appropriate methods. Rather, we are suggesting that in a developmental evaluation we can no longer hide behind them because the foreground is a relational space that we must acknowledge, engage in, and inhabit for the life of our evaluation.

Patton (2011) and more recently Kathy Brennan (2013) describe the positioning of an evaluator as one of the distinguishing features of developmental evaluation. That is, the evaluator is positioned as one of the project team, rather than as distant and independent of it. This positioning implies the need for deeper and more intimate relationships between the evaluator and project staff and management than in a more traditional evaluation.

An effective relationship is founded on trust, and this takes time to develop. Trust is a function of the capacity of the people in the relationship to engage, listen, understand, and collaborate, as well as of the competence they demonstrate to act skillfully, credibly, and reliably (i.e., to do as they say they will) (Maister, Green, & Galford, 2000).

Our roles and responsibilities as developmental evaluators are quite different from the roles we play in more traditional forms of evaluation. While we have people's best interests at heart, and it's in our job description to support their work, we also need to be able to have courageous conversations about what's actually happening, how well it's happening, and what this might mean for the next decision or action taken. Our job is not to tell people (i.e., the projects or the funders) what to do; it's to help them think critically about what they are doing, and what the next step might be.

Developing and Maintaining Relationships in Practice

Our relationships with each other were developed and maintained through regular, mostly face-to-face, open, and transparent discussion, debate, and sharing of data and information. We met fortnightly with the MPEI manager, sometimes more often if needed. With each of the projects, at least two evaluators met regularly (every 2–3 months) with the project's staff and jointly planned and reviewed the type and extent of evaluation support that the staff members felt they needed and wanted at that point in time.

As the MPEI vision statement quoted earlier in this chapter made clear, our responsibility in working alongside each of the projects was to allow its participants to speak for themselves as Māori and Pacific. And so we looked to Māori and Pacific principles, theory, and frameworks for guidance about our practice. Cultural ontologies, epistemologies, nuances, meanings, metaphors, customs, and beliefs all had a major influence on our practice and methods at both the individual and the collective levels (Anae, 2010). Exhibit 7.1 outlines some of the Māori cultural dimensions that informed our developmental evaluation practice.

Early in the evaluation journey, we gathered the leaders and staff of all the projects together and asked them what vision they had for evaluation (see Exhibit 7.2). They told us it was important that we do the following:

- Collaborate with them.
- Help them build their evaluation capacity.
- Keep things simple.
- Be there when needed, and be accessible.
- Demonstrate an understanding that they are all unique.
- Acknowledge that there is no one-size-fits-all approach.
- Look hard for the "difference that makes a difference."

Toward the end of the evaluation process, we gathered independent feedback from the MPEI projects about how well we had done, in a relational sense. Providers rated our performance on a range of relational attributes they had told us were important to them, and that are also evident in the literature on building trusted relationships (Maister et al., 2000). The projects confirmed that our approach was experienced as practical, relevant, collaborative, affirming, creative, reciprocal, and respectful. The staff of one project put it this way:

EXHIBIT 7.1

A Māori Cultural Framework for Developmental Evaluation

Māori cultural dimension	Dimension (in English)	Developmental evaluation application
Kaupapa	Philosophy/ vision/purpose	• The models, pathways, and theories of change that we developed for each project were based on each project's underpinning cultural philosophies and practices.
Horopaki	Context	• We took seriously the need for the developmental evaluation team to be culturally responsive and credible in each project context. Our team was culturally diverse, with Māori, Pacific, and Pākehā team members.
Whakapapa	History/ background	• Throughout the evaluation, we had to balance the importance of the MPEI's history and development within the philanthropic context with respecting and acknowledging the social, political, and cultural history of each individual project.
Tikanga a iwi	Worldview	• The complexity of the evaluation and implementation context required us to take account of and pay attention to how we might privilege the diverse Māori and Pacific realities, perspectives, and needs operating in each of the different places and contexts. • Wherever possible, project voices were honored and privileged in our reporting and presentations about the projects.
Ngā ūaratanga	Values and beliefs	• Each of the project's own values and belief systems provided guidance and grounding for the evaluation team's decisions about all evaluation tasks and directions (e.g., all evaluation learning opportunities and capacity building were grounded in culturally relevant examples and experiences wherever possible).
Kawa and Tikanga	Protocols and rituals	• Māori and/or Pacific protocols were observed throughout the evaluation process (e.g., formal welcoming processes, acknowledgment of ancestors, spiritual blessings).
Ngā Pūrakau	Storytelling	• Storytelling was validated in multiple ways throughout the evaluation process—for example, use of digital stories, hui and fono (cultural group meetings), infographics, and tailored performance stories.

(continued)

Source: Adapted from Pipi (2012). Used with permission.

Māori cultural dimension	Dimension (in English)	Developmental evaluation application
Whakawhānaungatanga	Relationships and connections/ systems thinking	• We took time to build relationships up front with all key stakeholders. We also ensured ongoing opportunities for providers, funders, and evaluators to come together to share and strengthen connections and build relationships.
Tika, Pono, Aroha	Rights and responsibilities; truth and love	• We regularly reflected on the roles, responsibilities, and accountabilities that each of us had—to providers, to the foundation, and to one another (checking, discussing, debating what's right in whose eyes). • We built in regular opportunities for projects to review our data and writing, in order to maintain the integrity of information they gave us. We checked in regularly on projects' progress and development, often going beyond the call of duty, doing things with our heads and hearts and "in spirit."
Tino Rangatiratanga	Self-determination	• We were committed to working to ensure that data were useful and meaningful for projects' development. • Part of the way we demonstrated this commitment was to give authority (mana) to the Māori and Pacific projects and communities to decide what mattered and what was important to them. • We were also mindful of the Treaty of Waitangi principles of protection, partnership, and participation (e.g., working toward ensuring the program funding was protected, working in partnership with the funder and the providers, ensuring ample opportunities for participation in strategic and tactical decision making). • In our team, we were clear that non-Māori and non-Pacific participants in the evaluation would have "guesthood" status (i.e., that their perspectives would take a supportive back seat where appropriate, rather than play a leading role).

"They were affirming, and it was about us. It's a real gift when you have people around who just listen to your vision; it's that focused attention. They did really well with us."

However, just as in everyday relationships, we didn't always get it right. In the early days, our evaluation team had no Pacific capacity, and we had to acknowledge to the projects and to the foundation that this was a significant shortcoming and we would work to resolve it. It took us a year before we found a Pacific evaluation colleague to work with us, and together we had to work out what kind of role he would have. It is easy, when there is a single Pacific person on an evaluation team, for the work to take account of Pacific perspectives tokenistically, and we did not want this. He spent a good deal of time getting to know the people and the projects, and assuring himself that our evaluation practice to that point had been culturally responsive and beneficial to the projects. He went on to play a strategic cultural advisory role on the team, at the same time helping to keep our evaluation practice safe and respectful, as well as reassuring Pacific communities about our work.

For one of the MPEI projects that came into the initiative later, we didn't get the opportunity to engage initially with the people on the project in a culturally appropriate way. The consequence of not getting this initial relational engagement right was significant. We struggled throughout the evaluation process to develop the trust needed to work productively together on a developmental evaluation journey. We never got there in the end. This became a very important lesson for us about the importance of taking the time to get the introductions and early engagement right. The costs (relational and actual) of not doing so are high for everybody involved in evaluation.

EXHIBIT 7.2

MPEI Provider Vision for Evaluation

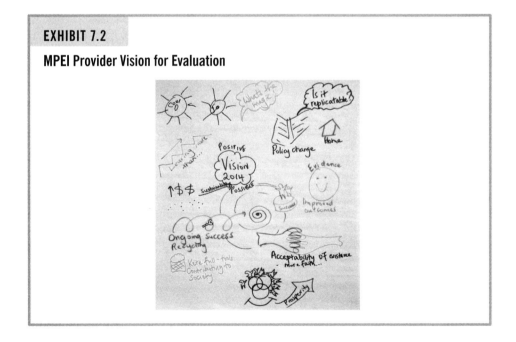

Balancing Different Expectations

The evaluation had to balance the tension between the trustees' expectations that we would be able to say something meaningful about the value of their investment at a strategic level, and the individual projects' needs and expectations for ongoing evaluation capacity support and development.

Early in the evaluation, we worked with a group of trustees to define, in their terms, what it would look like if the MPEI was highly effective. This process resulted in the development of a performance framework that we used throughout the evaluation. The framework identified seven strategic evaluation criteria, together with the levels of performance expected by the trustees on each of these criteria. Exhibit 7.3 shows the high-level critieria we developed.

A real challenge for the evaluation was to be able to ensure that our collection of data cumulatively built a robust performance story with evidence relating to each of the criteria, so that we would have a solid enough basis for saying how effectively each strategy was unfolding, as well as how effective the MPEI was overall. We were quite intentional and deliberate about ensuring there were multiple sources of evidence for each project, and for each of the evaluation criteria. Exhibit 7.4 provides an overview of the range of data collection we undertook for each project.

There was nothing linear about the data collection process. It was far more organic than a more traditional evaluation. There were several factors driving the way in which the data collection process unfolded. One of these was the need to maintain the trustees' buy-in to the MPEI overall, as well as to the evaluation process. The trustees were at times impatient for evidence of outcomes and effectiveness. And yet the project development process was very uneven: Some projects developed more quickly than others, and for some projects, the ability to demonstrate their

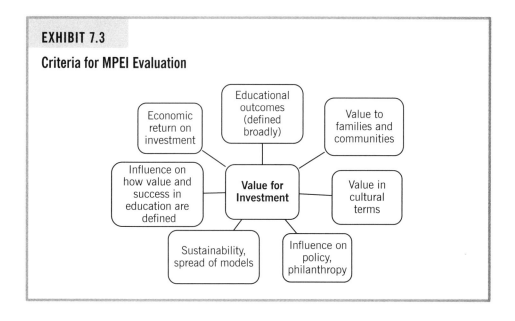

EXHIBIT 7.3

Criteria for MPEI Evaluation

EXHIBIT 7.4

Forms of Data Collection for MPEI Projects

MPEI project	Economic analysis	Analysis/review of educational data	Hui/fono/focus groups and interviews	Review of administrative data, including milestone reports	Regular face-to-face visits	Photovoice/testimonies from young people	Digital impact story
C-Me	×	×	×	×	×	×	×
Sylvia Park	×	×	×	×	×		×
Rise UP	×	×	×	×	×	×	×
Ideal Success	×	×	×	×	×		×
Leadership Academy	×	×	×	×	×	×	×
Unitec		×	×	×	×		
High Tech Youth Network	×			×	×	×	
Manaiakalani		×	×	×	×		
MITE			×	×	×	×	

effectiveness and measure outcomes was always going to be a longer-term process. So we developed our data collection process tactically to ensure that each time we reported to the trustees, we were able to present some quantitative data such as individual outcome data or economic analyses; we mingled the quantitative data with qualitative data, such as digital and infographic stories and other qualitative feedback on project implementation.

Balancing these diverse reporting expectations was a new and unexpected challenge for us with the MPEI. In traditional evaluation, most of the formal reporting is done for funders; it usually takes the form of an evaluation report with fairly standard layout, and may also include PowerPoint presentations. We pretty much "learned as we went" about reporting in a developmental evaluation. Some of our early reporting experiences, even with the trustees, were a bit rocky. We were inclined to include too much detail in our reports and presentations, and this wasn't all that well received. So we came to realize that we needed to work collaboratively with management and staff at Foundation North in preparation for reporting and presenting to the trustees. It took us about midway through the evaluation to get it right for the trustees.

And so it was at this midway point that we gave a major presentation to the trustees on the initiative's progress. We received really positive feedback about the presentation, and our reporting was also well received. On this occasion, we had decided against one large report, and had produced several smaller reports focused on key topics of interest to the trustees.

Buoyed by the positive response, we presented the same material to the project leaders at a large meeting—but their response was not what we expected. They said to us, "Where are we in there? We can't see ourselves." From Māori and Pacific perspectives, the reporting didn't capture the essence of who they were or the value they were creating at all. The reports were in our words, not theirs. It was a very salutary lesson. Because of our commitment to ensuring that providers' voices would be strong and clear in the evaluation, we changed tactics in terms of our planning for reporting. We developed infographic stories with some of the projects, and digital stories for some as well. We also engaged with some of the projects in using an adapted form of photovoice, so that the voices of the young people themselves would be more audible in our reporting. Exhibit 7.5 is an example of one of the infographics developed for one of the projects.

One of the other lessons we learned at this point was not necessarily to rely on ourselves to provide "voices" for projects. Foundation North had demonstrated a commitment to including providers' voices from the beginning of the MPEI. The foundation had engaged a very experienced narrative researcher and writer to gather each of the project's stories, and to document and compile a narrative of the MPEI's progress. The narrative stories and publications produced by the foundation are a rich resource that has been well received by the projects, the trustees, and a wider range of interested stakeholders.

EXHIBIT 7.5

An Infographic Developed for the Rise UP Trust

Developmental Evaluation and Evaluation Capacity Building

We had dual roles on the MPEI project: supporting and evaluating the development of an innovative approach to philanthropic investment, as well as supporting the evaluative capacity development of each of the individual projects. Each project was innovative in its own right—each trying to disrupt the systemic inertia preventing Māori and Pacific young people from succeeding in education. And most of the projects were also "startup" organizations, so they were developing their own internal capacity and capabilities to implement their visions.

There are stages of organizational capacity development, and the transitions from one stage to the next in the MPEI were not necessarily linear. We learned that this process can't necessarily be rushed. For some projects, it went relatively smoothly; for others, it was full of ups and downs, opportunities and setbacks along the way. Each project had its own unique combination and interplay of organizational characteristics and dynamics, and being effective in supporting each of them to develop the capacity to become evaluative depended on our having a nuanced understanding of the context for each project and organization.

This evaluation capacity developmental pathway was unique to each project; there were no simple "off-the-shelf" recipes. Across the MPEI providers, we found a really diverse range of provider mindsets and buy-in to evaluation capacity building. Some immediately recognized the importance of evaluation, prioritized their efforts to engage in it, and were highly motivated to build their own capacity. Others already had evaluation capacity and felt they didn't really need our support. Still others, while they recognized the importance of evaluation, struggled to prioritize it and would have preferred us to be more "hands-on" (i.e., to do more of the actual evaluative work ourselves). Not surprisingly, for some projects the ultimate drivers of their motivation and desire for evaluation capacity support were sustainability and ongoing funding.

A key learning from our experience is that just as there is no one-size-fits-all developmental evaluation approach, there simply is no one-size-fits-all approach to evaluation capacity building. It's a dance between doing evaluation *with*, building capacity to do evaluation *as*, and just doing evaluation *for*. It all depends on the context.

As our approach evolved, some key aspects of evaluation capacity building that we have learned are important include these:

- Focusing on and prioritizing our relationships with the key people in the organizations. As our relationships developed with the different projects and people within the organizations, we came to know their different skills sets and knowledge, and we gradually got better at working out who was best to contact for different evaluation needs.

- Committing to building a trusted relationship with each other over time.

- Having a mutual respect for each other's expertise, so we can pool our resources and harness our mutual energy and passions.

- Working collaboratively to co-produce tools, systems, and practices that contribute to the outcomes valued by each organization.

- Having transparent and open dialogue with each other about what we are doing, and how it's working (or not).

- Getting the buy-in of the funding bodies at both operational and governance levels, for both the developmental evaluation process and its costs.

- Focusing on what is pragmatic and possible within the resources available.

Cultural Politics and Ethics

The evaluation of the MPEI posed a number of political and ethical challenges that were constantly visited and revisited throughout the evaluation process. On the one hand, the evaluation client was grounded in Western systems of knowledge, politics, and power, albeit expressing a desire to support Māori and Pacific communities to determine the solutions for themselves. On the other hand, most of the MPEI projects were from, and of, Māori and Pacific communities. The evaluation team was commissioned to use a developmental evaluation approach to support evaluation capacity development within the projects, and also to evaluate the overall worth of the initiative's investment. So the evaluation had to face two ways: It had to try to balance being both client- and project-facing. In this respect, the evaluation was going to have to walk in several cultural spaces in the Western, Māori, and Pacific worlds. We recognized from the beginning that we would be reaching across and straddling cultural divides, and that we had a responsibility to advance understandings on all sides where we could—while at the same time questioning and potentially challenging systemic inequalities that did not support the aspirations of Māori and Pacific communities, given the vision of the initiative.

There is now a considerable body of literature on what is generally considered good evaluation practice in Māori and Pacific contexts (Barnes, 2013; Chilisa, 2012; Cram, 2001). Indigenous people express emancipatory, aspirational goals for themselves in this literature, as well as a strong desire for research and evaluation practice that is respectful as well as enriching for those participating in it. However, there is only a small amount of literature that speaks to the challenges of undertaking evaluation in historically contested and highly politicized contexts in ways that might authentically and with integrity recognize the aspirations of key evaluation partners (Jones with Jenkins, 2008).

Although the MPEI evaluation team comprised Māori, Pacific, and Pākehā evaluators, right from the outset we were faced with the political and ethical challenge of who should hold the MPEI contract. Our commitment, as a team, to evaluation that upholds Māori and Pacific aspirations and self-determination was tested when it became clear that the senior Māori evaluator was not in a position to hold the contract in this instance. So it came to be that a senior Pākehā evaluator held the contract for an evaluation of a Māori and Pacific initiative. This was not an easy situation to reconcile, and one that we were constantly challenged about, by our evaluation peers as well as by some of the project staff members themselves. In this instance, we made a choice to be Western-facing; it was a decision we made collectively, in full knowledge of the thin line we were treading.

The ethical and political challenges were many and varied throughout the evaluation process. The lesson we learned as each new challenge emerged was the importance of demonstrating a commitment to building connections and sustaining relationships with the Māori and Pacific communities we were engaging with. For us to have credibility in these communities, we needed to be seen and perceived as being prepared to walk alongside them for the long term. We didn't get it right in every case. But wherever possible, we worked to try to give the communities the option of choosing their evaluators, and then to sustain a relationship with the same evaluators over the course of the project.

Another important lesson reinforced during the MPEI evaluation was the importance of being able to recognize the limits of our cultural capabilities, in different contexts. There is simply no substitute for Māori and Pacific cultural expertise, leadership, and knowledge when it comes to knowing and understanding what is going on in Māori and Pacific communities (Bell, 2014).

What Did We Learn?

Through the MPEI developmental evaluation, we learned that fundamentally, developmental evaluation is relational. It is through relationships that the evaluation process unfolds, and that learning and change happen. Relationships are not something an evaluator simply pays attention to; they are inextricably the core business of developmental evaluation. How we as evaluators are positioned in relation to each other, and to programs and funders, matters. Our histories and other relationships are often more important than our evaluation skills and knowledge, particularly in Māori and Pacific contexts.

In a developmental evaluation, the evaluators become part of the development and history of the initiative, and therefore an integral part of the knowledge, stories, and memories that are shared about the initiative. The nature of our accountability as evaluators becomes a critical aspect of our way of working. That is, we need to critically examine and consider the many expectations of our relationships with those we are engaging with.

In the MPEI situation, where we were navigating Māori, Pacific, and Western contexts, the complexities of our accountabilities and relationships took on political and ethical significances that were constantly in play. Our positions as Pākehā, Māori, and Pacific evaluators in regard to each other were already pretty complex—and added to these were our relationships with each of the projects, and with the foundation staff and trustees.

We have learned that there are no simple recipes or "best practices" for respectful relationships. Relationship building is an ongoing process that is fluid and unfolding. It requires commitment, attention, awareness, and communication.

There are ups and downs, but through them all there are tremendous opportunities to work in solidarity and to make changes that will result in a more just world for present and future generations (Davis & Shpuniarsky, 2010, p. 347).

Summary of the MPEI's Achievements

The MPEI was a new way of working for Foundation North. It was a courageous move. And today there is no doubt that the MPEI has been been a success. Projects have achieved improvements in a wide range of educational outcomes for students and their families—including (but not limited to) academic achievement, engagement, retention, attitudes, and aspirations. The vast majority of projects are achieving outcomes that their families and communities value.

All projects have demonstrated good evidence and examples of educational success occurring in its wider framing. The examples include improved student attitudes to learning and life aspirations; families that are more engaged in their children's education, with higher aspirations for themselves and their children; improvement in family functioning and relationships; and increased rates of digital literacy, student engagement, and retention.

The spread and increased scope of several projects are strong indicators that the projects' outcomes are widely valued.

A number of the projects provide solid examples of what success for Māori and Pacific learners looks like when education is culturally grounded and strengths-based. The projects' models of delivery provide strong examples that reinforce existing policy settings and research evidence for achieving success for Māori and Pacific learners.

Evaluative economic analyses suggest that a positive return on investment seems highly plausible over the longer term, considering the impacts of the MPEI projects to date.

The foundation's high-engagement funding approach has gained interest among other philanthropic organizations and funders. Moreover, the success of the MPEI has contributed to the adaptation of this first approach into the foundation's longer-term investment strategy, with the formation of a Centre for Social Impact that will lead the foundation's high-engagement investment into the future.

There is no doubt in our minds that the foundation's deep commitment to the vision of the MPEI, and its courage to innovate in its investment approach as well as its evaluation approach, have been key ingredients in the success of the MPEI.

It seems fitting that we should end with the words of one of the young Pacific people:

> "Everything has an outcome, and if you cannot vision it, then you cannot achieve it. There are many opportunities that lie before us, things that are still to discover, and all we need to do is open our eyes."
>
> —ADAM KING (age 12 years)

REFERENCES

Abma, T. A., & Widdershoven, G. A. M. (2008). Evaluation and/as social relation. *Evaluation, 14*(2), 209–225.

Anae, M. (2010). Research for better Pacific schooling in New Zealand: Teu le va—a Samoan perspective. *MAI Review, 1*, 1–24.

Barnes, A. (2013). *What can Pākehā learn from engaging in Kaupapa Māori educational research?* (Working Paper No. 1). Wellington: New Zealand Council for Educational Research.

Bell, A. (2014). *Relating Indigenous and settler identities: Beyond domination.* Basingstoke, UK: Palgrave Macmillan.

Brennan, K. (2013, November). *Developmental evaluation: An approach to evaluating complex social change initiatives.* Paper presented at the conference Next Generation Evaluation: Embracing Complexity Connectivity and Change, Stanford University, Stanford, CA.

Chilisa, B. (2012). *Indigenous research methodologies.* Thousand Oaks, CA: Sage.

Cram, F. (2001). Rangahau Māori: Tona Tika, Tona Pono. In M. Tolich (Ed.), *Research ethics in Aotearoa* (pp. 35–52). Auckland, New Zealand: Longman.

Davis, L., & Shpuniarsky, H. Y. (2010). The spirit of relationships: What we have learned about Indigenous/non-Indigenous alliances and coalitions. In L. Davis (Ed.), *Alliances: Re/envisioning Indigenous–non-Indigenous relationships* (pp. 334–348). Toronto: University of Toronto Press.

Hancock, F. (2009). *Māori and Pacific Education Initiative thinkpiece.* Auckland, New Zealand: ASB Community Trust.

Hancock, F., & MPEI Contributors. (2012). *He Akoranga He Aratohu, Māori and Pacific Education Initiative: Lessons to guide innovative philanthropic and social practice.* Auckland, New Zealand: ASB Community Trust.

Hancock, F., & MPEI Contributors. (2013). *Nga Maumaharatanga, Māori and Pacific Education Initiative: Our journey of forging philanthropic innovation together.* Auckland, New Zealand: ASB Community Trust.

Jones, A., with Jenkins, K. (2008). Rethinking collaboration: Working the Indigene-colonizer hyphen. In N. K. Denzin, Y. S. Lincoln, & L. T. Smith (Eds.), *Handbook of critical Indigenous methodologies* (pp. 471–486). Thousand Oaks, CA: Sage.

Maister, D., Green, C. H., & Galford, R. M. (2000). *The trusted advisor.* New York: Free Press.

Patton, M. Q. (2011). *Developmental evaluation: Applying complexity concepts to enhance innovation and use.* New York: Guilford Press.

Pipi, K. (2012, January). *A Māori cultural framework for developmental evaluation.* Workshop presented at the annual conference of the African Evaluation Association, Accra, Ghana.

Wehipeihana, N. (2011). *Developmental Evaluation Workshop Series.* Australasian Evaluation Society.

Westley, F., Zimmerman, B., & Patton, M. Q. (2006). *Getting to maybe: How the world is changed.* Toronto: Random House Canada.

CHAPTER 8

Developmental Evaluation in the McKnight Foundation's Collaborative Crop Research Program

A Journey of Discovery

Marah Moore and Jane Maland Cady

A journey is a person in itself; no two are alike. And all plans,
safeguards, policing, and coercion are fruitless. We find that
after years of struggle that we do not take a trip; a trip takes us.
—JOHN STEINBECK

EDITORS' INTRODUCTION

Here's a portrait of complexity: well over 100 agricultural research grants in four parts of the world (the Andes and eastern, southern, and western Africa); four regional communities of practice made up of diverse experts coordinating and developing these projects; both technical and programmatic leadership essential at the overall coordination level; two major philanthropic funders, the McKnight Foundation and the Gates Foundation; a dialogic, consensus-oriented, inclusive decision-making process; and a process of supporting specialized agricultural researchers to become systems thinkers, deal with issues like gender and equity, buy into an overarching theory of change, and (oh, yes) embrace evaluation. And that's only the proverbial tip of the iceberg.

This chapter tells the story of how this global initiative, which continues to this day, has developed in its current iteration since 2008. It also tells the parallel story of the developmental evaluation that has been an integral part of this phase of the initiative's development. Central to that story is the close working relationship between the evaluator and program director "as they traversed the landscape of developmental evaluation." In this chapter, they engage in open and honest dialogue about their experiences, and they generate important insights that are deeply personal—while at the same time generally relevant for anyone engaged in complex systems change.

143

Utilization-focused evaluation emphasizes the importance of the personal factor. That is, who are involved in an evaluation, how they think, and what they care about make all the difference. Marah Moore, lead evaluator for the Collaborative Crop Research Program (CCRP), and Jane Maland Cady, director of international programs at the McKnight Foundation, are *naturals*. They are natural collaborators; it's the way they prefer to operate. They are natural visionaries, operating from a place of deep value commitments to social justice, equity, and the elimination of hunger worldwide. They are naturals in working at systems change through the lens of complexity; it's how they think. And they have a natural inclination toward developmental evaluation.

Here's an example of Marah Moore's natural inclination toward developmental evaluation. She served as the evaluator for a community partnership for some 10 years, working closely with its leaders to track and inform their very dynamic, emergent work. This work was instrumental in helping the partnership adjust its approaches to be more effective in developing new programs for its neighborhood-based work. She remembers telling a colleague about her close working relationship. "But that's not evaluation," he protested. She recalls, "All I could say at the time was, 'Well, that's how I do evaluation.' Had I had the terminology, I could have said, 'Yes, it is—it's developmental evaluation,'" but this conversation took place before the term *developmental evaluation* was coined. That's evidence of a natural developmental evaluator.

Years ago, Jane Maland Cady and Michael Quinn Patton worked together on a farming systems project for the Minnesota Extension Service. A major challenge was getting agricultural specialists (agronomists, soil scientists, crop specialists) to think in terms of whole farm systems. Jane was adept at helping specialists broaden their perspective. She demonstrated a natural predilection for systems thinking and bringing others into that perspective. Now, as this case illuminates, she's doing these things on a global level on one of the most urgent issues of our time: nutritious food security for people in poverty through sustainable agro-ecological intensification.

We think you'll both enjoy and learn from Jane and Marah as they tell together the story of CCRP, reflect on what they've learned, and offer insights about developmental evaluation.

This is the story of a journey.

More accurately, it is three journeys, three braids woven into a single complex story. The first journey—our primary focus—is the long road of an evaluation, that of the McKnight Foundation's Collaborative Crop Research Program (CCRP), unfolding over a number of years. But interdependent with that journey is the story of CCRP, which is itself a journey with a complex and unique evolution. And tied to these two interwoven stories is the sense of journey on a personal level: the paths taken by an evaluator and a program director as they traversed the landscape of developmental evaluation. All of these have been journeys of discovery—discovery that has grown out of both challenges and successes. And for each of these three threads, we gradually grew to understand that the journey became an end in itself. In other words, to fully engage in and stay present with each moment of the journey was to experience the destination.

Marah Moore, the lead evaluator for CCRP, and Jane Maland Cady, the director of international programs at the McKnight Foundation, are the "we" telling this story. Although we strive to tell a story that is accurate and somewhat objective, we acknowledge that there are multiple truths, and that our experience is always shaped by our subjective experience. But this is the power of developmental evaluation: It doesn't try to erase differences of perspective and experience; rather, it facilitates the understanding of difference and informs forward movement that embraces difference. With that caveat, we begin by introducing CCRP, the moving landscape across which we have traveled; we describe the introduction of a systematic evaluation into that evolving landscape; we chart our journeys through four key challenges we met and overcame; and at the end of this story, we tell you what discoveries we brought home from our journeys—to inform our next adventures, and to share with others ready to set out on similar paths.

The Landscape: The Collaborative Crop Research Program

In the mid-1980s, the board of the Minnesota-based McKnight Foundation became increasingly concerned about the world food crisis. Millions of people in developing countries were starving due to a combination of poor crop production, increasing population, an economic downturn, and political conflict. Food production and distribution systems did not reach the growing number of mouths to feed. In response, the foundation launched its Plant Biology Program to promote interdisciplinary research in plant science. Anticipating breakthroughs that would lead to greater crop yields, the McKnight Foundation hoped to help reduce world hunger.

The Plant Biology Program laid the groundwork for the reformulated CCRP, established in 1993. Together, these long-term efforts have provided over $130 million through grant funds to further collaborative research among smallholder farmers, leading local researchers, and development practitioners. CCRP reflects the

---

EXHIBIT 8.1

Program History: What and When

PLANT BIOLOGY PROGRAM

1983, $18.5 million (U.S. dollars throughout). Focus: Promoting interdisciplinary research in plant science to help reduce world hunger.

COLLABORATIVE CROP RESEARCH PROGRAM (CCRP)

1993, $15 million. Focus: Supporting collaborative agricultural research in developing countries, with leadership from developing countries and partners from northern universities.

2000, $41.5 million. Focus: Adding three communities of practice (CoPs) for stronger local leadership and collaboration.

2008, $47 million + $51.5 million from external private foundation. **Focus:** Adding a fourth CoP; expanding local grant-making capacity through regional consultants; increasing technical support to grantees; and increasing emphasis on programwide evaluation.

foundation's long-time commitment to place-based grant making and learning from those working on the ground. Exhibit 8.1 provides a brief history of CCRP, and Exhibit 8.2 sets forth its vision and mission.

In the spring of 2008, Jane Maland Cady was hired by the McKnight Foundation to fill a new position as its director of international programs. As part of this role, she was presented with the challenge of reintegrating CCRP into the McKnight Foundation grant-making processes, as well as responding to the potential doubling of grant funds through a pending grant from the Bill and Melinda Gates Foundation.

In July of that year, Jane brought in a team of people to begin designing an evaluation system for CCRP. Marah was part of that team.

A Call to Action: Designing an Evaluation System for CCRP

The journey of a thousand miles begins with one step.
—LAO TZU

The McKnight Foundation's CCRP has evolved and expanded from its beginnings in 1993. The intent and approach of the program remain true to the "DNA" of the McKnight Foundation, whose mission is to "attend, unite, and empower through grant making, collaboration, and strategic policy reform"—all with a commitment to innovation and relationships with local leaders and practitioners on the ground. These are the broad principles that undergird everything the foundation engages in. By focusing attention on smallholder farmers, CCRP prioritizes place-based knowledge and values decentralized innovation. In order to minimize the disempowerment that grows out of a "tyranny of experts," CCRP supports meaningful alliances among farmers, nongovernmental organization practitioners, researchers, and policy makers, all linked through a regional community of practice (CoP).

However, when CCRP's scope more than doubled in 2008, it became increasingly complex and unwieldy: 65 projects in four regions and 12 countries working with 24 different crops and addressing challenges across the agrological spectrum, including breeding, agronomy, markets, food preparation, storage, and postharvest value addition. The program leadership grew to include an expanded advisory

Marah: "Jane and I first met in 2004 at the American Evaluation Association (AEA) annual meeting, and at the time we were both practicing evaluators. We crossed paths again in 2005 through our engagement in the Human Systems Dynamics Institute, where we were learning about systems thinking and its application to practice. As two of only three evaluators in a group of organizational development practitioners, we bonded over the effort to understand how to apply systems thinking and complex systems concepts to our evaluation work. When Jane was hired by the McKnight Foundation to direct its international programs, she invited me to become part of a team to design and implement an evaluation for CCRP. It was very exciting to have a program like CCRP to work with: Not only was the program a perfect fit for a systems-based evaluation, but having a program director who didn't need convincing and was fully on board felt like a gift."

Jane: "I was hired to direct McKnight's international programs because of my background as an evaluator, my experience in agricultural research and development, and my interest in systems science. I was excited about the potential to infuse evaluation into a program's operational system, and I had a hunch that the opportunity would exist at the McKnight Foundation. I remember talking with Marah shortly before I was hired at the McKnight Foundation about the potential to advance systems approaches to evaluation as part of program planning and evaluation. We shared similar dreams. As I settled into the new job at the foundation, I clearly saw that all the transition in CCRP called for a systems-based, emergence-oriented approach. The program was changing even as we were trying to design the evaluation; it was a bit like building a bicycle while you are riding it. I could see that we needed to introduce more coherence and order—not through heightened bureaucracy, but through policies and processes that allowed us to remain flexible, reflective, and responsive to change. At that time, developmental evaluation and systems evaluation had begun to be talked about at AEA quite extensively. The McKnight Foundation's CCRP was a great place to utilize and advance both approaches."

committee; four regional teams providing support to and representing four CoPs in each of the four CCRP regions; a program director and scientific director; and the evaluation team. With the addition of all these new people contributing to program leadership came a commensurate increase in the diversity in understanding what the program should be about and how it should be implemented. This disciplinarily diverse group was striving to know each other and build trust among themselves, as well as to understand the program.

Prior to 2008, CCRP held minimal systematic evaluation requirements. Project evaluation happened through annual reporting; program-level evaluation was limited to periodic external evaluation reviews; and researchers shared progress at annual CoP meetings. Beyond that, there were limited frameworks, little reflective consciousness, and few formal protocols for sharing findings. Monitoring and evaluation (M&E) consisted largely of the individual projects' documenting their research process and results. The synthesis of evaluation findings happened either during the 5- to 6-year program reviews, or when results were compiled in an ad hoc way, responding to situation-specific program-level inquiries.

When Jane brought in a team consisting of an evaluator, a systems-based organizational development practitioner, a food systems expert, and an evaluation thought leader as a "critical friend" to design an evaluation system for CCRP, she was hoping for an evaluation that would encourage coherence, help to deepen understanding of the interrelated systems that underlie all aspects of CCRP, and document results more rigorously (Eoyang, 1997; Parsons, 2010; Westley, Zimmerman, & Patton, 2006). In essence, the hope was to construct a program "operating system" informed by systematic and iterative evaluation practice. In support of this intent, we began referring to the CCRP evaluation system as Integrated Monitoring, Evaluation, and Planning—which was quickly shortened to IMEP.

When we began to work together to design the evaluation, we hadn't determined that IMEP would be a developmental evaluation. The term *developmental evaluation* had only recently appeared on the landscape, and Michael Quinn Patton's seminal book on the approach, released in 2011, was still more than 2 years in the future. Understanding the complexities of the program, we were committed to designing a systems-based evaluation, but when we talked about the application of developmental evaluation to CCRP, it wasn't yet clear which parts of the program should be addressed through a developmental lens and which called for more traditional approaches. In what ways was the program itself developing, and how much was development constrained by grant-making processes and protocols? Could the project-level research be approached with a developmental perspective, or must this type of research be conducted in a more controlled setting?

Although we weren't clear about how developmental evaluation might apply at the program and project levels, we were fairly confident that we could, and perhaps should, apply a developmental evaluation approach to the CoP work that was happening within the four CCRP regions. The four CoPs were in very different stages: One had just been formed, and the oldest had been together about 4 years. The newly constituted regional teams were figuring out how best to support the projects, based on the projects' needs and the evolving circumstances in the regions. In addition, the foundation was investing a lot of resources into regional support for projects, and particularly into the CoP model. Not only did the foundation hope to understand whether these were resources well spent, but it would serve everybody well to have an evaluation in place that could guide the work of the regions as it was unfolding.

But what would it mean to implement a developmental evaluation at one of the three program levels, while doing something different at the other two? We were, after all, interested in an *integrated* evaluation in which information flowed seamlessly among all levels. We acknowledged these questions and quandaries, and held them lightly as we continued to design the evaluation.

The First Challenge: Building Credibility

Don't try to lure me to believe in what you believe, if your
believe [*sic*] is worthy to be believed, then I will believe.
                                —Michael Bassey Johnson

The first phase of the evaluation was exploratory. We reviewed project documents, spoke extensively with project staff members, and conducted interviews with regional teams and advisory committee members. This process confirmed what we had suspected: Different stakeholders had different interpretations of the purpose and approach that CCRP took and/or should take. We knew at this point that one important function for the evaluation would be to build coherence across the program. We began by developing a series of guiding questions that were to be used by projects, the regions, and the program. These questions were shaped by the "simple rules" of "attend, unite, and empower" (the McKnight Foundation mission), and were built on an adaptive action framework: "What? So what? Now what?" (Eoyang & Holladay, 2013). The idea was that regular structured conversations would take place at least twice per year to review and interpret information, and these conversations would inform planning for the next steps. We called this a *generative dialogue*. Results of the project-level generative dialogues would feed up to inform the regional dialogues; likewise, the regional dialogues would inform the program-level dialogues. We believed that this process would increase coherence and foster data-based decision making.

In October 2008, 3 months after we began to work on the CCRP evaluation, the two of us went together to Mozambique to participate in a CoP meeting and to pilot the generative dialogue. In Mozambique, crop scientists presented scientific findings in a very formal setting. There was a lot of talk about scientific methods and the isolated technological outputs; there was not much talk about farmers. The response to the generative dialogue by the regional team was less than positive: "What is this 'generative dialogue'? *This* is how you are going to evaluate CCRP?" We left with a deeper understanding of the program, and slightly less social capital. We knew that we did not yet have credibility, and that we had to earn trust. We still believed strongly in the concept of adaptive action, but we saw that people heard "generative dialogue" as empty jargon. We regrouped, dropped the term *generative dialogue*, and continued with our exploratory work.

Following the trip to Mozambique, we identified four core principles that seemed to undergird the work of CCRP: equity, sustainability, self-determination, and resilience. Together with the overarching outcomes of the program—productivity, livelihoods, and nutrition—we hoped that these principles would help to shape our inquiry. Using these principles and outcomes, we did a thorough review of project documents. We read all of the project proposals and 3 years' worth of annual reports to assess the extent to which the projects focused on these principles and outcomes. We also assessed the quality of project evaluation across the program. We presented the results of this assessment in January at the first CCRP leadership team meeting in Brazil, in January 2009. Once again, the response was less than positive. The leadership team members did not feel that they had been adequately involved in identifying the core principles. The regional teams (which were part of the leadership team) were upset that they hadn't had a chance to vet the assessment process and the results that came from it prior to that meeting. In general, the leadership team was wary of the systems language being used. All of these reactions were heightened by the fact that Marah did not have a background in agriculture—she was leading the evaluation because of her evaluation experience and her focus on systems-based evaluation—and those who had lived, eaten, and breathed agriculture over the course of long careers were skeptical. As before, our credibility was low, and we had to earn trust. We left with an even deeper understanding of the program, and still less social capital.

Although the assessment results were not well received, they provided valuable information. The results revealed key areas for improvement at the project level. Most projects lacked a truly functional M&E plan, with most existing M&E focused almost entirely on process monitoring. The task for IMEP, we thought at the time, would be fairly straightforward. We would support researchers to tighten up their M&E plans by asking more evaluative questions and identifying clear and appropriate methods for data collection and analysis. At the same time, the program would clarify the CCRP goals and adjust grant making to fit.

Marah: "That first leadership team meeting in Brazil, and its aftermath, were demoralizing. We had done a lot of work in a very short amount of time, and the feedback was fairly negative. There was pushback on our systems-based approach, on our analytical framework, and even on the attempt to do a baseline cross-project assessment. While the foundation felt a need for greater coherence, the members of the regional teams who had been working on the ground for the past few years did not feel the same need. For them, the program was working fine the way it was; why were we stirring the pot? What was wrong with the way things had been done up to now, and what made us think that we knew better than they? In many people's minds, there was nothing broken, so why were we coming in and trying to fix it? And conflict had begun to surface within our evaluation team. Some of the team members wanted to keep things very simple; they felt that the generative dialogue alone would provoke change in a deep and sustainable way. Others of us felt that we needed more—more focused evaluation questions, and higher-quality data and data analysis. I was an experienced evaluator, with over 20 years working on a wide variety of projects—many quite large and complex—and yet I began to feel tinges of doubt creeping in. Did I really know what I was doing? Was I setting myself up for failure? In the midst of this doubt, it was important that Jane and I were on the same page. Fundamentally, we trusted and respected each other."

Jane: "I knew that there was an opportunity here to advance some needed and important work for CCRP. Having been an evaluator, I had a bias toward thinking that infusing evaluative thinking into program processes was a way to do that—but I knew that it had to be a systems-based, emergent approach that was useful and could support the geographical scale and the complexity of food and agriculture systems aiming to improve nutrition, support holistic sustainability, and improve livelihoods for smallholder farmers. At the same time, I was entering philanthropy from the other side: I was just learning about grant making, about the McKnight Foundation's organizational systems and culture, and about CCRP. The systems thinking made sense to me, having been studying it for several years. I was taken aback by the negative reactions from our initial sharing of concepts. After the first leadership team meeting, I knew that I had to stay highly involved to make this evaluation work. Developing the focus and the evaluation system, and turning that into practice for the program, were challenging, and the stakes were high. I had a lot riding on this in terms of my own credibility at the foundation, and I wanted to make sure it worked to best support the program. My deep involvement early on was important, but it caused some tension down the road. There came a point where I had to back off a bit when it no longer served the process."

As we approached the end of our first year of work, we realized that moving to an M&E system that supported the complexity of CCRP required a paradigm shift at both the project and program levels, and we had to adjust our expectations and approach. We realized that the CCRP evaluation had to serve two broad functions. First, the evaluation needed to guide decision making about program implementation and improvement at the project, region, and program levels; second, it needed to document project and program success. To achieve this, we needed to focus attention both on developing systems to embed a reflective learning process, and on strengthening M&E capacity, skills, processes, and structures. Both tasks would need to be effectively implemented across all levels of CCRP, and both would have to contribute to program coherence. We understood our mandate to extend well beyond supporting individual project M&E. The design and implementation of the CCRP evaluation, we understood, would have to be driven by a bigger question: "How can we maximize our impact by generating insight and learning that are bigger than 65 projects?"

And the message had been loud and clear: We could not do that without full support and buy-in by the leadership team. We knew that we needed to find mechanisms to engage the entire leadership team in the evaluation process, while still being able to move forward. And we would not do that without trust and credibility. We decided on two strategies: (1) continue to use the adaptive action framework ("What? So what? Now what?") in all meeting planning and facilitation; and (2) bring the leadership team together to collectively develop a CCRP theory of change (ToC).

We had dropped the term *generative dialogue*, but we didn't walk away from the underlying concept: At every opportunity, we asked, "What? So what? Now what?" Like magic, the questions stuck. The leadership team members began to use the framework explicitly in their CCRP work, and regional teams used it with their projects. When people saw that the process was effective for deepening reflection and arriving at shared understanding, they began to trust us more. The framework became the template upon which meetings were planned. It brought coherence to the reflective process, and with coherence of process, there was support for building coherence of concepts.

The Second Challenge: Finding Conceptual Coherence

He who loves practice without theory is like the sailor who boards ship
without a rudder and compass and never knows where he may cast.
—LEONARDO DA VINCI

The first big push to bring coherence to the concepts driving CCRP came at the end of the first year, when we engaged the leadership team in two webinars to collectively develop a CCRP ToC. This was a transformative moment, when, for the first time, the entire leadership team wrestled with the what, why, and how of CCRP. The ToC continues to evolve from that early version, and it provides a common framework for planning and evaluating the work. It is important to note here that while the process of coming together to create a ToC brought people together in a profound way, it took a number of years to build the *habit* of using the ToC to inform all planning.

This was the point at which we stopped wondering whether and where to incorporate developmental evaluation into the CCRP program-level evaluation. We didn't *decide* to conduct a developmental evaluation; we just realized that we were *doing* it, and the adaptive process became part of the collective vocabulary.

With that realization, we were able to begin articulating the importance of encouraging the projects to take a more developmental approach to their research. Just as the program was in a continuous state of "becoming" in response to the environment within which it was operating, we knew that the projects too could continue to adapt and adjust to changes—not just to changes in the environment, but also to changes in their own understanding of the issues they faced.

Excited by the success of the ToC work with the leadership team, we decided to incorporate ToC work with the projects. Although the research itself was somewhat set, the context within which the research was being conducted and the connections between the research outputs and the farmer-focused outcomes were more dynamic. If, we reasoned, project personnel could understand their work and conduct their project evaluations within a larger and more dynamic context, then there would be a greater chance that the research would actually have an impact on farmers' lives. We hoped that by understanding the larger picture, the grantees would be encouraged to develop more effective partnerships and implement participatory methods that were more likely to lead to outcomes. And we were designing the ToC work to provide coherence and transparency among the program, regions, and projects.

Full of enthusiasm and convinced that grantees would be as excited by this approach as we were, we initiated the project-level ToC work at a 5-day CoP meeting in Tanzania in fall 2009. While the grantees were polite, and some were even curious, there was confusion about why we were asking them to do something different. Most of them had logic models or logframes (logical frameworks) for their projects (the approach expected by most funders in international development programs), and they didn't see the ToC as substantially different. In addition, the limited time that we had to work on the ToCs at the CoP meeting wasn't adequate for project representatives to fully understand the process.

Undaunted, we took this as an opportunity to address the M&E skill gap in the projects while building ToC skills. There was a limit to the support we could provide from the other side of the world—and building local capacity is a core value for the McKnight Foundation—so we spent the next few months finding four local evaluators to provide M&E support in each region. In spring 2010, Marah spent 3 weeks in Africa working with the regional support people there to provide training in ToC and M&E planning. She then went to Ecuador that summer to introduce these concepts to projects in that region.

We learned some important lessons through this process. First, the projects were thrown into the ToC process full sail, and many of them were at a midpoint in their project implementation; it is not surprising that the process was a bit stormy. In retrospect, it probably would have been easier on everybody had we begun with projects at the beginning of their funding cycle, and engaged in a stepwise process of capacity building, moving slowly toward full implementation. And, in fact, the new projects were the ones that were most receptive to structuring their projects around ToCs.

Second, although building local capacity has merit, the way we approached it was not effective. We found that local evaluators had the same challenges that we had found in the projects: Most were used to focusing on process measures, and accustomed to implementing fairly static evaluation. Of even greater concern was the message that was conveyed through having M&E support separate from the other regional support functions. We had moved away from a logframe or logic model approach to a ToC approach, in order to better implement an evaluation

Marah: "After the theory-of-change [ToC] work with the leadership team members, I felt pretty good: They were on board, and we finally had a common framework to drive the evaluation. Not only that, but the ToC provided a framework that could serve to integrate evaluation, design, planning, and implementation across all levels of CCRP. Then we dove into the work with the projects, and the feeling of success began to unravel. The projects didn't understand the value of the approach, and the local support people we had brought on were taking more time to manage and train than we had anticipated. As this was unfolding, I realized that not only was CCRP continuously developing (making it a great fit for a developmental evaluation), but, just like the program, the evaluation was under development too. It sometimes felt like for the first 3 or 4 years we learned more about what worked in the evaluation by initially getting it wrong and by crawling through windows of opportunity. Looking back, I can appreciate the process, and I see that the trial-and-error approach was necessary for maneuvering the complexities of the program and the diversity of people involved. But going through it, I continued to have moments (hours, days, weeks) of doubt, questioning my competence and wondering if I was the right evaluator to guide this process. Most of the projects I had worked on previously had been developmental in nature, and I prided myself on my ability to live in the realm of ambiguity. CCRP brought this to a new level, and I had to do a lot of soul searching (and venting) to stay with the unfolding."

Jane: "My excitement about the progress of creating ToCs with the leadership team reinforced my conviction that we could do this at the project levels. Each turn we took at the project level that caused pushback was another challenge to overcome. I knew we could make this operating system work. But after continuous pushback from multiple places—grantees, evaluation approaches, support in the field—combined with my growing understanding of philanthropy, I began to question that conviction. Was all this effort to do something effective from a developmental systems perspective really worth it? I began to wonder if all the extra effort really mattered for program learning, planning, and implementation. Perhaps annual reports and occasional interactions were enough. Perhaps it was just another funder mandating grantee priorities? Marah and I had many long talks about this. We were able to ask deep and important questions about how it should work, what was wrong; we could examine our contribution to the pushback, and so on. I trusted Marah, and I trusted the other members of the IMEP support team. And, fundamentally, I trusted what we were trying to create—a complex and adaptive global grant-making program that utilized evaluative thinking at its core to implement the program."

design that was integrated into project planning and implementation. Eventually, we realized that having M&E support coming in from outside reinforced the idea that M&E was something separate from the actual project work—exactly the opposite of what we were trying to reinforce. Ultimately, we trained the regional teams to integrate M&E support into the research support they were providing to the projects. We came to this decision through a back door, when one of the evaluation support people quit suddenly, and the regional team stepped in "temporarily." But it stuck and it became a perfect fit for IMEP; this modeled the fully integrated approach we had envisioned. Not only were the regional team members in a better position to support the project M&E because of their familiarity with the projects, but working through the ToC and M&E planning with projects helped them to understand the projects at a deeper level.

The Third Challenge: Systematizing a Dynamic Process without Losing Its Heart and Soul

I would not give a fig for the simplicity this side of complexity, but I would give my life for the simplicity on the other side of complexity.
—OLIVER WENDELL HOLMES, JR.

By now we were a good 3 years into the CCRP evaluation. We had embedded reflective practice into CCRP at all levels, using adaptive action and instituting regular, mandatory reflection times. We had embedded a ToC approach at the program, regional, and project levels, so that we could clearly articulate, test, and adapt the change hypotheses in play. The program ToC had been revised a couple of times, and was being used to structure discussions and planning. Most projects had ToCs and an evaluation plan, albeit most still needed some improvement. And we had data coming in from multiple directions. The 60+ projects were producing data through their research and, increasingly, through their evaluation. The regions were producing data when they completed annual Regional Analysis, Strategy, and Planning documents. And the program was producing data as its personnel interacted both within and outside the program boundaries. We found ourselves swimming in this data, and spending an inordinate amount of time combing through project reports to fill out spreadsheets in order to answer specific inquiries. It was clear that this was not sustainable and that we had arrived at a point where we needed to streamline the process of analyzing and synthesizing data so we could use the ToCs as a basis for identifying patterns, insights, and actions. This required that we put systems in place, and that we build the skills to make use of these systems.

From our work up to this point, we knew that the systems had to be robust enough to support a high degree of "back-and-forth" interpretation; they had to enhance our ability to work with the data, develop interpretations, get feedback, adapt, and revise. After the experience of reviewing annual project reports (some of which are hundreds of pages long) multiple times to answer different questions, we realized that we needed a system that would allow us to open a project report only once—to extract the key data and consolidate it for future use. In response, we took the following steps to systematize our data collection and analysis.

- *Developing a data system.* Given the complexity and diversity across the CCRP program, we knew that we needed to develop data systems that embraced heterogeneity while building coherence. Building on a database that was being developed in one of the regions, we developed a system called System for Monitoring or SyMon, which allows us both to aggregate (when appropriate) and to synthesize the vast array of diverse and disparate quantitative and qualitative data already available, in order to respond to the program evaluation questions. In addition to using the secondary data provided by the projects, we are also implementing interviews, surveys, and observations.

- *Building M&E skills.* We continue to work at building technical as well as conceptual skills related to evaluation at all levels of the CCRP—project, region, and program. We have developed a *Social Science Methods for Agronomists* handbook and an IMEP handbook, trained regional teams in CCRP's M&E approach, invited key strategic members to the American Evaluation Association's annual meeting, and engaged in regular IMEP phone calls. We have found that as a result of embedding iterative and reflective evaluation, research becomes more iterative and reflective as well.

- *Communicating and returning analysis to stakeholders at all levels.* Analysis is provided to stakeholders for further iterative interpretation that guides strategy and action. Every meeting at both the program and regional levels is now accompanied with slides and print material of aggregated and synthesized evaluative data. We encourage team members at project, region, and program levels to back up statements and planning with evidence.

When IMEP was first introduced, one of its mandates was to help build coherence within and across the program. The CCRP leadership team is a group of highly intelligent, creative, innovative individuals. New ways of organizing concepts and framing the work have grown out of the work that the CCRP leadership team has engaged in over many years. Although this process was often stimulating and productive, the introduction of new conceptual frameworks sometimes created chaos and division when they had not been vetted and agreed to by all stakeholders. The reflective practice that was embedded early on created a space and a process to vet conceptual frameworks that were introduced by various leadership team members. The ToC work helped to bound the creative energy so that the conceptualizing remained somewhat within the agreed-upon scope of CCRP. Building tools and processes for systematizing data collection and analysis has further helped support the creative process to remain productive and inclusive. As various frameworks have been adopted, data collection systems are built in response to them, allowing them to be "tested" and adapted in a way that is transparent to all stakeholders.

Marah: "To me, it was obvious: If we were expected to inform the program through cross-project, cross-region analysis, we needed a comprehensive database to manage the vast influx of information produced by CCRP. When we presented the idea, the leadership team was supportive. But when the database was ready to be piloted and populated, there was an outcry of dissent. There was concern that entering data would take too much time, and would require a level of interpretation that not everybody was comfortable doing. I think also that some of the pushback was because SyMon put parameters around the data collection and analysis; people were used to having an infinite canvas upon which to create. In a way, SyMon was where the rubber hit the road in terms of information-based decision making: It demanded that we collect accurate data against the theories that had been articulated, and use the data to make change in those theories and practice. Finally, I think that the complexity of CCRP had been somewhat invisible up to that point. The system that was created to manage CCRP's data was overwhelming to some people, and there was concern that we had 'made things too complicated.' Unlike some of my earlier reactions to pushback, this time I didn't question my own instincts or capacities. I knew that SyMon was complex because CCRP was complex. I knew that SyMon was a breakthrough in its ability to help us synthesize both qualitative and quantitative data. I fought hard for it, and Jane supported me; we really went out on a limb on this one, and I hoped we were right. What if we failed? What if we had burned all of our social capital on something that didn't work? When people started experiencing the utility of the system, and actually became grateful for the time it saved down the road, I breathed a sigh of relief."

Jane: "When I first saw the database that was developed in the Andes CoP, I was impressed by the potential for the entire program. Marah had been articulating for quite a while that we needed a better way to collect data across the program, so that we could have input into our adaptive action process ('What? So what? Now what?'). SyMon, as a primary tool, allowed us the opportunity to have more systematic information for the 'What?' question. In this, I know that having the program director's support for the system was important. There was a lot of pushback (data entry took too much time, responses weren't initially entered in a usable way, etc.). However, we built the data entry requirement into the contracts and annual work plans. Over time, people began to see what SyMon could do to support us in better understanding CCRP at its varied levels. Continuous improvement is also part of the plan, so that SyMon is supported to work better and help us understand our conceptual frameworks."

The Fourth Challenge: Rethinking Scale through a Developmental Lens

By thinking globally I can analyze all phenomena, but when it
comes to acting, it can only be local and on a grassroots level
if it is to be honest, realistic, and authentic.
        —JACQUES ELLUL, *Perspectives on Our Age*

As we entered the fifth year of the CCRP evaluation, we had a system in place that helped us to aggregate, synthesize, and make decisions based on different levels of program results: the outputs and outcomes achieved by the projects; changes in relationships, networks, and capacity stimulated by the CoPs; and the development of new conceptual models and approaches to international agricultural research.

This worked within the CCRP family. But in order to make a difference in people's lives, we had to think about how the work would ripple out beyond the boundaries of CCRP. For one thing, in the grand scheme of international agricultural research, CCRP was small; its budget was dwarfed by programs receiving funding from other major private foundations and from governments. In addition, a substantial portion of CCRP funding has been provided by the Bill and Melinda Gates Foundation. In other words, we were not just doing the best work we could as a program of the McKnight Foundation; the McKnight Foundation was also a grantee of another foundation with somewhat different ideas. And that other foundation was asking about scaling results.

In CCRP's work with smallholder farmers with limited resources in diverse environments, it has become clear that "going to scale" must look very different from replication of best practices; what is "best" in one place for a particular group of farmers is likely not to be "best" for other farmers in different places. Furthermore, we know that ideas spread in different ways, and that change happens through pathways such as inspiring and influencing continued adaptation and innovation, providing fundamental principles that undergird change, contextualizing evidence, developing frameworks for understanding, and advocating for policy changes from local to global scales.

The CCRP ToCs and other frameworks support expanded and contextualized thinking about how change happens and what it looks like. IMEP has provided a structure to talk about *scaling* as something well beyond the replication and dissemination of findings that is more typical in this field. *Success* has been redefined to include adaptive capacity and scale achieved through multiple mechanisms. In Exhibit 8.3, Jim Hancock (World Bank, 2003) depicts the differences between a universalist and a contextualized approach to scaling. With the universalist

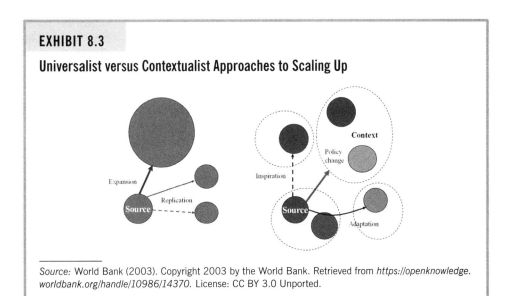

EXHIBIT 8.3

Universalist versus Contextualist Approaches to Scaling Up

approach, a model is pinned down and then expanded or replicated. Fidelity is measured by the extent to which the replication stays true to the model. A contextualist approach, on the other hand, goes beyond replication to include adaptation, inspiration, innovation, and policy change. It asks: What are processes that help take important elements and adapt them in new contexts, or that influence large-scale processes?

The evaluation questions that arise from a contextualized approach to scale include these: What are the factors for success, the principles that weave through difference? What are the drivers and influencers of change—that is, what catalyzes movement, and what helps it continue? What are the constraints and bottlenecks, and how can these be mitigated? What is the influence of the context, the enabling environment? What are the external triggers for change, and how can these be harnessed to nudge the work toward the desired outcomes? These are questions uniquely suited to a developmental approach to evaluation. IMEP systems are in place to encourage these lines of inquiry, and to collect and synthesize data about the what, why, and how of contextualized success.

To effectively implement a contextualized approach to scaling without losing the coherence we had fought so hard to create, we realized that we needed to articulate the underlying principles that shaped our work. When we began designing the evaluation in 2008, we recognized that we needed simple rules or agreements to keep us all moving in the same direction. As a newly expanded and restructuring program, we began then by using the McKnight Foundation's mission as a guide: to "attend, unite, and empower through grant making, collaboration, and strategic policy reform." Then we introduced the principles of equity, sustainability, resilience, and self-determination to guide the grant making and grantee support. From there, we have moved to explicit principles that have emerged more organically as we have all worked together. These include basic operating principles for the CCRP; principles for what constitutes and how to implement agro-ecological intensification; and principles for newly emerging farmer research networks. These principles provide a way to plan for, and measure the success of, "going to scale," and they provide fidelity measures that allow for a contextually responsive approach.

Coming Home: Lessons Learned

Act as if what you do makes a difference. It does.
—WILLIAM JAMES

Over the course of this journey—at this writing, 6 years of working together on the developmental evaluation of CCRP—we have learned a great deal. As we move forward with CCRP, this learning will continue to inform our work, both inside CCRP and as we engage with other projects. And though we know that all stories are unique, we hope that by sharing some of the most valuable lessons we have learned, we can help smooth the path for others as they engage in their own developmental evaluation journeys.

Developmental Evaluation Requires Time and Resources

We found that developmental evaluation and adaptive practice have a steep learning curve in an international research environment, and that this learning curve requires a paradigm shift about how to approach evaluation as well as research and development. This is probably true in situations outside the international development arena as well.

Because shifts in the fundamental ways people understand and implement their practice are not immediate, developmental evaluation can help move a program from abstract conceptual thinking to testing assumptions and hypotheses about how change happens "on the ground." For this to work, there has to be a commitment by all stakeholders to engage in the process of identifying key evaluation questions, collecting data against these questions, and using these data to inform adaptation. This requires a commitment of time and resources.

Developmental Evaluation Can Help Articulate and Reinforce Appropriate Boundaries

We found that the developmental evaluation process supports setting appropriate boundaries. At both the project and program levels, there were times and places where the scope and direction of the work were threatened because the goals and practices were overly ambitious and/or diffuse, and the work thus seemed to be losing its center. Developmental evaluation has been successful at helping to pull in the boundaries and focus the work by asking questions about purpose, methods, context, and capacity.

On the other hand, some projects and some program aspects have at times been overly rigid in their approach to their work. Some projects, for example, have had a difficult time shifting direction, even when the data point to the need; other projects have been inclined to remain narrowly focused on producing products without considering context or outcomes for people on the ground. The reflective, developmental approach to IMEP has pushed projects and the program to ask broader questions about the potential influence of their work, and to make adjustments or implement additional activities to strengthen this potential.

Developmental evaluation can become a powerful tool for identifying appropriate boundaries for a program or initiative—and these might be tighter or more expansive than the boundaries that are currently in place. Defining the boundaries makes it much easier to be clear about the scope and focus, to understand who needs to be at the table, and to identify the breadth of influence the project or initiative can expect to have.

Developmental Evaluation Supports Emergent Principles

At the start of this evaluation, CCRP did not have clearly articulated principles; we began by using the McKnight Foundation's mission, which proved useful as an agreed-upon core of the program. Beyond this, there was no shared understanding of the unspoken principles guiding CCRP's implementation. We found that the process of identifying the fundamental and shared beliefs about how change happens in a program or initiative can both build deeper coherence and allow for more freedom. When a group agrees to hold itself accountable to principles rather than to a set model, we found, there is room to innovate and adapt without compromising fidelity.

We have learned that it is not necessary, and maybe sometimes not even desirable, for a program or initiative to set out principles at the start of the work. Rather, through the process of working together and understanding how decision making takes place and what helps or hinders change, principles begin to emerge. When the principles are articulated this way, they become a mirror for the shared experience. Helping to articulate these principles as they emerge, guiding a program to understand the implications of these principles, and setting up systems to track fidelity to principles are roles uniquely suited to developmental evaluation.

Communication Matters

As the CCRP evaluation evolved, it became increasingly clear that one of the most effective tools we had for building coherence across the program was using common conceptual frameworks for understanding and implementing the work. We also realized that how these frameworks and concepts were communicated could either "make or break" their effectiveness. Naming something can be empowering; however, it can also be alienating if the names used don't resonate with people. Introducing new language to communicate a concept (e.g., *generative dialogue*) frequently led people to dismiss the language as jargon, and then to "throw the baby out with the bathwater." As we moved forward, we worked with reframing the concepts of complex systems into language that did not feel foreign, exclusionary, or overly precious. Sometimes, we learned, it is not important to name things; it is sometimes enough simply to integrate the concepts into the work, without calling attention to them.

At perhaps a more mundane level, it also became clear that there is no shared meaning, adaptive action, collaboration, or contextualized scaling without an effective communication strategy. Even among highly articulate people, we have had to facilitate the creation and articulation of new frameworks and the integration of existing ones. In practice, this has meant many hours of writing, revising, analyzing, and designing products in collaboration with colleagues and stakeholders. For developmental evaluation to fulfill its promise for integrated and iterative learning, time and resources need to be afforded for both formal and informal communications.

Partnerships with Program Staff Are Essential

Implementing an evaluation that is very different from what people are used to can provoke doubt, resistance, pushback, and even (occasionally) hostility. We experienced all of these at different points during the CCRP evaluation. It was very important that the foundation's director of international programs (Jane) was an unflagging ally and committed partner through this process. From our experience with CCRP and elsewhere, an evaluator cannot work in this way without at least one powerful ally. But while the partnership between the evaluator and the staff of the program being evaluated might build from a single relationship, part of the evaluation process must focus on expanding relationships more broadly—building mutual trust and credibility across the program. By design, a developmental evaluation is itself a partnership, and the evaluator acts in the role of an evaluation facilitator. Without relationships based on trust and a shared vision, this role is ineffective.

Jane: "Along with many of the lessons described above, this journey of integrating developmental systems-based evaluative thinking into a global grant-making program has become a key element of my journey of shifting from evaluator to program director in philanthropy. My gut told me it could and should be done—and it is still in its doing, as that is the journey. Through it all, I learned a variety of important lessons. It is very important to have an organization or institution that allows space for innovation to make change in the world. The McKnight Foundation is an organization that allows for new thinking, learns from its past, and expects concrete and important high-quality change on the ground over time; it was the basis from which the journey could operate. From the curiosity and strategic insight of the president, Kate Wolford, to the supportive teaching and challenging of Neal Cuthbert (vice-president for programs), guided by the deep wisdom of the McKnight Board, this allowed the journey to begin. Committed and passionate people also matter, from Marah Moore, who with grace and insight and expertise helped shape something from the chaos; Rebecca Nelson, CCRP scientific director, tireless contributor to improving the lives of smallholder farmers and their families; and the McKnight international team staff, who kept things running behind the scenes. Claire Nicklin, who wears many hats for CCRP, has both managed the IMEP workflow and contributed invaluable insight as a member of the IMEP team. The CCRP leadership team and grantees have been with us on this journey; without them, there would be no IMEP. Mentors and supporters along the way include Michael Quinn Patton and Glenda Eoyang, among others. Their expertise, key [advice,] and timely contributions helped us refine, refocus, and inspire this work, particularly in the tough spots."

Marah: "Reflecting on my personal journey over the past 6 years, the overriding feeling I land on is gratitude. Gratitude for the opportunity to work alongside so many gifted and passionate people. Gratitude for CCRP's being a safe place to learn together, to disagree (sometimes vehemently), to try things and fail, to work together to turn failure into success, and then to celebrate our successes—in effect, a safe place to implement a developmental evaluation. Through this process, I have learned to trust my instincts more, and to question my assumptions more. As this developmental evaluation has become more and more deeply embedded into the fabric of the program, I have learned when to sit back and let the process unfold, and when to step in and offer expertise or challenge the direction something is headed. Many years ago, I said to somebody who worked for me, 'If you leave a meeting with people thinking you're smart, you have failed; if you leave with them thinking that they are smarter than they were before the meeting, that is success.' This journey has affirmed for me that much of good evaluation work is invisible: We walk alongside our program colleagues, and facilitate their transformation of information into knowledge, and knowledge into wisdom. In the end, it is the people who are doing the hard work on the ground who hold that wisdom. And, if we're lucky, the wisest of them share it with all of us."

REFERENCES

Eoyang, G. (1997). *Coping with chaos: Seven simple tools.* Circle Pines, MN: Lagumo.

Eoyang, G., & Holladay, R. (2013). *Adaptive action: Leveraging uncertainty in your organization.* Stanford, CA: Stanford University Press.

Parsons, B. (2010). *Using complexity science concepts when designing system interventions and evaluations.* Fort Collins, CO: InSites.

Patton, M. Q. (2011). *Developmental evaluation: Applying complexity concepts to enhance innovation and use.* New York: Guilford Press.

Westley, F., Zimmerman, B., & Patton, M. Q. (2006). *Getting to maybe: How the world is changed.* Toronto: Random House Canada.

World Bank. (2003). *Scaling-up the impact of good practices in rural development: A working paper to support implementation of the World Bank's rural development strategy* (Agriculture and Rural Development Department Report No. 26031). Washington, DC: Author. Retrieved from *https://openknowledge.worldbank.org/handle/10986/14370.*

CHAPTER 9

An Example of Patch Evaluation

Vibrant Communities Canada

Mark Cabaj, Eric Leviten-Reid, Dana Vocisano, and Mabel Jean Rawlins

EDITORS' INTRODUCTION

This is the most comprehensive and complete developmental evaluation in this book. It was designed in phases over a 10-year period, as the innovative antipoverty initiative Vibrant Communities (VC) unfolded in 12 distinct cities across Canada. The overall evaluation synthesized results and lessons "patched together" from a plethora of different documents, data systems, and reports, including work by various evaluators working within and sometimes across different projects and communities. The evaluation used a range of tools, methods, processes, reporting approaches, and conceptual frameworks. Scores of diverse stakeholders were involved in a variety of capacities and relationships. Part of what is impressive about this case is the open and honest account of the evaluation's ups and downs, including times when it stalled completely and had to be resurrected with new energy through a negotiated process and reworked design. The developmental evaluation mirrored the complexity, turbulence, uncertainty, nonlinearities, and adaptations of the initiative itself.

Mark Cabaj, VC's executive director and co-leader of the developmental evaluation, was a pioneering participant in the world's first developmental evaluation training and coaching collaboration, conducted by Michael Quinn Patton. Mark and Michael subsequently collaborated on evaluation of a major social innovation that has become a teaching case (Parker, 2014). Mark's master's thesis at the University of Waterloo involved interviewing 18 developmental evaluators to analyze patterns in their practices and harvest wisdom from their insights (Cabaj, 2011b). You will see all of that knowledge and experience reflected in this case exemplar, as Mark and his colleagues reflect deeply and forthrightly about the twists and turns in the maze of large-scale, multidimensional, and multilayered developmental evaluation. Get ready for an extraordinary story.

This chapter describes an example of *patch evaluation*. This relatively obscure term refers to situations in which interventions have multiple moving parts and different users with different types of questions. These contexts require multiple and often overlapping evaluative processes, rather than one standard design. The evaluation of Vibrant Communities (VC)—a 10-year initiative in which over a dozen urban collaborations across Canada experimented with what would now be called a *collective impact* approach to reducing poverty (Kania & Kramer, 2011)—is an example of a patch evaluation. It required an ever-evolving combination of developmental evaluation, summative assessment, and accountability-oriented grant monitoring in one venture.

Although the results of the VC initiative are relatively well documented (Cabaj, 2011a; Gamble, 2010, 2012; Leviten-Reid, 2007), the evaluative processes that produced the findings for these reports are not. These included the challenge to develop a comprehensive evaluation strategy that was learning-oriented, manageable, and useful; the specific experiences with employing a theory-of-change approach to support complex local change efforts; and the general reflections on the enabling conditions for patch evaluation in general, and developmental evaluation in particular.

We, the authors of this chapter, were involved in VC in a variety of ways. We were part of the evaluation process, each from a different angle, as VC's executive director (Mark Cabaj); VC's coordinator of learning and evaluation (Eric Leviten-Reid); executive director of the Community Social Planning Council of Greater Victoria and founding Trail Builder member (Mabel Jean Rawlins); and senior program officer for the J. W. McConnell Family Foundation (Dana Vocisano). Although we have not worked together since the end of the VC initiative in 2011, we agreed to come together once again to describe what we agreed was the most challenging and rewarding learning and evaluation experience of our respective careers.

The Initiative

From 1996 to 2000, a diverse group of community leaders, nonprofit organizations, government agencies, and local businesses in southern Ontario's Waterloo Region sought to reduce the region's poverty rate to the lowest in Canada. Opportunities 2000 mobilized 86 organizations in support of 47 diverse poverty reduction initiatives, ranging from the development of community enterprises and workforce development initiatives to employer-driven changes in workplace practices. Although the initiative did not achieve its target of helping 2,000 families exit poverty by the year 2000, it did help 1,600 households make significant steps in their journey out of poverty, made poverty a public priority, and created a network of leaders and organizations committed to renewing and sustaining their collaborative work under the new name of Opportunities Waterloo Region (McNair & Leviten-Reid, 2002).

In its evaluation of Opportunities 2000, the Caledon Institute described the first phase of this endeavor as one of a growing number of Canadian- and American-based local initiatives that tackle complex issues through comprehensive, multisectoral efforts (McNair & Leviten-Reid, 2002). These initiatives shared the belief that the causes underlying complex problems like poverty are interlocked, and that communities can hope to make progress on them only by collaborating across organizations and sectors.

In late 2001, the found of OP 2000 and the newly established Tamarack Institute reconvened two organizations that had played a lead role in the effort—the J. W. McConnell Family Foundation and the Caledon Institute of Social Policy—to reflect on the lessons learned from the initiative (Born, 2010). They concluded that although Opportunities 2000's results were promising, it was not possible to generalize its approach to all communities. Specifically, further experimentation was required with other local initiatives guided by similar principles and perspectives to better understand the range of ways to unfold comprehensive, multisectoral efforts and the extent of their ability to reduce poverty.

In April 2002, representatives from 15 Canadian cities already involved in poverty reduction activities and the three national sponsors met for a 3-day forum in Guelph, Ontario, to create VC.[1] They jointly developed an experiment designed to test a "new" way to tackle poverty—one that acknowledged the complex nature of poverty and the challenge of achieving scale in poverty reduction efforts. The new way was not a model, but a set of five core principles that local communities agreed to follow in mounting locally unique campaigns:

1. *Poverty reduction:* A focus on reducing poverty, as opposed to alleviating the hardships of living in poverty.
2. *Comprehensive thinking and action:* Addressing the interrelated causes of poverty, rather than its individual symptoms.
3. *Multisectoral collaboration:* Engaging individuals and organizations from at least four key sectors—business, government, nonprofit, and persons who have experienced poverty—in a joint effort.
4. *Community asset building:* Building on a community's strengths, rather than focusing on its deficits.
5. *Learning and change:* Embracing a long-term process of learning and change, rather than simply undertaking a series of specific interventions.

VC was designed as a two-phase initiative. In the first phase, five communities—officially called *Trail Builders*—would receive a variety of supports from the three national sponsors to develop and implement poverty reduction initiatives, using the VC approach. (See Exhibit 9.1.) This included a commitment to collectively assist 5,000 households in their journeys out of poverty and to engage 450 leaders (from the private, public, and nonprofit sectors and from residents with lived experience) to help head local efforts. The remaining communities—unofficially called *early adopters*—would participate in a Pan-Canadian Learning Community (PCLC) and would follow the learnings of the Trail Builders. (Again, see Exhibit 9.1.)

---

[1]Each community was represented by individuals from the private, public, and nonprofit sectors, as well as by someone with experience living in poverty.

EXHIBIT 9.1

Trail Builders' Responsibilities

In exchange for the financial, coaching, and evaluation supports provided by VC's national sponsors, local Trail Builders were expected to continually meet a number of basic requirements:

- Commit to meeting numerical targets for assisting households in their journey out of poverty, and targets for engaging organizations and people from different sectors.
- Develop a community plan for poverty reduction, reflecting a comprehensive approach.
- Establish a multisectoral leadership table to include participation from government, business, nonprofit organizations, and people with lived experience of poverty.
- Secure the necessary financial and in-kind resources to support the convening, facilitation, research, and other work required to pursue a comprehensive, collaborative initiative.
- Design a learning and evaluation plan, and participate in the Pan-Canadian Learning Community (PCLC).
- Provide narrative and statistical reports on the progress of its work, as described in the Trail Builder Learning and Evaluation Package (see Exhibit 9.3).

These supports were "reviewed and renewed" annually during the grant review process.

Source: Cabaj and Leviten-Reid (2006).

If, after 3 years, Trail Builders were able to achieve a number of ambitious poverty reduction and partnership development targets, which would establish that the VC approach was "viable," then another group of PCLC members could apply for supports to launch their own multiyear campaigns. (See Exhibit 9.2.)

The responsibility of testing the VC approach would happen at the national level. As communities worked and learned from one another, evaluators and the VC sponsors would document their experience—tracking outcomes, distilling lessons learned, and drawing conclusions for local practice and for policies across all sectors. They would then disseminate their findings through the initiative's website; tools and papers; conferences and workshops; and a variety of tele-learning forums.

Scoping Out the Evaluation Strategy

The first step in scoping out the evaluation strategy for VC was mapping the various units of analysis and determining who needed what type of evaluative feedback. This was more complex than people had anticipated. As it turned out, VC had multiple units of analysis with multiple users who required evaluation to inform various uses. These were organized into four streams of evaluative work:

- *Stream 1: Developmental evaluation for Trail Builders.* The staff and leadership volunteers of each local group would require feedback on the effects of their poverty reduction activities and general operations, to help them make decisions about how to further develop and improve their strategies.

• *Stream 2: Grant monitoring for funders.* The staff and boards of organizations that provided Trail Builders with grant funding required feedback on the extent to which the organizations were meeting the terms of their granting agreements and using funds in a proper manner. As the largest funder (up to 50%) of local work, the J. W. McConnell Family Foundation was the primary user of this

---

EXHIBIT 9.2

National Supports

The national sponsors of VC were responsible for creating a variety of supports: for direct local action and learning by Trail Builders; for cross-community learning by members of the PCLC; and for the dissemination of VC updates, results, and learnings to communities and organizations outside VC.

SUPPORT TO TRAIL BUILDERS

- Matched grants to (1) support groups in exploring local interest in reducing poverty, (2) develop partnerships and plans, (3) undertake 3–4 years of implementation (also known as *action learning*), and (4) enable an additional 3 years of sustainability (after 2006).
- Coaching by experienced practitioners.
- Evaluation support to assist with implementing the VC evaluation package and developing locally customized evaluation design.

SUPPORT TO MEMBERS OF THE PCLC

- Monthly teleconference calls to provide local updates and discuss the design and administration of VC.
- A wide variety of tele-learning sessions focused on particular topics (e.g., living wages, engaging the private sector, policy changes).
- The production of case studies, tools, and papers on various issues related to the VC approach (e.g., comprehensive approaches to reducing poverty).
- Regular VC newsletters summarizing new projects, learnings, and resources.
- Periodic face-to-face meetings to more deeply explore results, lessons learned, and questions.

SUPPORT TO WOULD-BE REPLICATORS

Various mechanisms were made available to share the learnings of VC partners horizontally to other communities, and vertically to organizations that might provide enabling environments for the VC approach (e.g., policy makers, philanthropists). These included VC websites; conferences, presentations, and workshops; and periodic coaching visits.
The type, design, and delivery of these national supports would evolve over time in response to (1) new goals for the project, (2) advances in web-based and telephone technologies, and (3) learnings surfaced through annual reviews and three external assessments.

Source: Cabaj and Leviten-Reid (2006).

feedback; however, each group had from two to eight additional local funders that also required feedback on their investment.

  • *Stream 3: Practice building for the field.* The national VC team, the communities participating in VC, and those interested in the VC approach to reducing poverty were eager to understand the effectiveness, feasibility, and viability of the VC model in general. This included how the VC principles were practiced in diverse settings, what types of effects this might yield, and which capacities and conditions were required to make this work.

  • *Stream 4: Developmental and formative evaluation for the PCLC.* The national VC team and the communities participating in VC needed evaluative feedback to help inform the design and delivery of the various supports to Trail Builders and PCLC learning. Within this stream, the six funders that provided various levels of investment into the PCLC also required data on the extent to which Tamarack was meeting the terms of its grant or contribution agreements.

These evaluation "patches" were distinct but overlapping. The work of Trail Builders depended on funders' receiving the information they required to make annual disbursements, while the ability of Trail Builders to produce funder reports depended on their ability to gather data related to their local strategy. The operations of the PCLC depended on the Trail Builders' being able to produce and share data on their results and learnings, while the effectiveness of the Trail Builders and PCLC activities depended on evaluative feedback from Trail Builders on the various national supports. The field-building work depended heavily on the evaluation results of the three other clusters. For each evaluation cluster to be effective, the clusters would have to be developed and managed as an integrated package.

Although the national sponsors were unsure how to construct an evaluation strategy that was so complex, they were quite clear that it should be designed with the following features in mind:

  • A focus on designing evaluations that would be used.
  • A strong urge to use evaluation to encourage, rather than discourage, a learning culture.
  • An emphasis on manageability.
  • A priority placed on joint stewardship.

In early 2002, the national sponsors secured two evaluation firms experienced in community development and poverty reduction efforts. Representatives from both organizations participated in the founding meeting in Guelph. The first 2 days of the meeting focused on designing the VC initiative. The third day was given over to establishing a working group composed of the national team, contracted evaluators, and representatives from each community, to establish the intent, elements, and overall direction of the evaluation. This group explored and confirmed the "tightly coupled" nature of the evaluation clusters and key features of the strategy.

When they left the Guelph meeting, the group members had agreed on what they felt were the core ingredients of an evaluation design:

- A common definition of poverty and indicators to measure progress in reducing poverty.
- A shared methodology for gathering, analyzing, and reporting data on the effects of Trail Builder activities on local poverty, via a national database.
- The use of the logic model to describe and guide evaluation design, and provide the basis for comparing how Trail Builders manifested the VC principles.

The working group agreed to meet regularly via teleconference—and, if necessary, in face-to-face meetings—to develop a concrete evaluation design for the rest of the national team and local partners to review, discuss, and approve.

The Crumbling of a Cookie-Cutter Design

The initial efforts went well. After much wrangling about the complex and subjective nature of poverty, and a review of multiple definitions and measures commonly used in Canada, participants agreed that all Trail Builders would measure their progress in reducing poverty on the basis of five indicators: changes in household income of people affected by local activities, and changes in employment, financial assets, education/training, and housing. Although communities would be free to employ additional indicators for their own use, these measures were considered "core" and "minimum" expectations across all Trail Builder sites.

Committee members stumbled over the next part of the design. Try as they might, they could not settle on a shared approach to track their shared core outcomes. While the group supported the principle of a shared methodology and national database, its members struggled to develop a standard approach to gathering, analyzing, and reporting outcomes that could be usefully employed for a wide variety of interventions and settings.

The diversity of interventions was impressive. The group members from Waterloo shared how they had failed to capture the impact of a social marketing campaign to encourage employers to adopt human resource practices that reduced poverty. Although dozens of employers had reported making changes to their workplaces because of the campaign, they were unwilling to participate in the campaign survey, which was designed to capture the project outcomes of nonprofit programs and services. Group members from another community, in the throes of organizing support for the creation of a municipal housing trust fund, doubted that the fund administrators would be willing to contact the inhabitants of the affordable homes that had been created to ask them questions about the impact of the fund on their lives. Each of the dozen interventions that Trail Builders were developing seemed to require a different evaluation strategy.

The evaluation stalled entirely when it came to describing each community's comprehensive strategy in a way that might guide the evaluation. In most cases, VC evaluators were encouraging local groups to finalize their evaluation questions, measures, and designs at a level of detail that communities were unable—or unwilling—to do. The example of Opportunities Niagara illustrates the challenge. Its CEO, Peter Papp, noted:

> "We knew we wanted to assist 2,000 families out of poverty; we knew that the community wanted us to focus on wages, housing, and mental health; and we thought we could make things happen by brokering and facilitating multisectoral responses to these issues. We did not know more than that—we simply had to try stuff out and see if it worked."

The Niagara example was the norm.[2] Although each group was able to confirm its poverty reduction targets, commit to their domains of action, and sketch out the broad strokes of how they would "add value" in making things happen in those areas, the groups generally felt ill prepared to elaborate more on this until they had had opportunities to test their ideas on the ground. "You can only do so much strategy work in a boardroom," remarked an experienced community leader from Saint John. VC evaluators would have to settle on a broad-strokes evaluation design until Trail Builders had a chance to develop their approaches further.

The use of the logic model as the primary tool to describe the strategies amplified the difficulties. Although group members in almost every community had some experience with using the technique to describe relatively discrete and straightforward programs and services (e.g., a job search program), they found them too linear to be employed for a comprehensive, citywide poverty reduction campaign (e.g., the establishment of a workforce development pipeline with scores of partners). "There were too many moving pieces for a logic model to handle," said Mabel Jean Rawlins with the Quality of Life Challenge in Victoria, British Columbia. A member of another group reported that a preliminary description of the group's work looked like a "logic model on steroids." A third person added: "We took a pretty complex strategy and squeezed it into all these little boxes. We did it, but I did not recognize our strategy in it." The logic model had met its match.

Within 6 months of the Guelph meeting, the evaluation was stalled. While the expertise and professionalism of the evaluation team were valued, the tools and process were viewed as unproductive. "The air left the room during those evaluation discussions," recounted one person in Edmonton. "We had worked hard to get all these senior people in the room—including business leaders who don't usually get involved in these efforts because they don't like process—and the process was turning them off." In Victoria, the process was testing a carefully put together leadership group still trying to find its feet in the local effort. "We really had to

---

[2] The exception in this case was the Vivre Saint-Michel group in Montréal, which had been operating dozens of Citizens' Clubs for some time before VC and whose representatives were able to describe their strategy and evaluation questions in some detail.

hold back our leadership team [members], who felt that the process was narrow and confining. They were quite angry," says Rawlins. "We had even mused about backing out of the [VC] project at some point."

The evaluation was at a crossroads. Although everyone in the partnership was committed to making evaluation a useful part of the initiative, cookie-cutter, linear evaluation designs were simply unable to deal with the cross-scale, highly emergent, and complex nature of VC. The group would have to go back to the drawing board and start all over.

Back to the Drawing Board

That drawing board had two big questions: (1) "What is the most important part of the VC initiative?" (2) "How can evaluation be designed in a way to support this part of the work?"

The first question turned out to be easy when Paul Born, the CEO of Tamarack and the driving personality behind VC, stated simply: "Assisting Trail Builders in launching their VC-guided campaigns is the 'keystone' to the entire project; it is impossible to test the VC approach without local action." Trail Builder action—at least in the early phases—was the driver around which everything else had to be organized.

But how could evaluation help, not hinder, the Trail Builders' work? It would take several months of discussion and debate, but the working group would eventually draw on three developments in the field of complexity, strategy, and evaluation that would point the way.

The first development was getting a grasp of the level of detail that could reasonably be expected for a poverty reduction strategy. Brenda Zimmerman, an expert on management and complexity and a periodic advisor to VC sponsors, confirmed that the traditional "plan the work and work the plan" approach to tackling complex issues was often unviable and counterproductive.[3] Organizations that tried to work out all the details in advance often experienced "paralysis by analysis," while the shifting context of their work quickly made their hard-won assumptions and inputs outdated. Zimmerman also observed that poverty was a "wickedly complex" problem for which traditional planning approaches were completely unsuited.

A more productive approach, she offered, was to get diverse stakeholders to agree on the kinds of results they hoped to achieve and to establish a number of *minimum specifications*—such as principles, boundaries, or key processes—and allow actors to work adaptively, creatively, and flexibly within that container (Zimmerman, Lindberg, & Plsek, 1998). Zimmerman shared several examples of how this approach was used productively to tackle issues in health care, inner-city renewal, and the military. She confirmed that Henry Mintzberg, an international expert on

---

[3] The quote from Brenda Zimmerman occurred in a face-to-face meeting in Tamarack's offices in early 2003.

corporate strategy, referred to this approach as an *umbrella strategy* (Mintzberg & Waters, 1985), and that it was commonly employed by companies operating in complex business environments. The concepts of *minimum specifications* and *umbrella strategy* were liberating to the national team. These concepts accurately captured the kinds of strategies that Trail Builders had already developed on their own, and they legitimized their collective urge to work out the details through a learning-by-doing approach.

The second development that the group uncovered was how to capture this broader approach to strategy in a way that could guide the evaluation. The Aspen Institute's Roundtable on Community Change provided a way to conceptualize umbrella strategies in a way that was useful both for crafting local strategies and for guiding the design of evaluation. After a decade of wrestling with the limitations of conventional evaluation techniques to assess complex change efforts, the staff of the Aspen Institute's Roundtable on Community Change had embraced the *theory of change* as a viable alternative to the logic model:

> A theory of change can be a helpful tool for developing solutions to complex social problems. At its most basic, a theory of change explains how a group of early and intermediate accomplishments sets the stage for producing long-range results. A more complete theory of change articulates the assumptions about the process through which change will occur, and specifies the ways in which all of the required early and intermediate outcomes related to achieving the desired long-term change will be brought about and documented as they occur. (Anderson, 2005, p. 1)

The theory of change allowed Trail Builders to map out a strategy that had multiple, nonlinear moving elements so characteristic of comprehensive strategies (e.g., how a housing strategy and an employment development strategy in a neighborhood could be mutually reinforcing). It encouraged thinking about their work as a "hypothesis" or "bet" that required experimentation and testing. Finally, the process of developing a theory of change sharpened the groups' thinking about their expected results, their strategies to achieve them, and their priority questions for the evaluation. "I was sold on the usefulness of a theory-of-change approach within minutes of hearing about it," remarked a contracted consultant.

The third and final piece of the puzzle was the concept of developmental evaluation. Although Patton had not yet published his seminal work on developmental evaluation (Patton, 2011), VC participants found his early characterization of the approach compelling. Specifically, they liked the emphasis on providing social innovators with real-time feedback on their emerging strategy, the attention to the context-sensitive nature of social change efforts, and the need for continually adapting evaluation measures and designs to keep up with an evolving intervention. The most significant implication of developmental evaluation for the evaluation team, however, was the confirmation that requiring an elaborate, refined, and fixed evaluation design could be counterproductive to Trail Builders' efforts to get emergent processes off the ground.

These three overlapping ideas provided a conceptual framework that appeared to address difficulties that VC participants experienced in the original evaluation design: Trail Builders could use a theory of change to describe their umbrella strategy, while developmental evaluation activities could be used to provide their respective leaders with the feedback they needed to "test" their approach. As in the case of any theory or hypothesis, they might find the theory confirmed (and simply needing elaboration or improvement), completely off base (and needing to be dropped), or somewhere in between.

The evaluation team was relieved. The chance that these ideas would appeal to Trail Builders seemed strong. Moreover, the process of documenting, testing, and upgrading their theory of change would also be useful for understanding and comparing how different communities applied VC principles in their local settings. The team did a mockup of an entirely new evaluation strategy based on this complexity-sensitive paradigm of strategy and evaluation. (See Exhibit 9.3.)

However, the ability of VC participants to embrace a developmental approach to strategy and evaluation depended a great deal on whether the J. W. McConnell Family Foundation was willing to adopt an approach to its grant monitoring that enabled, rather than disabled, the type of emergent and adaptive action envisioned in this new approach. Luckily, the foundation was more than prepared to organize its grant-monitoring process to support a developmental process. The McConnell Family Foundation's CEO and director of programs, both of whom were on the VC steering committee, had extensive experience in international development circles and brought their grassroots understanding of community development to the foundation. Equally as important, they had invested significant time and energy into understanding and funding social innovation, and had embraced utilization-focused evaluation and developmental evaluation. Some of these insights were captured in the book *Getting to Maybe: How the World Is Changed* (Westley, Zimmerman, & Patton, 2006). The foundation staff immediately agreed to design a grant-monitoring process with three key features:

1. *One evaluation package.* The foundation agreed to organize its granting reports around the developmental evaluation approach used by Trail Builders.

2. *Embedded grant-making.* The foundation staff and national team participated extensively in the major learning events, went along with VC staff on selected coaching visits, and convened several learning circles about how philanthropists and policy makers could create an enabling environment for funding and policy dialogues.

3. *A joint review process.* Although the foundation made the final decisions on all funding, these were based on the recommendations of the senior staff members of all three national sponsors, who reviewed and discussed each proposal and funding report together in detail. This was a "learning-rich" process that offered national sponsors greater insight into the workings of each Trail Builder. It also allowed them to see the emerging patterns on the VC model over the 10-year period.

EXHIBIT 9.3

The Trail Builder Learning and Evaluation Package

The Trail Builder Learning and Evaluation Package included three broad elements that wove together the concepts of an umbrella strategy/theory of change and developmental evaluation:

THE THEORY OF CHANGE (ALSO KNOWN AS THE UMBRELLA STRATEGY)

Trail Builders were asked to articulate the following:

- A "working definition" of poverty, which must include the five core measures.
- The group's targets for assisting low-income households and multisectoral participation.
- A description of the current leverage points, domains, or priority areas for action.
- A description of how the local group "added value" to making change in these areas.
- A list of current and planned strategies, initiatives, or interventions.
- A governance structure reflecting the principles of multisectoral collaboration.

ANNUAL REFLECTION SESSION

VC coaches would facilitate an annual reflection session that was roughly organized to answer three major questions:

- What has changed over the last year (e.g., results, learnings, capacity, context)?
- What are the implications for the design or implementation of your theory of change?
- What are your priorities now, moving forward?

REPORTING

Trail Builders would provide two types of report to the national sponsors:

- *Semiannual VC By the Numbers reports to Caledon Institute:* A standard template to provide data on the number and variety of partners engaged in the local work, the number and types of strategies or interventions, and the numbers of households experiencing improvements in the five core poverty reduction measures.
- *Annual reports to the foundation:* A summary of the results of the annual reflection session, VC By the Numbers attachment, and an account of how the foundation's funds were employed.

Though the intent and broad elements of the package would remain roughly the same throughout the remainder of the initiative, the evaluation team and Trail Builders would continually elaborate and refine it across the next 7 years, and would work with each Trail Builder to adapt it to reflect the realities of its own context and campaign.

These measures made it easier for foundation staff to make funding decisions that concurrently embraced risk and rigor. "We were a lot more comfortable allowing grantees to let their work unfold over time and to accept that uncertainty, in part because we knew so much more about the grantees and their work," says Vocisano. At the same time, it did not mean that the grant-monitoring process was not rigorous and demanding: Of the original 15 groups, the foundation, on the recommendation of the sponsors' joint review process, would eventually refuse, withhold, or discontinue funding for 6 of them.

Developing Local Poverty Reduction Efforts

The new evaluation design immediately proved its value. Trail Builders found it easier to craft, communicate, and operationalize their comprehensive approaches to reducing poverty. By early 2004, all six Trail Builder communities had developed a theory of change for their work that was approved by their local leadership teams and accepted by the national sponsors. Perhaps just as importantly, Trail Builders had embraced the "tight–loose" evaluation design that allowed them to adhere to a VC-wide methodology for assessing their theory of change and to develop their own customized methods for assessing their diverse strategies and initiatives. All six Trail Builders were inventive in their evaluation efforts. The staff at the Quality of Life Challenge, in British Columbia's Capital Region, successfully adapted the outcome-mapping methodology to track the effects of this Trail Builder's social marketing campaign to encourage regional employers to make use of progressive human resource practices. The evaluation team in the Saint Michel district of Montréal experimented with ways to assess the cumulative effects of all their citizen-led committees, focusing on a dozen neighborhood issues. Opportunities Niagara staff explored how to test the extent to which "one-stop eligibility smart cards" for social recipients succeeded in improving their access to various services. The Trail Builders' interest in evaluation was so strong that VC participants established an Evaluation Community of Practice, which eventually turned out to be the most active and broadly subscribed learning group in the entire initiative.

Meanwhile, the national team members elaborated and refined the Learning and Evaluation Package. Their participation in each group's annual reflection session, in providing assistance to groups, and in filling out the statistical reports gave them insights into (and empathy for) how the methodology played out in each community. They regularly adjusted the criteria for reporting quantitative outcomes, adapted the process for facilitating annual reviews, and experimented with a "storytelling" format to describe each Trail Builder's theory of change. In response to consistent feedback that *theory of change* sounded too academic to local leadership teams, they adopted the *framework for change* language employed by the Hamilton Roundtable for Poverty Reduction. In the spirit of the shared stewardship model of VC, these adjustments would be reviewed and adapted during the monthly Trail Builder administration calls. VC participants had managed an evaluation turnaround. "It was imperfect, to be sure," commented Eric Leviten-Reid, the evaluation coordinator, "but it was a substantial leap forward from where we started."

The Emerging VC Approach: Common Principles, Local Variation

In 2006, the national sponsors, local communities, and evaluators met again in Guelph to review their collective experiences, results, and learnings. They had plenty of data with which to work.[4] Trail Builders had produced dozens of reports and had generously shared their struggles and learnings with the coaches and the national team during scores of site visits. Several hundred people had participated in eight distinct learning groups and in several dozen tele-learning sessions. VC participants had explored a variety of different topics in their monthly phone calls.

The first conclusion was that all VC participants had a much better handle on how differently VC principles played out on the ground in different settings. Several national leaders admitted that although no one had an entirely clear idea of what the local poverty reduction work would look like in each community, they had assumed that it would look somewhat like the 4-year experience of Waterloo Region's Opportunities 2000, the prototype for VC. It didn't. While the Trail Builder initiatives bore a family resemblance, each had its own distinct personality, which revealed the variety of forms these comprehensive, multisectoral initiatives may take. The national team identified nine points of variation in local efforts. For example:

• *Definitions of poverty.* Though all groups used the five core measures, they embedded them within different definitions of poverty and additional measures: social determinants of health, family economic success, economic and social inclusion, and quality of life.

• *Geographic scales.* Initiatives operated at different geographic scales (e.g., Saint-Michel in its immediate neighborhood; Saint John in a series of high-poverty neighborhoods throughout the city; Calgary and Edmonton on a citywide basis; Niagara and British Columbia's Capital Region on a more regional basis).

• *Time frames.* Some initiatives established tighter time frames for their work than others (e.g., Edmonton's relatively tight focus on its 3-year plan versus the 10-year poverty reduction targets set by Saint John or the 20- to 30-year perspective informing the work of the Quality of Life Challenge in British Columbia's Capital Region).

• *Demographic focus.* Some initiatives chose to concentrate on the circumstances of a particular low-income group (e.g., Saint John's emphasis on single

---

[4]The evaluation findings were eventually documented in three distinct but overlapping reports (Cabaj & Leviten-Reid, 2006; Cabaj, Makhoul, & Leviten-Reid, 2006; Leviten-Reid, 2007).

parents; Edmonton's focus on people working and earning low incomes), while others addressed the needs of low-income residents in more general terms.

Yet among this diversity, a number of patterns across the sites offered some insights into what might constitute the *core practices* or *minimum specifications* of a VC model. These included the following:

- Four different arrangements for convening a VC approach (e.g., one single organization—foundation, service delivery group, etc.; creation of a new legal entity; philanthropic organization; trisector partnership).
- Two different levels for multisectoral engagement: governance and concrete interventions.
- Success in engaging partners from the nonprofit, public, and private sectors, and significant struggles to provide low-income residents with meaningful opportunities to play leadership roles.
- A consistent focus on using a comprehensive lens to understand the interrelated elements of poverty and to pinpoint strategic interventions, with less emphasis on developing integrated strategies and/or integrated systems to tackle poverty.
- Eight overlapping pathways to reduce poverty comprehensively (e.g., housing, workforce development, income support, childhood development).
- Six major ways that Trail Builders "added value" to local efforts: public education, planning, direct management of programs, social marketing, advocacy, and networking/brokering relationships.
- A clear split between programmatic interventions designed to assist individuals or households directly (e.g., financial literacy programs) and strategic interventions that focused on changing the systems relating to poverty (e.g., welfare rules, employer wage rates).

If the practices of the VC model were becoming clearer, so too were the kinds of concrete initiatives and results that local actors could achieve. Some examples included these:

- A hard-won municipal subsidized fare structure for thousands of low-income residents using public transit in Calgary.
- A social marketing campaign with business associations and local press to encourage hundreds of private sector employers to adopt progressive workplace practices in British Columbia's Capital Region.
- A large-scale campaign to improve the uptake of government benefits, which in its first years enabled low-income residents of Edmonton to access millions of dollars of support for which they were eligible.
- Two projects that created 160 housing units for people leaving abusive family situations in the Niagara Region.

The results exceeded expectations. These initiatives had already affected 11,000 households and were projected to touch an additional 24,000 in the next several years. The participants in VC had dramatically exceeded their original targets of 5,000 households and were eager to set even higher targets for the next phase of their work.

Perhaps the most significant learning across sites was an even deeper appreciation of the complex nature of poverty and poverty reduction. Whereas the entire VC initiative was based on the idea that successful poverty reduction required communities to attend to the multiple factors of poverty, participants tended to focus on the idea that there was a select number of "root causes" of poverty. Three years of trying to address these multiple factors revealed that they were in fact highly intertwined, and that the lines of cause and effect connecting them ran in many different directions. This dynamic is captured in the following passage (Shipler, 2004):

> Every problem magnifies the impact of the others, and all are so tightly interlocked that one reversal can produce a chain reaction with results far distant from the original causes. A rundown apartment can exacerbate a child's asthma, which leads to a call for an ambulance, which generates a medical bill that cannot be paid, which ruins a credit record, which hikes the interest rate on an auto loan, which forces the purchase of an unreliable used car, which jeopardizes a mother's punctuality at work, which limits her promotions and earning capacity, which confines her to poor housing.
>
> If problems are interlocking then so too solutions must be . . .: a job alone is not enough. Medical insurance alone is not enough. Good housing alone is not enough. Reliable transportation, careful family budgeting, effective parenting, effective schooling are not enough when each is achieved in isolation from the rest. (p. 11)

The tangled-up nature of poverty reaffirmed the case for comprehensive, cross-sectoral efforts to reduce poverty. The simple act of framing it as a complex challenge led sponsors and communities to conclude that their current poverty reduction framework—which focused on five measures of poverty reduction—was inadequate for planning, communicating, and evaluating the work. They committed themselves to creating a new, more holistic framework.

For all this progress, there were also serious questions. Three stood out:

1. *What were the depth and durability of household reductions in poverty?* The evaluation package provided a reliable account of the number of households affected in their journey out of poverty, but it was not designed to offer insight into the depth and durability of these changes. This type of data was required to provide a fuller picture of the effects of Trail Builders' efforts.

2. *What are the best ways to engage residents who have experienced poverty?* The success in engaging public, private, and nonprofit leaders in local work was offset by the significant lack of progress in meaningfully engaging residents in the work. What new models of leadership were required to make this critical part of the approach work?

3. *What does comprehensive action look like?* Trail Builders had all used a comprehensive lens to assess poverty in their community (also known as *comprehensive*

thinking), but very few of the initiatives appeared to be designed to tackle the multiple factors of poverty concurrently (also known as *comprehensive action*).

These results, learnings, and questions energized VC participants. Said one participant, "We now have a decent grasp on what this VC approach looks like and that it can lead to interventions and outcomes that we had hoped—but did not know—were possible." But it remained to be seen whether the emerging questions were sufficiently compelling to trigger the second part of the VC plan.

They were. In December 2006, the foundation approved a proposal for an ambitious second phase. It included an expansion of the number of Trail Builders from 6 to 13, the extension of funding from 3 to 7 years, and the introduction of a new outcome framework. In exchange for expanded infrastructure, Trail Builders were expected to assist 40,000 households in their journey out of poverty, while national sponsors and communities were charged with stepping up their efforts to mine and distil the emerging practice of the VC model. Finally, in a vote of confidence on the general viability of the approach, the number of communities in the PCLC would also jump from 13 to 34. VC was officially in growth mode.[5]

Upgrading the Evaluation Design

The discussion of how to evaluate the next iteration of emerging practices for Trail Builders sparked a fierce debate about the purpose and methodology of the second phase of the VC assessment. Some participants argued that it was time to settle into a traditional summative evaluation. This would require the VC participants to agree on a shared set of practices to emerge from the original Trail Builders, to stabilize them as the "VC model," and then to develop shared measures and common measurement methodology. Although it would not be possible to employ the gold-standard methodology of summative assessment—a randomized controlled trial that might shed light on the link between Trail Builders' activities and their outcomes—VC evaluators could at least point to a VC model, activities, and outcomes based on that model.

There were two arguments against this approach. The first was that it was not feasible. The first six Trail Builders had already demonstrated the necessity of customizing the VC principles to reflect their unique contexts. Moreover, each group continued to adapt its approaches—in ways ranging from modest to radical—over the 3 years. Getting the original cohort of communities to agree to a common set of fixed practices was impractical. Getting the new cohort of seven communities to adopt these practices—rather than develop their own community-responsive versions of VC practices—was downright wishful thinking.

The second argument was that judging the merit or worth of the VC principles was misdirected because the case for the VC approach was already clear. If poverty was shaped by multiple root causes, then poverty reduction strategies needed to

---

[5]While the foundation provided a core grant for the activities of the PCLC, the major funding for this part of the work came from a variety of other sources, including a large 5-year grant from Human Resources and Social Development Canada, a significant contribution from the Ontario Trillium Foundation, and support from a variety of other public and corporate donors.

tackle multiple causes concurrently and comprehensively. If strategies needed to be comprehensive, then communities had to work across artificial organizational and sectoral boundaries. If communities had to work across artificial boundaries, then they should focus on their assets (rather than their deficits). If the practice of comprehensive and multisectoral strategies was complex, then communities needed to work adaptively and focus on continual learning and change. Why should VC participants spend their time trying to prove these relatively self-evident principles?

The central evaluative challenge, instead, was to assess the relative merit or worth of different ways to manifest the VC principles. For example, what were the different multisectoral leadership models? What were the strengths and limitations of each model? What were the contexts and conditions under which each model thrived or withered? These were the questions that Trail Builders—and would-be replicators—wanted assessments to answer.

The latter framing of the evaluation challenge for the next iteration best captured the spirit of the enterprise and the wishes of VC participants. "It still feels like a second-best paradigm," concluded the most skeptical person on the evaluation team, "but it makes sense to me, and it's practically the one that fits what most people want and the most feasible, so I'm in!"

The task of reorganizing the outcome-tracking frameworks of Trail Builders to answer questions about the depth, durability, and complex nature of poverty reduction turned out to be somewhat easier. To do this, VC participants turned to the *sustainable livelihoods framework* (SLF), developed in international development circles (U.K. Department for International Development, 1999). Its major features included the following:

- An asset-based approach that framed and measured the progress of reducing poverty as a household's building of "resiliency assets" that could assist vulnerable households.

- A focus on building assets in a variety of interrelated domains, including financial (e.g., income), physical (e.g., housing), social (e.g., supportive relationships), human (e.g., education), and personal (e.g., self-esteem, hope), reflecting the tangled-up nature of factors relating to poverty.

- A distinction between programmatic interventions, designed to assist vulnerable households directly in accumulating assets (e.g., a matched savings program for teen parents receiving social assistance), and strategic interventions, aimed at reshaping the systems and contexts that make people vulnerable in the first place (e.g., welfare rules that prevent households from accumulating savings).

The framework so closely reflected the principles and new insights of VC that it seemed like a perfect match. Ironically, the members of the original evaluation team had proposed using the SLF approach in the early days of VC, only to be told that it was too abstract and complex. "I think we had to experience poverty reduction work more deeply before we really understood how useful this approach was," remarked a Trail Builder member from Edmonton.

Unfortunately, the SLF evaluation process fit less well. The approach relied on program administrators and participants to jointly track changes in participants' household "assets" over time, and to continually assess and judge their progress by using a self-assessment rating schema. Although the technique provided insights into effects of an intervention on individual households, the process (1) made too many demands on resources and relations for the hundreds of intervention partners in local initiatives, and (2) did not provide a base to aggregate data across interventions and communities.

The evaluation team's efforts to develop a customized longitudinal survey instrument that contained standard scales of progress for each core asset were unsuccessful for the same reasons they encountered in the original evaluations: The variations in local interventions and contexts were too great to permit the development of a satisfactory shared assessment tool.[6]

In the end, VC participants agreed to settle on a modified version of the SLF approach: Trail Builders would track and report on the number of people accumulating each kind of assets from each intervention. This assessment would provide a rough sense of the depth of poverty reduction across households, interventions, and communities. Although Trail Builders might elect to track the longer-term effects of their specific interventions on their own, they would not be asked to report these data to the evaluation team. In the end, the national team and VC participants agreed on these primary focus and evaluation upgrades in the next iteration of the VC evaluation campaign:

1. *A focus on assessing, not just describing, Trail Builders' practices.* What were the different "archetypes" in manifesting VC principles? What were the strengths and limitations of each practice? What capacities and conditions needed to be in place in order for this practice to be effective?

2. *A more multidimensional framework to tracking reductions in poverty.* Trail Builders agreed to employ the SLF to track and report on the effects of their interventions.

3. *The use of a modified version of contribution analysis.* Trail Builders would employ a contribution analysis technique to assess their relative contributions to launching and supporting poverty reduction interventions.

The implications of these upgrades did not change the relationship of the evaluation clusters within the patch evaluation design; developmental evaluation was still the keystone of the entire enterprise. But it did shift the design and emphasis. While the evaluation team, Trail Builders, and sponsors rolled up their sleeves again to upgrade the Trail Builder evaluation processes and grant-monitoring processes, they would need to put a much greater focus on their PCLC processes for mining, distilling, documenting, and assessing VC practices.

---

[6]Several attempts to develop a set of scales for asset accumulation in all 26 categories were unsuccessful, due to the difficulty of crafting scales that reflected the unique nature of different circumstances.

Elaborating on VC Practices

The participants in VC took the challenge of assessing VC practices seriously. Throughout the period 2006–2011, they collectively produced over 200 papers, tools, and learning seminars that explored concepts and practices related to the major VC principles. These were made available on the VC website and organized under the following thematic areas:[7]

- Understanding Poverty and Poverty Reduction
- Approaches to Comprehensive Strategies
- Working across Sectoral Boundaries
- Operational Issues
- Sustainability and Resiliency
- Policy Making and Funding

In each of the six sections, the material included papers, podcasts of tele-learning seminars, and a variety of tools and techniques.

There was a cautionary note in the accounts of various practices as well. Whereas the earlier efforts highlighted the potential of different approaches, the focus in the second phase emphasized the limitations and the challenges of each practice. For each story of success, there was also one of struggle. The Caledon Institute had documented the variety of instances in which Trail Builders struggled to mount and sustain their local efforts: for example, an initiative that failed to launch despite a strong leadership team and good engagement process (Makhoul, 2007b), an initiative that stumbled after a solid start (Loewen & Makhoul, 2009), and an initiative that survived many years but never regained the vitality it had had in its first 4 years (Makhoul, 2007a). The Tamarack Institute used the *adaptive cycle*—increasingly employed to help make sense of social innovations—as a way to track the various stages and traps a group employing the VC approach might experience along the way.[8] A VC coach noted:

> "We now had a lot of dirt under our fingernails, furrows on our brows, and crowfeet around our eyes. We understood that there was a lot of value in the VC approach—more than we anticipated, maybe. Yet it takes a lot more effort than we thought it would; [it] was by no means a recipe; and even if you did a good job on the fundamentals—like engaging business—there were so many things that had to go well that you could still struggle a lot or not achieve what you set out to do."

The documentation of this body of practice appeared to be both an accurate reflection of the Trail Builder experience and a fair distillation of the emerging VC approach. A long-time local participant of VC added: "Can you imagine how much

---

[7] *http://tamarackcommunity.ca/g2_topics.html#boundaries.*

[8] *http://tamarackcommunity.ca/g3s61_VC_2009g.html.*

easier this would have all been had we had all of this insight at the start of Vibrant Communities? Very little of this existed 10 years ago—how far we've come!" Her Trail Builder peers agreed: When asked to assess the relative value of VC supports to their local efforts by allocating 100 votes, they awarded an average of 41 votes to foundation funding, and 59 votes to the practice-building activities of coaching, peer learning, and tools.

Evaluating the Merit of the VC Approach: Revisiting Old Ground

It was time for the patch evaluation design to enter into its final stage. VC participants were largely satisfied with the progress in mapping out the emerging practice of VC: A total of 13 communities had now applied and tested the VC principles, and the general sentiment was that VC participants had done a thorough job of elaborating their experiences and practices and documenting their results. VC participants turned their attention to answering the last major evaluation question in the initiative: Was the VC approach sufficiently effective in reducing poverty that it was worth replicating? What capacities and enabling conditions were required for the approach to be effective?

In truth, VC participants and the evaluation team had been preparing to answer these questions since 2007 and felt ready to tackle them. However, in the process of establishing a more detailed scope for this assessment, a key member of the VC steering committee reintroduced a question that had caused considerable commotion 3 years before: To what extent had the evaluation design produced sufficiently robust evidence to answer the question of whether this was an effective approach to reducing poverty? Were the data on households' outcomes sufficiently valid and reliable to permit VC to make any kind of claim? Did the reliance on local Trail Builders to produce the data lead to highly subjective data? In short, to what extent were we able to prove the effectiveness of the concept that the VC initiative had been exploring?

The discussion caused mild panic in members of the evaluation team. They were well aware of the strengths and limitations of their "compromise design," and had encouraged the VC steering committee and VC participants to make an "eyes wide open" decision when approving it. They also felt that they had done a reasonable job in designing and delivering the approach. "I was pretty frustrated that we were revisiting an issue that we already had been over several times, particularly at this late stage of the game," admitted one member of the evaluation team.

As the scoping discussions dragged on, the members of the evaluation team brainstormed ways to complement their existing evaluation data if the steering committee decided that these were required. Some of these included contracting an external group to carry out a metaevaluation of the VC evaluation, to assess the robustness of its methods and findings; developing a retrospective assessment of the poverty reduction effects on a smaller sample of projects and households; and bringing in a panel of experts to participate in a *jury assessment*—a particular kind of evaluation that uses a courtroom-style process in which advocates argue for and against the merit of an intervention, based on whatever evidence is available.

The breakthrough in the debate came when one member of the evaluation team suggested that in the spirit of utilization-focused evaluation, the steering committee should ask the other "primary users" of the data about the merit of the VC approach— the leaders of key networks (e.g., philanthropists, grassroots poverty reduction groups, provincial governments) who had significant influence on whether and how the VC model would be replicated outside the VC network. The steering committee agreed and asked Imprint Consulting, Inc., to interview a dozen "bellwether" leaders in the poverty reduction field in Canada, to identify (1) their questions about the VC approach and (2) their preferences regarding how these questions were answered.

The feedback from these bellwether informants was mixed. On one hand, only 1 of their 10 questions focused on the poverty reduction results, while the other 9 focused on questions about how and where the VC approach might be usefully employed. On the other hand, they provided little guidance regarding their expectations concerning what constituted "sufficiently robust evidence," or their preferences for the methods that VC might use to answer their questions.

In mid-2009, the steering committee approved an evaluation scope of work for a two-phase evaluation project that reflected a "compromise" design:

- *Phase 1 (December 2009 to July 2010):* Identify the questions that VC stakeholders would like addressed in the evaluation; bring initial conclusions to the surface by drawing on the large volume of existing VC data (e.g., statistics, case studies, reports); and generate questions for Phase 2.

- *Phase 2 (July 2010 to spring 2011):* Deepen the understanding of Phase 1 conclusions with additional data collection and analysis, and address new questions generated through Phase 1 of the evaluation.

The virtue of this approach was that it would draw on the extensive existing data on the VC initiative, but would allow for additional investigations (using other methodologies) to answer targeted questions raised by the VC steering committee, Trail Builders, and the bellwethers representing would-be replicators. The final chapter in the VC evaluation was ready to proceed.

The Penultimate Tally

In 2010, Gamble published a 94-page end-of-campaign report entitled *Evaluating Vibrant Communities: 2002–2010.* The document described the intent, design, and activities of the overall initiative, and reviewed the results to date. It described nearly two dozen working conclusions about the VC approach, based on this data. Some of the highlights included these points:

- *There are a variety of "archetypes" for applying VC principles.* There are at least four archetypes of comprehensive, multisectoral efforts to reduce poverty, organized around different drivers (i.e., programmatic push, policy change, transformational change, and bottom-up citizen engagement).

- *The VC approach can—in the right conditions—generate a variety of results.* These include the following:

  ○ *Community will and capacity.* In many instances, Trail Builders raised the communitywide knowledge of poverty, encouraged greater action on poverty reduction, and attracted new resources for poverty work.

  ○ *Systems and policy change.* Trail Builders were successful in shifting nearly 40 policies and practices in government, private, and nonprofit sectors; these shifts generated nearly one-half of the household outcomes achieved by the overall initiative.

  ○ *Reductions in individual and household poverty.* Trail Builders helped over 170,000 households accumulate a variety of different resiliency assets, helped a large proportion of these accumulate multiple types of assets, and helped approximately 20% of households accumulate significant assets (e.g., new home, above-poverty-level wages).

- *A variety of factors shape whether and how a community applies the VC approach, and the kinds of outcomes it can achieve.* VC participants identified 35 such outcomes (e.g., local history with collaboration, the current public debate on poverty, and the structure and performance of the local economy).

- *The higher-performing Trail Builders demonstrated a number of shared characteristics.* These included local convenors with a high degree of credibility, ambitious targets, broad leadership base, and easy-to-communicate purpose and strategy.

The Gamble (2010) report echoed and added to the earlier findings of the internal VC evaluation team about the limits of the approach: A good many Trail Builders struggled to make the VC approach work in their local contexts; the VC approach often caused tension and a perception of duplication with various other local initiatives; and the results of the effort were somewhat unpredictable. In fact, there was an informal bell curve of experiences; five groups that managed to create resilient and high-producing results; groups whose efforts were fragile and whose results were inconsistent; and roughly one-third of the communities falling somewhere in between.

The report also raised a number of questions about the VC approach that VC participants and bellwether informants felt should be explored in the second phase of the assessment. These were organized into three thematic areas:

1. *The results.* What additional data might shed light on the depth and durability of changes to VC-affected households? What are the most promising program and policy innovations emerging from the VC experience?

2. *Patterns of effectiveness.* What are the different phases, conditions, and challenges of launching and sustaining the VC approach?

3. *National supports.* What are the effects, benefits, and dynamics of providing Trail Builders with different types of funding, technical, and policy supports? What does a positive enabling environment for VC-type approaches look like?

The evaluation document was generally well received. The national team felt that the process had uncovered new insights and results that would probably not have emerged through an internal assessment alone, and agreed with the working conclusions and new questions. The representatives of the Trail Builders reported that the findings provided a broader lens on the VC model through which to understand their local work, and invited the members of the national team to present the findings to their local partners. Although several of the bellwethers reported that some of the answers were not sufficiently specific to their own unique contexts, they were satisfied with the findings and endorsed the report and the VC initiative in their respective circles of influence.

The first part of the final assessment was complete. It also nicely set up the second part of the research. Yet, in keeping with the many twists and turns in the life of the VC initiative, that second phase would look very different from what anyone had anticipated.

Events on the Ground Take Over

The end-of-campaign assessment turned out to be oddly anticlimactic. While people appreciated the quality of the report, they had already made their own summative judgment of the VC model—and what they planned to do next—well before it was published.

Trail Builders were already convinced of the VC approach. Of the 13 communities, 10 had secured sufficient resources to continue with their poverty reduction roundtables. The three that formally ended their campaigns—British Columbia's Capital Region, Edmonton, and the Niagara Region—would reestablish citywide poverty reduction initiatives under new leadership within a few years.[9]

Communities outside the VC network were already adopting and adapting the VC approach without the summative results.[10] Poverty reduction roundtables— some of which actually called themselves "Vibrant"—were popping up all over the country. One-quarter of the survey respondents reported that they were modeling a local initiative based on the VC resources. In 2010, the national team and VC Trail Builders were providing structured coaching support to 14 urban collaboratives, as well as less structured support to many more. They were also advising senior civil servants in 5 (out of 10) provincial governments, and in all 3 territorial governments, who were tasked to develop poverty reduction strategies, plans, and policies

---

[9]By 2014, all three communities had revived local poverty reduction roundtables.

[10]In 2011, at the height of VC dissemination activities, visitors to the VC website downloaded over 890,000 document files (e.g., tools, papers) and 60,000 podcasts of VC tele-learning events. Over 3,000 people from 520 different organizations in 366 communities participated in VC tele-learning calls; over 1,400 people from 350 communities were from outside the VC network. Just under half of the participants were working on poverty reduction efforts, while the others were focused on other complex issues (e.g., early childhood education, health care, gang violence). In one study (Gamble, 2012), 95% of respondents to a web-based survey reported that they found VC resources to be very useful (71%) or somewhat useful (24%).

for their jurisdiction. "The VC network was a 'go-to' institution in the arena of poverty reduction," noted a senior leader of the national United Way office in Ottawa.

Events south of the border would increase broader interest in the VC approach. In 2011, two partners at FSG in the United States published an article titled "Collective Impact" in the *Stanford Social Innovation Review* (Kania & Kramer, 2011), exploring how communities were using a highly structured collaborative approach to achieve greater impact on complex issues. Although the authors used slightly different language from that of VC (e.g., *mutually reinforcing activities* vs. *comprehensive strategies*, and *backbone organization* vs. *convenor*), the core concepts were largely the same. "The 'Collective Impact' language resonated so deeply with us—and it affirmed and simplified what we had been doing all along," reported Tamarack's Paul Born, an unknowing pioneer of the collective impact approach.

The article triggered a response that exceeded the expectations of its authors. The *Chronicle of Philanthropy* identified the phrase *collective impact* as the #2 buzzword in the field in 2011. The concept became a regular topic in field publications, conferences, and workshops. The staff at FSG would eventually refer to VC as one of the premier examples of the collective impact approach in North America, and the participants of VC found themselves spread thin sharing their experiences with others.[11] "The VC approach seemed to become mainstream almost overnight," recounted Liz Weaver, formerly Executive Director of the Hamilton Roundtable for Poverty Reduction and now Tamarack's Vice President.

Adjusting the Evaluation Design . . . Again

The irony of the situation was not lost on the VC steering committee and evaluation team. Eric Leviten-Reid said:

> "It was difficult to reconcile our own internal questions about the strength of evidence supporting the VC approach and how broadly—even enthusiastically—it was embraced by communities. We worried so much about generating meaningful data, albeit within the limitations of what was practically manageable, but it wasn't clear how much this mattered to others. Or then again, perhaps we reached a threshold that was sufficient to give people the assurance they needed that there was substance behind this approach."

This shift in context created another fork in the road for VC. The steering committee and evaluation team began to rethink the second part of the end-of-campaign assessment. There was little appetite to explore the case for the VC approach more deeply (the original intent of the second phase), given that so many communities and leaders had already adopted the approach based on the current level of evidence. The more valuable question now appeared to be to focus exclusively on the

[11] FSG and Tamarack would eventually develop a strategic partnership in which they provided approximately six to eight joint training sessions a year in the United States and Canada.

third stream of questions raised by the bellwether reference group: What had VC participants learned about how best to assist this work through national supports related to funding, learning, and policy development?

In response, the steering committee and VC participants agreed to adjust the evaluation design yet again. In late 2011 and early 2012, the evaluation team and Imprint Consulting mined and distilled the vast amounts of statistics, reports, and minutes maintained by VC sponsors and participants on the use and feedback of national supports. They complemented all this with a series of key informant interviews, surveys, and profiles with the local participants on the ground. The report, *Inspired Learning: An Evaluation of Vibrant Communities National Supports: 2002–2012* (Gamble, 2012), would be downloaded thousands of times from the VC website and became an important resource for VC participants to draw on when speaking with governments, intermediaries, and philanthropists about how to create an enabling environment for efforts to tackle complex challenges.

A New Beginning

While local participants were winding down their 10-year campaign, and VC sponsors were tying up loose ends at the national level, both groups were also quietly setting the stage for the next iteration of VC. Paul Born and Liz Weaver, the leadership of 6 of the 13 Trail Builder communities, and representatives from a half-dozen new communities explored how they might build on the success of the "grand VC experiment" of 2002–2012 and take advantage of the greater-than-anticipated interest in and uptake of the VC approach. In late 2012, they launched the Cities Reducing Poverty network. The successor to VC was designed to create cross-community learning on the VC approach, with the goal of signing up 100 Canadian communities to assist 1 million Canadians in their journey out of poverty.[12] The Tamarack-administered network offers its paid members access to up to 20 learning themes and opportunities to shape public awareness and policy and support one another's local campaigns. By mid-2014, the network's membership had increased to 55 communities.

Conclusion and Reflections

The VC initiative is an example of a relatively successful effort to develop, test, and scale an approach to a puzzlingly difficult complex social issue. A patch evaluation design was a central element in the initiative. It gave local Trail Builders a structured way to assess and adapt their local campaigns. It generated data required by the principal national funder to make tough decisions on whether to continue investing in complex and unpredictable change efforts. It yielded insights required to describe an emerging body of practice that transcended 13 different project sites.

---

[12]See *http://vibrantcanada.ca/learn*.

It also produced evaluative feedback to other users and purposes not described in this chapter. A local Trail Builder likened it to an "evaluation Swiss Army knife" that was useful in a variety of situations.

The VC evaluation was a demanding and rewarding evaluation for everyone concerned. Mabel Jean Rawlins reported it to be "the most ambitious, exhausting, and rewarding initiative" she had ever been involved in: "It tested us in every way possible." Noted Eric Leviten-Reid, "It's hard for me to be fair, I suppose: I see all the things we missed and could have done better, but we worked hard at it and did a reasonably good job." Dana Vocisano added, "VC was a benchmark for the [McConnell Family] Foundation. We frequently reference, talk about and think back on VC when designing new initiatives, particularly the approach to evaluation."

It was also learning-rich. Together, we have identified seven major reflections on our experience that may contribute to the growing body of practice of developmental evaluation.

1. *The VC evaluation demonstrates the importance of aligning, not standardizing, evaluation designs in complex initiatives.* A cross-scale, emergent, and complex change effort such as VC meant that it had multiple users who required evaluative feedback for diverse uses. This required a patch evaluation design, the various elements of which needed to be closely managed so that they yielded the data required by their distinct users, yet were also effectively orchestrated and efficient.

2. *The evolutionary nature of complex change initiatives requires that the evaluation design coevolve as well.* This basic premise of developmental evaluation was borne out in VC. Whenever VC participants had new questions, prompted by new learnings or shifts in directions, they had to upgrade their evaluation design to answer those questions. If VC users had remained fixated on their preliminary design, the initiative might not have gotten off the ground; if they had stuck with their design of 2003, they would not have been able to track the richer measures offered by the SLF; nor would they have developed a deeper understanding of the different "modalities" of VC practice.

3. *It is possible to employ a theory-of-change technique productively in complex change initiatives.* Finding useful methods is a central concern of many people interested in developmental evaluation. The use of a theory of change (or framework for change) to conceptualize a group's emergent or umbrella strategy, as well as to serve as a marker in the evolution of a group's strategy, turned out to be a useful technique and an area that we feel deserves further testing and elaboration in other complex change efforts.

4. *It was important in VC that evaluation be primarily managed in-house.* The intent, design, and delivery of the evaluation were central elements in every stewardship discussion and decision in VC; occupied a great deal of the central staff team's time; and required evaluation firms to be in constant contact with and work

as partners alongside VC participants. It is difficult to imagine that the assessment would have been as relevant, flexible, and adaptive if it had been positioned as an external, distantly engaged, and periodically performed set of activities.

5. *The initiative required a high level of evaluation expertise.* Unlike many simple evaluations, in which the evaluators are chosen because of their competence in a particular methodology (e.g., social return on investment), the volume, diversity, and unpredictability of evaluation subjects in VC required the evaluation team to have a great deal of knowledge and experience from which to draw—often with only a moment's notice. Even then, the national team, local partners, and contracted evaluation firms often felt that the demands of the project outstripped their collective capacity.

6. *The mindset and relationships of project partners created the conditions for a patch evaluation in general and developmental evaluation in particular.* Had participants not felt a shared mission to do whatever it took to test a new approach, felt some level of joint ownership for the entire initiative, and deeply trusted one another, the evaluation might well have splintered into a variety of independent, rigid, and less useful evaluation activities. The importance of this "social contract" became evident later in the initiative, when newly arriving staff in Trail Builder organizations were substantially less "ready, willing, and able" to work with the Learning and Evaluation Package.

7. *There is continued uncertainty about what represented an appropriate burden of proof for demonstrating the effectiveness of the VC approach.* The question of whether the VC evaluation generated the kind of evidence to demonstrate the effectiveness of the "VC approach" was never fully resolved for initiative partners. Although this uncertainty did not appear to get in the way of the field's dramatic uptake of the VC model (and now the collective impact model), determining what constitutes sufficiently robust evidence is likely to be a tricky question to answer in all developmental evaluations.

REFERENCES

Anderson, A. (2005). *The community builder's approach to theory of change: A practical guide to theory development.* Washington, DC: Aspen Institute.

Born, P. (Ed.). (2010). *Creating vibrant communities: How individuals and organizations from diverse sectors of society are coming together to reduce poverty in Canada.* Waterloo, ON, Canada: Tamarack.

Cabaj, M. (Ed.). (2011a). *Cities reducing poverty: How Vibrant Communities are creating the comprehensive solutions to the most complex problem of our time.* Waterloo, Ontario, Canada: Tamarack—An Institute for Community Engagement.

Cabaj, M. (2011b). *Developmental evaluation: Experiences and reflections of 18 early adopters.* Unpublished master's thesis, University of Waterloo, Waterloo, Ontario, Canada.

Cabaj, M., & Leviten-Reid, E. (2006). *Understanding the potential and practice of comprehensive, multisectoral efforts to reduce poverty: The preliminary experiences of the Vibrant Communities Trail Builders.* Unpublished manuscript, Tamarack—An Institute for Community Engagement, Waterloo, Ontario, Canada.

Cabaj, M., Makhoul, A., & Leviten-Reid, E. (2006). *In from the field: Exploring the first poverty reduction strategies undertaken by Trail Builders in the Vibrant Communities initiative.* Unpublished manuscript, Tamarack—An Institute for Community Engagement, Waterloo, Ontario, Canada.

Gamble, J. (2010). *Evaluating Vibrant Communities: 2002–2010.* Waterloo, Ontario, Canada: Tamarack—An Institute for Community Engagement.

Gamble, J. (2012). *Inspired learning: An evaluation of Vibrant Communities national supports: 2002–2012.* Waterloo, Ontario, Canada: Tamarack—An Institute for Community Engagement.

Kania, J., & Kramer, M. (2011, Winter). Collective impact. *Stanford Social Innovation Review,* pp. 36–41.

Leviten-Reid, E. (2007). *Reflections on Vibrant Communities: 2002–2006.* Ottawa, Ontario, Canada: Caledon Institute.

Loewen, G., & Makhoul, A. (2009). *When a collaboration stumbles: The Opportunities Niagara story.* Ottawa, Ontario, Canada: Caledon Institute.

Makhoul, A. (2007a). *Opportunities 2000's year of change.* Ottawa, Ontario, Canada: Caledon Institute.

Makhoul, A. (2007b). *The tale of the Core Neighborhood Development Council in Saskatoon.* Ottawa, Ontario, Canada: Caledon Institute.

McNair, D., & Leviten-Reid, E. (2002). *Opportunities 2000: Creating pathways out of poverty in Waterloo Region.* Kitchener, ON, Canada: Lutherwood Community Opportunities Development Association.

Mintzberg, H., & Waters, J. A. (1985). Of strategies, deliberate and emergent. *Strategic Management Journal, 6*(3), 257–272.

Parker, S. (2014). *Evaluation of the J. W. McConnell Family Foundation Social Innovation Generation (SiG) Initiative.* Washington, DC: Center for Evaluation Innovation.

Patton, M. Q. (2011). *Developmental evaluation: Applying complexity concepts to enhance innovation and use.* New York: Guilford Press.

Shipler, D. (2004). *The working poor: Invisible in America.* New York: Knopf.

Torjman, S. (1999). *Are outcomes the best outcomes?* Ottawa, Ontario, Canada: Caledon Institute.

U.K. Department for International Development. (1999). Sustainable livelihoods guidance sheet: Introduction. Retrieved from *www.livelihoods.org/info/info_guidancesheets. html#1.*

Westley, F., Zimmerman, B., & Patton, M. (2006). *Getting to maybe: How the world is changed.* Toronto: Random House Canada.

Zimmerman, B., Lindberg, C., & Plsek, P. (1998). *Edgeware: Lessons from complexity science for health care leaders.* Irving, TX: VHA.

CHAPTER 10

Outcome Harvesting

A Developmental Evaluation Inquiry Framework
Supporting the Development of an International
Social Change Network

Ricardo Wilson-Grau, Paul Kosterink,
and Goele Scheers

EDITORS' INTRODUCTION

One of the 10 questions addressed in the opening chapter is this: What methods are used in developmental evaluation? The answer is that *developmental evaluation does not rely on or advocate any particular evaluation method, design, tool, or inquiry framework.* Methods can be emergent and flexible; designs can be dynamic. In essence, methods and tools have to be adapted to the particular challenges of developmental evaluation. This chapter exemplifies how that is done, featuring an innovative approach developed by Ricardo Wilson-Grau and colleagues (including coauthor Goele Scheers) called *outcome harvesting*.

Based in Rio de Janeiro but working internationally, Ricardo Wilson-Grau has become deeply engaged with developmental evaluation, contributing to both its theory and practice. As coeditor Michael Quinn Patton wrote the *Developmental Evaluation* book, Ricardo provided extensive feedback and contributed the "acid test" for determining whether developmental evaluation is an appropriate approach—that is, whether those working to bring about change face uncertainty and complexity (Patton, 2011, p. 106). Ricardo developed outcome harvesting for precisely those situations where social innovators do not have plans that can be conventionally evaluated because either what they aim to achieve, and what they would do to achieve it, are not sufficiently specific and measurable to compare and contrast what was planned with what was done and achieved; or they have to cope with dynamic, uncertain circumstances; or both. This complexity is the "nature of the beast" in contexts where social innovators are attempting to influence changes in the behavior of societal actors over whom they have no control, as is

typically the case in major systems change initiatives. Outcome harvesting is thus an evaluation approach that collects evidence of what has been achieved and then works backward to
determine whether and how the efforts of social innovators and their interventions contributed
to observed and documented changes.

A second major contribution of this chapter is demonstrating how emergent and highly
dynamic networks can be evaluated. Networks have developed as one of the primary ways
social innovators connect with and support each other to bring about change. From the moment
we began discussing what kinds of cases we wanted to include in this volume, we knew it
would be crucial to include an exemplar of a network evaluation. Networks present different
challenges, compared to evaluation's usual task of determining the effectiveness of projects and
programs. Innovative networks require innovative evaluation approaches, which is how outcome harvesting and developmental evaluation became integrated. Indeed, outcome harvesting
emerged, in part, from Ricardo's active participation in the worldwide network of hundreds of
evaluators using a related approach, *outcome mapping*. The use of networks as a form of social
organization has exploded with the rise of the Internet and with the increased understanding
that many significant issues are global in nature—such as climate change, human trafficking,
endangered species, economic development, human migration, new and potentially epidemic
diseases, and (as in the case in this chapter) preventing armed conflict. This chapter features a developmental evaluation of the Global Partnership for the Prevention of Armed Conflict
(GPPAC), using outcome harvesting as an inquiry framework; coauthor Paul Kosterink continues
to steward the use of the findings. Preventing armed conflict is, on the face of it, a dauntingly
complex endeavor. This example demonstrates that the initiatives of a dynamic global network
enmeshed in real-world complexities at all levels can be evaluated and thereby be accountable
for concrete, verifiable, and significant results. This is breakthrough work. Read on.

This is a story about how the Global Partnership for the Prevention of Armed
Conflict (GPPAC) used *outcome harvesting* as a developmental evaluation inquiry
framework to support its emergence as a collaborative social change network operating in complex circumstances. To this day, there does not exist a tried and proven
network model for organizations such as GPPAC, much less a ready-made mechanism for tracking its performance and learning from its successes and failures.
Therefore, GPPAC had to create them.

In 2006, GPPAC adapted the methodology of *outcome mapping* to the needs
of a global network, and from 2009 onward, GPPAC integrated outcome harvesting into its monitoring and evaluation (M&E) system. This enabled the network to
move away from the prevailing "What is planned needs to be achieved" mode, and
toward learning from what is emerging in order to continue developing. Today the
network systematically registers, reflects upon, and learns from the planned and
especially unplanned *developmental* outcomes of its autonomous affiliates and the
development outcomes of the United Nations (UN), regional intergovernmental
organizations (such as the League of Arab States), state actors, the media, and aca-
demia. Thus outcome harvesting has supported GPPAC's continual innovation in
what it is and what it does.

Preventing Conflict through Global Action

GPPAC (pronounced "geepak") is a member-led network of civil society organizations from around the world that are active in the field of conflict prevention and peace building. GPPAC seeks a world where violence and armed conflicts are prevented and resolved by peaceful means. GPPAC works toward a fundamental shift in how the world deals with violent conflict: moving from reaction to prevention. Founded in 2003, the network consists of 15 regional networks of local organizations, each with its own priorities, character, and agenda.

GPPAC informs policy by connecting civil society with key decision makers at national, regional, and global levels. As a network of peace builders, GPPAC presents civil society analysis of conflicts from a human security perspective, generating knowledge and fostering collaborative mechanisms to prevent violent conflict. GPPAC builds capacity through learning exchanges on conflict prevention, involving civil society practitioners, state institutions, UN representatives, regional organizations, and other key actors. In addition, since its inception GPPAC has had an internal strategic focus that concentrates resources on its own development—on strengthening the network.

In Exhibit 10.1, the fruits of GPPAC's multipronged efforts are exemplified. It was to support this development that, initially, Goele Scheers (as the client) working with Ricardo Wilson-Grau (as the external developmental evaluator) employed outcome harvesting, although we only came to realize that our concerted efforts could be called *developmental evaluation* when the approach was presented in Michael Quinn Patton's (2011) book.[1]

GPPAC's Special Challenges for Global Peace Building in Complex Situations

When Goele Scheers joined the Global Secretariat of GPPAC in 2005, the network was using the *logical framework* approach (commonly known as the *logframe*). There was great dissatisfaction with the approach, however, as it turned out to be inappropriate for GPPAC's M&E needs. As do other networks,[2] GPPAC faces a high degree of environmental and operational complexity (Scheers, 2008). There are two principal reasons for the complexity: uncertainty and diversity.

First, GPPAC faces a high degree of *dynamic uncertainty*. The actors and factors with which GPPAC has to contend change constantly and in unforeseeable ways. Thus the relationships of cause and effect between what the network plans to do and what it will achieve are simply unknown until the results emerge. All

---

[1]Ricardo was one of four evaluators who read and provided feedback to Michael Quinn Patton on the manuscript of *Developmental Evaluation: Applying Complexity Concepts to Enhance Innovation and Use* (Patton, 2011).

[2]GPPAC was eventually featured as a *global action network* in Steve Waddell's (2011) book *Global Action Networks: Creating Our Future Together*.

EXHIBIT 10.1

GPPAC Outcomes in 2012–2013

Strategic Focus / Thematic Priorities	Network Strengthening and Regional Action	Action Learning	Public Outreach	Policy and Advocacy
Preventive Action	*The Organization for Security and Co-operation in Europe (OSCE) employed GPPAC conflict analysis to train personnel as its Regional Early Warning Focal Points in Eastern Europe and Central Asia.* Representatives of the League of Arab States announced plans to open up the organization to civil society and strengthen cooperation channels. *The League of Arab States appointed a Secretary General's Special Envoy for Civil Society and established a Secretariat for Relations with Civil Society.*		*The UN Secretary General's 2013 Report on Human Security acknowledged GPPAC's role in advancing the human security concept.* *The United Nations Institute for Training and Research (UNITAR) agreed to officially partner with GPPAC to produce an SSR e-learning curriculum on the UN Learning Portal.* *The UN Secretary General invited GPPAC to speak at the UN High-Level Event on Human Security.*	
Dialogue and Mediation				
Peace Education				
Human Security				

GPPAC members operate in an environment subject to innumerable variables—political, economic, social, cultural, technological, and ecological—that influence the network's collaborative activities globally, regionally, and in over 100 countries. In addition, GPPAC has 12 categories of internal actors[3] and hundreds of stakeholders with varying missions, ways of working, forms, and sizes—national and multilateral, governmental and civil society. The network operates with a Global Secretariat, 15 Regional Secretariats, and dozens of national focal points representing affiliated organizations. The 15 Regional Steering Groups have 5, 10, 15, or more independent member organizations, which enter and exit with such fluidity that GPPAC does not know at any given moment the exact composition of its membership.

Second, GPPAC member organizations and their representatives have a *diversity* of motivations and resources, as well as varying levels of commitment—of course, within the unity of their common purpose to work together to prevent conflict and build peace. Indeed, the conviction that they cannot achieve some political objectives by working alone drives GPPAC members to participate in the network. The 200-plus member organizations participate in GPPAC of their own free will. At most, one or two staff members of a regional network are paid part-time by GPPAC; all other staff members volunteer their time.

---

[3]GPPAC members, GPPAC regional networks, thematic focal points, thematic working groups, Regional Secretariat, Regional Steering Groups, International Steering Group (ISG), Global Secretariat, Program Steering Committee, ISG liaisons, GPPAC board, and regional liaison officers.

The complexity is heightened because many of GPPAC's stakeholders, from regional staff to donors, have expectations (especially of management) that are rooted in the organizational realities they know best, those of their home institutions. In GPPAC's case, these are primarily nongovernmental organizations (NGOs) or government offices. In addition, donors and strategic allies tend to expect GPPAC to function as if it were a more conventional civil society organization. These stakeholders confront a dilemma, however, because networks are not NGOs. As a result of the complexity, when GPPAC contributes to an outcome, the effect may be direct but is often indirect, partial, and even unintentional, and usually comes about through the concerted actions of other actors (sometimes unknown to each other) along with GPPAC's initiatives. Also, an outcome generally occurs some time—even years—after the GPPAC activity. This means that the conventional M&E practice of comparing what has been done and achieved with what was planned is of dubious value to GPPAC or its stakeholders.

Initially, GPPAC tried to manage according to these conventional expectations, but they clashed with reality. This complexity made it extremely difficult— essentially an exercise in predicting the unpredictable—to develop a results-based framework such as the logframe, which produces a causal chain (scheduled inputs → activities → outputs → outcomes → impact) in which results are predefined in specific, measurable, achievable, realistic, and time-bound terms. Furthermore, reality changes so quickly across the network that within months plans prove not to be useful guides for action, and much less bases for learning and accountability.

Due to the nature of GPPAC as an international network, the implementation of its strategic plan, as well as of monitoring and evaluation, hinges on the buy-in and support of stakeholders. Therefore, by 2005, these dilemmas had to be resolved. GPPAC had realized it required an alternative approach to planning, monitoring, and evaluation (PM&E) if it was going to be able to assess efficiency and effectiveness in a useful manner and be accountable to its stakeholders.

Customizing Outcome Mapping for Planning and Monitoring

Therefore, even while commitments to donors required that the Work Plan for 2007–2010 (European Centre for Conflict Prevention, 2006) be a 4-year logframe with 21 targets, 85 worldwide activities, and hundreds of activities in the regions, GPPAC began to explore alternative PM&E approaches.

In 2006, Goele introduced a customized application of outcome mapping, a PM&E methodology developed by the Canadian International Development Research Centre.[4]

Outcome mapping was relevant for GPPAC for three reasons. First, outcome mapping would allow GPPAC to plan to adapt to continual change and take into account unexpected results. Second, the approach focuses on contribution and not

---

[4]The International Development Research Centre's outcome-mapping methodology is a results-oriented but very flexible methodology whose principles and procedures are readily adaptable for an international social change network's PM&E needs. See Earl, Carden, and Smutylo (2001).

attribution, which for GPPAC is important because conflict prevention and peace building come about when a multitude of actors interact to achieve change. Thus it is usually impossible to attribute this change to an intervention by a single actor. Furthermore, the essence of a network such as GPPAC is not the sum of its parts, but the interaction among its parts. Consequently, much of GPPAC's added value lies in the relationships among its members and contributing to the work each one is doing. Third, outcome mapping focuses on outcomes that can be the actions of key social actors that GPPAC helped *prevent* from happening, as well as those that GPPAC influenced to happen (Aulin & Scheers, 2012).

For the 2007–2010 Work Plan, GPPAC used outcome mapping to formulate *outcome challenges* for its five global programs.[5] These objectives presented what the social actors that GPPAC aimed to influence to change would be doing differently, and how, when, and where they would be doing these things, by 2010. A distinction was made between *internal* outcome challenges (related to the GPPAC actors) and *external* outcome challenges (related to actors outside of the network that GPPAC was trying to influence). GPPAC also agreed on up to 15 *progress markers*[6] for each outcome challenge per global program, and agreed to monitor progress on these markers by using a customized version of the outcome-mapping monitoring journals. By 2008, however, Goele realized that progress markers and outcome mapping's monitoring journals were too cumbersome for the network.[7] Nonetheless, GPPAC desperately needed to track what it was achieving in order to be accountable to donors, as well as to improve performance. This led Goele to ask what today we recognize was a developmental evaluation question: What monitoring and evaluation tool would be compatible with outcome mapping, but would

---

[5] An *outcome challenge* is a goal in outcome mapping that describes the *ideal* changes in the behavior, relationships, activities, and/or actions of the actor the program is trying to influence. An outcome challenge is visionary and describes what the intervention will achieve if it is very successful. For example:

> The Network Program intends to see autonomous GPPAC Regional Secretariats functioning as the heart of the Global Partnership, taking initiative and leadership in driving regional GPPAC processes, and actively shaping the global agenda and processes. The Regional Secretariat will be hosted by an organization in the region actively engaged in conflict prevention and peace building that has the capacity and institutional infrastructure to coordinate and administer the regional network, fundraise for and facilitate implementation of the Global and Regional Work Plans in the region, facilitate processes embedded in local realities that foster ownership of GPPAC in the region, and interact with the broader GPPAC network—nationally, globally, and other regions in the Global Partnership.

[6] *Progress markers* are a set of graduated ("expect, like, and love to see") indicators of changed behaviors for the subject of an outcome challenge that focus on the depth or quality of change. For the GPPAC outcome cited in footnote 5, the network *expected* that by 2007 its Regional Secretariats would "fundraise and acquire the necessary resources (financial, skilled human resources and office) to implement the Regional Work Plan." GPPAC would *like to see* the Regional Secretariats "planning, monitoring and evaluating the regional process including regular reporting," and would *love to see* them "facilitating credible national and regional processes through which National Focal Points are established and Regional Steering Group members are selected (transparent and inclusive processes)."

[7] Eventually GPPAC would conclude that making a full-fledged outcome-mapping strategic plan (*intentional design*) was too time- and money-consuming, and that the actual benefits would be minimal. In a network where spaces to meet and discuss planning are limited, and the context is rapidly changing, planning has to be kept light. GPPAC members now mainly focus on developing and agreeing on common outcome challenges and strategies. See Aulin and Scheers (2012).

encourage (if not ensure) the participation of voluntary, autonomous, and very busy informants in identifying and reporting the outcomes they were achieving, both intended and especially unintended?

To pursue an answer, Goele hired Ricardo[8] in 2007 to develop a baseline study of the network-building program (Wilson-Grau, 2007), and from 2009 onward to support the ongoing innovation of the methodology. Although neither of us explicitly talked of our engagement as an exercise in developmental evaluation, with hindsight we realized that it turned out to be the beginning of long-term developmental evaluation support for the ongoing development of the GPPAC network and especially of its PM&E system.

Introducing Outcome Harvesting for Evaluation

In late 2008, Goele decided to lead a Mid-Term Review of the 2006–2010 strategic plan, with support from Ricardo who had continued to contribute to GPPAC's understanding of the complex challenges of monitoring and evaluating its work (Wilson-Grau, 2008). The overarching review question that GPPAC decided should guide the collection of data was to be this: "To what extent were GPPAC's activities contributing to strategically important outcomes?" We were to focus on internal and external outcomes achieved by GPPAC regions and working groups in 2006–2008. Therefore, we seized this opportunity also to explore an alternative tool for monitoring and evaluating the work of GPPAC.

Independently of GPPAC, Ricardo and his coevaluators had been developing an instrument over the previous 3 years that would eventually be known as *outcome harvesting*. This is a tool inspired and informed by outcome mapping, which he had used to track and assess the performance and results of international social change networks similar to GPPAC, as well as the programs of the Dutch development funding agency Hivos (whose policies were similar to those of GPPAC's donors). The essence of the tool was to focus on outcomes as the indicators of progress; it constituted, as the UN Development Programme (2013) came to describe it, "an evaluation approach that—unlike some evaluation methods—does not measure progress towards predetermined outcomes, but rather collects evidence of what has been achieved, and works backward to determine whether and how the project or intervention contributed to the change." For the GPPAC Mid-Term Review (Scheers & Wilson-Grau, 2009), Goele acted as an internal evaluator and Ricardo as an external evaluator to apply the principles of what would become a six-step tool, although at the time we did not refer to the process as *outcome harvesting*.

We defined *outcomes* as the changes in the behavior of social actors (*boundary partners*, in outcome-mapping language) that GPPAC influenced but did not control. In recognition of the uncertainty and dynamism generated by complexity, these changes could be expected or unexpected, as well as positive or negative. GPPAC's contribution to these changes could be small or large, direct or indirect.

---

[8] Ricardo was having a similar experience introducing outcome mapping into the Global Water Partnership (*www.gwp.org*).

In addition to formulating the outcome, we briefly formulated its significance and the way in which GPPAC contributed to the change.

As the name implies, at the core of outcome harvesting is the collection of data. Between March and September 2009, Goele and Ricardo engaged every GPPAC region and program manager through email, Skype calls, or personal interviews—including field visits to central Asia, eastern and central Africa, and South Asia—to help them identify and formulate the most significant outcomes. In total, 14 GPPAC regions participated in the harvest.

In the light of GPPAC's uses for the outcomes, and in recognition of people's limited time, we asked each region or working group to identify up to five outcomes that they considered to be the most significant in 2006–2008. The idea was to have a representative sampling and not an exhaustive inventory of outcomes achieved, simply because working retrospectively would make that exercise too time-consuming.

The outcomes were of two types:

1. *Internal outcomes*: demonstrated changes in the actions of GPPAC members that strengthened and developed their collective capacity to achieve GPPAC's purpose. These outcomes enhanced meaningful collaboration among members, the functionality of network secretariats, and the improvement of GPPAC members' own practices. They were (and are) important bricks in building a strong network capable of influencing external actors.

2. *External outcomes*: similarly demonstrated changes in individuals, groups, or organizations outside the GPPAC network that represented significant contributions to conflict prevention and peace building.

The GPPAC members identified a potential outcome and then did the following:

- *Formulated the outcome*: Who did what that was new or different? Specifically, they described who changed; what changed in their behavior, relationships, activities, or actions; and when and where this occurred.

- *Described its significance*: They briefly explained why the outcome was important for GPPAC. The challenge was to contextualize the outcome so that a user of the findings would understand why the outcome was important for conflict prevention or peace building.

- *Described how GPPAC contributed*: The members indicated why they considered the outcome a result—partially or totally, directly or indirectly, intentionally or not—of GPPAC's activities.

In the end, we harvested 68 outcomes (an average of 3.3 for each of the 14 regions reporting); the number per region varied from 1 to 11. (See Exhibit 10.2 for an example of an outcome.) The variation was due to different factors. Generally, regions where the GPPAC network is not strong or not fully operational reported fewer outcomes. Also, people reported the changes that were foremost in their minds, and these tended to be the most recent outcomes or those that were

---

EXHIBIT 10.2

Example of a GPPAC Outcome

Description: In 2008, the UN Peacebuilding Commission (UNPBC) incorporated civil society organizations' recommendations regarding the importance of accountability and human rights training for the security services in its semiannual review of peacebuilding in Burundi.

Significance: The review is a valuable tool for civil society to encourage both the Burundian government and its international partners to attach conditions to their technical and resource support to the security services, particularly the intelligence service, to address ongoing human rights abuses. (The recommendations concerned human rights abuses in Burundi in 2007–2008.) As a result of the UNPBC's recommendations, international actors pledged support for security sector reform. This fact demonstrates the rapid response capacity of the civil society organizations and their ability to speak with one voice, as well as the recognition by the UNPBC of the organizations' role in the country's peace-building process.

Contribution of GPPAC: GPPAC member WFM-IGP (based in New York), along with the Biraturaba Association (the GPPAC national focal point in Burundi), organized briefings for the UNPBC with Burundi-based civil society organizations and international civil society experts on Burundi, followed up by a position paper and lobbying aimed at the 2008 draft report of the UNPBC. The added value of GPPAC was in connecting the New York UN arena with the local and national level in Burundi. While channeling the voices from local organizations in Burundi strengthened WFM-IGP's advocacy in New York, the Biraturaba Association and its Burundi network were able to directly access the policy makers in the international arena.

---

most memorable. The quality of the outcomes also varied: The average length of the formulation of the outcomes was just under one single-spaced page and averaged 450 words each, but many if not most were poorly written. One standard criterion for an outcome in outcome harvesting is that the formulation be sufficiently specific and measurable to be verifiable. In the course of the review, GPPAC decided that identifying the sources would suffice, although some outcomes were verified with independent, knowledgeable third parties. For example, for the UN Peacebuilding Commission (UNPBC) outcome in Exhibit 10.2, we spoke with the head of the UNPBC in Burundi. In the light of the Mid-Term Review's process use to develop GPPAC staff capacity in identifying outcomes, it was more important to involve people in formulating outcomes even if these were imperfect than it was to burden them with crafting sounder ones. Thus, for example, some outcomes did not have specific dates, although it was understood that they occurred some time between 2006 and 2009.

The First Strategic Innovations Supported by Outcome Harvesting

The "proof of the pudding" of outcome harvesting as a developmental evaluation tool is that the process and findings usefully answer a developmental evaluation question. The review process demonstrated that outcome harvesting was a compatible and a viable means to monitor and evaluate what GPPAC actors were achieving throughout the network. More specifically, to what extent did the 68 outcomes answer the review questions in a manner useful for the ongoing development of GPPAC? The strategic decisions GPPAC took on the basis of information from the review are outlined in Exhibit 10.3.

All these strategic decisions were incorporated in the GPPAC Strategic Plan for 2011–2015. In addition, GPPAC members reflected on the outcomes gathered through the Mid-Term Review. Under Goele's guidance, they looked at what had emerged for their specific program and discussed the next steps for their GPPAC work.

The process, however, highlighted important structural challenges for PM&E in GPPAC. First, time is perhaps the most precious nonrenewable resource of a network such as GPPAC. This Mid-Term Review took twice as much time as planned because GPPAC members did not deliver their outcomes within the planned time frame. In part, this was because GPPAC's peace-building activists had higher priorities than M&E. Thus, although we worked with informants in crafting their outcomes, their limited time was a major constraint. Second, and also related to time, informants tended to remember and report the most important and most recent outcomes, to the detriment of smaller, incipient, and earlier changes. Third, when an outcome was a result of GPPAC's influencing change in a social actor with whom the network was collaborating, informants were hesitant because they were concerned not to be perceived as claiming they had influenced a behavioral change in someone else. Fourth, there was an issue of political sensitivity because GPPAC's advocacy and campaigning were often ongoing at the time when outcomes were harvested.

A different complication was language: Informants were formulating outcomes in English, which for the majority was their second, third, or fourth language. Also, the harvesting process revealed a communication problem independent of the informants' native language: Regardless of variables such as education, profession, occupation, and available time, most people are not comfortable in expressing themselves in writing even in their native language, and few do so well.

Further Integrating Outcome Harvesting into the GPPAC PM&E System

Through the Mid-Term Review and follow-up by Goele, the essence of outcome harvesting had been woven into the evolving GPPAC PM&E system. As Goele says, "Instead of reporting on the outcome-mapping progress markers, the Global and Regional Secretariats were charged from 2009 onward to harvest outcomes: report every year on changes in social actors, their significance for conflict prevention and how GPPAC contributed." Also, due to the high turnover in GPPAC staff, the network implemented ongoing training of new staff to identify and communicate outcomes and how they were achieved. Goele, as the PM&E coordinator, coached

EXHIBIT 10.3

GPPAC Strategic Decisions Informed by the 2006–2010 Mid-Term Review

Review findings	Strategic decisions
GPPAC's outcomes in 2006–2008 mainly contributed to the mission of "building a new international consensus," "promoting peace building," and most notably "pursuing joint action to prevent violent conflict." It was too early to conclude what GPPAC members were contributing to the eventual impact that GPPAC envisioned.	1. Resist pressure from stakeholders to describe in detail the "impact" GPPAC will achieve. That is, GPPAC will not pretend to document the fundamental changes in the lives of people that result from the network's contributions to dealing with violent conflict, and specifically to a "shift from reaction to prevention." GPPAC will be accountable for contributing to changes that are upstream from sustainable development and human security.
GPPAC programs were generating more outcomes than were the regional activities.	2. Intensify the support to regional activities, including funding, but avoid the Global Secretariat's being seen simply as a donor. 3. Establish a better connection between the programs and the regional activities.
The contribution of GPPAC to outcomes was through GPPAC-funded activities, but also from members' being part of a global network.	4. Define networkwide criteria for what constitutes a "GPPAC activity" versus members' other conflict prevention and peace-building activities.
A third of the outcomes demonstrated the motivation of GPPAC members to drive the network by getting together to exchange and collaborate, take on leadership roles, and carry forward activities without help from the Global or Regional Secretariats.	5. Develop criteria for regional affiliate sustainability goals as a means to decide when and where current GPPAC activities are no longer necessary.
GPPAC was suffering from the common tension in networks around the right mix of centralized and decentralized decision making, fund raising/disbursement of funds, and responsibility for implementation of activities.	6. Set up a Program Steering Committee. 7. Allocate more resources to translation. 8. Define mutually agreed-upon criteria for allocating funding, and strictly and transparently enforce their application.
GPPAC was generating outputs and outcomes through its regions and programs, with, however, significant differences in quantity and quality. Nonetheless, although this diversity was expected in a dynamic network, the problems were not minor.	9. Give more resources to network strengthening.

them all and supervised the development of the system. During regular monitoring and learning meetings, the program managers and network members discussed outcomes. They reflected on trends and patterns in the outcomes, discussed next steps, and formulated suggestions for strategic decisions. The Program Steering Committee that was set up as a result of the Mid-Term Review used this input to make the nine strategic decisions presented in Exhibit 10.3.

In spite of the Global Secretariat's training and coaching, however, by 2011 it was clear that inconsistency in the reporting of outcomes continued to be problematic across the network. A useful harvest of outcomes from beginning to end continued to consume a great deal of both clock and calendar time. Furthermore, in complex and dynamic circumstances, the usefulness of outcomes has a very short half-life. Not only must they be harvested in a timely manner, but also in GPPAC, the right way to learn systematically from the outcomes through periodic monitoring meetings was still emerging.

Throughout the network, monitoring meetings consumed much time and many resources. People would rather spend money on a content meeting than on discussing outcomes. Consequently, the next developmental evaluation question GPPAC posed was this: "To what extent is GPPAC overcoming its weaknesses and building on its strengths to develop as an international network?"

A new opportunity arose that same year to pursue this question systematically and to hone the outcome harvesting tool as it had been integrated into GPPAC's PM&E system. The GPPAC PM&E cycle included an external evaluation of GPPAC's program. Goele contracted with Ricardo and a coevaluator[9] to carry out this major 2006–2011 evaluation, to provide substantial evidence of what outcomes GPPAC had achieved and how.[10] Although this exercise was going to be used for accountability with donors and would therefore serve the purpose of a summative evaluation, Goele made it very clear that Ricardo and his colleague were evaluating a network and a program that were in development and constant innovation. It was above all a part of GPPAC's own monitoring and learning cycle; the process and findings, like those of the Mid-Term Review, would serve the development of GPPAC too. Consequently, Goele avoided calling it a *summative evaluation*, and today we all consider it to have been a *developmental evaluation*.

For the evaluation terms of reference and the evaluation design, Goele and the evaluators agreed to use outcome harvesting, which GPPAC had started using in 2008 as described above.[11] By 2011, Ricardo had evolved outcome harvesting from a simple data collection tool into a six-step developmental evaluation *inquiry*

---

[9]Natalia Ortiz was the coevaluator. She is an independent consultant, based in Colombia, who advised GPPAC on its use of outcome mapping.

[10]Since both Natalia and Ricardo had been working as consultants to support the development of the GPPAC PM&E mechanisms, the ISG weighed the propriety of their serving as external evaluators. The ISG decided that the danger of conflict of interest (they would be evaluating in part the results of a management system they had helped create) was outweighed by the importance of their understanding of GPPAC and its evolution over the years in a rapidly changing environment.

[11]GPPAC ISG members developed a systems map for GPPAC globally under the guidance of Peter Woodrow, during their meeting in Buenos Aires in 2008.

framework. (For more on inquiry frameworks, see Patton, 2011, chap. 8.) Thus Goele and the evaluators agreed to use this full-fledged tool to design the evaluation. This was in addition to using it as the instrument with which to collect data on outcomes, which since 2009 had increasingly been the established practice in GPPAC.

What this meant practically was that while the 2006–2011 evaluation (Ortiz & Wilson-Grau, 2012) was the responsibility of external consultants, it was focused on the needs of the *primary intended users* (see Patton, 2012), and it was participatory.

The evaluators' role was that of facilitators in a professional, systematic, data-based joint inquiry with GPPAC actors globally and regionally, rather than as detached external experts wielding "objective" measuring sticks.

As noted above, the full-fledged outcome harvesting inquiry framework consists of six steps. (Goele and Ricardo had followed only the third step in the Mid-Term Review.) A description of these steps and their use follows.

1. Design the Outcome Harvest

The primary intended users of the 2006–2011 evaluation findings were the GPPAC board, management, and global and regional staffs. They were to *use* the findings of the evaluation to adapt and strengthen the 2011–2015 strategic plan. There were two important *process uses*: (a) further developing the GPPAC PM&E system by building the capacity of staff at the global and regional levels of GPPAC to identify and formulate outcomes; and (b) stimulating a learning environment in the GPPAC network. Furthermore, the broader audience for the evaluation included GPPAC donors, especially the Dutch and Austrian governments.

In outcome harvesting, the questions that guide the next five steps are derived from the users' principal uses; they must be *actionable* questions (i.e., ones that enable users to make decisions or take actions). For the GPPAC evaluation, Goele and the evaluators agreed on four questions. We focus here on the one that involved an assessment of the network-strengthening strategy of GPPAC:

> *Strategic effectiveness*—What patterns or features did the evaluators find in the way GPPAC contributed to its outcomes, and what did those patterns suggest about how effectively GPPAC works?[12]

---

[12]The other three questions were as follows:

- GPPAC's results—The impact of GPPAC's outcomes. How did the behavior, relationships, activities, or actions of the people, groups, and organizations with which GPPAC works directly change? What are the most successful pathways of change?
- *Theory of change*—To what extent do the 2006–2011 outcomes support the assumptions in GPPAC's rationale for its strategies, the social actors it aims to influence, and the outcomes to which it aims to contribute?
- *GPPAC's current performance*—In the light of what GPPAC members consider is the level of performance of, on the regional level, networks, steering groups, and secretariats, and on the global level, the ISG, board, Program Steering Committee, working groups, and Global Secretariat, what areas should be strengthened in the next 5 years?

2. Gather Data and Draft Outcome Descriptions

As explained earlier in the chapter, both GPPAC programs and the environment in which they operate are highly complex, open, and dynamic. Faced with this evaluation challenge, a linear, cause–effect mindset of comparing what was done and achieved to what was planned would not have been useful. Therefore, without concern for what had been planned as activities, outputs, or outcomes, Ricardo and his coevaluator simply identified and formulated approximately 250 potential outcomes extracted from the 51 reports for 2006–2011 on file with the GPPAC Global Secretariat, including the Mid-Term Review.

3. Engage Change Agents in Formulating Outcome Descriptions

The evaluators then communicated virtually with the GPPAC Global and Regional Secretariats to support them in reviewing our draft formulations and answer questions aimed at turning them into verifiable outcomes. Paul Kosterink played an important role in this process by facilitating the participation of the 15 staff members in the Global Secretariat. Those GPPAC change agents consulted with others within the network with knowledge of what had been achieved and how. They suggested additional outcomes. Working iteratively with the evaluators, together they whittled down the outcomes to 208.

By the end of April 2012, the evaluators had a set of solid outcomes that represented a considerable quantitative improvement over those of the Mid-Term Review (see Exhibit 10.4). Overall, there was a threefold increase in outcomes harvested. With the exception of two regional affiliates, all regions appreciably increased the number of outcomes registered. Equally important, the length of each outcome was slashed by more than half, to an average of 215 words. The evaluators, instead of compiling them into what would have been 75 pages of outcomes, stored them in a Drupal database so that the information could be more usefully managed.

Qualitatively, the evaluation deepened and broadened the harvest of outcomes, which, in contrast to a sizable number of the Mid-Term Review outcomes, were concise enough to be quantitatively and qualitatively measurable. Each outcome was sufficiently specific that someone without specialized subject or contextual knowledge would be able to understand and appreciate the "who, what, when, and where" of things that were being done differently. Equally important, there was a plausible relationship, a logical link, between each outcome and how GPPAC had contributed to it. That contribution was described in similarly hard and measurable terms—who did what that contributed to the outcome. The outcomes were qualitatively verifiable.

Even though the Mid-Term Review had only requested up to five outcomes from each informant for 2006–2009, and the 2006–2011 evaluation attempted to harvest *all* significant outcomes that each informant knew of since 2006, the sources of outcomes were basically the same—program managers at the Global Secretariat and regional liaison officers. Thus the increase in the number of outcomes harvested was an indicator both of improved capacity on the part of GPPAC actors to influence change and of improved reporting on outcomes.

EXHIBIT 10.4

GPPAC Outcomes

Outcomes by source	Mid-term review	Evaluation 2006–2011
Regional Secretariats	**47**	**165**
Caucasus	1	12
Central and Eastern Africa	11	16
Central Asia	3	3
Latin America and the Caribbean	2	8
Middle East and North Africa	2	6
North America	2	6
Northeast Asia	4	22
South Asia	5	16
Southeast Asia	6	14
Southern Africa	3	0
The Pacific	1	18
West Africa	1	9
Western Balkans	4	31
Western CIS	2	4
Global program	**21**	**43**
Total	**68**	**208**

Note. CIS, Commonwealth of Independent States (an organization of former Soviet republics).

4. Substantiate

Evaluation in general, and identifying and formulating outcomes in particular, will always have an element of subjectivity. For example, when a person who identifies a change in another social actor is also responsible for GPPAC's activities that are intended to influence that change, there is an undeniable element of bias. Similarly, different people will have different knowledge of what happened and different perspectives on how GPPAC contributed. Therefore, outcome harvesting strives for more objectivity by providing for substantiation of outcomes in a way that enhances their understanding and credibility.

Initially, the evaluators proposed to check on the veracity of the evaluation's outcomes through a random sampling of independent third parties with knowledge of each outcome. In the end, however, in consultation with GPPAC, the evaluators decided against substantiating the outcomes. These were deemed to be sufficiently accurate for the uses of the evaluation, for these reasons:

a. The outcomes were reported in documents produced by the GPPAC activists who contributed to the outcomes.

b. All informants understood that the external evaluators could verify their outcomes.

c. Two or more GPPAC program and regional staff members responsible for contributing to the outcomes cross-checked 177 of the 208 outcomes. An additional 25 incomplete outcomes[13] were excluded from the data set.

d. The evaluators examined all 208 final outcomes to ensure that there was a plausible rationale for what was reported as achieved and the reported contribution of GPPAC.

Furthermore, although the outcomes were not exhaustive of GPPAC's achievements in 2006–2011, GPPAC and the evaluators also considered that they were representative of the network's most significant achievements, and therefore a solid basis for decision making and accountability to donors.

5. Analyze and Interpret

The evaluators also involved the program managers in classifying the outcomes (with their critical oversight, of course). They placed the classified outcomes in the Drupal database in order to be able to make sense of them, analyze and interpret the data, and provide evidence-based answers to the useful harvesting questions.

GPPAC's stakeholders' interest went beyond aggregating outcomes; the stakeholders wanted to understand the process of change the network was supporting. This was one of the values of outcome harvesting for this evaluation.

For example, with the GPPAC Western Balkans regional network, the evaluators compiled the majority of its 28 outcomes into a two-and-a-half-page story of how this network had influenced peace education over the years 2008–2012.[14] In Exhibit 10.5, we extract a single year, 2010, from that story. (The numbers in brackets in this exhibit refer to the outcomes.)

Mixed-Methods Interpretation of External Outcomes

Outcome harvesting's *analysis* function is about aggregating outcomes into clusters, processes, patterns, and stories of change. The *interpretation* function is to explain what the outcomes, and the stories, mean. In the GPPAC evaluation, the interpretation involved answering the evaluation questions. The relevant question for the Western Balkans was this: To what extent did the 28 outcomes contribute

---

[13]That is, a change in a social actor was identified, but it was unclear whether it was an output or an outcome, or GPPAC's contribution was unclear.

[14]Even this is a partial story—what the GPPAC regional network in the Western Balkans achieved in terms of *outcomes*. The full story would include the *contribution* of GPPAC to each outcome, as well as its *significance*.

EXHIBIT 10.5

One Year in an Outcome Story

In 2010, practitioners-teachers and Ministry of Education representatives from the Western Balkans and Western Commonwealth of Independent States (CIS) regions wrote articles that they collected into a booklet, which the Development Center for Information and Research in the Ukraine published. The booklet consists of various methodological materials on peace education (PE)—experts' texts either on voicing the need for PE or on certain topics related to PE. [131] This same year, the Serbian Deputy Minister of Education committed to follow-up on recommendations on the integration of PE programs outlined in the Declaration on Joint Cooperation with Civil Society Organizations in the Field of Peace Education (signed in 2009). [124]

In July 2010, the Montenegrin assembly incorporated school mediation into the new law on education. Article 9b of the law highly recommends school mediation as a tool for conflict resolution. [269] And then in September, the Ministries of Education from Serbia and Montenegro officially supported the GPPAC-sponsored art competition by sending letters encouraging both teachers and pupils to participate in the competition. [139]

---

to change in the willingness and ability to act of the different actors playing roles in the Western Balkans conflict prevention system? For this question, the evaluators used a complementary inquiry framework—*complex systems change* (Patton, 2011, pp. 240–243).

During Ricardo's visit to the Western Balkans GPPAC affiliate in Montenegro, Regional Steering Group members agreed with him that the system they were working to influence had three dimensions: the components of the system and their *interrelationships*; the different *perspectives* on those interrelationships; and the *boundaries* determining what components made up the system and which interrelationships and perspectives were taken into account (see Exhibit 10.6).[15]

These dimensions would vary, of course, from system to system. In the Western Balkans system, the components might be the same as in other regions of the world, but the interrelationships between, for example, civil society and governments would necessarily be quite different. In addition, the perspectives on the boundaries—on who was in and who was out of the system—would vary.

The 28 outcomes of GPPAC in the Western Balkans tell an impressive story of how a group of dedicated women[16] influenced change at two tipping points in the

---

[15]See Williams and Hummelbrunner (2011, pp. 18–23). The idea of the systems map was based on work by Peter Woodrow of the CDA Collaborative Learning Project, Boston, Massachusetts, together with GPPAC members in 2008.

[16]All but one of the RSG members are women, as are the GPPAC team members. They explain that the absence of men is not due to the fact that men in the region have both historically and recently been warriors, as an outsider with superficial knowledge of the region might assume. Rather, the women believe that by and large men throughout the region have been traumatized by war and by the reality that no one was a victor, since NATO imposed peace by force of arms.

EXHIBIT 10.6

Complex Systems Change: The Dimensions of the System in the Western Balkans GPPAC Affiliate

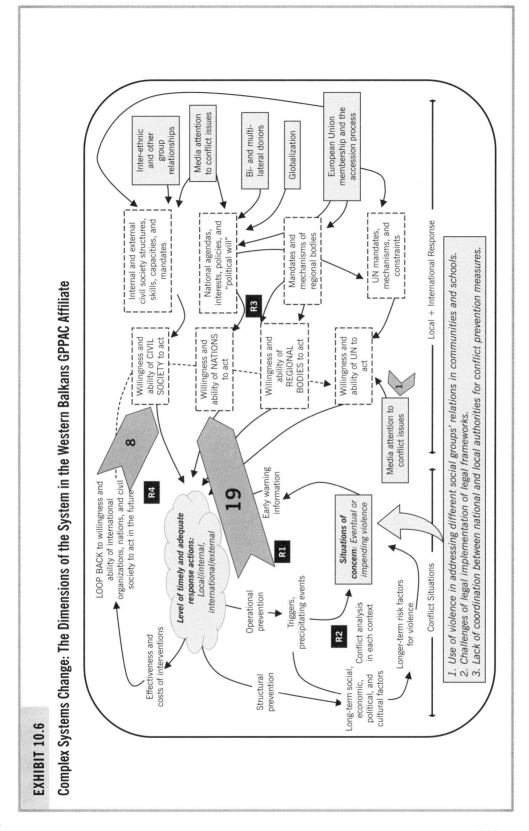

Local + International Response

1. Use of violence in addressing different social groups' relations in communities and schools.
2. Challenges of legal implementation of legal frameworks.
3. Lack of coordination between national and local authorities for conflict prevention measures.

system: the willingness and ability of nations and civil society to act. Two-thirds of the outcomes related to state actors, and the majority were focused on influencing the national and municipal schools and educators. (In Exhibit 10.6, the numbers in arrows refer to outcomes.) Intertwined with 5 years of influencing state actors to make changes in their policies and practices that would represent a more significant process of peace education in the Western Balkans, the GPPAC regional network influenced complementary changes in civil society and one change in the media. In other words, this successful, ongoing story of introducing peace education, including mediation, into the Western Balkans required working simultaneously to influence civil society, the education system, the media, and government.

Internal Outcomes as Evidence of Network Strengthening

Since 2006, GPPAC had made great efforts to consolidate as a true network, including a restructuring of investment to strengthen the regional networks. Notably, in 2009 GPPAC received the ISO 9001 quality management certification given by the United Kingdom Accreditation Service, the sole national accreditation body recognized by the UK government to assess, against internationally agreed-upon standards, organizations that provide certification, testing, inspection, and calibration services. To assess the degree of success, financial analysis was combined with the outcomes data. GPPAC's income between 2007 and 2010 increased by 80%, but the direct allocations to strengthen the regional networks increased by 750%. Although as a percentage of GPPAC's overall budget the investments to strengthen the regional networks were in low single digits, the rate of increase was greater than the increase in investments in the global programs or the Global Secretariat (Exhibit 10.7).

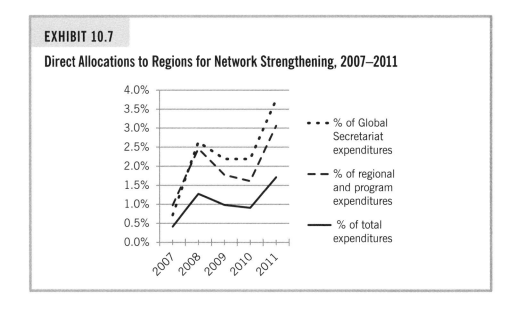

EXHIBIT 10.7

Direct Allocations to Regions for Network Strengthening, 2007–2011

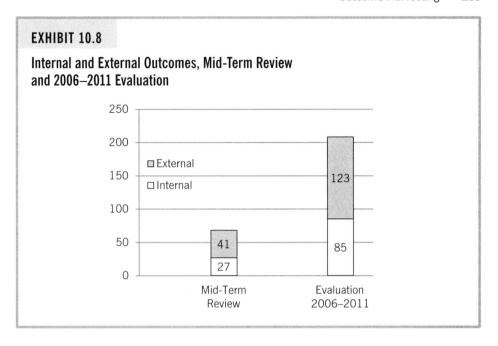

EXHIBIT 10.8

Internal and External Outcomes, Mid-Term Review and 2006–2011 Evaluation

In 2006–2011, GPPAC progressively consolidated both its internal structure and its internal functions; it also improved the practices of its members through greater exchange of knowledge and experience and more collaboration between them for lobbying, advocacy, and actions. The increased investment in strengthening the regions corresponded to the hefty increase in internal as well as external outcomes harvested during the evaluation (Exhibit 10.8).

In sum, the use of outcome harvesting enabled the evaluators to harvest outcomes from a sufficiently diverse group of GPPAC staff members to ensure that the findings (a) were sufficiently representative of the most significant changes achieved by GPPAC, and (b) would permit evidence-based answers to the evaluation question of GPPAC's effectiveness in 2006–2011.

6. Support Use of Findings

The last step in an outcome-harvesting process is to raise issues that have come up in the process of collecting, analyzing, and interpreting data; to propose evidence-based points for discussion to the users; and to support them in making use of the findings. In collaboration with Ricardo and his coevaluator, Paul prepared the workshop to discuss the findings and follow-up of the evaluation with the board and Program Steering Committee. In the GPPAC evaluation, half of the recommended points for discussion were developmental evaluation questions for the continuing development of the network's PM&E system:

a. How can GPPAC ensure that everyone who is accountable for outcomes and everyone who must use them give due priority to PM&E?

b. Since complexity means that at the moment of planning, much is uncertain and unpredictable because the cause–effect relationship between what actors do (activities and outputs) and what they will achieve (outcomes) is unknown, what is the right balance of involving people in GPPAC in monitoring and evaluation versus planning?

c. What alternative ways should GPPAC consider to identify outcomes that will ensure (i) harvesting the significant outcomes in as close to real time as possible; and (ii) processing them in a manner that involves analyzing and interpreting them so that they are available to inform decision making in a timely fashion?

As with the Mid-Term Review, the usefulness of the evaluation's findings to GPPAC was evidenced by the strategic decisions GPPAC's leadership took to further strengthen the network (see Exhibit 10.9).

Supporting Ongoing Strategic Innovation

In sum, through the use of outcome harvesting, we were able to serve a developmental evaluation function of introducing innovations into the GPPAC PM&E system, and thus contributed to developing GPPAC as a social change network. Between 2009 and 2012, Ricardo served as an external developmental evaluator to support Goele and Paul as internal GPPAC developmental evaluators. Goele and then Paul were able to influence a change in the network's emphasis from extensive planning to ongoing tracking of and learning from outcomes, through interaction among a variety of GPPAC actors. This is a process Paul continues. We used outcome harvesting as an inquiry framework, formulating what we eventually came to see as developmental evaluation questions, and then generating outcomes to answer them. Goele and Paul worked with GPPAC leaders and staff through an interactive learning process to use the findings to improve their policies and procedures.

In addition to the possibilities and advantages of using outcome harvesting to generate real-time evidence, this case shows that learning from M&E findings was a key to GPPAC's development. The use of such findings needs to be planned and organized carefully. It was the close cooperation between Goele and Paul (representing GPPAC and working internally) with Ricardo (working externally) that enabled GPPAC to overhaul its PM&E system and generate useful and timely learning to enhance its development. Today outcome harvesting and the internal developmental evaluation function continue to support the network as it copes with an uncertain and dynamic environment for conflict prevention and peace building.

In conclusion, through a multiyear developmental evaluation process, GPPAC learned that outcome harvesting led to a variety of significant advantages. As Paul summarizes these advantages, the network was able to develop a PM&E system that enables GPPAC to do the following:

EXHIBIT 10.9

GPPAC Strategic Decisions Informed by the 2006–2011 Evaluation

2006–2011 Evaluation findings	Strategic decisions 2012–2014*
In spite of considerable improvement in some regions, outcome reporting—and learning from the outcomes—continued to be deficient.	1. Invest human and financial resources in harvesting regional outcomes through direct interaction and dialogue, rather than through written reports only. 2. Store outcomes in a web-based GPPAC Monitoring Information System.
GPPAC was influencing four of the six external social actors it had targeted: state actors, civil society, traditional and new media, and the UN. The business sector had not been influenced, and it was too early to expect outcomes for the regional intergovernmental organizations (RIGOs).	3. Recognize that the business sector is not a priority for GPPAC in the foreseeable future. 4. Give special attention to monitoring GPPAC outcomes influenced by the RIGOs.
The evaluators found sufficient evidence to question, but not to conclude, whether GPPAC was overstretching organizationally and in its programming.	5. The network took up this finding and translated it into two related questions: "Are we spreading ourselves too thin?" and "Should we focus on a few common issues?" These were further addressed in strategic planning meetings of the network in 2012 and 2013. An increased focus is noticeable in the 2014 operational plans, and in the process to formulate the next 5-year strategic plan.
Among the consequences of the limited outcomes was that the evaluators could not conclude whether GPPAC's theory of change was validated. The strategies were working; the targeted social actors were being influenced; expected and unexpected outcomes were being achieved; there was evidence that GPPAC was influencing the system of interacting actors and factors that is the source of conflict and an obstacle to peace building. Nonetheless, there was not enough information about outcomes achieved over time to assess in a conclusive way whether the assumptions—and they are the heart—of the theory of change were well founded.	6. Define individual theories of change for the priority issues and processes in the strategic plan for 2016–2020. 7. Support regional networks to formulate theories of change for their regional priorities.

(continued)

*By the GPPAC board and Program Steering Committee, unless otherwise stated.

2006–2011 Evaluation findings	Strategic decisions 2012–2014*
GPPAC's achievements have principally been in three areas: a. Influencing the policies and practices of state actors that promise to change the practice of reaction to prevention of conflicts. b. Mobilizing civil society (organizations in particular, but the general public as well) to engage with state actors and the UN. c. Developing the GPPAC network on the global and regional levels.	8. Decide that linking local, regional, and global levels should be one of the leading strategic principles for the network.
GPPAC's four strategies were being effectively applied. They were influencing outcomes. For some of the substrategies, however, either it appeared premature to try to understand (because they were so new), or there was insufficient evidence to understand how some strategies might complement and reinforce each other in achieving the same outcome.	9. The global programs and the 15 regions reviewed their strategic progress in 2013 on the basis of harvested outcomes from the PM&E system. This new Mid-Term Review was set up to be "light" and participative, with the emphasis on reflection, learning, and adapting the current strategic plans, and on formulating new priorities where necessary.
GPPAC's performance as a network itself was better than good, and reasonable for a young, international network. There were numerous suggestions identified for ways to improve; most were obvious, but quite a few were novel.	10. Conclude that GPPAC is "on the right track," and yet "we can and should improve" and take next steps in the process to become an experiential, self-learning organization.

- Identify achievements more quickly and more comprehensively.
- Enhance learning about success and failure, rather than serving as a mechanism of operational or budgetary control.
- Appraise collectively the progress in the development of the network itself.
- Serve as a mechanism for accountability to internal and external stakeholders.
- Preserve the historical memory of the common processes that gave birth to and sustain the advocacy network.

Equally important is GPPAC's recognition that it makes much more sense to focus on what is emerging than on what is planned; thus the network devotes less time to the planning and more time to the monitoring and evaluation in PM&E. Also, ongoing annual developmental evaluation has demonstrated itself to be more useful to the network than conventional formative and summative evaluation. Outcome harvesting has proven to be suitable for evaluating and learning from complex change processes. And, lastly, GPPAC members and management have found that they can be accountable for results that lie between what they do and the conflict prevention and peace-building impact to which they ultimately aim to contribute.

REFERENCES

Aulin, J., & Scheers, G. (2012, October). *Measuring progress in conflict prevention: GPPAC's adaptation of outcome mapping* (OM Ideas No. 5). Ottawa, Ontario, Canada: International Development Research Centre.

Earl, S., Carden, F., & Smutylo, T. (2001). *Outcome mapping: Building learning and reflection into development programs.* Ottawa, Ontario, Canada: International Development Research Centre. Retrieved from *www.idrc.ca/EN/Resources/Publications/Pages/IDRCBookDetails.aspx?PublicationID=121.*

European Centre for Conflict Prevention, in consultation with Global Partnership for the Prevention of Armed Conflict International Steering Group. (2006, July). *GPPAC Work Plan 2007–2010.* The Hague, The Netherlands: European Centre for Conflict Prevention.

Ortiz, N., & Wilson-Grau, R. (2012, September), *GPPAC evaluation 2006–2011: An assessment of the outcomes achieved and the current performance of the Global Partnership for the Prevention of Armed Conflict.* The Hague, The Netherlands: Global Partnership for the Prevention of Armed Conflict.

Patton, M. Q. (2011). *Developmental evaluation: Applying complexity concepts to enhance innovation and use.* New York: Guilford Press.

Patton, M. Q. (2012). *Essentials of utilization-focused evaluation.* Thousand Oaks, CA: Sage.

Scheers, G. (2008). Measuring success in complex settings: GPPAC's experiences with planning, monitoring and evaluation. In G. Scheers (Ed.), *Assessing progress on the road to peace: Planning, monitoring and evaluating conflict prevention and peacebuilding activities* (GPPAC Issue Paper No. 5). The Hague, The Netherlands: European Centre for Conflict Prevention.

Scheers, G., & Wilson-Grau, R. (2009, September), *GPPAC Mid-Term Review 2006–2008: Final report.* The Hague, The Netherlands: Global Partnership for the Prevention of Armed Conflict.

United Nations Development Programme. (2013, August 23). *Discussion paper: Innovations in monitoring and evaluation.* New York: Author. Retrieved from *www.outcomemapping.ca/download/UNDP%20Discussion%20Paper%20Innovations%20in%20Monitoring%20and%20Evaluation.pdf.*

Waddell, S. (2011). *Global action networks: Creating our future together.* Milan, Italy: Boccioni University Press. Retrieved from *http://networkingaction.net/networks-change/global-action-networks.*

Williams, B., & Hummelbrunner, R. (2011). *Systems concepts in action: A practitioner's toolkit.* Stanford, CA: Stanford University Press.

Wilson-Grau, R. (2007, August). *Capacity-building baseline and outcome challenges for GPPAC.* The Hague, The Netherlands: Global Partnership for the Prevention of Armed Conflict.

Wilson-Grau, R. (2008). Evaluating the effects of international advocacy networks. Available at *http://mande.co.uk/blog/wp-content/uploads/2008/12/evaluating-the-effects-of-international-advocacy-networks-ricardo-wilson-grau-20071.pdf.*

CHAPTER 11

Adapted Developmental Evaluation with USAID's People-to-People Reconciliation Fund Program

**Susan H. Allen, David Hunsicker, Mathias Kjaer,
Rebekah Krimmel, Gabrielle Plotkin, and Kelly Skeith**

EDITORS' INTRODUCTION

This chapter describes the kind of situation and programming for which developmental evaluation is, in principle, ideal: conflict management and mitigation. Bringing diverse people together for reconciliation in areas of conflict is inherently uncertain, dynamic, emergent, and likely to be nonlinear in important respects. On the other hand, the funder, the United States Agency for International Development (USAID), has established standardized evaluation procedures and templates; emphasizes accountability and compliance; and has bureaucratic decision-making processes that limit flexibility, responsiveness, and rapid adaptations. How does developmental evaluation mesh with traditional accountability evaluation requirements and expectations? What emerges is an effort at adapted developmental evaluation, with a heavy emphasis on learning, but with other developmental uses limited by the realities of bureaucracy. The chapter authors have striven to overcome, sidestep, and/or convert bureaucratic constraints into developmental evaluation opportunities, with mixed results. The authors conclude by sharing lessons for engaging with developmental evaluation principles under these circumstances.

This chapter presents reflections on the use of developmental evaluation in a conflict resolution context. Specifically, the design of an evaluative learning review that included a developmental evaluation approach is discussed as it was applied in evaluating the People-to-People Reconciliation Fund Program, managed by the United States Agency for International Development's (USAID's) Office of Conflict Management and Mitigation (CMM). Although the chapter highlights the compatibility of developmental evaluation and conflict resolution, as both operate in complex adaptive system contexts and emphasize ongoing learning and adaptation, the case study also presents insights on ways developmental evaluation can be integrated as an approach within an evaluation design that includes traditional tools and a focus on accountability and assessment of program performance.

Key contributions from developmental evaluation are noted: shaping the reflective process to encourage long-term ongoing learning; creating conversations that themselves have a reconciliation effect; and setting in motion the possibility of changes to the program, once such changes go through the large decision-making structures in the U.S. government. The chapter also notes that developmental evaluation can be compatible with reconciliation program evaluation at the project level, where it can support implementers in making adjustments on the ground for rapid adaptation to changing needs. The full value of developmental evaluation may be more readily visible there than at the global program level described here, where its longer-term contributions are still emerging.

The Innovative Reconciliation Fund Program

Since 2004, USAID/CMM has held an annual Reconciliation Fund Program small-grants competition through an Annual Program Statement (APS). This competition is funded through a Congressional appropriation mandating projects that "support people-to-people reconciliation programs which bring together individuals of different ethnic, religious, and political backgrounds from areas of civil conflict and war" (*www.usaid.gov/who-we-are/organization/bureaus/bureau-democracy-conflict-and-humanitarian-assistance/office*).

Over time, the fund has grown from $8 million to $26 million annually, with approximately $10 million reserved for Middle East programming and $16 million for other global programs, supporting over 135 peace-building projects in 35 countries. Although the definitions have shifted slightly over time, the fund has always been focused on community and people-to-people (P2P) reconciliation work, particularly at the grassroots level. Grants typically range from $100,000 to $1.2 million, last from 12 to 36 months, and are managed by USAID missions around the globe. The range and types of P2P reconciliation programming supported under the fund are also broad and focused on varied strategic ways to contribute to and support peace building.

Challenges in Evaluating Diverse Reconciliation Processes in Different Complex Dynamic Contexts

The decentralized nature of USAID management of individual grants at the country mission level, and the broad range of reconciliation approaches, challenge CMM's ability to assess the aggregated effectiveness of all activities from this central level. In addition, CMM's ability to assess the effectiveness of the APS grants is complicated by the mercurial and complex nature of conflict-related programs, which are difficult to monitor and evaluate using standard, linear monitoring and evaluation

(M&E) approaches. Furthermore, conflict-related interventions rarely produce short-term, measurable results and are very context-sensitive; these characteristics make it difficult to establish meaningful baselines, identify properly sequestered counterfactual examples, successfully plan for target outputs, and attribute outcomes and results back to inputs.

Evaluation Phases and Purposes

In the fall of 2011, CMM contracted with Social Impact, Inc. (SI) to conduct a 2-year evaluative learning review of targeted awards and activities under its APS through a pilot application of the developmental evaluation methodology, along with other evaluation techniques. The objectives of this review were not only to learn about the APS projects themselves, but also to build CMM's technical leadership in evaluation of complex programs.

CMM's evaluative review of its programs included three nonsequential phases: (1) knowledge management and study of the Reconciliation Fund Program APS; (2) field evaluations of selected APS projects (specifically those in Israel/West Bank/ Gaza, Bosnia-Herzegovina, and Burundi); and (3) reflective learning, in which a learning group consisting of six experts in peace building and evaluation was utilized as a forum for discussion, technical review of learning products and data, and further inquiry. The final product was an overall synthesis report that drew together the lessons derived through these three phases. This report encompassed a desk study, three field evaluations, and a meta-analysis and metaevaluation over the course of the 2 years of the project. That report (SI, 2014) was issued in March 2014, but some lessons uncovered during the process of implementing the evaluative learning review had already begun to be considered and/or implemented before the report's release, as appropriate and as would be expected for a developmental approach.

The next sections provide some details about the various aspects of the evaluation, showing elements that were more traditional accountability-focused evaluation and elements that constituted developmental evaluation. A primary focus of this chapter is the challenge of integrating different evaluation purposes and processes within a large governmental bureaucratic context. Thus, elements of the evaluation had to address traditional accountability and compliance concerns, while also engaging in developmental evaluation for the more innovative and adaptive elements of the program at the implementation level.

Knowledge Management and Study of the Reconciliation Fund Program

The first deliverable product of the evaluative learning review was a desk review of a wide assortment of project designs and M&E documents from 94 APS grantee projects. This was a form of retrospective developmental evaluation (Patton, 2011, pp. 294–303)—looking backward at what has developed in the past to set the stage for understanding developments in the present and future. The review examined the strength and adaptability of the project designs; it reported implementation, the quality of the projects' reporting, challenges faced by the projects, and the larger impact on or contribution to peace and reconciliation (as reported by the implementers themselves). However, the inconsistent and incomplete nature of the documents reviewed limited the team's ability to draw definitive conclusions on any of these four topics. This was due to a variety of factors, including the facts that many projects were several years old; that implementers and USAID missions did not possess complete sets of records, due to the often decentralized approach to project implementation; and that no commonly understood standard for documenting P2P projects existed then (or exists now). In the spirit of developmental evaluation, the desk review study was conducted in a highly collaborative and iterative manner that encouraged ongoing learning from a range of stakeholders. This approach also served to maximize potential utilization of the review's findings. The data collection was guided by a list of questions identified in close consultation with CMM and the evaluation's learning group.

Metaevaluation and Meta-Analysis

The evaluative learning review also included a metaevaluation and meta-analysis of existing APS grantee evaluation reports as another desk-based study of project documents. The review of APS activity evaluations utilized a sample of P2P APS grant evaluation reports to assess the degree to which traditional evaluation criteria had been attempted in APS evaluations to date.

The assessment was driven by two sets of questions:

1. *The metaevaluation:* What methodologies have been used? Using evaluation standards, identify the strengths and weaknesses of the evaluation methodologies and products.

2. *The meta-analysis:* What can we learn about how to implement an effective P2P program? What can we learn about how well P2P programs are delivering results?

The metaevaluation was intended to provide a richer understanding for the evaluative learning review team and CMM about what evaluations had been conducted on APS activities to date, the strengths and weaknesses of the evaluations, and any findings related to outcomes of the APS programming. In addition, it helped to provide insights into better options for future APS activity evaluative efforts and opportunities for skill building among CMM's partners. The assessment of activity evaluations used a modified metaevaluation and meta-analysis framework, promoted by USAID's evaluation policy and its Program, Policy, and Learning

Office for use in the agency's evaluation work. Unlike the other learning products or processes, the approach to this component of the evaluative learning review did not employ a particularly iterative or collaborative approach in order to generate findings, conclusions, or recommendations regarding the quality of evaluations conducted on APS grantee projects. Although the metaevaluation was conducted with standard, traditional criteria and did not, by itself, constitute an aspect of developmental evaluation, it did help set the context for developmental evaluation by making explicit how evaluations had traditionally been conducted. This can be important when developmental evaluation is being introduced into a new context. It is an example of how traditional evaluation and developmental evaluation serve different purposes, even as one may inform the other.

Field Evaluations

The field evaluations were conducted in three sites: (1) Israel, West Bank, and Gaza; (2) Bosnia-Herzegovina; and (3) Burundi. While the Reconciliation Fund Program covers a wide geographic range, with grants issued on four continents, some countries and regions have had a higher concentration of grants over the years for a variety of reasons. CMM chose to focus on these three field sites due to their geographic diversity (i.e., three different continents), the very different nature of the three conflicts, and their relative concentration of several grant activities implemented over the years. It will be helpful to provide some details about how the program and evaluation operated in these three different places because developmental evaluation emphasizes contextual sensitivity. Both the P2P program processes and the evaluation had to be adapted to the three contexts.

Israel/West Bank/Gaza Evaluation

The first of the three field evaluations that served as part of the evaluative learning review was a case study of the APS grants in Israel, the West Bank, and Gaza (IWBG). In the IWBG region, the APS has distributed $42.7 million worth of grants between 2004 and 2011, to fund 60 P2P projects implemented by 42 different organizations, reaching tens of thousands of beneficiaries. The projects selected employ a wide range of intervention approaches and engage a variety of target populations, reflecting the diversity of the Israeli–Palestinian peace-building field and CMM's pluralistic definition of P2P work. Grantee approaches include civil society activism; dialogue; economic development; education; empowerment of youth, women, and minorities; environmental peace building; human rights and issue advocacy; media; psychosocial work and trauma healing; research; sport; and technological cooperation.

Developmental evaluation was well suited to the study of Israeli–Palestinian peace-building initiatives because it demands attention to a project's ongoing development within a context defined by emergence, nonlinearity, and dynamism.

During a period of profound political upheaval at the time in the Middle East, this was a useful approach. The evaluation team employed traditional qualitative methods—interviews, focus groups, and site visits during the initial field phase, and a survey distributed following the fieldwork in order to validate preliminary findings and conclusions. Analytically, the team focused on identifying salient themes regarding three primary areas of inquiry:

1. The contemporary context of P2P peace-building work in IWBG, and features limiting or potentially enhancing project impact.
2. Successful "emergent" strategies that APS grantees had adopted/adapted in response to the challenges and opportunities of the present context.
3. Successes/impacts of APS-funded projects.

In addition to these three overarching evaluation lines of inquiry that guided each of the field studies, another question emerged in response to the data gathered during the course of the fieldwork. The question sought to understand ways in which CMM could most successfully support and facilitate effective, responsive, relevant peace-building work in the contemporary regional context, throughout the grant process and administrative procedures as well as through technical interventions. In the spirit of developmental evaluation, this was incorporated as a fourth, unofficial question:

4. How do APS grantees experience the grant process? How can CMM most effectively strengthen grantee capacity and enhance project impact in the contemporary context?
   a. What CMM policies or practices do grantees identify as most effective/beneficial?
   b. What CMM policies or practices do grantees recommend changing, why, and how?
   c. How does CMM evaluate the effects of grant management policies and practices on the overall impact of the APS?

The study resulted in a final report that examined these four themes. However, it is important to note that this particular field study also generated some important unintended by-products—namely, opening a dialogue among the USAID West Bank Gaza mission and its Israeli and Palestinian counterparts regarding some of the more contentious elements of the grant management process. This is discussed below in the section on the synthesis report.

It should also be mentioned that in the intervening period between the time when the evaluation team was in the field in September 2012 and the time when the follow-up survey was sent, renewed violence broke out between Israel and Gaza. The survey questions were therefore adapted to explore how that flare-up had affected respondees' views.

Bosnia-Herzegovina Evaluation

The second field study looked at APS grant projects in Bosnia-Herzegovina (BiH). In BiH, six grantees have received funding since 2008, with four still being implemented at the time of the fieldwork, and each had very different visions, mandates, and operational modalities. The evaluation employed a nonexperimental, multilevel, qualitative, mixed-methods design including document review, key informant interviews, and small-group interviews. Through these methods, the evaluation was designed to capture a general understanding of projects and their outcomes, to better understand their suitability to the Bosnian context, and to identify and reflect on any emerging lessons. The team sought to take a comprehensive view of the contextual situation in BiH and the P2P projects designed to address reconciliation, and to contextualize this view within the theoretical and academic literature, as well as in guidance on the practice of reconciliation more broadly. From the perspective of the evaluation team, this understanding was critical in undertaking an evaluation of the effectiveness of any reconciliation program.

The evaluation centered on the three primary evaluation questions listed below. Each primary question had individual subquestions:

1. How has the context of P2P peace building in BiH changed in recent years, due to developments (political, economic, etc.) in BiH and the region?

2. Which of the strategies adopted by APS-funded projects were most effective for coping and adapting to changes in the context in recent years?

3. In the contemporary context, are APS projects contributing to changes at the communal or societal level (beyond the individual persons who participate directly in project activities)? What features of the contemporary context enhance or limit wider impact?

Several process-based learning outcomes occurred during the BiH evaluation. Based on the findings regarding the diverse approaches that P2P projects took, the evaluation team concluded that key actors did not have a shared sense of what reconciliation would look like in BiH. This was most pointedly revealed during the fieldwork "out-brief," during which mission personnel stated that they lacked a clear or consistent enough definition of *reconciliation*; thus they did not really know how they could develop activities best designed to produce it, or how they would measure whether it had been achieved. By strongly engaging with the evaluation team early, and establishing what amounted to a secondary purpose for the evaluation team that existed outside the frame of the performance evaluation questions the team was working toward answering, the mission director was able to influence the direction of research activities and ensure that the evaluation produced a meaningful conceptual reference for *reconciliation*. This was of particular utility for the mission.

Furthermore, during several of the interviews, it became obvious that the specific research questions the evaluation team was pursuing were not relevant to the interviewees; however, the team recognized opportunities to mine information on what reconciliation in BiH would look like. Therefore, in deference to the flexibility and dynamic emergence that are hallmarks of qualitative methods and developmental evaluation, the team allowed the interview to morph away from the rigid pursuit of answers to questions contained in the questionnaire. The evaluation findings have helped the USAID mission in BiH develop its own vision of reconciliation and how to achieve it, thus serving as an intervention in the peace-building space in BiH. This led to a more clearly articulated reconciliation-oriented grant solicitation issued by the mission, separate from the CMM-managed fund, and more directly focused on BiH's specific reconciliation needs.

Burundi Evaluation

The third and final field study of the evaluative learning review examined APS grants in Burundi. Responding to lessons learned during the previous two field studies (IWBG and BiH), the team made significant adjustments to its methodology, such as staggering its field visits and having local team members conduct separate follow-up interviews (as opposed to the two previous evaluations, which had relied entirely on 2-week field visits), to better identify and test possible outcomes and impacts of APS projects. The evaluation was organized around three main questions:

1. Is a P2P approach relevant for the Burundi context?
2. How effective have APS Burundi projects been in producing attitudinal and behavioral change?
3. What are the links, if any, between APS Burundi projects and the concept of *peace writ large*? (The concept of peace writ large focuses on large-scale, long-term social change.)

The team employed a nonexperimental, qualitatively focused approach involving (1) a desk review and simple content analysis of relevant primary and secondary sources; (2) key informant and focus group interviews with APS donors, implementers, and beneficiaries, as well as comparison groups with other donors, implementers, and other community members engaged in similar but non-APS projects; and (3) additional interviews with community members and individuals in camps for internally displaced persons, to test and validate information about program impacts received in the presence of expatriate team members.

The evaluation team adopted a more purposeful developmental evaluation approach than the approaches taken in the two preceding studies, in part due to an increasing understanding by CMM and SI of how it could be better integrated into the design. Following each day of data collection, the full team (including translators) met for a semistructured session to discuss what evidence they had gathered to answer the three primary evaluation questions, as well as to discuss any patterns, discrepancies, or surprises they had heard. Each evening, team members wrote up their notes from the interviews, sharing them with one another through a cloud-based shared drive. Team members were asked to continue to reflect on emerging themes throughout the evaluation process. This rolling analysis was further strengthened by a half-day, midpoint check-in, when the team discussed its preliminary impressions, which were vetted and agreed upon by group consensus. In line with good evaluation practice, all team members were also asked to do a number of other things: identify any underlying assumptions they held that might color their analysis, suggest any additional questions that should be included in the interviews, and identify key stakeholders that might have been overlooked. On their last day of data collection in country, the team met for a final session to discuss the group's overall impressions and to identify and discuss dissenting or divergent views. Once the U.S.-based team members returned home, they analyzed the data, using the criteria developed at the beginning of the evaluation process and the themes that emerged from the rolling analysis in country. Based on this analysis, the team drew conclusions and developed recommendations, which were validated with the Burundi-based colleagues.

As in the other two field studies, this effort culminated in an evaluation report that examined the findings, conclusions, and recommendations pertaining to the three primary evaluation questions. However, the process of conducting the evaluation itself, particularly the fieldwork, also resulted in important learnings for evaluators and evaluands alike. Similar to the experience of the BiH evaluation team, although members of the team possessed expertise in reconciliation, they found that conducting interviews provided them with further education on the real nature of reconciliation and how it was operationalized by communities in Burundi. Likewise, many interviewees asked questions of the team to gain a better understanding of what kind of programming was appropriate. Through this mutual exchange, it was evident that the intervention inspired learning and discovery that could not have been anticipated in advance.

Synthesis Evaluation Report

The final written product of this adaptation of a developmental evaluation was a synthesis report. The synthesis report summarized the program-relevant conclusions on the strengths, weaknesses, opportunities, and threats, as well as recommendations for new developments, of USAID's People-to-People Reconciliation Fund Program APS. Another set of conclusions in the synthesis report focused on improving the evaluation of the APS, and offered suggestions on ways to incorporate developmental evaluation approaches into USAID evaluation processes. The synthesis also included reflections from USAID, SI, and other stakeholders on the process of conducting the evaluation. We found that the processes of the adapted developmental evaluation approach were highly useful in encouraging ongoing learning, and also in facilitating continued conflict resolution conversations. And perhaps the processes themselves were as important a result as any of the written products.

Reflections: Utilizing Developmental Evaluation in Long-Term Governmental Programs

The challenges to utilizing a developmental approach not only in a project of this scale, but also in large governmental donor projects more generally, include the slow pace, decentralized nature, multiple stakeholders, and rigidity of government procurement processes. To realize the full potential utility of developmental evaluation in such a context, the evaluation would need to continue and be sustained longer than the 2-year engagement of this evaluation effort. Among the primary advantages of utilizing developmental evaluation are the immediate feedback it is able to provide, and the focus on adaptability and flexibility as an integrated part of the process. This feedback and reflection on process provide routine opportunities for real-time adjustments to programming. In the case of CMM's APS, however, making significant changes takes time.

This is due in part to the fact that CMM's APS is just what its full name indicates: a statement issued annually. So on the macro level at which changes might be integrated into the design of the overall program, it could require a year or more for those changes to have any eventual influence on the solicitation. Add to that the time required for nongovernmental organizations (NGOs) to respond to the new criteria set forth; for procurement processes to identify successful applicants and to negotiate and fund awards; and for implementation on the ground to begin. All of those additional steps would mean that some changes might not be visible in programming until 2 or more years later than originally identified and recommended by evaluators.

These processes are further complicated by the fact that there are multiple levels of stakeholders within the U.S. government, both internal and external to the evaluation process, who can influence the shape of the program. Most notable among those stakeholders is the U.S. Congress. The funding for CMM's P2P programming is appropriated annually by Congress. The appropriation and accompanying report language establish the main parameters of the programming, determine funding levels, and to some extent establish the geographic scope of the projects. It also includes a requirement that USAID consult with the appropriations committees before obligating funds, to ensure that Congress concurs with the funding choices USAID is making. All of this means that there are legal constraints to making significant changes to the program. Those constraints do not mean that the informed recommendations of evaluators cannot be implemented, but simply that the authority for such implementation does not ultimately lie with the program managers at CMM, or even with USAID. Most of the recommendations that were produced by the evaluative learning review were in the manageable interests of USAID and did not necessarily require Congressional review or concurrence. However, Congressional engagement may also provide an opportunity, as highlighted below.

The most significant constraint to utilizing recommendations from this developmental evaluative approach is to making changes in programming results from the level at which USAID operates. As a donor, USAID does have significant influence on the shape this programming will take—something that the *Evaluative*

Learning Review Synthesis Report (SI, 2014, p. 57) highlights and emphasizes. But despite this fact, CMM is still removed by several layers of bureaucracy from implementation on the ground. So there are limitations to the influence that CMM (as the primary audience for the recommendations of the evaluation) can have at the activity level—the level where we found that developmental approaches can have the most immediate impact in this context. At the global level, it is expected to take a number of years for results or changes to be seen, so at this time we are not able to determine precisely how this evaluation will influence CMM and other stakeholders in the immediate term. Nor at this time are we able to fully predict the manifestations and timelines in which change will occur and/or be incorporated, as those processes will need to be reflected upon throughout various stages and by various stakeholders in the bureaucracy. However, what is clear is that the reflective processes encouraged by the developmental evaluation have had an immediate impact on the dynamics of how CMM managers approach the fund, as well as on the structure of the dialogue about future adaptation.

One specific example where the reflective learning process did bring about real-time change in the implementation of the program was a shift that was made in the APS solicitation for the Middle East. As mentioned above, one of the overarching findings of the evaluative learning review as a whole and in the IWBG field evaluation in particular was that while activities were successful at bringing about change in individuals and communities taking part in P2P interactions, they were less successful in demonstrating change at the level of peace writ large (as defined above). This learning was incorporated into the solicitation as the overall project was continuing by including new requirements for applicants to demonstrate how their activities would link with other ongoing efforts, so that aggregate effects could be better understood and demonstrated.

The bottom line, however, is that the bureaucratic constraints of making changes to a project such as the Reconciliation Fund Program APS are not insignificant and therefore need to be weighed when evaluators and donors are considering implementing a developmental approach with similar programs. But some of these same constraints can also be viewed as opportunities.

One advantage of the slow pace of change in a grants program such as CMM's is that the developmental approach provides an opportunity to embed reflective practice into more traditional evaluative processes. In intending to evaluate an ongoing grant program in a developmental manner, a donor can perhaps modify and augment more traditional evaluation tools to utilize them as a means to check in periodically on emerging trends evident from programs in a particular region or emerging general themes. Analyzing those trends or themes may provide a basis for adjusting future grant giving to build upon strengths that may be emerging or gaps that are manifesting themselves. But this is, at best, only a slight change from how traditional evaluation tools are used.

The primary shift, however, is in using the evaluation tools primarily for learning and adjusting programming rather than as accountability tools. Whereas it is much more common for an implementing organization to utilize evaluation tools for learning across their projects, donors tend to focus more on performance and accountability. As laid out in USAID's (2011) evaluation policy, both accountability and learning are important evaluation functions for the agency. This model might allow USAID to better utilize performance evaluations aimed at accountability toward informing its learning and decision making beyond the activity level.

Similarly, and as alluded to above, the close supervision of CMM's Reconciliation Fund Program exercised by Congress provides an opportunity to make legislators and their staffers more direct users of evaluation than they perhaps would be otherwise. This and future evaluations will serve as the basis for ongoing discussions with Capitol Hill on how to adjust P2P grant giving for maximum effectiveness. Evaluation may thereby become a tool that can inform law and policy, not just programmatic implementation. So while change in this context may come slowly, it may allow evaluation to become a tool that inserts reflective learning practice to be appreciated not just at the point of grant implementation and day-to-day management, but at much higher levels as well.

Despite the challenges, developmental evaluation may be very useful over the long term, even when there are significant bureaucratic hurdles to introducing changes into programs. Aligning the time frame for evaluators' engagement with the timing with which programmatic changes can be introduced will support maximum utility of a developmental evaluation approach in such contexts.

Process as a Key Product

The processes of reflection that the adapted developmental evaluation approach brought to the interactions among stakeholders engaged in P2P reconciliation programs are the same processes employed for conflict resolution reflection. In other words, the processes of developmental evaluation are conflict resolution processes. When stakeholders from across a conflict divide are brought together to consider their shared conflict resolution program in an atmosphere of open reflection, developmental evaluation conversations become conflict resolution conversations. Developmental evaluation facilitates working toward a shared goal—which is itself a reconciliation process. Therefore, developmental evaluation can change the way people work together. Rather than seeking one "right way" and sticking to it, groups can improve gradually, through trial and error, constant feedback, and continual learning. We found that when it was applied to the conflict resolution programs we were assessing, developmental evaluation could serve as a conflict intervention.

Our learning process involved several activities. A learning group was convened to engage with the evaluative learning review, providing advice CMM considered as it steered the project. Individuals from the learning group provided feedback on the overall learning review design and the field evaluation processes and products, and led the metaevaluation team. Other members of the learning group joined the shared learning as team leaders for the field evaluations. CMM's managers of the APS and of the evaluative learning review joined with the SI team leaders in periodic (usually monthly) leadership meetings. The leadership meetings had a dual purpose: fine-tuning the implementation of the adapted developmental evaluation approach, and reflecting together on what we were learning about the process and substantive findings of the overall project. Finally, the learning process was greatly enriched by a learning summit that gathered evaluation experts together to help us make sense of the overall evaluative learning review, and particularly the scenarios for future development of evaluation of P2P reconciliation programs. Together, these pieces of the learning process created an atmosphere of open learning. No questions were stupid questions; all areas were approachable areas of inquiry; and no one person was assumed to have all the answers, or even access to all the relevant perspectives. We created an atmosphere in which it was clear we all needed each other to develop more multifaceted understandings and explore potential developments together.

This attitude toward evaluation as process-oriented, much as reconciliation is process-oriented, emerged as a key theme in leadership meetings among the evaluative learning review's managers at CMM, relevant managers at SI, and (periodically) learning group members. At the conclusion of most of those meetings, a few minutes were dedicated to reflection on the project's development, allowing space for new insights or approaches to emerge (see Exhibit 11.1). These insights informed the development of the evaluative learning review, and the flexible space for creative reflection became a regular practice. Through regular use, these evaluative practices became a routinized part of the team's work, but over time they were sometimes uneven in terms of the originality of the ideas that resulted. It has yet to be seen how long this reflective way of working will last, and whether it will become adopted as a new culture of the APS stakeholders' ways of working with each other. Over time, it may have more impact on future programming than any of the substantive suggestions for specific new innovations in APS projects.

The process of engaging with CMM program managers as active partners in the evaluative learning review, including through leadership meetings that involved these active partners in all decision-making components of the review, served to spur thinking at CMM. In other words, the process helped raise questions even if it did not immediately provide answers, and brought to the surface challenging areas for ongoing consideration. Rather than producing any set of conclusions regarding the definitive "best practices" or the best ways to do something, the evaluative learning review led to scenarios for potential development of P2P reconciliation programs. CMM program managers reported that the review, through the process

---

EXHIBIT 11.1

Reflection Questions Used during Leadership Meetings

- What decisions have we made, and why?
- What approaches have we not adopted, and why?
- What have we learned about evaluative learning reviews of reconciliation programs?
- What challenges are we facing?
- What assumptions are we making?

of leadership team meetings, greatly increased their awareness of the difficult balancing acts required in evaluating the P2P reconciliation programs.

Similarly, the field evaluation teams found that their presence in the field served as a catalyst for learning among the stakeholders with whom they worked. Rather than treating stakeholder interactions as data collection, the evaluators discovered that the interactions took on importance as part of the overall learning process in the evaluative learning review. As stated above, in BiH, the field evaluation team learned that the USAID mission there wanted an additional question explored in the evaluation: What is *reconciliation* in the Bosnian context? Later, in a separate meeting, another USAID mission member questioned whether reconciliation would ever be possible in BiH. In response, one of the local evaluation team members, an expert practitioner of reconciliation process activities, shared his personal journey of reconciliation and some of his ongoing work toward broader social reconciliation. He described his wartime experience as a concentration camp prisoner, and told a number of anecdotes about people with whom he had worked. He also described, in evidently reconciled terms, how he currently viewed people from the other ethnic group that had been responsible for his traumatic experience. This personal testimony contributed significantly to group learning in ways that would be difficult to convey fully in the field evaluation report.

For the Burundi field evaluation team, the learning process was highly inclusive, and again and again the evaluation led to learning in unexpected places. For example, in meeting with a community council leader in a remote region, the evaluation team raised a question about the ways the local council could influence the national council. The local council leader took the question quite seriously, was open to approaches he had not previously considered, and left the discussion with some potential actions he and his council colleagues might take. When the evaluation team driver began to sit in on some focus groups, he was impressed with the discussions and shared that he was learning much about reconciliation in the various regions they visited. The learning often generated more questions. In the team discussions regarding the potential for the Truth and Reconciliation Commission to serve as an effective reconciliation tool for Burundi, many more questions were raised than answers offered.

The IWBG field evaluation team, by structuring its evaluation debriefing session to include substantial discussion, served to facilitate multiple stakeholders' communicating with each other about big questions regarding USAID policies and procedures. Many of these questions arose from misunderstandings. A Palestinian grantee thought that only Palestinian vendors and participants had to go through the vetting process, but USAID mission staff explained that the same vetting procedures applied more broadly. Similarly, evaluation discussions allowed a grantee to ask about required indicators; this gave a USAID mission staff member a chance to explain that, beyond the standard "changing perceptions" indicator, all other indicators could be developed and tailored specifically for each unique project. For the 2 hours of the evaluation debriefing, the evaluation team established a forum for open-ended, problem-solving communication between grantees and mission staff, which allowed several differences to be revealed and resolved.

This compatibility of the processes of developmental evaluation and conflict resolution should not be surprising. Both are utilized in complex adaptive system contexts and thus, to be effective, must develop as their contexts do. Informing both processes are shared values that include ongoing learning and balancing of multiple concerns with care. For example, both conflict resolution and developmental evaluation require working within an appropriate time frame and acknowledging that things change over time. Introducing innovative programming or trying out new steps in confidence building requires sensitivity to the current context gained through regular reflection—something that developmental evaluation fosters. Similarly, both conflict resolution and developmental evaluation require engaging multiple levels of the system; for example, work at a global headquarters must be connected to work in a local village, and vice versa. Both provide space for defining and redefining a problem over time, allowing efforts to shift as the context of the work shifts. And both encourage a team approach, in which the facilitators (of the conflict resolution effort) or the evaluators (of a program) work collaboratively together with a broad range of stakeholders.

Lessons from Our Work with Developmental Evaluation

Developmental evaluation is intended to work in partnership with program decision makers to support innovations in social change efforts. Our learning has been that evaluative input can be useful when program managers engage in ongoing program development, adapt programs to new local or national contexts, pilot or adopt innovative approaches in a program, and adapt programs flexibly in response to shifts in the program context. And the program decision makers whom developmental evaluation engages can be at any level of the program, or from a broad range of program levels, provided that the evaluation's time frame is adjusted appropriately to support the kinds of changes each decision maker can consider. Developmental evaluation is often used to support developments in a social change intervention through direct work with the leaders or managers of that social change initiative; in these contexts, where the evaluation is done at the project implementation level, it directly helps those decision makers who work closely with a target population. But headquarters-based policy makers are also important decision makers in the shape of a program, and developmental evaluation can also be supportive in that context.

In contrast to the activity level of focus, where developmental evaluation is most often employed, the focus or unit of analysis for this evaluation was on the global APS managed by CMM in USAID's Washington office. Rather than looking at one specific project within the global program, and suggesting appropriate shifts in that particular project, the evaluation's purpose was to look at the whole global set of many projects and to consider the countrywide program impact in a sample of countries. This meant that the evaluation was one step removed from the projects' direct implementers, although it should be noted that implementers of over 37 projects were consulted during the field evaluations. These consultations sought input from the implementers, but the primary learning was aimed at managers of the global program at CMM, not any particular implementer.

The activities of the Washington program management team do not include interference in the project implementation managed by local USAID missions in the relevant countries where grantee projects are implemented. Instead, Washington's activities include envisioning future years' solicitations of applications, managing the selection process for grantees, and then referring winning grants to USAID missions for contracting and management. Ultimately, this means that the kinds of innovations or changes the managers of the global program can consider are long-term in nature. Any changes CMM chooses to make in the APS will be ones that will require years to implement, as contracting procedures must be approved in advance of issuing the program call for proposals, and the parameters of application review and selection cannot be shifted once they are set.

In order to utilize the developmental evaluation approach to inform significant changes at the project level in a shorter time frame, or as the project is being implemented, the appropriate unit of analysis would be one P2P reconciliation project. The approach would then be utilized for the full life cycle of that project. Here, a *project* refers to one grant to one specific implementer for one set of activities in one country over a period of approximately 1–3 years. For example, a developmental evaluation team might support the project manager at NGO X in implementing a 2-year grant for "Supporting Reconciliation." This team would work with the project implementation team to infuse evaluative thinking into the project's work and to bring evaluation insights to inform project decisions. With feedback early during the project, shifts in project design could be considered and, after discussion with USAID, implemented according to new approaches suggested by the evaluation insights. The evaluation would last for the full time period of the project and would have an opportunity to inform significant changes in the project as the specific country's context changed.

For this approach to work, the local and global management team would also need to actively encourage and support adaptive implementation. Although this may sound easy in theory, in practice constantly adapting or changing a project's focus or implementation plan can go against governments' and other donors' contracting regulations and standards of practice. Typically, a project implementer has signed a contract with a specific scope of work and work plan, and it is difficult to amend this significantly once the project has begun. In order to implement a developmental evaluation approach, adaptive implementation must be supported. This could be done by further developing program management procedures and by actively requiring annual work plans to explicitly identify and articulate any planned changes in program directions or adaptations due to changes in the context. If, in the course of an entire year of a project, the implementers find no way it can possibly be improved, then evaluation is probably not being used effectively to support adaptive implementation in that situation. The idea is that adaptation of a plan would be the expected normal course of action as a project proceeds, rather than being an exception that requires extra review. This would help to systematize periodic renewed analysis of the situation and the role of the project in that situational analysis. Projects would be adapted on the basis of updated analysis and evaluation of the project up to that point. Encouraging adaptive implementation would thus be encouraging innovation. Adopting an organizational culture with this in mind would require sharing the lessons learned, celebrating successes, and even celebrating the learning that comes from mistakes or missteps. If the evaluation culture embraces adaptation as a useful result, then even dead ends can be helpful steps along the way to adaptation. Adaptation can be a measurable value in an evaluation culture that encourages people to recognize failures and move forward. Being accountable to a complex system that shifts over time requires adaptability.

Although this approach to utilizing developmental evaluation at the individual project level would help to effect change more quickly, it is still important to consider how developmental evaluation approaches can be useful in supporting decision makers located at the headquarters funding level, several steps removed from the direct participants in the funded projects. Practical steps might include the following:

• Adopting an appropriate time frame for the evaluation, based on the time required for steering policy shifts at the global level of a program.

• Focusing evaluative thinking on ways in which global program policy influences project impact, but remaining open to unexpected learning beyond this focus.

• Complementing the global-level focus with additional evaluative efforts at the national and local levels.

• Engaging multiple levels of the project system. Useful evaluation recognizes the interconnections between different parts of the system—from micro-level local communities to regional, national, and global levels. By looking at the global level of the project, the evaluation described in this chapter has illuminated ways the often invisible work done at headquarters is part of reconciliation work, too. Washington is where policy is set and large-scale financing decisions are made; what happens in Washington shapes what project proposals are written and what projects are awarded funding. The project designs shape what reconciliation activities are implemented. At the same time, however, participants form the heart of reconciliation; by bringing their voices to conversations, they shape the dialogue to be most meaningful and effective for them. The work of reconciliation happens at all of these various levels.

In addition, the evaluation process can be used as an intervention itself, as described earlier in the chapter. Our team adjusted evaluation methodologies, lines of questioning, analysis of data, and recommendations as learnings were reflected upon and insights sought in the learning group, thereby creating an evolving learning process and (ultimately) more effective and useful evaluation for all stakeholders.

The utility of the evaluation process was not limited to evaluation; it also served a reconciliation function. For example, when the evaluation conversation opened the space for one Bosnian former prisoner of war to describe his reconciliation process, his openness touched others in that conversation, and changed the heart and mind of at least one person who had thought reconciliation never could really happen. Developmental evaluation conversations are highly relevant for conflict resolution contexts, as they raise the same questions about shared analysis and desired changes that conflict resolution dialogues do. We offer this chapter in the hopes that others will find the developmental evaluation approaches useful in conflict resolution contexts, too.

ACKNOWLEDGMENTS

Portions of this chapter have been adapted from the *Evaluative Learning Review Synthesis Report: USAID/CMM's People-to-People Reconciliation Fund, Annual Program Statement (APS)*, March 2014, available online (*http://pdf.usaid.gov/pdf_docs/pbaaa370.pdf*). That publication was produced by Social Impact, Inc., for USAID under Contract No. AID-OAA-TO-11-0046. The views expressed therein and in this chapter do not necessarily reflect those of USAID or the U.S. government, but are ours alone.

REFERENCES

Patton, M. Q. (2011). *Developmental evaluation: Applying complexity concepts to enhance innovation and use*. New York: Guilford Press.

Social Impact, Inc. (SI). (2014, March). *Evaluative learning review synthesis report: USAID/ CMM's People-to-People Reconciliation Fund, Annual Program Statement (APS)*. Arlington, VA: Author. Retrieved from *http://pdf.usaid.gov/pdf_docs/pbaaa370.pdf*.

United States Agency for International Development (USAID). (2011, January). *Evaluation: Learning from experience. USAID evaluation policy*. Washington, DC: Author. Retrieved from *www.usaid.gov/sites/default/files/documents/1868/ USAIDEvaluationPolicy.pdf*.

CHAPTER 12

Creating Safety to Explore

Strengthening Innovation in an Australian Indigenous Primary Health Care Setting through Developmental Evaluation

Samantha Togni, Deborah Askew, Lynne Rogers, Nichola Potter, Sonya Egert, Noel Hayman, Alan Cass, and Alex Brown

EDITOR'S INTRODUCTION (BY KATE McKEGG)

I first met Samantha Togni, the first author of this chapter, in a developmental evaluation work-shop in Adelaide, Australia. I was facilitating the workshop, with Michael Quinn Patton beam-ing in by Internet. I could never have imagined that this would be part of the impetus for Sam to take the lead in a developmental evaluation. A year later, I saw Sam give a presentation at the Australasian Evaluation Society Conference in Brisbane. Her presentation encapsulated all the principles of developmental evaluation—but I was struck by the way she modeled the col-laboration principle by presenting with her evaluation team, made up of Indigenous[1] and settler Australians. This developmental evaluation was an exemplar of bringing together traditional and Indigenous methodologies in an innovation that has created systemic change for Aboriginal and Torres Strait Islanders. When we were discussing this book, I knew this case had to be here. It demonstrates the power of developmental evaluation, well executed, to make a real difference in Indigenous settings, with Indigenous people, for Indigenous people. In these settings, too much time and too many resources have been spent doing things in traditional Western ways that have no impact on really tough, intractable, complex problems.

This case describes an exploratory collaboration between an Indigenous primary health service and researchers/evaluators who set out to develop an innovative model of care aimed at improving the quality of life of, and the quality of care for, Aboriginal and Torres Strait Islander people living with chronic medical conditions (e.g., heart disease, renal disease, and diabetes). In this real-world setting, developmental evaluation was used to take respectful account of, and to help inform, a situation of considerable complexity. More importantly, the case shows

---

[1] *Indigenous* is used in Australia to mean Australian Aboriginal and Torres Strait Islander peoples.

how the evaluation process engaged and respected the perspectives of practitioners and health service staff at the center of the developmental process, contributing to a higher-quality, more integrated, strengthened model of care that had strong uptake and diffusion. It demonstrates how the members of a developmental evaluation team with long-standing, trusting relationships can leverage their collective knowledge and expertise to strengthen the diffusion and dissemination of innovation and make a real difference in the lives of Indigenous Australians.

Setting the Scene

Our story of developmental evaluation is set on the east coast of Australia. It involves a collaboration between the Inala Indigenous Health Service (IIHS), an urban Aboriginal and Torres Strait Islander primary health care service, and the Kanyini[2] Vascular Collaboration (KVC), a research collaboration aimed at improving the quality of life of, and the quality of care for, Aboriginal and Torres Strait Islander people living with chronic conditions such as heart disease, renal disease, and diabetes.

The KVC, formed in 2005, is led by Aboriginal and non-Aboriginal health researchers; it brings together health and medical research institutes and more than 10 Aboriginal and Torres Strait Islander primary health care services (including the IIHS) across three states and one territory. Through a series of competitive research grants, the KVC has developed and implemented a program of research within its partner health services that focuses on improving health care and health outcomes for Aboriginal and Torres Strait Islander peoples, while simultaneously developing the research capacity of Aboriginal and Torres Strait Islander researchers (Mentha et al., 2012).

Research in this real-world setting is challenging and demanding, as the context is complex and dynamic. Competing priorities between research and service delivery emerge, particularly as the latter is core business for health care services. On a day-to-day basis, the time investment and potential disruptive effects of research on clinical care may make it difficult for the personnel of busy, underresourced health services to undertake research. Effective relationships between researchers and health services, and responsive and adaptive processes, are therefore essential for the successful implementation of research in these contexts.

The IIHS is located in a southwest suburb of Brisbane, Queensland, and is funded by the Queensland Government. Its founding and current clinical director is an Indigenous medical practitioner and one of the first Indigenous medical graduates in Queensland. The IIHS has a proud and impressive history of improving access to health care for Aboriginal and Torres Strait Islander people over the last two decades (Hayman, White, & Spurling, 2009). In 2010, the IIHS received

---

[2] The term *kanyini* is used by a number of Aboriginal language groups in Central Australia, including Pitjantjatjara and Pintupi. The closest English equivalent translation of kanyini is "to have, to hold and to care" (Institute for Aboriginal Development, 2001). The concept has been further described as "a verb which reflects a commitment, a full engagement" (Franks, 1996). The principle of kanyini guides the philosophy, actions, and perceptions of caring as lived within Aboriginal communities.

funding from the state government to expand its clinical services, teaching, and research programs and establish the Southern Queensland Centre of Excellence in Aboriginal and Torres Strait Islander Primary Health Care (Hayman, Askew, & Spurling, 2014). The Centre of Excellence remains commonly known as the IIHS.

In this chapter, we share our experiences of using developmental evaluation within an exploratory research project at the interface of research collaboration, research and evaluation capacity development, innovation in Aboriginal and Torres Strait Islander primary health care, and integration with service delivery. We describe how we applied developmental evaluation, what we believe it has contributed, the challenges we faced, and the lessons we have learned. We also reflect on the potential of developmental evaluation to support and strengthen the uptake of innovations within primary health care settings.

The HOME Study

The Home-based Outreach Chronic Disease Management Exploratory Study (HOME Study) aimed to determine whether a patient-centered outreach model of chronic disease care was acceptable to, feasible for, and appropriate for Aboriginal and Torres Strait Islander people with complex chronic disease and their primary health care providers. Initially, broad ideas about developing this model of care emerged independently within the KVC and IIHS, and both organizations had secured funding to support such an initiative. When this serendipity was realized, the study's methodology and approach were developed collaboratively and implemented at the IIHS, with supporting resources contributed by both the KVC and IIHS.

We initially planned to conduct the study as a pilot trial of a model of care. However, as discussions evolved, our uncertainty about many of the specific details of the model of care became clear; we realized that proceeding to *test* a specific model was premature, as we needed the flexibility to identify and incorporate the needs of participants and the health care service into the model of care as it was developed and implemented. Thus a different methodology was needed.

We chose an exploratory study approach that allowed us to start with what we knew about outreach models of care, multidisciplinary care coordination, the characteristics of Aboriginal and Torres Strait Islander peoples living with complex chronic disease, and the health care service. From this starting point, we could iteratively develop the model of care through a continual evaluative and learning process about what was effective in terms of taking care into the homes of our study participants.

The key research questions underpinning the study focused on addressing the overarching aim outlined above, as well as on understanding the model of care's key components and features. The study protocol defined the inclusion criteria, outcome measures, and general approach to the delivery of the model of care. An evaluation plan was developed, again collaboratively, that incorporated the collection of qualitative and quantitative data into the quest for answers to the research questions. A developmental evaluation framework was used to implement the plan, and so the plan was adapted over time. Ethical and community approvals for the study were received from the local human research ethics committee and the Inala Community Jury for Aboriginal and Torres Strait Islander Health Research (a group of local Aboriginal and Torres Strait Islander people who guide all research undertaken by the IIHS; Bond, Foley, & Askew, in press), respectively. Informed consent was obtained from all participants before any data collection occurred.

Case managers collected quantitative data directly from participants at regular intervals, including assessments of participants' social and emotional well-being, quality of life, self-rated health status, and lifestyle risk factors. Case managers also conducted regular audits of the participants' medical records to document health service utilization, clinical indicators, medical history, medications, and any new diagnoses. The case managers recorded all contacts with participants, whether these were planned or ad hoc, and noted whether these occurred in the participants' homes, in the health service, via the telephone, through accompanying participants to specialist outpatient appointments, or through visiting participants if they were hospitalized. Case report forms were developed to capture this information in a systematic way, and this information was also recorded in the participants' electronic medical records within the health service, to facilitate integration and coordination of care.

The HOME Study was implemented by a core team composed of five IIHS staff members and one employee of a research institute affiliated with the KVC. The IIHS staff included the research director, a program coordinator, two registered nurse case managers (initially), and a KVC-funded Indigenous research officer (IRO), who joined the team 9 months after the study commenced. The external team member (also funded by the KVC) was the developmental evaluator, who lived in central Australia approximately 3,000 kilometers to the west of the IIHS, and made regular visits to the IIHS over the course of the study.

The core team brought together relevant skills, experience, and knowledge to support and implement the study. The research director is an established primary health care researcher with an academic track record, and the case managers (who delivered the model of care) brought their clinical skills and knowledge of health care systems. One case manager (non-Aboriginal) had previously worked in a similar outreach case manager role in the United Kingdom, and the other, an Aboriginal woman, brought her Aboriginal health worker and community nurse background to the team, in addition to her cultural and community knowledge. The program coordinator has more than 25 years' experience working within the state health department, and therefore has a thorough knowledge of its systems. The IRO is a member of the local Aboriginal and Torres Strait Islander community, and so brought an in-depth understanding of, relationships with, and knowledge of this community. The evaluator has considerable experience in developing and implementing applied research and evaluation projects within Indigenous primary health care settings, as well as experience in organization development. Research governance and strategic oversight were provided by KVC senior researchers, the IIHS clinical director and research director, and the study evaluator.

After 18 months, our model of care proved to be acceptable to, feasible for, and appropriate for Aboriginal and Torres Strait Islander people with chronic disease and their primary health care providers. It was multidisciplinary and holistic in its approach, and focused on the social, cultural, and health needs of the participants. For participants, this model of care contributed to improvements in their social and emotional well-being, clinical indicators and self-reported health status; encouraged and supported them to take a more active role in their own care; and supported improvements in the health care they received. In addition, the model of care was effectively integrated into the health service to ensure comprehensive and coordinated care—the essence of high-quality primary health care (Askew et al., 2014).

These outcomes, together with the effective engagement of and timely sharing of information with decision makers, have resulted in ongoing funding for incorporating the model of care into usual practice at the IIHS. Developmental evaluation is being used to continue to adapt the model of care and more fully understand its features of value.

How the Team Utilized Developmental Evaluation

Developmental evaluation offered the team a framework to capture, understand, and contribute to the development of a model of care within the complex and uncertain environment of an exploratory research project being conducted in a busy primary health care service. Not surprisingly, given the relatively recent emergence of developmental evaluation, the evaluator was the only member of the team who was familiar with this evaluation approach. In what was perhaps a leap of faith for some of the researchers on the team, the team adopted developmental evaluation as an approach to support the learning processes of this exploratory study.

Two main strategies were used for the developmental evaluation. The first was an ongoing series of in-depth, one-on-one interviews with staff and study participants, and the second was a regular series of reflective workshops with the core study team. The evaluator conducted the semistructured interviews throughout the duration of the study, interviewing other members of the core team, other IIHS staff members, external service providers, and study participants. The IRO assisted the evaluator in accessing the study participants and conducting these interviews, thereby enhancing cultural safety and bringing a local Indigenous perspective to the data collection, analysis, and interpretation.

The reflective workshops with the core team members were held every 6–8 weeks during the development and implementation of the study. Each half- or full-day workshop was a safe space where the evaluator guided evaluative thinking, reflection, and discussion about the components of the model, how it was working, and what needed to change. The workshops also enabled reflection on and consideration of real-time data, including the stakeholder interviews. Although the evaluator prepared an agenda for each workshop, she took a flexible approach to workshop facilitation—ensuring that the workshops were responsive to emerging issues, and encouraging the team to address or clarify issues, develop shared understandings, and identify learnings. The evaluator prepared a comprehensive report following each workshop, which formed an essential component of the study documentation.

> ### 🐚 Reflecting on the Developmental Evaluation Process
>
> **Sonya Egert, Indigenous Research Officer (IRO):** "My experience of the workshops was very good. I was able to get a better understanding of the HOME Study through each individual team member's perspective. I felt as though I was able to contribute to the workshops by bringing a lot of my community knowledge and experience.
>
> "I liked the opportunity for our team to meet and have deeper discussions regarding all aspects of the HOME Study. We had our weekly team meetings, but I found that our workshops enabled us to have more time to discuss and resolve things. I think the team workshops contributed greatly to the success of the HOME Study. To be able to have the opportunity to reflect on the work you are doing and look at what is working effectively and what may not be working so well, you actually have a chance to be able to change the way you do things to have a better outcome."

The workshops were part of the information-sharing and decision-making processes supporting the development and implementation of the model of care. Weekly meetings of the core team, chaired by the research director, supported the day-to-day operations of the study and the delivery of care to the participants. The evaluator participated in these team meetings via tele- or videoconferencing. Over time, the team meetings and workshops became more complementary, as the team members came to understand better each forum's purpose and functions and how these supported the team's work.

Counting the Ways: The Contributions of Developmental Evaluation

Developmental evaluation greatly benefited both the development of the model of care and the implementation of the study in this real-world setting. The evaluation was built on trusting relationships and on shared values and vision, which enabled ongoing collaborative and participatory processes. The developmental evaluation approach informed the ongoing adaptation of the model of care—specifically through the workshops, which promoted evaluative thinking and facilitated reflective practice and active learning within the whole study team. This in turn strengthened the team's ability to navigate the complexities and the inevitable challenges that emerged, and thus supported the pragmatic implementation of the study.

Supporting the Study's Implementation and the Innovation's Development

Developmental evaluation provided the team with systematic processes for considering and making sense of real-time data and information to inform the iterative development of the model of care and strengthen its implementation. Importantly, the processes positioned the engagement of practitioners and health service staff members as central to the development and implementation of the model, which we believe strengthened the quality of the model of care and improved its uptake, as discussed below. Furthermore, these processes enhanced our understanding of the feasibility, acceptability, and appropriateness of the model of care for participants and the health service.

The developmental evaluation approach contributed to clarifying the research process; the data collection tools; and the roles, relationships, and expectations of the core team members. This was particularly important during the initial few months of the study, as three of the initial core team members were new to working on research projects and the research director was new to research of this nature, which aimed to develop, implement, and evaluate an innovation simultaneously. The workshops provided a forum for these issues to be discussed, explored, clarified, and revisited, which supported the effective implementation of the study. For example, the case managers initially resisted completing some of the case report forms, as they felt their activities were "just what we did"; through workshop discussions, however, they gained an appreciation of the importance of comprehensive documentation to inform our understanding of the model of care.

When challenges or issues arose for any or all of us as team members, the developmental evaluation processes enabled us to consider whether these challenges were related to the research process, the specifics of the model of care, and/or the context of the health service. In this way we were able to better manage the messiness and uncertainty of what we were doing in this complex environment, and to acknowledge the effect that these conditions had on us as team members. We achieved some clarity about the things we could change and those that were beyond our control.

Reflecting on the Workshops

Deborah Askew, Research Director: "The workshops were a really useful experience for us as a research team. They gave us the chance to come together as a group of equals. They gave us time to stop and reflect on what we were doing. We got out of the hurly-burly, everyday busy work and stopped and really thought about what we were doing, why we were doing it, and could we do it better.

"[Our evaluator] would come in and ask us, 'What have you been doing? So what happened? What was the impact of that?' and she helped us tease out what exactly it was that we'd done. We knew what we'd been doing, but it was not until you stopped and thought, 'Well, that happened, and then that happened, and then that happened, and then that led us to do that.' 'OK, so why did you do that?' [the evaluator] asked. We could say, 'Well, that was because of this . . .' And, importantly, she asked us, 'And where is that being recorded? Not only for the research side of things, but for the health service as well.'

"This was a complex model of care that we were delivering, and this approach with the workshops enabled us to tease apart what the actual model of care was, its different components, and to read between the lines to understand what was going on in the study."

Reflecting on Reflective Practice

Nichola Potter, Case Manager: "I think the way in which we used reflection, applying it to what we were doing in real life, brought our work to a whole new level, and I think that opened lots of different doors to find out new information and where to go with my work . . . so I think that was probably the best part . . . it was a spiral of learning, really."

Samantha Togni, Developmental Evaluator: "Our understanding of the model of care, what it was, and how it was working became 'three-dimensional' through the case managers' reflections at the workshops. This reflective practice brought the work of the case managers to life and enabled the team to develop a deeper, shared understanding of the model of care and the importance of the human relationships that were being developed. Without this process, we would not have had meaningful data to make sense of the model of care and how it was achieving the outcomes with participants."

Importantly, we were then able to develop strategies for change in situations where this was possible, or to reduce the impact of issues and realities we could not control.

With this new and emerging model of care, the roles, responsibilities, and relationships of the case managers to others within the health service needed to be developed and clarified. As nurses, the case managers were used to working with clear protocols and defined roles. The uncertainty associated with this emerging role took them outside their comfort zones—and, understandably, at times was a source of some stress and frustration. The workshops created safe spaces for these issues to be considered and clarified, resulting in the case managers' feeling supported and valued, as the exact nature of the breadth and comprehensiveness of their role was defined and understood by the team. Over time, workshop discussions also highlighted differences in the practices of the two case managers, and we all were able to consider the implications of these differences and clarify practices going forward. This strengthened our understanding of the case managers' role and the implementation of the model of care.

The developmental evaluation processes also enabled us to understand the different components of the model of care and identify its features of value. In particular, the workshops enabled us to explore the complex work of the case managers, and together to develop an understanding of the activities, processes, and relationships that were being developed between the case managers and the participants. The rich information and understanding that were generated through the reflective practice and evaluative thinking in the workshops contrasted sharply with the information recorded on the case report forms that were designed to capture the work of the case managers. A document analysis alone would have provided very little understanding of the case managers' skills, the sensitive work that was being done, and the ways in which this work was making a difference. The workshops facilitated the exploration of the model of care in all its dimensions, enabled meaningful analysis and interpretation, and brought an understanding of the human component in the model's features of value.

Strengthening the Team

The innovation team is central to the developmental evaluation process. Through our workshops, each team member contributed to developing and adapting the model of care, implementing the study, and interpreting information to strengthen our understanding of the model of care. Discussions contributed to a "bigger-picture" perspective of the model of care, its purpose, and the team's work in achieving this purpose. This process positively challenged team members, particularly those who had not previously contributed in this way in the workplace.

Because our team was specifically formed for the HOME Study, relationship building was an early priority. The workshops enabled a shared understanding of each team member's role and responsibilities in the study, increased all members' professional and personal respect for each other, and developed trust within the team. The team members came together as equals and were able to contribute their expertise, knowledge, and experience to discussions; these discussions highlighted that it was *the team* that was required to deliver the model of care and conduct the study. This further encouraged effective teamwork. Importantly, the workshops provided the research director with opportunities for reflection, and freed her from being "the leader" and having to have "all the answers."

Notably, the workshops created safety for team members to raise and clarify issues and ask questions to support them in their work. The workshops were facilitated in a way that promoted respectful interactions; this atmosphere of respect enabled team members to talk honestly about issues that were considered "tricky" and work to resolve these, which served to strengthen the team's cohesiveness further. As a result, the team members demonstrated high levels of engagement and participation. Communication was improved both within and outside the workshops, and the importance of effective communication across and beyond the team was realized. The diversity within the team not only aided the analysis and interpretation of information, but acknowledged the real, lived experience of team

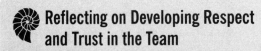

Reflecting on Developing Respect and Trust in the Team

Deborah Askew: "Another important aspect of the workshops was that we were coming together as a team. It enabled us to get a sense of the role of each member of the team, and this increased the respect for each other and we realized that none of us could do this by ourselves.

"It really increased the cohesiveness of the team, and the workshops meant much, much better communication. The workshops gave us a safe space to not necessarily vent, but to be honest, and that certainly increased the trust within the team."

members as something not separate from the development and implementation of the model of care. The range of expertise and experiences among us enabled us to better understand and address the complex conditions in which we were working.

Developmental evaluation processes thus strengthened the team's effectiveness in such a way that a deeper, shared understanding within the team of the model of care and its implementation emerged. This strengthening of the team and the individuals within it contributed directly to improving the research process, as well as the model's development, implementation, and uptake.

Benefit of the Insider–Outsider Embedded Evaluator

The active role of the evaluator is a defining characteristic of the developmental evaluation approach. In our experience, there were numerous benefits to having the evaluator embedded within the core project team. Key to this was the unique positioning of the evaluator as both an insider and an outsider. The evaluator was an insider in her roles of contributing to the study design and methodology; facilitating the workshops; gathering and analyzing data; and contributing to the development, adaptation, and evaluation of the model of care. However, the evaluator was also an outsider, as she was employed by an external organization and was not involved in the day-to-day implementation of the study or the model.

As an insider, the evaluator developed knowledge of the context and the model of care, and shared the values and vision of the other team members. As an outsider, the evaluator brought "fresh eyes" and was not "blinded" by the intimacy that the other team members had as insiders. This unique perspective enabled the evaluator to ask questions that challenged and clarified assumptions, and that other team members felt less comfortable about asking.

This position also meant that the evaluator became a *trusted* outsider and was able to develop respectful relationships with the other team members based on mutual trust. In turn, these relationships made her an *informed* facilitator of the workshops, which strengthened her ability to create a space safe for the team to explore emerging issues and apply evaluative thinking to resolve issues and support the development of the model of care.

As an outsider, the evaluator brought new energy into the team and offered a different perspective to events. At times the implementation of the study within the changing and uncertain context was hard work, but she was able to highlight and encourage team members to celebrate the team's achievements. Through the workshops, the evaluator facilitated discussions of the challenges and the identification of strategies to eliminate or reduce their impact.

Navigating the Tensions between Research and Provision of Care

A key challenge in applied research is the tensions that emerge in relation to the competing priorities between research and practice—in our case, health care service delivery. As mentioned above, most of the core team members were new to research, and this increased the challenges for them in developing and implementing a new model of care within the constraints of a research project and in an already complex environment. The developmental evaluation processes alerted us to these tensions as they emerged, and assisted us to understand these tensions and their consequences for team members, the research process, and the delivery of health care. Consequently, as a team, we were able to navigate and manage these tensions so that their impact was minimal. The documentation of these tensions and of the pragmatic decisions for their management was important, especially with regard to the research process, data analysis, and understanding the features of value of the model of care. Through this process, a number of learnings emerged that strengthened the ongoing implementation of the study.

Embracing Complexity

As with program development in any real-world setting, there was considerable complexity at different levels of our project. The HOME Study took place at a time of significant change, reform, and uncertainty within the state health department, of which the IIHS is part. A new conservative state government had come into power with a reform agenda and changes in health policies and priorities, resulting in significant job cuts. These circumstances understandably created stress and uncertainty for the team members, both with regard to their own job security and in managing the study participants' expectations with regard to the ongoing delivery of the model of care.

Within this broader turbulent context, the team was developing and implementing a complex model of care within a busy and dynamic health service—and, as noted earlier, some team members were initially working outside their comfort zones. At times this complexity threatened to become overwhelming. However, the developmental evaluation processes enabled us to acknowledge, explore, navigate, and negotiate this complexity, and provided a framework in which we could make effective progress. The interview data complemented the quantitative data in enabling us to identify what we were achieving; furthermore, the interview data gave us insights into why we were achieving these things. The workshops enabled us to enhance our understanding of how we were achieving things, and to develop and adapt the model of care within a complex environment. Exhibit 12.1 provides a representation of this environment; indicates the space the developmental evaluation processes provided; and shows how we were able to use these processes to develop the model of care iteratively, despite the reality and uncertainty of our context.

Strengthening Integration of the Innovation

We were able to harness our ability to integrate the model of care effectively within the IIHS's existing practices of care through the application of developmental evaluation. This was achieved in four main ways. First, the core team members' knowledge about the clinical, management, and administrative structures, systems, and processes of the IIHS informed adaptations of the model to enable integration as we went along. Second, the evaluator interviewed other IIHS staff members at key intervals to explore, among other things, their perspectives on integration of the model of care within the health service systems. Information from these interviews was discussed in the workshops and informed changes to improve integration. This engagement with the broader health service was well received and may have contributed to people's willingness to incorporate the model into the existing systems. As one health professional stated in an interview, "The fact that you're here interviewing us . . . to find out how we all feel about it is very good."

EXHIBIT 12.1

The HOME Study's Systematic Framework to Support Innovation Development and Implementation

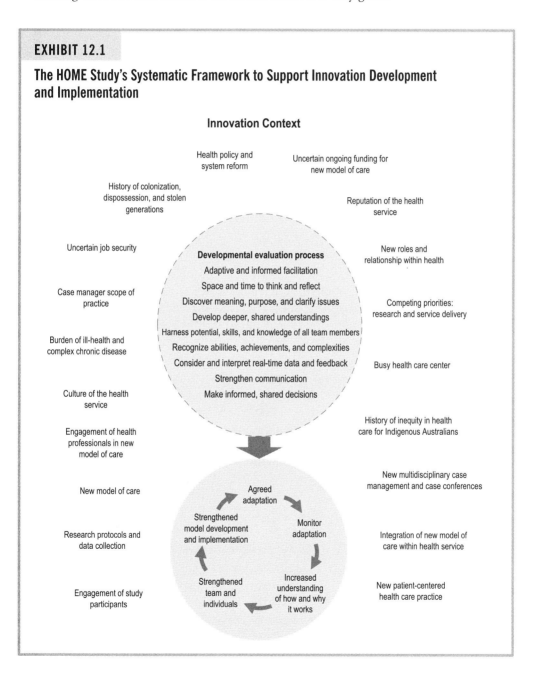

Third, as mentioned above, a focus of the workshops was the clarification of what and where information was recorded. In addition to supporting high-quality data collection, this process ensured that information recorded by the case managers that was relevant to the participants' ongoing care through the health service was included in the participants' medical records, to support the integration of the model of care within the health service and coordination of participants' care.

Finally, the developmental evaluation processes enabled the team to consider and clarify the roles, responsibilities, and relationships of other health service staff members with regard to the new model of care, and to specify the expectations of their engagement with the model. Once the team had clarified all these, they were discussed with the broader health service staff. This improved communication with the health service and further supported integration.

Supporting Diffusion, Dissemination, and Uptake of the Innovation

As previously discussed, the success of the model of care in improving social and emotional well-being and health outcomes for participants, and its acceptability to the participants and the health service after the first 18 months, contributed to the model's incorporation into the usual practice of the health service. We believe that this outcome was in part due to the developmental evaluation approach. A strength of the developmental evaluation approach was its ability to enable the team members to use their knowledge and expertise to meet and adapt to the health service's information needs with regard to diffusing and disseminating the innovation. In turn, this strengthened the ability of the team and the health service to communicate about the model of care and influence decision making in regard to its uptake. This aspect of developmental evaluation demonstrates its position and effectiveness within the broader field of utilization-focused evaluation (Patton, 2008).

Access to current information and emerging findings enabled the team members to disseminate information about the model of care and its outcomes within the health service through formal presentations in meetings and informal conversations with their colleagues and other stakeholders. This was effective in spreading the word about the model of care and its outcomes within the health service and the local community.

The information to which the team had access was shaped in part by the research protocol; however, the developmental evaluation process enabled the team members to be adaptive and responsive to emerging information needs within this real-world setting. The research director was able to identify particular aspects or areas of impact and outcomes that she knew would be of interest to the health department's decision makers. At times, the research director would shape the focus of discussion at the workshops to explore what we knew about how the model of care was working in certain areas and what outcomes were emerging in this regard. Examples of these areas included prevention of potentially avoidable hospitalizations, ways the model of care was working at the interface between primary and tertiary care, and participants' stories. During the workshops, the team could then identify relevant data or identify any needs to collect additional data.

This information could be presented formally or informally by the research director or the clinical director at key high-level meetings within the health department. Following one such meeting in which the research director had spoken about the outcomes of the HOME Study, she was invited to submit a business case for conducting a trial of the HOME Study model of care in three Aboriginal Community Controlled Health Organizations in the health district. The business case was successful, and funds were committed for this trial.

While the IIHS's track record of success in improving access to high-quality health care and health outcomes for Aboriginal and Torres Strait Islander people meant that it was already well positioned to influence decision makers, we believe that the developmental evaluation process was able to strengthen this position. It is therefore not surprising that the developmental evaluation approach incorporates or offers the ability to incorporate and/or address many of the determinants identified in Greenhalgh, Robert, Macfarlane, Bate, and Kyriakidou's (2004) conceptual model for the diffusion, dissemination, and implementation of innovation in health service delivery.

Developing Research and Evaluation Capacity

The embedding of developmental evaluation within the HOME Study, and the evaluator's process of guiding evaluative thinking through asking questions and facilitating reflection, increased team members' evaluation skills and capacity. This was consistent with the IIHS's commitment to ongoing professional development and the strengthening of a research and evaluation culture within the organization. The process created the space for, and encouraged team members to "think outside the box" with regard to making sense of and resolving issues. Over time, in the workshops, we noticed an increase in evaluative questions asked by team members other than the evaluator. There were also anecdotal accounts of team members' applying these new skills in their work outside the study.

Capacity development of Aboriginal and Torres Strait Islander researchers is a key focus of the KVC's work. Within the HOME Study, the evaluator had a key

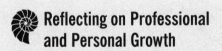

Reflecting on Professional and Personal Growth

Lynne Rogers, Program Coordinator: "For me personally . . . having those workshops, it just made me feel empowered and able to do things to help and contribute to the overall model of care . . . it contributed to my feeling of worth, my sense of worth.

"You could safely raise things in the workshops. How the evaluator explored everybody's information and teased that out helped people in their own thinking . . . my challenge was to look outside to the bigger scheme of things. I had to challenge myself to think of other ways to help, maybe put a solution in place, whereas before I'd have the path to follow for those solutions. The developmental evaluation approach makes you think outside the box."

role in mentoring the IRO. The interactive nature of the developmental evaluation processes supported the development of the IRO's applied research skills and abilities and provided opportunities for her to engage and learn, while at the same time contributing her unique knowledge. This created a positive and supportive learning environment in which to develop her research capacity, and one in which her existing community knowledge and expertise were recognized and valued.

The Value of Developmental Evaluation in Supporting Innovation in Primary Health Care

Primary health care is generally not a setting where concentrations of social entrepreneurs are found. Necessarily, health care services are generally characterized by protocols and risk aversion, and a context in which "innovations [are] defined as health technologies and practices supported by sound research evidence" (Greenhalgh, Robert, Macfarlane, Bate, and Kyriakidou, 2004, p. 590). Innovation in primary health care settings can therefore be challenging. In our case, we were embarking on an exploratory study with the aim of developing a new model of care within a primary health care setting. Our initial scoping of the model's design was guided by an evidence base, but we wanted to explore and learn about what worked, how it worked, and how it needed to be developed and implemented in our particular context. As a team, we brought a range of relevant skills and experience to this undertaking, but most of us had not worked on this type of research project before. We were working within a health service with a national profile for excellence in health care for Aboriginal and Torres Strait Islander people, as well as a health system undergoing significant reform. Within this complex and dynamic context, there was a considerable degree of uncertainty and risk in what we were setting out to do.

The developmental evaluation approach provided us with a framework in which we could *safely* explore and develop the model of care. There were sufficient

✦ Reflecting on the Developmental Evaluation Process

Deborah Askew: "It gave me the opportunity to not be the leader, to not be the person that had all the answers. It gave me a space to say, 'Well, I don't know; I don't have the answer. What are the options? What do you think?' It acknowledged that because we were developing the model, there wasn't an answer. The workshops gave us the space to develop a solution, and then next time around think about it and ask, 'Did it work?'

"It affected the development of the model of care, because we were learning from what we had done.

"Developmental evaluation gave us the permission to change as we went along. It gave legitimacy to the fact that we could change the model as we learned—not only learned from our mistakes, but also learned from those things that went really well too."

checks and balances in place for us to feel confident in our exploration. It provided a structure without curtailing the changes that we needed to make—changes that were informed by the information and data we were collecting and analyzing as we went along, to strengthen the model of care and its implementation. It created a space in which we could say we did not have *the* answers and that there was no *one* expert; it thus enabled a process that brought together the skills, experience, and expertise of all team members to tackle complex issues and contexts.

Lessons from Our Developmental Evaluation Experience

Key features of the developmental evaluation process that we believe contributed to its effectiveness in our case were these:

- It provided a framework and processes in which the team felt safe to explore and develop the model of care and strengthen its implementation.
- It facilitated reflective practice and active learning.
- It enabled the recognition and utilization of all team members' skills, knowledge, experience, and abilities.

However, it is important to recognize and acknowledge the part that we all played in applying this approach to evaluation. Developmental evaluation is nothing without people and their relationships; these factors cannot be underestimated. The features of the developmental evaluation processes that we have identified as contributing to its effectiveness in our context were underpinned by the individual qualities of all core team members and the relationships among us, as well as the skills, abilities, and attributes of the evaluator. The individual qualities that we believe supported effective developmental evaluation processes were a willingness to participate in the process, develop trusting and respectful relationships, and work collaboratively, and an openness to sharing skills and knowledge. In addition, team members displayed their ability to be self-reflective or a desire to learn the practice of self-reflection. It was also important that the team shared values in wanting to improve quality of life for Aboriginal and Torres Strait Islander peoples, and to develop a more holistic approach to health care.

The skills, abilities, and attributes essential for the developmental evaluator in this process included good "people skills"; an ability to foster trusting relationships and identify and build on people's strengths; adaptive facilitation skills, flexibility, and agility; an ability to observe and respond constructively to situations; an ability to sit comfortably with ambiguity; and an understanding of organizations and their systems and change processes. In our case, it was also beneficial that the evaluator had content knowledge in implementing health services research projects.

We experienced few challenges in using developmental evaluation in our context, but it is worth identifying those we did. An initial challenge was to gain support from the KVC leadership to utilize this new form of evaluation within a research project. Developmental evaluation was not known within the broader KVC or the IIHS at this time, and thus the value and credibility of this new and emerging evaluation approach as an approach to the HOME Study were not clear. The evaluator, who introduced developmental evaluation to the KVC, had developed trusting relationships with her research colleagues over several years of working together, and these relationships inspired confidence in considering its use. Following discussions regarding its attributes and suitability for our context, the researchers agreed to support its utilization.

Securing resources to support developmental evaluation as an integral part of the research project might have proved challenging, as evaluation is often not funded for the duration of large research projects. However, we were fortunate in this respect: The KVC had secured funding that gave us flexibility in how it was used to support the research program.

Our evaluator was very experienced and well suited to the collaborative nature of this approach, and therefore the actual implementation of developmental evaluation was relatively simple. In addition, developmental evaluation processes enabled any challenges to be addressed as we went along. The considerable time commitment from the team to participate in the workshops might have proved challenging if the workshops were not experienced as useful and therefore valued in supporting the team's work.

The main challenge we faced was managing the confidentiality of stakeholders who participated in interviews when this information was fed back to the core team in the workshops as part of the consideration of real-time data. Although the evaluator did not use stakeholders' names, the identity of the stakeholders was difficult to disguise fully, given the size of the health service and the familiarity of staff members with one another. This issue requires further consideration for research projects such as this one.

Conclusion

Overall, developmental evaluation was an effective approach for the aims of our exploratory study to develop a model of care in a primary health care setting. It offered us a framework and processes that not only supported innovation development and strengthened the pragmatic implementation of real-world research, but also supported diffusion, dissemination, and implementation of innovation within the primary health care service. Through the process, the health service staff and practitioners who were part of our core team were engaged in developing and implementing the innovation and in identifying issues and learnings. This engagement increased the team's and the innovation's effectiveness. The process harnessed the knowledge and expertise of all team members in a focused and purposeful way, and facilitated access to real-time data that were responsive to the information needs. We were informed about what we were doing and what was being achieved, and this enhanced our ability to respond in a timely fashion and take up opportunities when they occurred in a complex and emergent political environment.

Developmental evaluation embraces iterative and emergent processes within complex systems and uncertain, dynamic contexts. It recognizes that innovation and its uptake within these spaces are not linear processes, but are determined by people, their relationships, and their interactions with the systems and structures in which they operate. However, it is important to remember that developmental evaluation is relationship-based, and that its effectiveness depends on the qualities and abilities of those engaged in the process.

ACKNOWLEDGMENTS

We wish to acknowledge funding from the Australian Primary Health Care Research Institute, which is supported under the Australian Government's Primary Health Care Research, Evaluation and Development Strategy, and from Queensland Health, which supported this research project. We also wish to acknowledge the contributions of Roslyn Wharton-Boland, who was a case manager within the HOME Study until June 2013.

REFERENCES

Askew, D. A., Togni, S., Schluter, P. J., Rogers, L., Potter, N., Egert, S., et al. (2014). HOME, but not alone: Home-based, multidisciplinary case management for Aboriginal and Torres Strait Islander peoples with complex chronic disease. In *2014 Primary Health Care Research Conference: Program and abstracts*. Bedford Park, South Australia, Australia: Primary Health Care Research and Information Service. Retrieved from *www.phcris.org.au/conference/abstract/7999.*

Bond, C., Foley, W., & Askew, D. (in press). "It puts a human face on the researched": A qualitative evaluation of an Indigenous health research governance model. *Australian and New Zealand Journal of Public Health.*

Franks, C. B. (1996). *Keeping company: An intercultural conversation.* Wollongong, New South Wales, Australia: Centre for Indigenous Development, Education and Research, University of Wollongong.

Greenhalgh, T. R. G., Robert, G., Macfarlane, F., Bate, P., & Kyriakidou, O. (2004). Diffusion of innovations in service organizations: Systematic review and recommendations. *The Milbank Quarterly, 82*(4), 581–629.

Hayman, N. E., Askew, D. A., & Spurling, G. K. (2014). From vision to reality: A Centre of Excellence for Aboriginal and Torres Strait Islander primary health care. *Medical Journal of Australia, 200*(11), 623–624.

Hayman, N. E., White, N. E., & Spurling, G. K. (2009). Improving Indigenous patients' access to mainstream health services: The Inala experience. *Medical Journal of Australia, 190*(10), 604–606.

Institute for Aboriginal Development. (2001). *Pitjantjatjara/Yankunytjatjara to English Dictionary* (2nd ed., rev.). Alice Springs, Northern Territory, Australia: Institute for Aboriginal Development Press.

Mentha, R. A., de Vries, J., Simon, P. R., Fewquandie, B. N., Brady, J., & Ingram, S. (2012). Bringing our voices into the research world: Lessons from the Kanyini Vascular Collaboration. *Medical Journal of Australia, 197*(1), 55–56.

Patton, M. Q. (2008). *Utilization-focused evaluation* (4th ed.). Thousand Oaks, CA: Sage.

CHAPTER 13

Leadership's Role in Building the Education Sector's Capacity to Use Evaluative Thinking

The Example of the Ontario Ministry of Education

Keiko Kuji-Shikatani, Mary Jean Gallagher, Richard Franz, and Megan Börner

EDITORS' INTRODUCTION

We often encounter questions about whether developmental evaluation can be done in the public sector. Government accountability processes and demands are often positioned as barriers to innovation, adaptation, and learning. This case example shows how system reform, ongoing adaptation, and learning by doing can occur in the public sector. A critical facilitating factor illustrated in this case is engaged leadership committed to embedding evaluative thinking and developing evaluation capacity throughout the different levels of the Ontario Ministry of Education's programs and initiatives. System leadership is crucial in providing coherence and focus across a hugely diverse and complex educational system, while supporting relevant adaptation and contextual innovation at the local level. Dialogue, trust, and capacity to use research and evaluation information are all key factors within and across organizational levels. This example also illustrates the use of traditional evaluation tools (e.g., logic modeling, monitoring test scores, and other indicators) in support of ongoing adaptation through a developmental evaluation mindset. To fully appreciate this example, note that the authorship is shared by people with different kinds and levels of responsibility in the system: an assistant deputy minister, a director, a manager, and an education officer. We can attest that this has been a collaborative reflective practice and writing exercise by these authors. We can also attest that the educational leadership described in this case is knowledgeable about and committed to developmental evaluation, and fully engaged with the internal developmental evaluators. This is why we especially wanted to include this example of public sector developmental evaluation in the book. It doesn't happen often. It's not easy. But as this case illustrates, public sector developmental evaluation can be done—and can be done well.

This case study focuses on the example of the Ontario public education sector, where infusing evaluative thinking through the use of the developmental evaluation approach is positioned as a responsibility for internal evaluators, and informal and formal leaders at all levels of the system, who are focused on organizational learning and improvement. Leaders' valuing of evaluation and modeling of evaluative thinking are essential to transforming and building the Ontario education sector's capacity to use evidence to inform decisions and implementation for increasing student achievement and well-being (Patton, 2013). Transforming a large system within the public sector requires a form of social innovation that can be described as "a complex process of introducing new products, processes or programs that profoundly change the basic routines, resource and authority flows, or beliefs of the social system in which the innovation occurs. Such successful social innovations have durability and broad impact" (Westley & Antadze, 2010, p. 2). This case study illustrates the role of leaders and internal evaluators as social innovators who are involved at all levels of the system. It also shows how logic modeling is used as a tool to infuse evaluative thinking and guide developmental evaluation—enabling us in the ministry to "learn as we go" in our relentless pursuit of successful educational outcomes for every student.

Education in Ontario

Ontario is among the top education systems in the world (Mourshed, Chijioke, & Barber, 2010; Organisation for Economic Co-operation and Development [OECD], 2012). Forty percent of Canada's 33.6 million people reside in Ontario, and 40% of all immigrants to Canada come to Ontario. Approximately 95% of all students attend the four publicly funded education systems (English public, English Catholic, French public, and French Catholic). These systems serve 2 million students through 72 district school boards, involving 4,897 schools with 115,000 teachers. In 2003, the government introduced a large-scale reform in response to limited improvement in student achievement in elementary and secondary schools. Since its launch, Ontario has made a multimillion-dollar investment annually in system reform. The following eight features characterize the entire reform strategy (OECD, 2012):

- A small number of ambitious goals.
- A guiding coalition at the top.
- High standards and expectations.
- Investment in leadership and capacity building related to instruction.
- Mobilizing data and effective practices as a strategy for improvement.
- Intervention in a nonpunitive manner.
- Reducing distractions.
- Being transparent, relentless, and increasingly challenging.

The results show overall increases in the numbers of students meeting the elementary school provincial standards[1] for reading, writing, and mathematics, and graduating from secondary school. Based on Education Quality and Accountability Office (EQAO)[2] data, the overall combined 2013–2014 Grades 3 and 6 result of 72% of English- and French-language district school board students meeting the provincial standard represents an increase of 18 percentage points since 2002–2003. The high school graduation rate[3] has increased by 16 percentage points (from 68% in 2003–2004 to 84% in 2013–2014), representing approximately 163,000 more students who have graduated than would have done so if the strategy had not been in place.

The core of the strategy—capacity building, led from the Student Achievement Division of the Ontario Ministry of Education—is constructed from many specific initiatives that target different parts of the school improvement challenge. Although drawing from the same theory of action and targeting the same goals, initiatives may focus on different challenges and on different populations of students and educators. A *prism* (Ontario Ministry of Education, 2013), adapted from Elmore's references to the *instructional core* (City, Elmore, Fiarman, & Lee, 2009), has been used as the key visual device to represent the strategy across the province and within the ministry. (See Exhibit 13.1.)

The prism represents the alignment and coherence that are needed throughout the system in reaching every student. Each level needs to inform and reflect the core of the system: teaching and learning for student achievement and well-being. It extends this instructional core to engagement and action at every level. The interconnectedness of the educational enterprise means that classrooms, schools, district school boards, and the province all need to work together, since decisions and actions affect others and the system as a whole. System leaders have to bring together many initiatives and policies, so that the resources of time, personnel, and efforts are targeted on the goals in their improvement plans (Mourshed et al., 2010).

Ontario public education has received recognition for its success while the work continues. After a recent public consultation process, the ministry renewed its vision with four goals that are interconnected, as success in one contributes to success in the others (Ontario Ministry of Education, 2014, p. 3):

- *Achieving Excellence:* Children and students of all ages will achieve high levels of academic performance, acquire valuable skills and demonstrate good citizenship. Educators will be supported in learning continuously and will be recognized as among the best in the world.
- *Ensuring Equity:* All children and students will be inspired to reach their full

---

[1] Ontario's provincial standard is equivalent to a letter B grade.

[2] EQAO is an arm's-length agency of the provincial government that administers provincial, pan-Canadian, and international assessments in elementary and secondary schools. EQAO's tests measure student achievement in reading, writing, and mathematics in relation to Ontario curriculum expectations. EQAO's assessments provide information about student achievement that teachers and parents can use to improve learning for all students.

[3] The Ministry of Education's method for calculating the provincial graduation rate is based on a cohort approach, which measures the percentage of students who graduated within 4 or 5 years after starting Grade 9.

EXHIBIT 13.1

The Prism: A Representation of the Ontario Ministry of Education's Capacity-Building Strategy

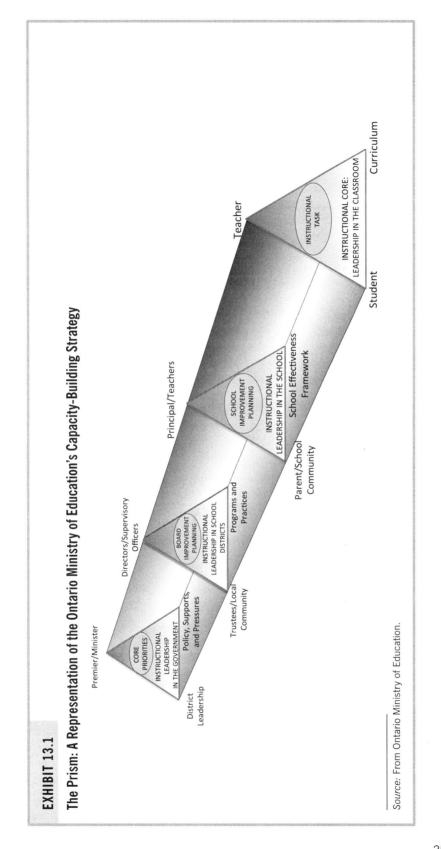

Premier/Minister

Directors/Supervisory
Officers

Principal/Teachers

Teacher

Curriculum

Student

CORE
PRIORITIES

INSTRUCTIONAL
LEADERSHIP
IN THE GOVERNMENT

Policy, Supports,
and Pressures

District
Leadership

Trustees/Local
Community

BOARD
IMPROVEMENT
PLANNING

INSTRUCTIONAL
LEADERSHIP IN SCHOOL
DISTRICTS

Programs and
Practices

SCHOOL
IMPROVEMENT
PLANNING

INSTRUCTIONAL
LEADERSHIP IN THE SCHOOL

School Effectiveness
Framework

Parent/School
Community

INSTRUCTIONAL
TASK

INSTRUCTIONAL CORE:
LEADERSHIP IN THE CLASSROOM

Source: From Ontario Ministry of Education.

potential, with access to rich learning experiences that begin at birth and continue into adulthood.

- *Promoting Well-Being:* All children and students will develop enhanced mental and physical health, a positive sense of self and belonging, and the skills to make positive choices.
- *Enhancing Public Confidence:* Ontarians will continue to have confidence in a publicly funded education system that helps develop new generations of confident, capable and caring citizens.

The world in which today's youth are growing up and going to be leaders and learners throughout their lifetimes is a complex and a quickly changing place. In order to make sure that the students are the best they can be, those in the system need to *work smarter* and use *evaluative thinking* to guide every facet of improvement efforts. Patton (2013) defines *evaluative thinking* as "systematic, intentional and ongoing attention to expected results. It focuses on how results are achieved, what evidence is needed to inform future actions and how to improve future results." But what does *working smarter* in regard to evaluative thinking involve, and how does a ministry facilitate this in a way that translates into better learning for students?

Evaluative Thinking as a Leadership Responsibility and Function

Keeping initiatives coherent and aligned, while maintaining their relevance, requires partnership and collaboration from the entire sector. Leaders in schools and district school boards focus on ongoing teacher capacity building in order to maximize learning for students. They focus and ask the right kind of questions in order to make advances.

> Our role at the province is to support learning at all levels of our system and provide resources, time and programs to assist. But also we need to be prepared to ask ourselves the questions to ensure that the support we are giving is appropriate and is able to move the agenda forward. The coherence and alignment that drives our success forward really requires an evaluative inquiry mindset all the way through the system. (Gallagher, Franz, & Malloy, 2013)

It is essential for leaders at all levels to continually communicate the value of evaluative thinking and guide the developmental evaluation approach by modeling/mentoring the use of evidence to understand more precisely the needs of all students and to monitor and evaluate progress of improvement efforts. The existence of a branch within the Student Achievement Division that focuses on research, evaluation, and capacity building reflects a leadership belief in the importance of "having skilled practical program evaluators who can really help in being more rigorous with the questions that are raised" (Gallagher et al., 2013). The branch's goal is to build ministry and sector capacity for the use of evidence to inform decisions and implementation. Research, monitoring, evaluation, and capacity building are integrated into the work through evidence-informed practice that does the following:

- Improves the coherence of planning, implementation, and ongoing learning.
- Facilitates capacity building for improved student learning, well-being, achievement, and engagement.
- Supports good decisions and promotes increased public confidence.
- Builds a culture of evaluative thinking through collaborative inquiry, action, and reflective practice that are adaptive, coherent, precise, and personalized.

The work of the Research, Evaluation and Capacity Building Branch focuses not on being prescriptive, but on supporting the sector to think evaluatively (Gallagher et al., 2013). The "learn as we go" approach, analogous to developmental evaluation, is the approach to the use of evidence in practice that enables the branch to adapt, improve, and evolve over time. The division models evaluative thinking through developmental evaluation by having evaluators intentionally embedded in program and policy development and implementation teams. The emphasis is on being a learning organization through evidence-informed, focused improvement planning and implementation. The division as a whole, then, is participating in the building of developmental evaluation capacity by applying evaluative thinking to conceptualizing, designing, and testing new approaches in a long-term ongoing process of continuous development, adaptation, and experimentation, while being keenly sensitive to the possibility of unintended results and side effects. In fact, this embedded approach means that evaluative thinking is not the exclusive responsibility of the evaluators of the branch, but becomes the commitment of all in the division.

Research-Informed and Evidence-Based Practice

"An early focus on research-informed and evidence-based policy and practice led to recognition of the need to embed evaluation and evaluative thinking into ministry initiatives" (McWhorter & Franz, 2014); the strategies that concern literacy and numeracy, the graduation rate, leadership, parent engagement, and early learning were all designed on the basis of foundational research. For example, in 2004, externally commissioned research unpacked the low high school graduation rate of 68% to reveal that in fact students were at risk of not graduating if they missed even one credit by Grade 10, and findings showed that 40% of Grade 10 students were missing at least one credit (King, 2004). Research conducted in 2005 identified student disengagement as a critical component of students' leaving high school before graduation (Ferguson et al., 2005). Together, these studies provided the body of knowledge to inform the development of a range of programs designed to help every Ontario student to acquire the necessary 30 credits to graduate from secondary school (Directions Evidence and Policy Research Group, 2014). Credit accumulation for Grades 9 and 10 became and still is an indicator of student success and progression toward graduation that is monitored by schools, district school boards, and the ministry. Graduation rates and other student success data are reported publicly every year.

System reform in Ontario's public education system has been able to develop, adapt, and evolve over the past decade through consistent and constant attention to building a culture of research and evaluation practices in which educators and policy makers alike are engaged in understanding the importance of data and evidence to informing the life cycles of policy and programs (Fullan, 2010). High-level, measurable targets; internally led evaluations and the monitoring of key performance indicator data; and externally commissioned research and evaluations, consultations, and external assessments all give a multidimensional picture of the division's impact on outcomes for students.

Using Logic Modeling as a Tool to Infuse Evaluative Thinking and Guide Developmental Evaluation

The division uses logic modeling as a tool to infuse evaluative thinking in its work as a "formal rigorous discipline" in all of its initiatives (Kuji-Shikatani, Franz, & Gallagher, 2014). Embedded internal evaluators are assigned to every initiative and facilitate the developmental evaluation process through asking evaluative questions, applying evaluation logic, and gathering real-time data to inform ongoing decision making and adaptations. Logic models are evolving into the pivotal documents/tools to build in evaluative thinking and guide developmental evaluation throughout the annual work cycle, which includes the following:

1. Planning and budgeting for the coming year.
2. Using carefully co-constructed language in communication materials.
3. Articulating implementation activities into a cycle, showing the programming, initiatives, and interventions for the year.
4. Developing/refining support materials for external stakeholders, based on what was learned.
5. Developing internal support reference materials and implementation details, based on what was learned in the previous year.
6. Identifying when and how to collect, analyze, and use timely data for monitoring and developmental evaluation throughout the year.

As educators, we understand the value of experiential learning, and the same can be said about the fit of developmental evaluation for a learning organization such as the ministry: The key program and policy stakeholders' willingness to monitor and reflect on the results of the initiatives supports programs' improvements in the long run. Using logic models as tools to anchor evaluative thinking and guide developmental evaluation enables the ministry to activate the "learn as we go" culture and to support others in the system as they try to do the same. Collaborative development and examination of logic models offer highly participatory learning opportunities, allow documentation of explicit expected outcomes, clarify knowledge about what is thought to work and why, and offer strategic means to critically review and improve thinking. The clarity of thinking that occurs from building these models is critical to the overall success of the desired change process (Knowlton & Phillips, 2012).

Logic modeling became part of the division's work through several phases. The first phase was at the initiative level, in which evaluators modeled the use of how logic modeling can support evaluative thinking and guide developmental evaluation. Then, in 2010, the logic-modeling initiative was introduced in a divisional all-staff meeting by the chief student achievement officer/assistant deputy minister (Mary Jean Gallagher), who stated the importance of using logic modeling as a way of being more precise and intentional in the division's work. Acquiring evaluative thinking and developing social innovators within the public sector necessitate a thorough understanding of how their efforts in the policy and program areas contribute and relate to the transformation objectives of the overall system. Therefore, learning sessions were held to introduce staff to both theory-of-change and program/theory-of-action logic models. Evaluators from the Research, Evaluation and Capacity Building Branch worked with 37 initiative teams in the division (both the Literacy and Numeracy Secretariat, and Student Success Learning to 18 branches) to co-construct logic models. Ministry teams often commented that they had never consciously explored the assumptions underlying their initiatives; testing the meaning, coherence, plausibility, and sustainability of the change they were hoping to see.

Logic modeling allowed the teams to come to a shared agreement on the conceptualization and language they would use to communicate the initiative to the system. Once this common ground was established, and depending on the teams' readiness, the evaluators moved on to intentionally weaving evaluative thinking into the work. To do this, they used a program theory like a map or a blueprint, to articulate the shared understanding that would enable complex programs to function, despite changing realities that were sure to occur throughout the school year. Evaluators differentiated their approaches according to the comfort level of each team, as determined through ongoing discussions. Specialized terminologies were kept to a minimum, and the evaluators used plain language to layer in evaluative thinking as resources were developed to support the teams. Once each initiative had a logic model, an all-staff, divisionwide logic-modeling session was held to co-construct a divisional theory-of-change logic model. The session, involving over 180 staff members, required careful planning culminating in numerous logic-modeling conversations among various teams working on similar initiatives. In many cases, these teams had never had deep conversations about their work, since they functioned fairly separately.

Through significant annual investments, the Ontario strategy for system reform targets many aspects of the school improvement challenge. The complexity of the ministry's work is reflected in the logic models developed, which encompass the perspectives of the many parties involved and tend to be relatively text-heavy, to allow the articulation of the evidence, experience, knowledge, and theory that inform the direction of the work and each aspect of an initiative's development and implementation. Using qualitative and quantitative data collection instruments specifically developed for each work area, teams track and monitor progress toward outcomes and deliberately consider the implications of each decision. A set of cumulative decisions can establish a direction for something without allowing for an explicit decision about that change in direction (Patton, 2008). Throughout the year, the ministry's various teams support those who are implementing the policies and the programs in district school boards and schools. Recording changes and incremental learning through collaborative inquiry yields a wealth of information and illuminates the responsive efforts made. The developmental evaluation process is helpful in enabling a group working on an innovation that addresses adaptive challenges to provide some accountability by reporting on the evolving process. Processes and tools used for developmental evaluation are closely related to the ministry's implementation cycle. Utilizing information for ongoing development and adapting effective principles to local contexts require careful attention to details that affect programs at critical decision points.

Leaders at All Levels

An education strategy that centers on a ministry's being a learning organization requires significant investment in leadership at all levels, as well as capacity building focused on learning about and addressing the learning challenges experienced by the students in the system. Through the roles of leaders, there are focused efforts to embed evaluative thinking in various facets of this complex system, in order to clarify major goals and to implement and monitor progress toward achieving those goals. Leaders' valuing and modeling of evaluative thinking are essential to building the education system's capacity to use and learn from evidence to inform decisions and implementation: "It is a belief that we are evaluators, change agents, adaptive learning experts, seekers of feedback about our impact, engaged in dialogue and challenge, and that we see opportunity in error, and are keen to spread the message about the power, fun and impact that we have on learning" (Hattie, 2012).

To meet the outcomes of the ministry's education vision and its goals, the Ontario provincial government has made major investments in providing additional staff and resources at all levels of the system, in order to lead and implement finely tuned strategies based on both universal and intervention approaches. Functioning at the classroom and school levels, a Student Success Teacher, who focuses on students at risk of not graduating, is in every high school (800 schools), and additional specialist teachers for literacy and numeracy learning are in elementary schools. District school boards have student achievement officers supporting their elementary schools and one or more Student Success Leaders for their high schools. At the district school board and regional levels, school effectiveness leaders, Aboriginal education officers, special education officers, external Student Success education officers, and regional education officers are all leaders in their roles as change agents, adaptive learning experts, and seekers of feedback about impact, and are engaged in dialogue and challenge (Hattie, 2012). An array of resources and strategies support and frame the work of these leaders to help improve teaching and learning in Ontario schools.[4] Evaluative thinking is contributing to intentionally building a solid foundation of professional, social, and decisional capital (Hargreaves & Fullan, 2012) in Ontario. At each level, the division and the system are using developmental evaluation processes to work together to build evaluative thinking capacity and to create and sustain social innovation, in order to meet the collective goal of providing a successful educational outcome for each student.

Classroom: Diverse Teams Engaging in Professional Learning through the Use of Collaborative Inquiry–Action Cycles

The essential work of education centers on the students and their learning. The ministry's initiatives aim to support teachers in their instructional tasks to be very precisely focused on the details of the work that the students are doing, what they are thinking, and the instructional design, to provide challenges and opportunities for them to move from where they are to where they need to be. Increasingly, educators collectively understand data—words, numbers, and observations—as information that is collected and organized in a systematic way, so that it can be used to make instructional or organizational decisions. Various collaborative inquiries for professional learning across the system engage teams of educators in an iterative process that is informed by the ongoing assessment of the impact of planned actions on learners' needs. The intent is to create a culture of reflective practice.

A system involved in collaborative inquiry that promotes evaluative thinking values different points of view and recognizes the function of dissonance as part of a collaborative inquiry–action cycle. The operating belief is that successful leaders for instructional improvement cannot operate in isolation.

> Engaging in the cycle is more about changing norms, habits, skills, and beliefs than about changing formal structures. It is about organizational learning, and at the heart of organizational learning is the ability to enter into a professional community, to develop modes of inquiry, and to take risks. . . . One structure for a meaningful collaboration is the community of practice (often called a professional learning community). Such communities consist of professionals who are "engaged in the sustained pursuit of a shared enterprise" (Pallas, 2001, p. 7) and who interact with each other "in particular contexts around specific tasks" (Spillane et al., 2004, p. 5). Members of school communities for practice collaborate with the goal of supporting their work toward

---

[4]The resources include a School Effectiveness Framework (see later discussion), a leadership framework, professional learning institutes, webinars, and instructional guides. The strategies include the Ontario Focused Intervention Partnerships (OFIP), Schools in the Middle, the Differentiated Instruction Professional Learning strategy, Credit Recovery, the Student Engagement/Student Voice strategy, and the School Support initiative. For more details, see the ministry's website (*www.edu.gov.on.ca/eng*).

instructional improvement. As the name implies, communities of practice examine their own practice: They analyse data related to their work to inform their planning and decisions; the dialogue results in learning that builds coherence and capacity for change. (Militello, Rallis, & Goldring, 2009, p. 29)

Use of the collaborative inquiry–action cycle, which is both grounded in and propelled by evaluative thinking, is crucial to improving educator practice and enriching student learning experiences that build on each other iteratively (Zegarac & Franz, 2007).

School and District School Board: School Improvement Planning and the School Effectiveness Framework

The K–12 School Effectiveness Framework (SEF),[5] built in partnership with school districts and schools, is a self-assessment tool that can engage school and district school board improvement planners in reflecting on their own practices and their impacts. It is designed to ensure that improvement planning is a collaborative process that uses a wide range of sources of student data at the classroom, school, and district school board levels. Based on their school self-assessments, schools select components from the SEF that will assist them to coordinate curriculum, instructional strategies, and assessments of students among teachers within a grade level or department (Ontario Ministry of Education, 2013). District school boards across Ontario have created tools based on the SEF to suit their needs as they use evaluative thinking and the developmental evaluation approach to become more precise in their school improvement planning and implementation efforts.

District School Board: The Board Improvement Plan for Student Achievement Process

The structure created to systematize evaluative thinking and the processes of developmental evaluation across the province is the Board Improvement Plan for Student Achievement (BIPSA) (Ontario Ministry of Education, 2012). The BIPSA builds evaluative thinking through a cyclical process involving developmental evaluation activities (see Exhibit 13.2). It addresses each district school board's own most urgent student learning needs, based on ongoing needs assessment through the cycle of planning, implementation, monitoring, and evaluation. The ministry supports the process through professional learning opportunities, resources, and a regional team of educational experts who visits each district school board's BIPSA team to engage in conversations as a professional community, and, when requested, to serve as a "critical friend."

The BIPSA cycle is a robust process that allows district school boards to pursue their own inquiries about their practices, so that these practices can become more effective and more precise. To varying degrees, district school boards are embarking

[5]*www.edu.gov.on.ca/eng/literacynumeracy/framework.html.*

EXHIBIT 13.2

Board Improvement Plan for Student Achievement (BIPSA) Cycle

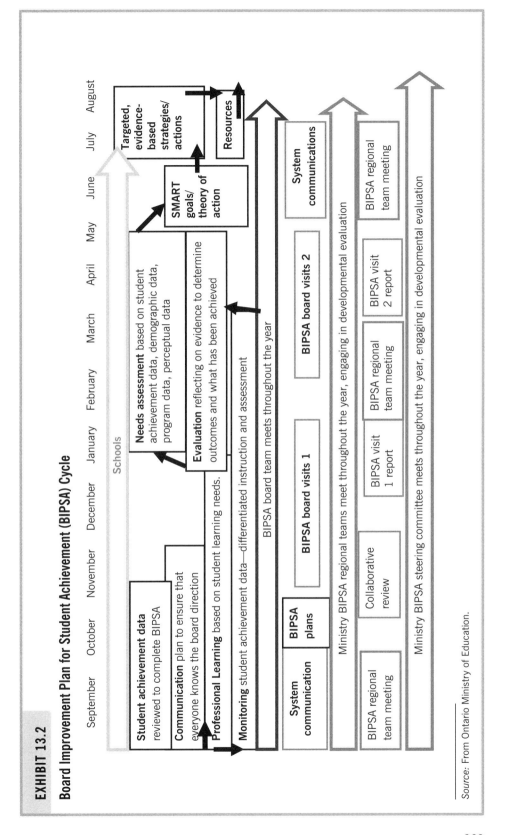

Source: From Ontario Ministry of Education.

on a systemwide collaborative inquiry model to align the school improvement focus with the administrators' capacity building and the system's annual improvement plans. Central to this work is the "learn as we go"/developmental evaluation approach: conducting needs assessments; identifying success criteria; considering what evidence constitutes success at the front end of the plan; and observing, evaluating, and reflecting (Gardner & Malloy, 2013).

The ministry's BIPSA teams visit district school boards twice during the school year for conversations to support their BIPSA process. To establish relationships and foster trust with district school boards, the makeup of each four-member BIPSA regional team of education officers (who have diverse areas of expertise among them—e.g., regional context, Aboriginal education, student achievement, special education) remains consistent throughout the school year. The BIPSA regional teams are asked to preplan, develop protocols, schedule meetings, and tailor/differentiate support, based on each district school board's context and BIPSA plan. As a "critical friend" and source of support, the ministry leverages existing structures to help the district school boards work through their challenges. In turn, the ministry BIPSA teams gain valuable field knowledge and understanding of each region when they engage in developmental evaluation activities by collaboratively analyzing and learning from what the district school boards have learned individually and collectively. The resulting knowledge and insights are shared broadly across the system and inform the ministry's own improvement planning and next steps.

Among the key responsibilities of leaders at all levels of the education system are to clarify system goals and to articulate and monitor the progress being made toward achieving them. Developmental evaluation structures and processes (e.g., logic models, improvement plans, collaborative inquiry) and evaluative thinking play essential roles in that effort and are positioned as leadership responsibilities. Leaders are agents of change at all levels of the system, building a culture through reflective practice that is adaptive, coherent, precise, and personalized.

What has become evident is that evaluative thinking is a process that enables ongoing adaptations to address the ever-changing learning needs within the classroom, school, district school board, and government environments. Leaders think and talk about the real value of evaluation and evaluative thinking, as well as ways to turn this value into something that actually influences decision making and direction setting at all levels of the system.

> One of the big challenges for any leader is to sustain that evaluative thinking as part of the organization. Leaders need to constantly articulate the message that we want people to be looking at the data. We want people to be looking at the results of programs . . . [to] go back through the logic models and figure out where the gaps might be, where the place is that we can tweak this in order to get a better outcome for our students. Leaders need to model the fact that they are open to those conversations that challenge their ideas . . . [and] staff need to be free to be able to raise those issues with them as does anyone across the system. It's also important for leaders to continually articulate the reasoning of their support for evaluative thinking[—]that it is an important part of the everyday work of the organization[—]if we are going to continue to

leverage better and better results with our students in our classrooms. It is important that we both model and mentor other leaders in approaching that and that we use logic modelling tool[s] as . . . powerful tool[s] to identify the differentiated approaches in various parts of the organization and to identify the places in which we need to change. (Gallagher et al., 2013)

Educational leaders in the schools, district school boards, and the ministry mirror the precise work required in the classroom: If teachers need to be very precise in designing their instructional tasks, leaders need to be equally precise in designing the supports and assistance that are put in place, so that teachers and leaders can increase their knowledge of what will enhance student learning.

Developmental evaluation provides the structural design for the culture of evaluative thinking for a complex system; such thinking must, to reach its goals, be adaptive, coherent, precise, and personalized. Work in the division involves a cycle of implementation, monitoring, and evaluation parallel to the school year; it provides inputs into the budgeting cycle in the fall, and culminates in the government's decisions in early spring. (See Exhibit 13.3.) The budgeting process is when the value of developmental evaluation is most clearly realized. This is when the various data and findings collected from different efforts are utilized in an overall developmental evaluation process to inform the next steps.

Systemwide Collection and Use of Student-Level Data to Encourage Evaluative Thinking

Since the beginning of education reform in Ontario, a number of data management and assessment tools and processes have been introduced to enable systemwide collection of student-level data that can be integrated, tracked over time, and used to inform policy and practice. Using these data, not just collecting data, is a developmental evaluation priority. The ministry's work to support a movement toward encouraging evaluative thinking through evidence-informed decisions and practices required an increase in the capacity at the provincial, district school board, and school levels to ensure the availability and effective use of high-quality data. The Managing Information for Student Achievement initiative was created by the ministry to increase the capacity of teachers, principals, board administrators, and ministry staff to work with data in support of strategies for improved student achievement, and to help support the sector in gaining a common level of functionality in working with data (Gitterman & Young, 2007). This local capacity-building initiative, which has substantially transformed the data management capacity for all district school boards, underpins and scaffolds the efforts to create a culture of evaluative thinking across the system.

As the division supports board and school improvement, there is a critical need for ongoing monitoring and evaluation of the effectiveness of the division's initiatives and strategies, in order to continue to refine and advance organizational understanding and capacity to achieve the ministry's four goals. For Grades 9–12,

EXHIBIT 13.3

Mapping the Forks in the Road: Result-Based Planning (RSP), Implementation, Monitoring, and Developmental Evaluation

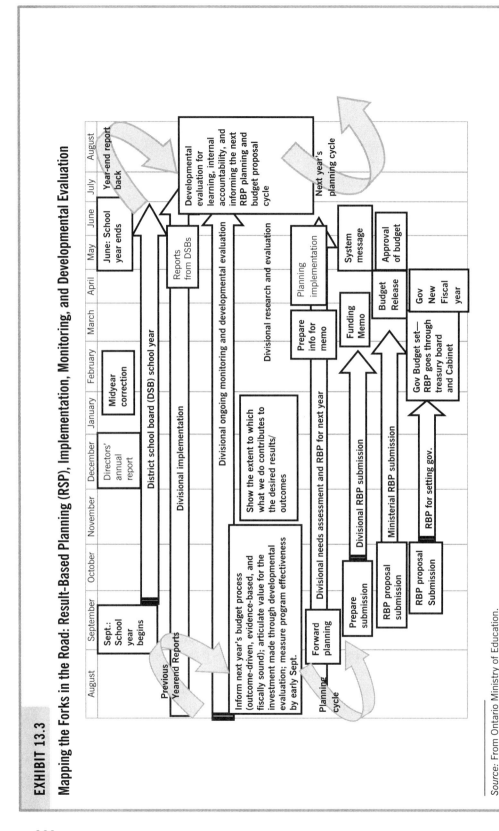

Source: From Ontario Ministry of Education.

for example, in addition to the provincial cohort graduation rate, new accountability requirements were introduced in 2004–2005 involving annual report-backs by boards on the Student Success Indicators.[6]

Building the capacity to use evidence takes place through ongoing internal research, monitoring, and evaluation, and through external studies examining for impact and effective practice. As an accountability component built into its annual implementation cycle, each Student Achievement Division initiative has an ongoing cycle of monitoring (including tracking indicators, field visits, reporting, and conversations) and internal developmental evaluations that are also informed by external evaluations.

Findings are analyzed and interpreted to identify successes and challenges, as well as to communicate new understandings to senior leadership, in an ongoing dialogue that serves to refine design and implementation of initiatives throughout the policy and program cycle from year to year.

At about the same time when logic modeling was being introduced by evaluators working in different initiative teams, the ministry, recognizing the importance of building research and evaluation capacity, invested in programs to train staff across the ministry. Sharing evaluation practices through presentations at conferences, professional learning sessions, communication to the sector, communities of practice (CoPs), and regular ongoing staff meetings also provided opportunities to build the capacity to understand and use evaluation. Progressively, leaders from across the ministry began to ask for support from the division's evaluators at the initiative, strategy, branch, and divisional levels. As they spread across the ministry, these experiences helped facilitate evaluative thinking and created common language and terms to articulate evaluation practices. The Ontario Ministry of Education's experiences are often shared through CoPs within Ontario Public Services, such as the Performance Measurement and Program Evaluation CoP.

In 2013, the ministry released a discussion paper outlining seven consultation questions for consideration. It then conducted eight formal regional and provincial consultations, as well as community, online, and digital consultations; these efforts resulted in over 1,100 written submissions, along with notes from hundreds of discussions. A cross-ministry team led by senior evaluators played a critical role in planning the data collection (including instrument development and training of consultation facilitators and note takers), and collaborative analysis and synthesis in both English and French of what the ministry learned from the consultations. The consultation formed the basis of the needs assessment, along with the developmental evaluation of our ongoing work to build on the system's successes and renew the system's vision, aspirations, and goals for our students (Ontario Ministry of Education, 2014).

Learning is a major component of the process of developmental evaluation. Adaptation and innovation to emergent and dynamic realities have become the norm in our work as evaluators, as we contribute to building the sector's capacity to learn and use evidence to inform decisions and implementation.

---

[6]*www.edu.gov.on.ca/eng/bpr/allBoards.asp?chosenIndicator=6.*

Conclusions

Evaluators, researchers, policy makers, and educators in Ontario's public education systems are social innovators in pursuit of the best possible outcome for all of our learners. Public sector work in an inclusive society of the 21st century means that adaptation and innovation must become the norm in providing services within quickly changing realities. Developmental evaluation suits the context and realities of work in the public sector, which is characterized by the following (Patton, 2011; Rowe & Kuji-Shikatani, 2013):

- Ongoing development, adaptation, and/or innovation as new conditions arise in complex dynamic systems.
- The ongoing need for preformative development of programs that can be scalable (from pilot to generalizable).
- The need for adaptation of effective principles to new contexts.
- Major system change and innovation.
- Developing a rapid response to a crisis or urgent need.

Program evaluation begins with the desire to seek information that can be utilized to improve the human condition. Public sector evaluators work in a decidedly complex environment. The mandate of public sector work in a democratic society is the realization of the agenda advanced by the elected government of the day. We serve the public; this is the bottom line of our work. And because we are social innovators working toward the vision of Ontario education reform, both we *and* the public need to know whether we are providing our best advice.

> Complexity-based developmental evaluation shifts the locus and focus of accountability. Traditionally accountability has focused on and has been directed to external authorities. . . . In contrast, for vision-and-values-driven social innovators the highest form of accountability is internal. . . . These become internalized questions, asked ferociously, continuously, because [innovators] want to know.

Public sector agencies engage in or commission evaluations with the intention to use the findings to learn and to inform the decision-making process. Some external evaluators may find it difficult to see how organizations are using and learning from commissioned evaluations. Due to the sensitive nature of the work that public sector evaluation users are engaged in, external evaluators may not immediately see the reach and the depth of internal conversations; they may not initially understand how the learning is being utilized and informing decisions. Internal evaluators, on the other hand, are very aware of how organizations value, use, and learn from the commissioned external evaluations as learning opportunities/events in the ongoing process of evaluative thinking that informs social innovation, as illustrated in this chapter.

Embedding evaluative thinking in social innovation supports building the sector's capacity to learn and use evidence to inform decisions and implementation through integrating research, monitoring, evaluation, and capacity building. Learning through evaluative thinking contributes to deepening and broadening the system's capabilities in meeting changing conditions; adding and using new skills, knowledge, and behaviors; and becoming an increasingly sophisticated system through reflection on its own actions and consequences (Rowe & Kuji-Shikatani, 2013; London & Sessa, 2007).

We are expected to have thorough knowledge of the work for which we are responsible. Yet our work environments are often complex and changeable, and adaptation is the norm. Thinking evaluatively and engaging in developmental evaluation ensure that we remain grounded in reaching our goals and outcomes, despite variable conditions. The ongoing and intentional use of a common logic-modeling process across the Student Achievement Division demonstrates the developmental evolution of our work. It increases our coherence, precision, clarity, and intentionality in responding to the needs of the system. It helps us gain understandings of knowledge and insights that provide direction for ongoing innovation and adaptation. Put simply, "If you want to get to where you want to go, you have got to know where you are."

REFERENCES

City, E. A., Elmore, R. F., Fiarman, S. E., & Lee, T. (2009). *Instructional rounds in education: A network approach to improving teaching and learning.* Cambridge, MA: Harvard Education Press.

Directions Evidence and Policy Research Group. (2014). *The Ontario Student Achievement Division Student Success Strategy Evidence of Improvement Study.* Toronto: Ontario Ministry of Education.

Ferguson, B., Tilleczek, K., Boydell, K., Rummens, J., Cote, D., & Roth-Edney, D. (2005). *Early school leavers: Understanding the lived reality of student disengagement from secondary school.* Toronto: Ontario Ministry of Education and The Hospital for Sick Children.

Fullan, M. (2010). *All systems go: The change imperative for whole system reform.* Thousand Oaks, CA: Corwin.

Gallagher, M. J., Franz, R., & Malloy, J. (2013). *Leadership's role in valuing evaluative thinking.* Paper presented at the Canadian Evaluation Society National Conference, Toronto, Ontario, Canada.

Gardner, M., & Malloy, J. (2013). *Board Improvement Planning for Student Achievement through a system-wide collaborative inquiry model.* Paper presented at the annual conference of the Canadian Evaluation Society, Toronto, Ontario, Canada.

Gitterman, A., & Young, D. (2007). *Developing a province-wide strategy to increase the role of research and evidence in Ontario education.* Paper presented at the annual meeting of the American Education Research Association, Chicago, IL.

Hargreaves, A., & Fullan, M. (2012). *Professional capital.* New York: Teachers College Press/Toronto: Ontario Principals' Council.

Hattie, J. (2012). *Visible learning for teachers: Maximizing the impact of learning.* New York: Routledge.

King, A. E. (2004). *Double Cohort Study Phase III.* Toronto: Ontario Ministry of Education.

Knowlton, L., & Phillips, C. C. (2012). *The logic model guidebook: Better strategies for great results*. Thousand Oaks, CA: Sage.

Kuji-Shikatani, K., Franz, R., & Gallagher, M. J. (2014). *Using logic modeling as a tool to infuse evaluative thinking and guide developmental evaluation*. Paper presented at the annual meeting of the American Educational Research Association, Philadelphia, PA.

London, M., & Sessa, V. I. (2007). How groups learn, continuously. *Human Resource Management, 46*(4), 651–669.

McWhorter, D., & Franz, R. (2014). *The evolving role of education research and evaluative thinking in shaping system reform*. Paper presented at the annual meeting of the American Educational Research Association, Philadelphia, PA.

Militello, M., Rallis, S., & Goldring, E. (2009). *Leading with inquiry and action: How principals improve teaching and learning*. Thousand Oaks, CA: Sage.

Mourshed, M., Chijioke, C., & Barber, M. (2010, November). How the world's most improved school systems keep getting better. McKinsey & Company. Retrieved from *http://mckinseyonsociety.com/how-the-worlds-most-improved-school-systems-keep-getting-better*.

Ontario Ministry of Education. (2012). *K–12 Improvement Planning Assessment Tool*. Toronto: Author.

Ontario Ministry of Education. (2013). *School Effectiveness Framework: A support for school improvement and student success K–12*. Toronto: Author.

Ontario Ministry of Education. (2014). *Achieving excellence: A renewed vision for education in Ontario*. Toronto: Author.

Organisation for Economic Co-operation and Development (OECD). (2012). *Strong performers and successful reformers in education: Lessons from PISA for Japan 2011*. Paris: Author.

Patton, M. Q. (2008). *Utilization-focused evaluation* (4th ed.). Thousand Oaks, CA: Sage.

Patton, M. (2011). *Developmental evaluation: Applying complexity to enhance innovation and use*. New York: Guilford Press.

Patton, M. (2013, April). *Making evaluation meaningful and useful*. Minneapolis: Minnesota Council on Foundations.

Rowe, W., & Kuji-Shikatani, K. (2013). *Learning process and tools for use in developmental evaluation*. Professional development workshop conducted at the annual conference of the Canadian Evaluation Society, Toronto, Ontario, Canada.

Westley, F., & Antadze, N. (2010). Making a difference: Strategies for scaling social innovation for greater impact. *Innovation Journal: The Public Sector Innovation Journal, 15*(2), Article 2.

Zegarac, G., & Franz, R. (2007). *Secondary school reform in Ontario and the role of research, evaluation and indicator data*. Toronto: Ontario Ministry of Education.

CHAPTER 14

Developmental Evaluation in Synthesis

Practitioners' Perspectives

Kate McKegg and Nan Wehipeihana

> **Kate:** "Kia ora, I'm Kate McKegg. I'm a sixth-generation Pākehā New Zealander, descended from Irish, Scottish, and English immigrants who came to New Zealand in the 1800s. I now live in Hamilton in the North Island of New Zealand, with my partner, Richard, and I have three beautiful children, Jessica, William, and Patrick. I've been doing evaluation for over 20 years."
>
> **Nan:** "Kia ora, I'm Nan Wehipeihana. On my mum's side, my tribal links are to Ngāti Porou and Te Whānau-a-Apanui, on the east coast of the North Island of New Zealand; and on my dad's side, my tribal links are to Ngāti Tukorehe and Ngāti Raukawa, just north of Wellington. I live with my partner, Bill, in Wellington, and I have two daughters, Kahiwa and Teia. I've been doing evaluation for more than 20 years."

In Aotearoa, New Zealand, in a custom drawn from Māori culture, it is typical in a formal meeting or other engagement to introduce yourself—who you are, where you come from, your interests, your work, your family, and how you come to be in this particular place contributing to this discussion or meeting. So we start this chapter in a way that is familiar and comfortable to us, and that provides some insight on who we are and how we come to this synthesis.

We are both "self-taught" developmental evaluators—something that it appears we have very much in common with other contributors to this book. We have followed a "learn as we go" approach since we commenced our first developmental evaluation in 2008, reflecting on our practice and honing our craft with each experience. This type of emergent, "learn as we go" practice is fitting in our cultural context because as New Zealanders we pride ourselves on being a "give it a go" kind of culture—stepping up and just trying things out, and then adapting practice, products, or processes to whatever the emerging situations or needs might be.

271

On the other hand, this "learning as we go" has at times felt personally and professionally scary. Nevertheless, it has been permission-giving, freeing us to respond to the innovation and evaluation as necessary. Developmental evaluation gave a name and credibility to much of what we were already doing; it allowed us to be transparent about our practice, and affirmed that our instincts about what kind of evaluative thinking and practice was needed in complex situations (honed over time with experience) were spot on.

As we began sharing our experience and knowledge about the practice of developmental evaluation, we were continually searching to add to our body of knowledge and skill set—and although there were a few things available, as our coeditor Michael Quinn Patton discusses in Chapter 1, we hankered after case examples from developmental evaluation practitioners. We really wanted to know what other people were doing: how they were applying developmental evaluation; how they responded to the challenges of complexity, method selection, and reporting—and, importantly, what they were doing that we might try out and apply in our own practice. We thought that if we were interested in and wanting this information, then so would others be.

Our suggestion for a book of developmental evaluation case studies coincided with the growing interest in developmental evaluation that Michael also talks about in the opening chapter. The publisher, The Guilford Press, had also had requests for exemplars and cases of developmental evaluation in practice. In October 2013, we got together with Michael at the American Evaluation Association Conference in Washington, D.C., and discussed our ideas for this book. Together, we suggested possible contributors and fleshed out an outline and key points for a prospectus for the publisher. And the rest is history, as they say!

Nan: "As an early adopter, I was really keen to see how others were applying developmental evaluation and what we could learn from what they were doing. We first presented on developmental evaluation at the 2009 American Evaluation Association Conference and I came to the realization—strange as it may seem—that we were at the forefront of developmental evaluation (along with many of the contributors to this book). You could go to as many presentations as there were; you could get copies of the presentations; but the snippets of information gleaned were insufficient on their own, without networking and more detailed follow-up. You got an appetizer-size portion when you really wanted a main course, with dessert."

Kate: "I think the idea for a developmental evaluation case study book initially came about when we developed our first developmental evaluation workshop for the 2010 Australasian Evaluation Society Conference in Wellington. What we realized in developing the workshop material is that we had few case examples that we could draw on and use to illustrate the application of developmental evaluation. We were able to use our own projects, but we really felt we needed a wider set of cases to provide a range of examples that were relevant to evaluators whose contexts (and countries) were different from our own."

As we received the case studies, one of the things we have been struck most by is the willingness of developmental evaluators (and their clients) to disclose their vulnerabilities, and the many ups and downs of developmental evaluation practice. The cases are all highly reflective and learning-oriented, which is what we had hoped for, but we didn't know if the chapters would all turn out that way. It's been a real joy to realize that we are part of an international community of evaluative practice, working alongside others to support innovation that makes a difference—that systemically changes lives.

We would like to acknowledge everyone who has contributed to the cases in this book. Your willingness to share your experience in deeply personal and professionally revealing ways has been humbling, to say the least. Thank you.

We would also like to thank Michael, who really did not need novice coeditors for this book, and whose advice and support have been unwaveringly affirming and encouraging. We have valued the opportunity to exchange ideas with him and to provide feedback on the iterations for the opening and concluding chapters of this book. And so we now move to our reflections on the cases.

One of the other things we noticed as we read the cases is that developmental evaluation has a transformative effect, not only for those people innovating and working alongside communities to create systemic change, but for evaluators. We doubt very much that any of us will find the same deep professional satisfaction in going back to doing traditional evaluation.

For the two of us, this deeply transformative effect on both ourselves and the communities and individual lives we touched along the way has inspired us to want to share our experience with others, and we encourage others to do the same. As we read the cases, we are more acutely aware than ever that developmental evaluation, undertaken in the appropriate contexts and with willing and amenable co-creators, makes a real difference to changing lives. And playing even a small part in creating a slightly more just, fairer, more equitable, more sustainable world really matters to both of us.

And so it was as developmental evaluators who care passionately about making a difference that we came to the synthesis process for this chapter; this perspective has strongly influenced how we read each case. To help us with the task of synthesis, we created a framework using the key systems concepts (so integral to developmental evaluation) of the perspectives, boundaries, and interrelationships through which we filtered each case; we then overlaid our perspective as practitioners. What emerged were the concepts of roles, responsibilities, and readiness, and these became intertwined with systems thinking. So, although the three systems concepts are not specifically discussed, they are woven throughout our synthesis—as are many other systems and complexity concepts, such as diversity and emergence.

This book as a whole, and this chapter in particular, aim to provide some insights from the collective experience of the contributing developmental evaluators and social innovators about what it takes to do developmental evaluation, and how we might improve its practice, processes, and outcomes. We are hopeful that everyone engaged in developmental evaluation will find our synthesis useful.

Developmental Evaluation: Flexing the Boundaries of Evaluative Thinking and Practice

Many of the cases described in this book demonstrate that more traditional evaluation approaches were judged not suitable for the context by the innovators working on the ground, such as in the cases of the United Way Toronto community of practice and the Musagetes arts initiatives (Chapter 5); He Oranga Poutama (HOP), the Māori sports initiative (Chapter 2), and the Grand Rapids Challenge Scholars initiative (Chapter 3). In other cases, traditional approaches were tried and found wanting, or simply failed to cope with the highly emergent and complex nature of the initiatives discussed, such as in the Global Partnership for the Prevention of Armed Conflict (GPPAC) outcome-harvesting initiative (Chapter 10).

Not all that surprising is that developmental evaluators are expected to be able to provide advice on evaluation design, tools, and methods to social innovators, funders, and other stakeholders involved in innovative change efforts. However, because developmental evaluation is embedded in innovative and complex situations, it has to be emergent, iterative, and adaptive, and these needs flex and challenge the boundaries of traditional evaluative thinking and practice. The cases point to several features of developmental evaluation advice and support that, in our interpretation, are different from those of more traditional evaluation and in some ways challenge some of traditional evaluation's fundamental tenets. These features include the following:

- Evaluative advice is ongoing, iterative, rapid, and adaptive.
- The developmental evaluator can expect to work closely and collaboratively on the development of the innovation, as well as the evaluation.
- The developmental evaluator will play a number of roles, and innovators will become evaluators.
- The tools and approaches that the developmental evaluator will draw on will come from many fields and disciplines.

- *Evaluative advice is ongoing, iterative, rapid, and adaptive.* The cases confirm one of Michael Quinn Patton's guiding principles: that developmental evaluators will need to be able to adapt, change, and develop evaluation designs over time, in order to continue to be useful to the development of innovative initiatives. This is quite a departure from more traditional evaluation. However, in the cases described in this book, it was not unusual for the evaluation design and process to be reviewed and adapted in quite major ways. Just as a development process consists of reasonably short cycles of design, action and reflection, so too must a developmental evaluation. For example, the McKnight Foundation's Collaborative Crop Research Program (CCRP) developmental evaluation (Chapter 8) went through several cycles of evaluative design, rethinking, and redesign. In applying the outcome-harvesting methodology to the GPPAC evaluation (Chapter 10), Ricardo Wilson-Grau and his colleagues continually adapted the evaluative approach to better fit the needs of the situation.

In all these cases, this adaptation of design was done to take account of the changing needs of stakeholders and communities, as the trajectory of development unfolded, shifted, changed, or sometimes diverged from expectations. As the innovative projects and initiatives unfolded, new and emerging opportunities and challenges were common—and so, as the cases illustrate, developmental evaluation has to be able to respond to these, and not become locked into a fixed or preordained design. For this to happen, evaluation advice and support cannot be provided at arm's length, or restricted to the more usual time frames for progress reports and final reports. Evaluation advice and support have to be available when needed, provided on a continuing basis, and adapted as the innovations are developed. The need for rapid feedback, in time to inform changes in strategy and implementation, was also a feature. In the Musagetes case (Chapter 5), insights and lessons were routinely brought back to the project for the evaluators to reflect on in conversation with each other, rather than using more traditional reporting formats and time frames.

• *The developmental evaluator can expect to work closely and collaboratively on the development of the innovation, as well as the evaluation.* The cases also show that the developmental evaluator or developmental evaluation team becomes a core member of the development team, working collaboratively on both the development of the innovation *and* the evaluation. This situation is quite a radical departure from traditional evaluation, where it is expected that the evaluator remain completely independent, at arm's length from the initiative. However, as the cases demonstrate, when developmental evaluation is effectively integrated into social innovation initiatives, all those involved become data-informed, critical, evaluative thinkers and decision makers.

In the development of the Indigenous health care model (Chapter 12), Sam Togni and the core team of five innovation collaborators worked alongside each other and created a change none of them had previously thought possible. In the United Way Toronto initiative (Chapter 5), the director reflected that this close collaboration helped the whole team build skills and develop a team culture of evaluation and learning that affected all of its work.

• *The developmental evaluator will play a number of roles, and innovators will become evaluators.* Although the developmental evaluator will still play a major role in providing evaluation advice and support, what the cases demonstrate is that the evaluator can expect to have many other roles as part of a developmental evaluation. In this book, we have seen developmental evaluators undertaking more traditional evaluation tasks such as designing and undertaking a wide range of data collection and analysis, as well as undertaking such varied roles as facilitators, negotiators, counselors, reconciliators, film makers, and strategic and community advisors. The cases also point to the transfer of evaluative expertise to innovators and others involved in the initiatives, as evaluative thinking and practice is infused into innovation. For example, in the Ontario Ministry of Education case (Chapter 13), people in a whole range of positions across the education sector and system developed adaptive evaluative expertise; they continually engaged in evaluative dialogue and challenge as they developed and evolved new ways of tackling the challenge of raising student achievement. This transfer of skills and evaluative capabilities could be conceived as quite challenging to some evaluators, who are used to being the "experts." However, our reading of the cases is that when evaluative thinking and practice are shared, transferred, and integrated into the development of innovative initiatives, they will have transformative results.

  • *The tools and approaches that the developmental evaluator will draw on will come from many fields and disciplines.* Although it is likely that traditional qualitative and quantitative tools and methods will be necessary in a developmental evaluation, it can be expected that the methodological boundaries of evaluation will also be permeated. Developmental evaluators throughout the cases reached for tools and methods from other disciplines and traditions (management and strategy, systems and complexity science, Indigenous knowledge, etc.) to meet the needs of the developing innovations. For example, in the HOP initiative (Chapter 2), many of the tools and approaches used to gather data and to reflect on and synthesize findings were drawn from the Māori world.

The ambiguity of complexity, and the dynamic and evolving nature of innovation development, challenge the boundaries of traditional evaluation approaches. For developmental evaluators to operate effectively amidst the action of unfolding and emerging development, they have to be prepared to work adaptively and rapidly, engage and collaborate with innovators, step into a number of roles when necessary, willingly part with their knowledge, and cast a wide gaze in their search for the tools of the trade.

The Credibility of Developmental Evaluation

As the niche of developmental evaluation develops, one of the central challenges is for the approach to establish its credibility and legitimacy. Questions and concerns among funders, managers, and evaluators about the robustness of developmental evaluation emerged in a number of cases—most pointedly in relation to its ability to establish the value or worth of initiatives. This indeed is a central challenge for evaluation in general, not only for developmental evaluation.

Our reading of the practice illustrated in the cases is that the credibility of developmental evaluation among many social innovators has been hard-won, and that there are still many challenges ahead and much to learn. The framing of developmental evaluation, and the boundaries of its niche and influence, are far from settled in many people's minds. There are examples where developmental evaluation was doubted not only in the early stages, but throughout the evaluation process. Even among evaluators, there was uncertainty and doubt at times. One strategy used early in the Challenge Scholars evaluation (Chapter 3) to build acceptance of and credibility for developmental evaluation was to spend time setting expectations among key stakeholders about what developmental evaluation actually is and how it differs from other approaches. In the Vibrant Communities initiative (Chapter 9), even as the initiative appeared to become well respected, evaluators were still in doubt about the strength of the evaluative evidence.

However, in all the cases—even when developmental evaluators struggled to gain traction, such as in the United States Agency for International Development (USAID) example (Chapter 11)—developmental evaluation was perceived as effective by those on the ground. Evaluative thinking, inquiry, sense making, findings, and results were used, and were found timely and useful by innovators and many other stakeholders.

In most of the cases, evaluation was integrated into the innovation's development, and the innovation and evaluation evolved together in a collaborative effort. Developmental evaluation contributed to ongoing deliberation and assessment about the value and worth of an innovative initiative (as well as all its various dimensions) as it developed, and in some cases, the evaluation also contributed to summative judgments of worth made by funders and communities about the overall worth of the initiative. In the Vibrant Communities case (Chapter 9), many communities had made summative judgments about the value of the approach well before the final reports were published. In the Māori and Pacific Education Initiative (MPEI) (Chapter 7), Foundation North decided that the high-engagement approach used was worth reinvesting in, based on the feedback the trust received from the developmental evaluation, well before the final report was finished.

Four key features emerged from the cases that we feel contribute to the credibility of developmental evaluation:

1. An organizing framework is developed.
2. Data are layered over time and aligned with the organizing framework.
3. Data collection, reporting, and sense making are timed to meet the needs of key stakeholders.
4. Engagement in values-based collaborative sense making takes place.

1. *An organizing framework is developed.* We noted that in many of the case examples, innovators and evaluators were guided by some kind of organizing framework that expressed what was valued or important to the innovators and the communities they were working with. There was no single recipe for how these frameworks were developed; they were context-specific and in all cases collaboratively developed by multiple stakeholders involved in the innovation. A developmental evaluator often plays a central role in facilitating the values-based inquiry and discussions necessary for such a framework to emerge. For example, in the Vibrant Communities initiative (Chapter 9), an umbrella strategy or theory of change became a key organizing framework for the evaluation and the innovation's development. In the evaluation of the Otto Bremer Foundation's youth homelessness initiative (Chapter 4), a set of principles was developed to guide the development of the initiative as well as the evaluation. In the MPEI (Chapter 7), a values-based performance framework or rubric was developed; in the HOP example (Chapter 2),

an Indigenous cultural framework that incorporated Māori principles and levels of performance was developed; and in the Frontiers of Innovation case (Chapter 6), a strong framework was developed for the innovation and the evaluation.

An organizing framework such as those described and used in these cases is a form of boundary setting. But rather than being rigid and inflexible, these frameworks are values- or principles-based, so the boundaries can be readily adapted and given expression in different ways in different contexts.

2. *Data are layered over time and aligned with the organizing framework.* We noted that when developmental evaluation is effective, a preset, rigid, and standardized approach to data collection is not followed; rather, data collection and evidence gathering are adapted for contextual appropriateness. In the Frontiers of Innovation case (Chapter 6), an evolving scorecard was developed to ensure that emerging changes in the innovation could be captured, and genuine progress could be reported. Over time, multiple types and forms of data and evidence are gathered; both planned and opportunistic data collection occurs, and high use is made of naturally occurring data collection activity and moments. In the USAID example (Chapter 11), in spite of having a planned data collection process, the evaluation team recognized opportunities to gather locally generated insights and feedback on reconciliation, so they adapted their data collection to ensure that this information was collected. It was subsequently used to develop a vision of reconciliation and peace building for the local mission.

In developmental evaluation, a layered body of evidence is gradually built that is aligned with the principles, values, or dimensions of the organizing framework. This is rarely a neat, linear process; rather, it progresses in short cycles, with many revisions to design and deliverable products along the way. Decisions about what kind of evidence will be needed and when are not set in concrete, but are aligned with the organizing framework and with the needs of the innovators and their communities. In the MPEI (Chapter 7), the members of the evaluation team were intentional about obtaining multiple sources of evidence for each of the strategic evaluation criteria, but they also realized that they had to be tactical and more organic in building a body of qualitative and quantitative evidence, to ensure the ongoing buy-in of the trustees. In the Challenge Scholars initiative (Chapter 3), the FSG team members were intentional about framing their data collection around key questions, but also found that they had to be open to collecting other data from a wide range of potential perspectives and experiences, to meet the information needs of the Partners' Group.

3. *Data collection, reporting, and sense making are timed to meet the needs of key stakeholders.* In more traditional forms of evaluation, it is fairly standard to see evaluation contracts specify some form of regular progress reporting, followed by a draft and then a final evaluation report. In developmental evaluation, as the cases in this book demonstrate, the timing of data collection, reporting, and sense making is driven by the needs of the initiative being developed in the first instance. The developmental evaluator's role is to work alongside the members of the innovation

team, supporting them to gather and use evidence evaluatively to inform cycles of design, inquiry, learning, and adaptation. As discussed earlier, the emergence of new and unexpected needs for data and information is common, and the developmental evaluator must be able to respond to such needs, within reason. As Michael Quinn Patton notes in Chapter 1, such flexibility is not easy. A major challenge for developmental evaluators is to be able to renegotiate the scope and deliverables, or boundaries, of evaluation—without necessarily extending the budget or time frame!

Meeting these dual challenges—ongoing delivery of useful and timely evidence, as well as successfully renegotiating and rescoping the nature of evaluative activity and deliverables (often within the same budget and time frames)—is often very difficult (and as the USAID example in Chapter 11 illustrates, not always possible). It requires a combination of these skills and attributes:

- A highly developed understanding of the context.
- Appreciation of the different needs of different stakeholders in relation to the innovation.
- Relational trust between the evaluator and the social innovators and funders.
- A deep well of evaluation and methodological experience.
- Clarity of purpose.

4. *Engagement in values-based collaborative sense making takes place.* Another key strategy of developmental evaluation that has emerged from these cases is what we are coming to call *values-based collaborative sense making.* In all the cases, collaborative and highly participative processes of evidence-informed sense making underpinned the developmental evaluations. Through data-informed dialogue and interaction, in trusted relationships, learning, adaptation, and change unfolded. In many of the cases in this book, we have seen the use of organizing frameworks—frameworks that express what is valued—guiding the presentation, reflection, and discussion of data. We have also seen the use of analysis frameworks (e.g., the adaptive action framework of "What? So what? Now what?") assisting the process of sense making and meaning making about what is valued, important, and worth doing. Innovators and developmental evaluators draw on multiple sources of evidence in ongoing cycles of sharing, deliberation, and decision making, as illustrated in the Frontiers of Innovation (Chapter 6) and CCRP (Chapter 8) cases.

The collaborative sense-making processes used in many of the examples in this book harness and value the collective knowledge and expertise that resides within the development team. In this context, the developmental evaluator is not the expert; rather, all team members are acknowledged as having valuable knowledge and expertise, pertinent to the context of the innovation, to contribute to the development of the initiative. When it is done well, collaborative sense making takes account of individual points of view and, importantly, creates the space for honestly and respectfully engaging with perspectives, experiences, and viewpoints different from one's own. The power of collaborative sense making lies in what is gleaned from the interrelationships between us—what is distilled and what is learned in dialogue *with each other*. The shared meanings of quality and value emerge from this dialogue, as do points of agreement and points of difference (Elkjaer, 2003; Schwandt, 2008). All life is profoundly dependent on communication, and out of this deliberative and participative process of dialogue, trusted relationships are built over time; such relationships allow further exploration and development to occur (Kurtz & Snowden, 2003). What results from values-based collaborative sense making is very often far greater than the sum of the parts.

These four features stand out to us as essential to the credibility of developmental evaluation as a legitimate evaluation approach—one that can usefully support the development of innovation, as well as provide sufficiently robust evidence about the value and worth of innovative initiatives. It is interesting to note that these features are not all that dissimilar to those Patricia Rogers shared at a conference in 2010 entitled Evaluation Revisited: Improving the Quality of Evaluative Practice by Embracing Complexity (see Guijt, Brouwers, Kusters, Prins, & Zeynalova, 2011). We believe it will be important for those practicing developmental evaluation to continue to share their experience about the dimensions of practice that contribute to its credibility, in order for confidence to grow among evaluators as well as social innovation funders about its legitimacy.

It would be fair to say that among some of the cases, we noted times when developmental evaluators were troubled by the challenge of establishing "stronger" evidence for the relationships between innovative initiatives and the outcomes being achieved. This pressure did not necessarily come from funders (although at times it did); it mostly appeared to be deeply rooted in evaluators' own views about what constitutes "good" evaluation (i.e., "good" evaluation is able to demonstrate the contribution or attribution of initiatives or programs to outcomes). There is no doubt that the questions of contribution and attribution are important questions in evaluation. However, we would argue that they are not the central questions in a *developmental* evaluation because under conditions of complexity, the assumptions (e.g., order, linearity, rationality, control, and choice) that underpin our use of more traditional causal designs and measurement approaches simply don't hold (Kurtz & Snowden, 2003). For example, (as the USAID example in Chapter 11 illustrates) in conflict and peace-building contexts, there is simply no possibility of establishing baselines or comparisons: The context is often highly volatile and chaotic, and very often success is defined by what's not happening, rather than by what is.

Complexity is defined by unpredictability, uncertainty, emergence, interdependency, nonlinearity, and feedback loops (Eoyang & Berkas, 1999). To understand better what is going on in complex situations, we need observers from multiple perspectives paying attention and taking notice of what is happening. This is why the layering of multiple data collection methods, combined with participative, iterative, collaborative sense making, is so appropriate for a developmental evaluation (Kurtz & Snowden, 2003). However, shifting from more traditional evaluation to doing evaluation with a complexity lens can be deeply challenging, as several of the cases attest. It can be particularly challenging when evaluators encounter their own doubts about what they are doing, as well as those of the organizations and structures around them.

In our view, the most important and central questions for developmental evaluation are the foundational questions posed by Michael Quinn Patton in his 2011 book. These questions pertain to what is being (or has been) developed and the value or worth of this, in order to inform decisions about ongoing action and further development. The adaptive action questions "What? So what? Now what?" are frequently used, and the present book's cases illustrate that they can be applied iteratively throughout a developmental evaluation and can also be addressed in a summative way about the overall value of an innovation or initiative.

Evaluative inquiry is what makes an evaluation developmental, and not something else. As Michael's principle of evaluation rigor suggests (see Chapter 15), this means inquiry informed by data, with specific questioning to ensure that those involved in the evaluation grapple with (1) what they consider is valuable about each part of the innovative process and why; and (2) how the boundaries and perspectives they bring to this valuing affect their decision making, as well as the dynamics and trajectory of the innovation. Without data and without evaluative questioning, it's not developmental evaluation.

This is not to say that there isn't a place in developmental evaluation for good strong data collection, measurement, and attention to building a solid evidence base (which may contain relatively good evidence about causality and/or contribution). Indeed, this book's cases are full of examples of sophisticated evaluation designs and data collection strategies. In a developmental evaluation, a solid evidence base is one that is contextually aligned to the principles or organizing framework of the innovation—one that in time, and over time, provides decision makers with good enough data to be confident of the value of what they are doing and to make decisions about what next. In a rapidly changing developmental situation, the central concern of evaluation is not about establishing cause-and-effect relationships.

Readiness for Developmental Evaluation

One of the overriding themes of the cases in this book has been what we call *readiness* to take on the journey of developmental evaluation. This concept of readiness applies to the individuals involved in the evaluation and the innovation, as well as the groups of stakeholders and organizations with a stake in the innovation.

The first aspect of readiness the cases point to is the need for evaluators to have a depth of experience if they are to successfully navigate a developmental evaluation process. Such evaluators possess a deep methodological toolkit and the ability to be methodologically agile; are prepared to use multiple methods from different disciplines, contexts, and cultures; and are adept enough to develop and adapt methods and approaches to work better in different contexts. We have discussed earlier the need for an emergent and iterative developmental evaluation design. It follows that the methods chosen for such an evaluation will also be contextual and capable of being adapted appropriately to the situation as it emerges. For example, in the HOP initiative (Chapter 2), Māori cultural practices were embedded in the developmental evaluation, and other evaluation approaches were adapted for contextual relevance. Such agility and adeptness require experience. In our view, developmental evaluation is not for the novice evaluator.

But at the core of readiness for developmental evaluation are three dispositions. The first is a disposition to "embrace unknowability" (Zimmerman, 2014)— to be comfortable about there not being a sure destination or known pathway, to acknowledge risks, and to begin the journey anyway. The second disposition is an inquiring mindset; that is, the developmental evaluator and others in the innovation team are open to multiple possibilities, perspectives, puzzles, and learnings (Westley, Zimmerman, & Patton, 2006). And the third disposition is perseverance—the capacity not only to begin an unknown journey, but to stick with it.

The situations and contexts described in this book have been characterized by high levels of uncertainty about how and in what ways the future might unfold, as well as diversity in terms of the interrelationships, perspectives, motivations, and expectations among all those who might have a stake or interest in the innovations and the evaluation. Faced with this complexity in combination with a strong desire to transform intractable problems, and very often dissatisfaction with previous monitoring and evaluation approaches, the leadership and key individuals within organizations have very often decided that a journey into the unknowable is worth the risk.

The inquiring mindset has been demonstrated in all the cases; it has been evidenced by the embedding of critical and evaluative questioning, reflection, and collaborative sense making into the everyday practice of the development of innovative initiatives. More importantly, this questioning, reflection, and sense making have been thoughtfully and strategically applied, testing even the most fundamental assumptions in some of the initiatives.

The third disposition has frequently been evidenced in the cases by the level of personal investment, courage, and commitment shown by individuals and teams of people to journey through feasts and famines, summers and winters. They have developed trusted relationships, which have given them the confidence to tackle so-called *wicked problems* and set about intentionally creating, at the very least, the possibility of systemically changing the status quo and making a positive difference in many people's lives.

For these dispositions—willingness to embrace unknowability, inquiring mindset, and perseverance—to hold true for the developmental evaluator, in contrast to standard evaluation parlance, the evaluator's values need to be aligned with the innovation. It's simply not possible to operate in this kind of environment without some form of alignment with and commitment to the vision and values of those working to create change. This alignment is essential for riding out the ups and downs of the evaluation process because the shared values as well as the time taken to build shared experiences and trust are what create the glue that holds us *in relationship* with each other.

Exhibit 1.5 in Chapter 1 highlights and summarizes the dimensions of readiness we have discussed for organizations and for developmental evaluators.

The Developmental Evaluator's Responsibilities and Roles

As the support and demand for developmental evaluation increase, it could seem reasonable to assume that it is increasingly better understood by social innovators and the evaluation community. However, as many of the cases suggest, developmental evaluation is not yet widely accepted or understood. For example, in the CCRP case (Chapter 8), the evaluation team was faced with building developmental evaluation's credibility among skeptical grantees, scientists, and the leadership team. Many funders, managers, and people working in programs or organizations have deeply embedded assumptions about ways of doing things, including evaluation—and developmental evaluation isn't what most people think of as evaluation.

Because developmental evaluation presents a challenge to many people's mental models of what evaluation should be, evaluators and internal champions of this approach often assume a number of roles and responsibilities to keep a developmental evaluation on track and viable—as the cases in this book illustrate. One of these responsibilities is the need to embrace the challenges of maintaining and holding onto developmental evaluation's principles and ways of working, often in the face of systemic and relentless pressure to "snap back" to old patterns, behaviors, and ways of thinking (Zimmerman, 2014). One of the ways in which the cases increased the chances of success was to ensure that there was at least one strong ally, if not more, within each initiative or organization who championed the developmental evaluation approach. In the CCRP case (Chapter 8), a new internal director of the McConnell Family Foundation with a strong conviction about the need for developmental evaluation became the internal champion for the approach. In the Indigenous primary health care case (Chapter 12), members of a small team within the organization came to trust each other; and working collaboratively they developed a deep commitment to the developmental evaluation process. The Ontario Ministry of Education case (Chapter 13) illustrates how more extensive system leadership can transform a sector's capacity to be evaluative. When leaders demonstrate the value of evaluative thinking by modeling it, innovative change can be more resilient and lead to systemic change, as the Ontario case shows. In the Vibrant Communities case (Chapter 9), the importance of internal stewardship and leadership of a developmental evaluation is also highlighted.

Alongside these internal allies, some of the developmental evaluators in these cases took responsibility for constantly looking for opportunities to advocate for developmental evaluation, educate those around them about it, and keep the momentum of the evaluation going. In the HOP initiative (Chapter 2), presenting and writing about developmental evaluation and the innovation, and sharing the learning in public forums, provided a measure of protection and secondhand affirmation for the approach and the initiative. (It also didn't hurt to win an international evaluation award.) In the case of the MPEI (Chapter 7), Foundation North intensely stewarded the initiative over many years. Along with dedicated staff members, the foundation also ensured that stories and publications were made available as the initiative played out; these kept the initiative in people's minds, highlighting its valuable and innovative aspects as well as providing learning opportunities along the way.

Furthermore, we have seen developmental evaluators in these cases taking on the primary role and responsibility for ensuring that the dynamics of the *wicked situations* (Williams & van 't Hof, 2014) in which innovations were occurring were critically explored, with different people's perspectives of the situations identified, framed, and valued within the evaluations and the initiatives. The evaluators paid attention to individual and stakeholder dynamics, working to ensure the equitable inclusion of multiple perspectives. Several of the cases illustrate ways in which developmental evaluators facilitated and created opportunities for multiple perspectives to be heard and to contribute to the developmental process and decision making; they took account of and managed the power dynamics that might otherwise mean that one or more perspectives might dominate. For example, in the USAID case (Chapter 11), the evaluators reflected that having developmental evaluation conversations with people from across a conflict divide facilitated shared goals; the developmental evaluation itself thus became a reconciliation process. This was by no means an easy task. Bringing together groups of passionate and committed individuals and stakeholder groups, each with personal, professional, and reputational motivations and points of view, requires a mix of subtle and more direct facilitation techniques.

In our view, what the cases highlight is that developmental evaluators and their internal champions have a responsibility to come to grips with systems and complexity principles and theory, as well as to develop expertise in applying this knowledge to the developmental evaluation inquiry and process. Most particularly, as all the cases illustrate, developmental evaluators as well as those they are working with need to have high levels of skill in managing complex relationships, as well as expertise in facilitating and engaging in deep, collaborative, and evaluative inquiry about the patterns, structure, nature, and strength of the boundaries, interrelationships, and perspectives that influence an innovation. A key responsibility for evaluators is to carve out this space, and it is imperative for the leadership of innovations to make space and resources available for deep relational engagement—for listening, and for deliberative, iterative, ongoing evaluative inquiry.

Exhibit 14.1 summarizes the key themes related to developmental evaluators' readiness, roles, and responsibilities.

Five Preparatory Practice Questions for the Developmental Evaluator

The 12 exemplars of developmental evaluation in this book represent reflective practice at its best. Of course, the real value of reflective practice is to prepare us for the future. In that spirit, we want to stimulate some anticipatory and preparatory ponderings. As we read and digested the cases in this book, thinking about developmental evaluators' readiness, roles, and responsibilities through a systems and complexity lens, what emerged were five *preparatory practice* questions—particularly for those evaluators who are still uninitiated to developmental evaluation, but who are thinking that a situation they are faced with seems appropriate for this approach. We conclude, then, with the questions that emerged for us as we journeyed through the cases and reflected on our own developmental evaluation experiences.

EXHIBIT 14.1

Developmental Evaluators' Readiness, Roles, and Responsibilities: Challenges, Strategies, and Lessons

Readiness, roles, and responsibilities: Cross-case themes	Challenges	Strategies and lessons
1. Readiness (individuals and organizations)	a. Sufficient experience/ methodological agility and adeptness/capacity to take on a developmental evaluation	a. Assess capabilities and capacity honestly at the individual and team levels, as well as within the organization; seek advice or hire a mentor as necessary.
	b. Ability to embrace unknowability	b. Ensure that the internal champion and organizational leadership are willing to experiment, and have a high tolerance for uncertainty and ambiguity.
	c. Openness to learning and inquiry	c. Ensure that evaluative inquiry is built into the innovation from the outset, at all levels of the system.
	d. Perseverance and courage in the face of adversity	d. Place high importance on the development and maintenance of trusting relationships, and on alignment of shared aspirations and values.
2. Roles	a. Explaining developmental evaluation	a. Remember that the explanation must be ongoing, not just a one-time, front-end presentation.
	b. Making developmental evaluation credible	b. Stay focused on the developmental evaluation's purpose, and on appropriate methods and tools for this purpose.
	c. Finding allies	c. Keep in mind that allies and leadership in evaluative inquiry are not just found; they must be nurtured and developed.
3. Responsibilities	a. Multiple perspectives authentically included	a. Facilitating genuine participation and collaboration is part of a developmental evaluator's job; ensure that multiple perspectives are at the table.
	b. Deep, collaborative, evaluative sense making informed by systems and complexity	b. Ensure that all evaluators and innovators are informed about systems and complexity thinking and practice. *And* make sure that space and time are made for deep engagement—for listening and for deliberative, iterative, evaluative sense making.

1. *Are you prepared to stand up to criticism of developmental evaluation as just the latest fad, or as an approach that is risky and not really robust?* This question raises for us the need for evaluators to have a deep understanding of the foundational theoretical influences of developmental evaluation (particularly evaluation, systems, and complexity), as well as of the significant paradigm shift that this approach represents to others. Developmental evaluation challenges very deeply ingrained ways of thinking and acting, at individual, organizational, and societal levels. There's a lot invested in traditional ways of doing things, and it doesn't take much for the system to reject the "new kid on the block."

2. *Are you prepared for moments of uncertainty and ambiguity? That is, how will you manage yourself and others when you experience these moments?* Some of the most moving moments in these cases for us were the points when developmental evaluators found themselves uncertain and not sure what to do, even doubting themselves and their years of experience. The cases demonstrate that these experiences are common in developmental evaluation; the journey is filled with many unknowns. But experienced evaluators use various strategies to overcome this discomfort and find a way forward. One of the most significant of these is to find allies within the system who embrace the process and understand the tensions that arise (Zimmerman, 2014).

3. *How ready are you to engage rapidly in systematic data collection of different kinds, at a moment's notice? And are you prepared to engage in regular, data-based reporting, feedback, reflection, and sense making with your clients, groups, and/or organizations?* In this chapter, we only touch lightly on the depth and breadth of methodological skill and experience, as well as other relational skills and qualities that (in our own experience, supported by the cases) we consider necessary for taking on a developmental evaluation. To be agile and responsive in his or her role, the evaluator has to have a range of experience with using different methods (qualitative and quantitative) in different contexts, including contexts where certain methods haven't worked. This range of skill and experience is not always found in one person, but the collective experience in a team can meet the challenges of developmental evaluation. The cases demonstrate that some evaluators have worked successfully without other evaluators alongside them; other cases are illustrative of a team approach. In our view, what is most important for evaluators is being honest about their capabilities in each situation—and reaching out for support if they need it.

4. *Are you and key people in the initiative, organization, or group you are working with prepared to prioritize the building of trusting relationships, and do you think they will be willing to bring you on the journey with them?* An important feature of most of this book's cases is that trusting relationships existed between the developmental evaluators and key individuals (usually at a senior level) in the initiatives or organizations being evaluated. Such relationships underpin so much of the developmental evaluation experience because it is "in relationship" that change and development happen. There have been times in our own experience when potential clients have asked for a developmental evaluation, but have given early indications

that the allocation of time (in particular) and resources for the development of relationships is not a priority for them. In our view, such indications are red flags signaling danger for developmental evaluation. Our advice is "Do not proceed past this point, or do so at your own peril."

5. *How well prepared are you and the organization or group for a responsive relationship in regard to defining evaluation activities, negotiating evaluation budgets, and unconventional time frames for deliverables?* This question speaks to one of the issues rarely discussed in detail about developmental evaluation, but one that we think is important: the costs of doing it, and the nuts and bolts of negotiating contracts and deliverables. We have touched briefly on this issue above, in our discussion of meeting the dual challenges of iterative evaluation design and renegotiation of evaluation deliverables. However, we feel that this issue needs a deeper conversation. We highlight the question here because several of the cases discussed changes of evaluation design and scope, but there was little discussion of what it takes to renegotiate contracts and budgets when such changes take place. If an organization is wedded to traditional time frames and delivery outputs, then it's unlikely that a developmental evaluation will be able to fit this context, unless the internal champions are extremely adept at working the internal system of an organization. In our own experience, developmental evaluation can be seen as more expensive than more traditional forms of evaluation because on top of data collection, it requires time and resources for people to come together on a continuing basis; moreover, it isn't always possible to ask for more money when new evaluation possibilities and needs emerge. Our approach (and, we suspect, the approach of other developmental evaluators) is to begin work within the agreed-upon total budget, allocating investment to cycles of expected engagement and data collection. When things change as they almost inevitably do, we renegotiate what can be done and delivered, created anew, changed, or discarded—and we talk about money and time frames in the same breath.

The Courage to Engage in Developmental Evaluation

When we are offering workshops on developmental evaluation, we talk about the need for courage to engage in it. What these case studies illustrate to us is the enormous courage that so many evaluators, innovators, and organizations have demonstrated as they work to address intractable, tough, complex issues that materially affect thousands of people worldwide. It takes courage to try something new, to step outside our comfort zones. It takes even more courage to stay the course—and, when things are not working out, to adapt the plan, and try again and again and again. Developmental evaluation is all about testing reality continually, and not simply acting with good intentions. Developmental evaluation is serious about holding our feet to the fire of reality and keeping them there—about focusing firmly on evidencing the impact of our actions on those with whom we interrelate as we act. And, in our view, developmental evaluation is an essential part of innovative design and implementation, if good intentions are to deliver real results. What these cases illustrate to us is that with courage and perseverance, it is possible to make a difference—at home, locally, regionally, internationally, and globally. In the opening of this chapter, we have noted that for some of us, our developmental evaluation experiences have been the most rewarding of our professional lives. From our perspective—and, it would appear, from that of our contributors also—the greatest reward is seeing developmental evaluation contribute to systemic change that makes a positive difference in the lives of so many people.

Throughout our own journey, we have found ourselves thinking about how we might contribute to developmental evaluation being taken more seriously, more often—to it being perceived as an essential and critical component of innovative design and implementation in the pursuit of systemic change. Indeed, the idea for this book emerged in part from this thought. We sincerely hope that in bringing together this rich tapestry of developmental evaluation practice in a reflective, open, and transparent way, we may have gone a small way toward making such a contribution.

Again, we thank all of our contributors to this case study book. These contributions, we are sure, will not only influence evaluation practice, but transform systems—and thereby change lives.

REFERENCES

Elkjaer, B. (2003). Social learning theory: Learning as participation in social processes. In M. Easterby-Smith & M. A. Lyles (Eds.), *The Blackwell handbook of organizational learning and knowledge management* (pp. 38–53). Malden, MA: Blackwell.

Eoyang, G., & Berkas, T. (1999). Evaluating performance in a complex, adaptive system. In M. Lissack & H. Gunz (Eds.), *Managing complexity in organizations: A view in many directions* (pp. 313–316). Westport, CT: Quorum Books.

Guijt, I., Brouwers, J., Kusters, C., Prins, E., & Zeynalova, B. (2011). *Evaluation revisited: Improving the quality of evaluative practice by embracing complexity. Conference report*. Wageningen, The Netherlands: Wageningen University Research Centre for Development Innovation.

Kurtz, C., & Snowden, D. (2003). The new dynamics of strategy: Sense-making in a complex and complicated world. *IBM Systems Journal, 42*(3), 462–483.

Patton, M. Q. (2011). *Developmental evaluation: Applying complexity concepts to enhance innovation and use*. New York: Guilford Press.

Schwandt, T. A. (2008). The relevance of practical knowledge traditions to evaluation practice. In N. L. Smith & P. R. Brandon (Eds.), *Fundamental issues in evaluation* (pp. 29–40). New York: Guilford Press.

Westley, F., Zimmerman, B., & Patton, M. Q. (2006). *Getting to maybe: How the world is changed*. Toronto: Random House Canada.

Williams, B., & van 't Hof, S. (2014). *Wicked problems: A systems approach to complex problems*. Wellington, New Zealand: Bob Williams. Retrieved from *www.gum.co/wicked*.

Zimmerman, B. (2014, October). *Preventing snap back: The challenge of resilient systems*. Keynote address presented at the Collective Impact Summit, Toronto. Retrieved from *www.youtube.com/watch?v=cnXRX0Y9io8&feature=youtu.be*.

CHAPTER 15

The Developmental Evaluation Mindset

Eight Guiding Principles

Michael Quinn Patton

Principles are like prayers. Noble, of course, but awkward at a party.
—VIOLET CRAWLEY, DOWAGER COUNTESS OF GRANTHAM,
    Downton Abbey

The party's almost over; this book is nearly done. But before you leave, it's time to talk principles. In Chapter 1, I have reviewed the state of the art and practice of developmental evaluation, in the form of answers to the 10 most common questions I get about it. The first question is this: What are the essential elements of developmental evaluation? The answer is that there are *eight guiding principles*:

1. *Developmental purpose*
2. *Evaluation rigor*
3. *Utilization focus*
4. *Innovation niche*
5. *Complexity perspective*
6. *Systems thinking*
7. *Co-creation*
8. *Timely feedback*

This concluding chapter elaborates and explains each of these eight guiding principles, as well as their integral interconnection.

    These principles come from my own experiences in developmental evaluation, as well as the insights of my coeditors and other developmental evaluators—both those whose work is featured in this book, and others in what has emerged as a global community of practice. I have been writing about evaluation for more than 40 years. I have never had as much engagement from colleagues on something I was writing as I have had in the process of developing the eight principles. I received detailed feedback about which principles to highlight as essential, how many to include, and how to word those included. Questions and thoughtful suggestions took me deeper into key points. The experience-based insights of others complemented my own. The substance these colleagues shared demonstrated a commitment to reflective practice unlike any I've previously experienced. The reactions to early drafts of the principles and later rewrites came with these messages: Developmental evaluation is hard work, challenging work, but (most of all) important work. The need and niche are real. The results are being used. Demand for developmental evaluation is increasing, and momentum is building. And developmental evaluation is, first and foremost, a principles-based approach.

The Principles-Based Developmental Evaluation Mindset

Developmental evaluation is not a set of methods, tools, or techniques. There isn't a set of steps to follow. There's no recipe, formula, or standardized procedures. Rather, developmental evaluation is a way of approaching the challenge of evaluating social innovation through guiding principles (Patton, 2015). A principles-based approach contrasts with prescriptive models, which, like recipes, provide standardized directions that must be followed precisely to achieve the desired outcome. For example, goals-based evaluation prescribes operationalizing clear, specific, and measurable goals in order to measure goal attainment. In contrast, guiding principles provide direction, but must be interpreted and adapted to context and situation, like advice on how to be a good student: *Make your studies your priority.* What that means in practice will depend on what you're studying and what else is going on in your life. The alternative principle is *Have fun, hang out, hook up, and study just enough to get your degree.* Different principles, different guidance. Pick your poison.

Standardized models, like recipes, are specific and highly prescriptive: *Add one-quarter teaspoon of salt.* Principles, in contrast, provide guidance: *Season to taste.* A time management "best practice" prescribes setting aside the last hour of the workday to respond to nonurgent emails. The principled approach guides you to distinguish urgent from nonurgent emails and manage email time accordingly.

The eight principles offered in this chapter are written to be succinct, pointed, and distinct enough to provide direction within the niche of developmental evaluation. The cooking principle *Season to taste* meets these criteria. The principle doesn't tell you what seasonings to consider, or even what a seasoning is. It doesn't tell you how to taste, exercise taste, or judge taste, or even who is doing the tasting. Novices learning to cook may be better off initially following the recipe that says *Add one-quarter teaspoon of salt*, and then experiencing how that amount of salt tastes as they develop confidence to season to taste. My point is that these developmental evaluation principles assume some knowledge of evaluation, innovation, complexity concepts, and systems thinking as presented and discussed in depth in *Developmental Evaluation* (Patton, 2011). This chapter goes beyond the book in converting those core ideas and elements into a set of guiding principles.

Taken together as a whole, the eight principles constitute a *mindset*—a way of thinking about evaluation's role in the development of social innovations and, correspondingly, a way of working with social innovators in the adaptive innovation process. As I go through the separate principles, I urge you to keep in mind that this is not intended as a laundry list, but rather as a set of interrelated and mutually reinforcing principles—a point to which I return after introducing and explicating the principles. Let me also note that the discussion of the first four principles is more detailed and therefore lengthier than the subsequent four because the elaboration of the first four principles involves a review of some basics about developmental evaluation that I hope will make the meaning and implications of the later principles more immediately understandable and usable.

The Developmental Evaluation Principles

> 1. ***Developmental purpose principle:*** Illuminate, inform, and support what is being developed, by identifying the nature and patterns of *development* (innovation, adaptation, systems change), and the implications and consequences of those patterns.

The first principle guides us in staying mindful of the *purpose* of developmental evaluation—to support innovation *development*. Developmental evaluation serves a distinct purpose in contrast to other evaluation purposes. Summative evaluation renders overall judgments of merit, worth, and significance. Formative evaluation supports improvements in a model. Improving a model, especially to get it ready for summative evaluation, serves an important purpose. But it is not a developmental purpose.

Developmental evaluation supports innovation, adaptation, and systems change. Innovations can take the form of initiatives, programs, projects, policies, collaborations, and interventions. The structure or form is not what makes something a social innovation; it is, rather, the degree and nature of change involved compared to the existing situation. Exhibit 15.1 identifies five specific types of developmental evaluation contributions: (1) evaluating a new, original approach to a problem as it is being created; (2) informing ongoing innovative development of a program or intervention in response to changing conditions and new understandings (basically, *adaptive innovation*); (3) adapting effective principles validated in one context to a different context; (4) supporting major systems change, including cross-systems/cross-scale innovation; and (5) developing rapid responses in crisis situations. These five types of developmental evaluation are discussed at length throughout the *Developmental Evaluation* book (Patton, 2011).

EXHIBIT 15.1

Five Types of Developmental Evaluation: Variations in the Nature of the Innovation and Adaptation

Focus of development, corresponding to five types of developmental evaluation	Nature of the innovation*	Contribution of developmental evaluation	Key concepts
1. Developing (creating/inventing) a new intervention aimed at a significant problem	Creating an *original* approach, or *inventing* a new intervention and/or innovative program; the emphasis is on *originality* within a complex context.	Clarifying the elements of the innovation; examining effectiveness, unanticipated consequences, and the emergent dynamics of the innovation.	• Invention • Original • New • Significantly different in important, identifiable ways
2. Ongoing adaptive development	Innovatively adapting an existing intervention, approach, or program to changing conditions, new knowledge, and new clientele	Clarifying the nature of the adaptive innovation: what is carried forward; what is changed; how these interact; and the consequences of ongoing innovative adaptation as a way of engaging in change through trial-and-error, double-loop learning.	• Adapting an existing initiative or program • Changes that go beyond marginal improvements • Ongoing innovation
3. Developing greater impact by adapting validated innovation principles and practices to a new context (scaling)	The adaptive innovation of principle-based practices from one context to another, or to a larger context; this means that what has become established in one context is experienced as innovative in a different context.	Clarifying and elaborating the ways in which different contexts affect adaptive innovation: the degree, nature, and consequences of adaptive innovation from context to context as ideas and approaches are shared and spread.	• Scaling • Expanding options by context • Adapting principles contextually (not replicating a model or recipe)
4. Developing changes in and across systems	Innovation through changed relationships, perspectives, and boundaries within and across systems.	Tracking, mapping, and interpreting systems changes both within and across systems; supporting adaptive innovation responses as systems changes become manifest.	• Systems as the focus of change • Complex dynamics in play
5. Developing rapid responses in crisis situations	"Building while flying"; rapid adaptive innovations in the face of humanitarian, political, social, and economic crisis.	Tracking, documenting, and providing real-time feedback about emergent challenges, urgent needs, flow of resources, and aligning interventions in highly turbulent, uncertain conditions.	• Urgent • Real-time feedback • Simultaneous planning, implementation, and evaluation

*Innovations can take the form of initiatives, programs, projects, policies, collaborations, and interventions. The structure or form is not what makes something a social innovation. It is, rather, the degree and nature of change involved, compared to the existing situation.

Let me reiterate: The purpose of developmental evaluation is *developmental*. Some kind of innovation is being *developed*. The evaluation tracks what is being developed and how it is being developed—the nature and implications of the innovative and adaptive processes. And because the innovation is developing, the evaluation must also be developed. The design and implementation of a developmental evaluation are emergent and adaptable as the innovative process emerges and adapts. Developmental evaluation is characterized by short cycles of design, data collection, feedback, and evaluative synthesis and reflection.

Let me provide a specific example of how developmental evaluation can accompany creation of an innovative systems change initiative. Sometimes a problem may be identified by social change agents who share a commitment to attempt major change, but the nature of that change has not yet been determined when the developmental evaluator is invited to join the process. The evaluator, then, especially when involved from the beginning, may play a significant role in helping shape the innovation vision and process. Donna Podems, an experienced developmental evaluator based in South Africa, tells of such an experience:

> "I was asked to work with innovators in the national health program of an African country. When I started working with the group, they said, 'We aim to shift the health system.' After listening for a few hours, I said, 'Honestly, I have no idea what you are doing, or what you are trying to achieve . . . and I haven't a clue how to measure it. I don't understand what it means to "shift the health system." ' And they looked at each other and burst out laughing and said, 'We have no idea, either.' I could not have helped this group of innovators if forced to do a traditional evaluation where everything has to be specified upfront. But using developmental evaluation, we developed what came to be a very successful initiative. Engaging together through developmental evaluation was an immense relief for everyone as we figured out how to innovate toward shifting the health system."

Innovation often begins with problem identification and a commitment to change (Westley, Zimmerman, & Patton, 2006). This is an example of using developmental evaluation to help create a response to a problem. It also illustrates the *principle of co-creation*, discussed below.

Mark Cabaj has studied ways in which developmental evaluation contributes to different kinds of development. His "growing list" includes the following:

- Deeper insight into the nature of the challenge being addressed.
- Working conclusions about what does and does not work.
- Emergent elements of what could become a broader intervention.
- Strengthened capacity of the innovation group.

Exhibit 15.2 presents his developmental framework, illustrated with examples drawn from his experience of working with a network of social service agencies

EXHIBIT 15.2

Examples of Developmental Evaluation Support in a Canadian City's Network of Agencies: Experimenting with Innovative Ways to Help Homeless Day Laborers Secure Housing and Better Income

What was developed through developmental evaluation	What this means	Examples
1. Understanding the challenges of innovation and systems change	The effort to tackle a complex problem may generate new and/or deeper insights about the nature of the challenge being addressed and/or the context in which it is being addressed.	The innovators realized the importance of social supports in the "homelessness puzzle," once some of the clients who secured housing were drawn back to the streets to regain the friendship and company of their previous networks.
2. Theory-of-change elaboration	The innovators may have new ideas about how they might address the challenge and/or the kinds of results they might expect from their efforts.	The innovators expanded from their strategy focused primarily on housing and employment income to one that included education, social networks, and mental and emotional health.
3. Change mechanisms	The establishment of concrete mechanisms (e.g., practices, regulations, relationships, policies) that have an influence on the challenge being addressed may represent the most tangible development of the innovation.	The innovators established (a) a protocol with local credit unions to provide clients with access to bank accounts, even before they had permanent addresses; and (b) an arrangement where laborers could bypass predatory, temporary job agencies (which took 50% of their wages) and use a nonprofit intermediary that allowed them to retain all their employment earnings.
4. Capacity development of social innovators	Developments that relate to the capacity and morale of the innovators and affect how they think about and pursue their innovation (e.g., skills, resources, membership).	The trust levels between previously disconnected service agency leaders increased after these early successes and allowed them to open up their work to discussing the deeper reasons why they found it difficult to integrate their services more closely (e.g., competition for resources).

(continued)

Source: Provided by Mark Cabaj from his developmental evaluation practice. Used with his permission.

What was developed through developmental evaluation	What this means	Examples
5. Deepening understanding of context	Developments that are not under the complete control of innovators, but in which what happens (emerges) contextually shapes the goals, design, delivery, and results of the innovation (e.g., economy, demographics, key events). All developments are important to track and assess in developmental evaluation. Whereas the previous four types in this exhibit refer to the development of the innovation, this fifth one (the context) is equally important because innovation does not emerge in a vacuum, but instead is highly influenced by the context in which it is unfolding.	A slowdown in the construction industry (the major employer for homeless day laborers) required the innovators to develop relationships with different types of employers and adjust their expansion plans.

in a major Canadian city; this network was experimenting with new ways to help homeless day laborers secure housing and better income. You will have found many concrete examples of these kinds of developmental evaluation contributions to innovation development throughout the cases in this book.

Developmental evaluator Meg Hargreaves adds her own examples of important developmental evaluation contributions: leveraging funding for social innovation and reframing issues through "new narratives," such as changing the focus of school discipline from punishment to a "broader issue of adolescent health and development." Coeditor Kate McKegg finds that developmental evaluation leads to "greater confidence among the innovation stakeholders to take action/change/adapt to emergent conditions and situations." She also emphasizes that as the innovative process emerges and adapts, the evaluation design is emergent and adaptable; this is "one of the most profoundly different features of developmental evaluation from other evaluations." Such flexibility is not easy. I hear often from practitioners that the need for continually redesigning the developmental evaluation process is a major challenge for evaluators and innovators alike. The case exemplars in this book show how experienced practitioners of developmental evaluation are handling this challenge.

Bottom line: Developmental evaluation is distinguished from other forms of evaluation by its *purpose*: to illuminate, inform, and support what is being developed, by identifying the nature and patterns of *development*, and the implications and consequences of those patterns.

> 2. *Evaluation rigor principle:* Ask probing evaluation questions; think and engage evaluatively; question assumptions; apply evaluation logic; use appropriate methods; and stay empirically grounded—that is, rigorously gather, interpret, and report data.

Developmental evaluation is *empirically driven:* Data are gathered and interpreted to understand the implications of what is being developed. Any high-quality evaluation is data-based, but this principle is included here because in some cases, organizational or community development processes, evaluator-facilitated program staff discussions, and development-oriented expert consulting are being labeled as *developmental evaluation* with no data collection. So let me be absolutely clear: *No data, no evaluation—developmental or otherwise.*

So I hope that's clear. But the principle calls for *rigorous* evaluation. *Rigor* is a loaded word for some, restricted to randomized controlled trials or external, independent evaluations. I reject such a narrow framing and emphatically insist that developmental evaluation can and must be conducted rigorously. Developmental evaluation is not *evaluation lite*, like a beer with fewer carbs (and little taste) that gives the impression to oneself and others that one is drinking beer, when in fact it's more like beer-flavored water. It's good that people restricting calories have a "lighter" alternative to real beer, but serious beer drinkers don't confuse lite beer with the real thing. Extending the beer analogy just a bit, I've noted that developmental evaluation designs are customized and contextualized, not standardized. A developmental evaluator is like a brewmaster at a local microbrewery—crafting a unique, high-quality product within and for a distinct milieu. Microbreweries don't produce lite beers. Developmental evaluators don't produce lite evaluations.

Now, to be fair, there are occasions (let's hope, rare ones) when a little *lite evaluation* is appropriate for small programs with few resources and simple questions. But serious developmental evaluation is *rigorous* evaluation. Because some are perceiving developmental evaluation as *evaluation lite*, or not serious evaluation, or not even evaluation, I want to reclaim and emphasize developmental evaluation's commitment to rigor. Let me explain, then, what I mean.

The problem, it seems to me, is the focus on methods and procedures as the primary, or even only, basis for determining quality and rigor. The notion that methods in and of themselves are more or less rigorous decouples methods from context and the thinking process that determined what questions to ask, what methods to use, what analytical procedures to follow, and what inferences to draw from the findings. In an evaluation, rigorous thinking is manifest in the full range of activities— from framing hypotheses; to seeking and validating information; to analyzing data; to collaborating to assess the meaning of findings; and to questioning, testing, and reexamining results and conclusions. Evaluation rigor resides in diligent, systemic situation analysis, principles-based evaluative thinking, and appropriate methodological decision making with primary intended users (Patton, 2015, pp. 701–703). Rigorous evaluative thinking combines critical thinking, creative thinking, design thinking, inferential thinking, strategic thinking, and practical thinking.

A rigorously conducted evaluation will be convincing as a presentation of evidence in support of an evaluation's conclusions, and will presumably be more successful in withstanding scrutiny from critics. Rigor is multifaceted and relates to multiple dimensions of the evaluation. . . . The concept of rigor is understood and interpreted within the larger context of validity, which concerns the "soundness or trustworthiness of the inferences that are made from the results of the information gathering process" (Joint Committee on Standards for Educational Evaluation, 1994, p. 145)

This quotation is also a reminder that developmental evaluation, as evaluation with a distinct purpose (informing and supporting development; see Principle 1), still must adhere to and be judged by the professional evaluation standards of the Joint Committee Standards for Evaluation, as well as relevant professional association standards, guiding principles, and ethical statements.[1]

Rigorous evaluative thinking forces clarity about the inquiry's purpose, those for whom it is intended, and its intended uses. This means being explicit about the criteria applied in prioritizing inquiry questions, making design decisions, determining what constitutes *appropriate* methods, and selecting and following analytical processes. It includes being aware of and articulating undergirding values, ethical considerations, contextual implications, and strengths and weaknesses (for there are always both) of the evaluation. Assessing evaluation rigor, then, involves examining the extent to which a multidimensional, multiperspectival, and critical thinking process was followed determinedly to yield conclusions that best fit the data, and therefore findings that are credible to and inspire confidence among those who will use them.

Approaching rigor in this way avoids "*research rigor mortis*: rigid designs rigidly implemented, then rigidly analyzed through standardized, rigidly prescribed operating procedures, and judged hierarchically by standardized, rigid criteria." (For an extended critique of and rumination on *research rigor mortis*, see Patton, 2015, pp. 701–703.)

In essence, rigorous evaluative thinking is grounded in intellectual rigor. Methods do not ensure rigor. A research design does not ensure rigor. Analytical techniques and procedures do not ensure rigor. Rigor resides in, depends on, and is manifested in *rigorous thinking*—about everything, including methods and analysis.

One final point about rigorous evaluation: It is a commitment shared with social innovators and their funders. James Radner, cited in Chapter 1 and a contributor to this book, has reflected on what the developmental evaluator contributes to the evaluative perspective of social innovators. His insights about the evaluation-focused interactions between social innovators and developmental evaluators captures both elements of the evaluation rigor principle: evaluation *and* rigor.

---

[1]See the American Evaluation Association's Guiding Principles; the Ethical Standards of the Australasian, Canadian, and European Evaluation Societies; and the Evaluation Standards of the Organisation for Economic Co-operation and Development's Development Assistance Committee as examples (Patton, 2012, Ch. 17, pp. 388–402).

"In my experience, social entrepreneurs, like all entrepreneurs, have a remarkable capacity to scan, sense, and integrate empirical phenomena, to respond to the complex environment around them. They are doing that every day, all the time. So why add an evaluator with her claim to empirical know-how? Because, I think, the tools of the evaluator's craft can complement and deepen the innovator's own empirical sense in a rigorous, productive way. The innovator, of course, is a collaborator in developmental evaluation, helping to gather and make sense of data. The innovator, to one degree or another, is also an evaluator. But the developmental evaluation frame means data collection is systematic, intentionally reaching out to places and people the innovator may not have considered, or may not have direct access to. The developmental evaluation process provides data the innovator otherwise wouldn't have. The combination of an 'outside' perspective and multiple 'inside' perspectives helps make sense of that data.

"A second key contribution of evaluative thinking relates to accountability. Even the most brilliant entrepreneur is at the same risk all of us humans are, the risk of being limited by our own ways of seeing and conceptualizing the world around us. We may honestly think we have a clear idea of what we're doing, that we know the key steps and how they produce results, but the reality may be (at least somewhat) different. We all need accountability to external reality—we need our frames tested and challenged. This is well aligned with the kind of accountability that funders appropriately want and need, but by the same token, empirically based evaluation is highly beneficial to the mission of the social innovator, the mission of catalyzing change."

The devil is in the details, of course, so details are what we need, and details are what the case studies in this book provide. I suggest that the case exemplars in this book exemplify both the application of developmental evaluation rigor and the challenges of doing so under conditions of turbulence, emergence, and ongoing innovation.

Bottom line: The credibility and utility of developmental evaluation depend on rigorous evaluative thinking and situationally appropriate rigorous evaluation methods.

Integrating Developmental Purpose with Evaluation Rigor

Determining the order of the eight developmental evaluation principles posed a challenge because they are interconnected and interactive (see Exhibit 15.5 at the end of this chapter). Thus the order in which the principles are discussed is not meant to imply priority or degree of importance. Rather, the first two principles lay a foundation that explicates and connects the two words in the nomenclature—*developmental evaluation*. Each subsequent principle is meant to delineate further what constitutes the developmental evaluation approach. Exhibit 15.3 depicts this foundational relationship between developmental purpose and evaluation rigor. The developmental purpose principle provides focus for the evaluation. Evaluation

EXHIBIT 15.3

The Foundation of Developmental Evaluation: Principles 1 and 2

1. Developmental purpose principle: Illuminate, inform, and support what is being developed, by identifying the nature and patterns of *development* (innovation, adaptation, systems change), and the implications and consequences of those patterns.

Focused purpose

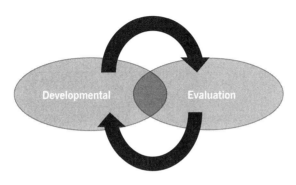

Data-based credibility and utility grounded in rigor

2. Evaluation rigor principle: Ask probing evaluation questions; think and engage evaluatively; question assumptions; apply evaluation logic; use appropriate methods; and stay empirically grounded—that is, rigorously gather, interpret, and report data.

rigor ensures the utility and credibility of the evaluation in support of innovation, adaptation, and systems change.

3. *Utilization focus principle:* Focus on intended use by intended users from beginning to end, facilitating the evaluation process to ensure utility and actual use.

Developmental evaluation emerged during an evaluation of a leadership development program, as a response to the director and staff, who chafed against the emphasis in formative and summative evaluation on demonstrating the effectiveness of a standardized model. They understood that as leadership trainers, they needed to be continually developing their program and adapting in the face of societal, political, cultural, and technological changes. (For the full story of the utilization-focused emergence of developmental evaluation, see Patton, 2011, Ch. 1.)

Utilization-focused evaluation centers on *intended use by intended users*. Social innovators, funders of social innovation, advocates and supporters of social innovation, and change agents are the primary intended users of developmental evaluation—and clearly identified as such in any specific developmental evaluation. The intended use (purpose) of developmental evaluation is to support adaptation and development of the innovation (Principle 1). This is done through rigorous evaluation (Principle 2). The developmental evaluation feedback and findings are used by social innovators and change agents to illuminate and adapt innovative strategies and decisions. That's intended use by intended users. That's utilization-focused evaluation. Funders of social innovation use developmental evaluation findings to inform funding decisions and meet accountability expectations and demands. That's also intended use by intended users. That's also utilization-focused evaluation. In short, developmental evaluation is a particular kind of utilization-focused evaluation. All that has been learned about enhancing use over 40 years of utilization-focused evaluation practice and research undergirds developmental evaluation (Patton, 2008, 2012, 2015).

In identifying and working with social innovators and their funders (primary intended users), some sophistication about the different kinds of social innovators engaged in different levels and types of developmental initiatives is essential. This includes sensitivity to how social innovators refer to themselves in various contexts. Some prefer nomenclature like *social entrepreneur, change agent, systems change catalyst, community organizer, difference maker, status quo disrupter, political activist*, and a host of other names. There is no orthodoxy about or insistence on labeling all primary intended users of developmental evaluation as *social innovators*. It is simply a shorthand way of referring here to those engaged in innovative social change and ongoing intervention adaptation. These can include innovation-minded program directors and initiative leaders, as well as funders of major innovations who make it possible to turn ideas, rhetoric, visions, and proposals into reality. Beyond contributing to a specific innovation under development, developmental evaluation can also contribute to the substantive field in which the adaptive experiment is unfolding (environmental issues, public health, poverty reduction, etc.) and, in some cases, to the development of an innovation platform for funders and their collaborators.

Given this broad view of the potential primary intended users of developmental evaluation, understanding different kinds of social innovators (and what they call themselves) can guide the developmental evaluator in working collaboratively to determine what information will be most useful to whom for what purposes as innovative processes unfold. Frances Westley holds the J. W. McConnell Chair in Social Innovation at the University of Waterloo, where she leads the Waterloo Institute for Social Innovation and Resilience. As an example of distinguishing different types of social innovators, she distinguishes *social entrepreneurs* from *system entrepreneurs*. Social entrepreneurs come up with innovative ideas, whereas a new and different kind of social innovator focuses on systems change: the system entrepreneur.

> The system entrepreneur identifies the promising alternatives to the dominant approach and then works with networks of others to stimulate and take advantage

of opportunities for scaling up those innovations. Working at the level of the whole system, system entrepreneurs develop the alternatives, attract the resources, and work toward the moment when the system tips. (Westley, 2013, p. 1)

Systems thinking, one of the developmental evaluation principles discussed below, is essential for working effectively and knowledgeably with system entrepreneurs. System entrepreneurs engage in innovation as systems-change leaders: "The deep changes necessary to accelerate progress against society's most intractable problems require a unique type of leader—the system leader, a person who catalyzes collective leadership" (Senge, Hamilton, & Kania, 2015, p. 1).

The utilization-focused evaluation principle guides developmental evaluators to know, understand, be able to work with, and adapt to the particular styles, approaches, and commitments of diverse social innovators, whatever they may call themselves. Likewise, developmental evaluators must be skillful and attentive in working with other users of developmental evaluation—specifically, those who fund and support innovation. For them, the tracking of the development process and emerging outcomes serves the need for accountability and learning.

Developmental evaluation can offer a meaningful solution to a real concern funders often have: accountability in complex environments, where, because of this very complexity, the innovative initiatives they fund simply can't have preset targets and indicators. At a philanthropic meeting on developmental evaluation involving both evaluators and funders, the consensus after much discussion was this: "Developmental evaluation isn't the enemy of accountability, providing some kind of free pass. Rather, it's a way to bring effective, constructive, and serious accountability to settings where traditional tools don't suffice." In dynamic environments where goals and targets are themselves changing, assuring accountability is a complex challenge, and developmental evaluation is tailored to meeting that challenge. (For more on developmental evaluation and accountability, see pp. 17–18.)

Bottom line: Developmental evaluation is guided throughout by the *utilization-focused principle* of focusing on intended use by intended users from beginning to end, facilitating the evaluation process to ensure utility and actual use.

4. *Innovation niche principle:* Elucidate how the change processes and results being evaluated involve innovation and adaptation, the niche of developmental evaluation.

Social innovators are unhappy with the status quo, so they work to change the way things are. That is the *innovation*—changing the way things are to some significant extent. The *innovation process* refers to how they go about changing things. Thus developmental evaluation documents, interprets, and provides feedback about both the processes and outcomes (products) of innovation. I am often asked for my definition of *innovation*. My response is that it is not my inclination or role to impose some standardized, universal, and operational definition. Rather, part of the developmental evaluation task is to find out what innovation means to those who are engaged in bringing about change within the context where the evaluation is occurring. The terms *innovation* and *adaptation* may, or may not, mean the same thing depending on how they are defined and employed within different contexts. Developmental evaluation supports efforts to create a fresh response to an emergent or intensifying crisis, an intractable challenge, or a *wicked problem* (Rittel & Webber, 1973; Williams & van 't Hof, 2014).

A recurring theme in delineating the niche of developmental evaluation is that invention, innovation, and development are different in degree and scope of change from program improvement. Mark Cabaj interviewed early developmental evaluation adopters about what stood out for them in their developmental evaluation experiences. One emphasized, "The act of creation [innovation] is very different

🐚 Wicked Problems and Social Innovation

Wicked problems are those that have no definitive formulation or time frame; thus there's no definitive way to test solutions to them. Every wicked problem is unique, yet also connected to and a symptom of another problem (Rittel & Webber, 1973). *Wicked* in this context means "difficult to deal with or resolve," not "evil." A wicked problem cannot be solved in any definitive way because the very nature of the problem defies a firm definition, due to its inherent complexity—multiple interacting factors and tightly intertwined interrelationships in a turbulent environment. The problem is like a dynamic maze where the pathway through the maze keeps shifting. Adding to the complexity of a wicked problem is that the problem and any potential solution are so intertwined that any solution identified and implemented changes the understanding of the problem. It is impossible to predict or control how things will unfold once an attempted solution is put in motion. Imposing clear outcomes will not solve the problem and may well make it worse. Nor can wicked problems be resolved with traditional analytic approaches that run roughshod over complexity, in the belief that simplification is essential to make problems manageable. Indeed, the effort to solve one aspect of a wicked problem—that is, its inherent complexity—is likely to reveal or create other problems (Churchman, 1967).

Social innovation approaches wicked problems through engagement, learning, and adaptation, rather than imposition of project-like solutions or models. *Double-loop learning* (learning how to learn about the nature of the problem and situation) is integrated into the social innovation through developmental evaluation.

> Wicked problems are systemic problems that are characterised by multiple stakeholders involved in complex and unpredictable interactions. Stakeholders are people or organisations with an interest in the (wicked) problem and its re-solution. Systemically designed interventions are needed because conventional understanding and management cannot address wicked problems. (Williams & van 't Hof, 2014, p. 2)

Emergent designs and mixed methods are especially appropriate for evaluating innovations aimed at wicked problems, because both problem identification and innovative interventions (attempted solutions) will be multidimensional, dynamic, and dependent on how the problem is understood over time as engagement deepens and learning occurs (Mertens, 2015).

than the act of improvement" (quoted in Cabaj, 2011, p. 38). Innovation can take the form of new initiatives, programs, projects, policies, collaborations, and interventions. As noted earlier, the structure or form is not what makes something a social innovation. It is, rather, the degree and nature of change involved compared to the existing situation.

Sometimes what is being developed is new to a particular context, but may not be viewed as "innovative" in a different context. In these cases, the innovation is the adaptation of the original innovation to a new context. Adaptation also includes initiating innovative changes in a program or other intervention (adaptive innovation) when knowledge, circumstances, and/or context change. Thus this advice from experienced developmental evaluation practitioners Hallie Preskill and Srik Gopal (2014) is important: "Pay particular attention to context and be responsive to changes as they occur" (p. 14).

Innovative processes are typically dynamic, so explicitly connecting innovation and adaptation is being mindful of the dynamic and adaptive nature of the innovative process—and thus of the developmental evaluation process. Frances Westley (2008) explains that social innovators engage in a "social innovation dynamic":

> Social innovation is an initiative, product or process or program that profoundly changes the basic routines, resource and authority flows or beliefs of any social system. Successful social innovations have durability and broad impact. While social innovation has recognizable stages and phases, achieving durability and scale is a dynamic process that requires both emergence of opportunity and deliberate agency, and a connection between the two. The capacity of any society to create a steady flow of social innovations, particularly those which re-engage vulnerable populations, is an important contributor to the overall social and ecological resilience.
>
> Resilience theory suggests that the processes of adaptation and transformation are dynamic, cyclical, and infinite. Social innovation is not a fixed solution either; it is part of a process that builds social resilience and allows complex systems to change while maintaining the continuity we rely on for our personal, organizational, and community integrity and identity.

Exhibit 15.1, presented earlier, distinguishes types of innovation and adaptation in relation to the five different types of developmental evaluation. Because developmental evaluation is innovation-driven, part of the documentation and data collection involves finding out what *innovation* means within a context and among specific social innovators—an approach I have discussed above in connection with the utilization-focused principle (Principle 3). We are attentive to their definition of what they are doing (*innovation*) to find out what they mean. We pay attention to and document what they are doing and how they talk about what they are doing. We interact with them about what is going on and the implications of their efforts and documented results. We gather data about what is unfolding and emerging. We observe and provide feedback about how what is actually happening matches expectations and hopes. We work with those involved to interpret what is happening and judge what is working and not working, and thereby to help them adapt, learn, and move forward. In so doing, we are engaging with them around, and deepening both their and our understanding of what is meant by, *innovation* and *adaptation* in that context. The definition and meaning of innovation are likely to evolve, deepen, and even morph as part of the developmental evaluation inquiry and engagement. For example, significant adaptations of an initial singular intervention (innovation, invention, or creation) thought to be sufficient for change can develop into *ongoing adaptive innovation* when informed by developmental evaluation observations and feedback.

Developmental evaluator Nora Murphy, a contributor to this volume (Chapter 4), reflects on the dynamic and iterative nature of the process of clarifying key concepts with social innovators.

> "Reflecting back to social innovators how they are defining key words related to the innovation, and revisiting and redefining these terms periodically, may be one of the most important jobs of the developmental evaluator. What is meant by *systems change? Innovation? Complexity?* And so on and so forth. At the start of a project, it's easy to assume shared understandings, so social innovators and other stakeholders are often surprised as they interact to surface variations in what concepts mean. They continue to be surprised when we come back to these central terms and learn how their understanding of the concepts [has] changed as their understanding of the context and intervention has developed and deepened. This is important to capture, but creating time to work on developing and revisiting shared understandings is a place I frequently experience pushback from action-oriented people. I have to help them see this as valuable because it is part of what is being developed."

Bottom line: The arena where innovation is occurring, or at least being attempted, is the defining niche of developmental evaluation.

Four plus Four

I have noted in introducing the principles that the discussion of the first four principles is more detailed than the discussion of the subsequent four because the elaboration of the first four principles has incorporated a review of some basics about developmental evaluation, aimed at establishing a foundation for understanding the meaning and implications of the later principles. I hope that this will be the case as I turn now to the remaining four principles, with shorter discussions of each.

> 5. *Complexity perspective principle:* Understand and interpret development through the lens of complexity, and conduct the evaluation accordingly. This means using complexity premises and dynamics to make sense of the problems being addressed; to guide innovation, adaptation, and systems change strategies; to interpret what is developed; to adapt the evaluation design as needed; and to analyze emergent findings.

The fifth developmental evaluation principle calls for understanding innovation, and designing and conducting the developmental evaluation, by applying complexity concepts. An evaluator needs to expect that plans, goals, and targets will all need to evolve as the innovation itself develops. No one, simple model can capture the complexity inherent in social systems. Why? Disruptive innovations aimed at major change are usually being introduced into a complex dynamic system in which multiple variables interact in uncertain and unpredictable ways to take on wicked problems. Nonlinear effects, turbulence, and emergence characterize complex dynamic systems. Unpredictability and lack of control make results uncertain. Change is multidimensional and multifaceted. Disagreements, even intense conflict, among key stakeholders about what can and should be done can add to the turbulence and uncertainty. In the face of complexity, serious attention to *emergence* is essential in the developmental evaluation findings, even as the design of the evaluation itself is emergent and adaptive. Both linear and nonlinear relationships, intended and unintended consequences, and anticipated and unanticipated interactions, processes, outcomes, and system changes are documented and evaluated. Here are insights on innovation and complexity as essential elements of developmental evaluation, from three experienced developmental evaluators:

> "A developmental evaluation touchstone is evaluation for people doing something innovative (purposefully, or emergently) in situations of high complexity."
>
> —JAMIE GAMBLE, author of *A Developmental Evaluation Primer* (2008)

> "In my experience, when I must clarify what developmental evaluation is and is not, two aspects ring especially true. Creating a new approach to a challenge or problem, that is, *developing* one from rudimentary ideas contrasts quite clearly with *improving* an approach by doing more or better. Similarly, people appreciate the distinction between developing something new in a complex, dynamic situation in which you cannot predict what will be the results, or even what you will be doing, versus replicating, transferring, or adapting an approach in a new but more or less stable and predictable environment."
>
> —RICARDO WILSON-GRAU,
> international developmental evaluation practitioner
> and coauthor of *Outcome Harvesting* (Wilson-Grau & Britt, 2012)

> "Had I not employed complexity concepts in a developmental evaluation, I would have missed all patterns and behavior that were unfolding before my eyes. Complexity helped me connect the dots, sooner rather than later, before having the full picture in place."
>
> —CHI YAN LAM, Canadian developmental evaluation practitioner
> and researcher on evaluation

Complexity concepts that have proven especially relevant to developmental evaluation include emergence, nonlinearity, adaptation, uncertainty, dynamical, and coevolution (Patton, 2011).

Bottom line: Complexity understandings inform and undergird all aspects of developmental evaluation.

> **6. *Systems thinking principle:*** Think systemically throughout, being attentive to interrelationships, perspectives, boundaries, and other key aspects of the social system and context within which the innovation is being developed and the evaluation is being conducted.

Developmental evaluation draws together complexity concepts and systems thinking to attune and orient the developmental evaluator to the dynamics of innovation development. Systems thinking provides a means for conceptualizing multidimensional influences, interrelationships, and interactions as innovative processes and interventions unfold. This in turn helps social innovators and evaluators, thinking together, to deepen their understanding of whether, how, how much, and in what ways systems changes are occurring. Together, complexity concepts and systems thinking provide powerful lenses through which to make sense of innovative situations and dynamics.

Experienced developmental evaluation practitioner Meg Hargreaves emphasizes the *nested reality* of systems and systemic thinking.

> "When people think of boundaries, they often stop after they have drawn one circle that surrounds the whole and separates it from its context. But thinking systemically is also profoundly about recognizing the interplay across levels, [and] between the parts, the whole, and the greater whole. Some system innovations effectively link and align innovations vertically, from changes in individual mindsets, to changes in organizational practice, the development of new programs, and broader changes in local, state, and federal policies. Systems innovations often span multiple systems boundaries."

In Chapter 1 of this book, I have discussed in more depth the relationship between and integration of complexity theory and systems, and the contributions of each to developmental evaluation.

Bottom line: Systems thinking is essential for framing, designing, and drawing conclusions in DE.

> **7. *Co-creation principle***: Develop the innovation and evaluation together—interwoven, interdependent, iterative, and co-created—so that developmental evaluation becomes part of the change process.

The seventh principle calls on developmental evaluators to acknowledge, document, report, and reflect on the ways in which a developmental evaluation becomes part of the intervention. The developmental evaluator gets close enough to the action to build a mutually trusting relationship with the social innovators. The quality of this collaboration derives in part from the capacity of the developmental evaluator to facilitate evaluative thinking, timely data-based feedback, and illuminative sense-making processes in support of innovation and adaptation. The developmental evaluator works *collaboratively* with social innovators to conceptualize, design, and test new approaches in an ongoing process of adaptation, intentional change, and *development*. Developmental evaluation is interactive—engaging social innovators, funders, supporters, and other core stakeholders to tailor and align the dynamics of innovation, development, adaptation, and evaluation. This dynamic amounts to the *co-creation* of both the unfolding innovation and the developmental evaluation design (Lam & Shulha, 2014). The co-creation principle is a manifestation of a more general observation about collaborative processes of evaluation, articulated by Cousins and Shulha (2006) in the *Handbook of Evaluation*: "Possibly the most significant development of the past decade in both research and evaluation communities has been a more general acceptance that *how* we work with clients and practitioners can be as meaningful and consequential as *what* we learn from our methods" (p. 277; original emphasis).

Co-creation becomes especially powerful in *principles-focused developmental evaluation*, where the principles guiding the innovation and those informing the evaluation are aligned. This is the distinguishing feature of the exemplar described in Chapter 2 of this book, in which the innovative program and the developmental evaluation were co-created, based on a holistic set of Māori cultural principles that guide ways of knowing and being in tribal and Māori contexts. This seamless blending of cultural and evaluation principles exemplifies principles-focused developmental evaluation. Chapter 4 also presents a principles-focused evaluation exemplar, in which the intervention and evaluation principles for a youth homelessness initiative were co-created, aligned, and integrated.

The consequences of how we work with social innovators on the change process itself constitute *process use* (Patton, 2008, 2012). *Process use* refers to the learning and behavior changes that occur among those involved in the evaluation as a result of their involvement—for example, becoming more adept at evaluative questioning and thinking. Changes based on feedback of findings is *findings use*. Changes based on the processes of collaboration and co-creation constitute *process use*. For example, social innovators' learning from a developmental evaluator how to articulate and use a complexity-based theory of change is process use.

A developmental evaluator can be either external or internal to an innovation, including being part of the innovation intervention team. Diverse structural and contractual arrangements have been used in the case exemplars in this book. What is evident as important across cases is that the developmental evaluators were willing and able to form mutually trusting relationships and work collaboratively with the social innovators in each initiative to co-create the innovation and evaluation design.

Bottom line: Developmental evaluation, fully engaged, implemented, and used, becomes part of the innovation.

8. *Timely feedback principle*: Time feedback to inform ongoing adaptation as needs, findings, and insights emerge, rather than only at predetermined times (e.g., quarterly, or at midterm and end of project).

We live in a real-time world, where things change rapidly, attention spans are short, windows of opportunity open and close quickly, and information flows continuously from multiple directions. This elevates the importance of timeliness as a developmental evaluation principle. But what is *timeliness* in a developmental evaluation?

Timeliness is defined by the nature of the innovation and by the needs of the primary intended users. As such, determining timeliness is part of situation analysis and negotiation, not a matter of adhering to a precise and fixed schedule. Feedback is not rapid for the sake of being rapid. It's rapid because it must be to support timely decision making, adaptation, and fork-in-the-road funding and strategy decisions. Timeliness is driven in part by the recognition that evaluation findings have a short shelf life, especially in turbulent environments. What is relevant and meaningful can change rapidly. Keeping findings fresh and useful requires speed. The capacity to work quickly is an essential capability in developmental evaluation.

Coeditor Kate McKegg emphasizes that timeliness is connected to utility:

"The usability of feedback is what's important. The issue of timeliness has struck me as one of the more important and potentially costly features of effective developmental evaluation—the need to build in regular, ongoing opportunities for feedback, discussion, sense making, and adaptive decision making."

One of the rewards of providing timely and useful feedback is having social innovators, funders, and other stakeholders understand and accept the insights offered, react appreciatively, and follow through with decisive action. On occasion, timely and astute developmental feedback leads to important reframing and a new direction. The impact can be profound, affirming the observation of American abstract painter Darby Bannard that "Most 'profound truths' are just timely ideas."

On the other hand, the extent to which speed matters is situational. Sometimes developments are unfolding slowly, leading to a slower pace for the developmental evaluation. While the pace of social innovation is often fast and almost always iterative, it can also be uneven (speeding up and slowing down in response to the pace of development). Developmental evaluation must adapt accordingly.

Timeliness also informs developmental evaluators' reporting to funders and other stakeholders for accountability purposes. Traditional evaluations serve accountability needs through predetermined midterm and end-of-project reports, or standardized quarterly monitoring reports. In contrast, rapidly changing conditions and opportunities in complex dynamic systems may mean that decisions about funding the developmental evaluation, revising its design, changing its scope of work, assessing the added value of its processes and findings, and related accountability queries can occur at any time. Timeliness rules.

Bottom line: Timeliness is essential for usefulness. Align and time evaluative feedback to inform and support intended use by intended users.

Developmental Evaluation as an Integrated, Principles-Based Approach

Exhibit 15.4 presents the eight developmental evaluation principles. The principles are interrelated and mutually reinforcing. The developmental purpose (1) frames and focuses evaluation rigor (2), just as rigor informs and sharpens understanding of what's being developed. Being utilization-focused (3) requires actively engaging with social innovators as primary intended users and staying attuned to the developmental purpose of the evaluation as the priority. The innovation niche (4) necessitates understanding the situation and what is developed through the lens of complexity (5), which further requires understanding and applying systems thinking

---

EXHIBIT 15.4

Developmental Evaluation Principles

1. *Developmental purpose principle:* Illuminate, inform, and support what is being developed, by identifying the nature and patterns of *development* (innovation, adaptation, systems change), and the implications and consequences of those patterns.

2. *Evaluation rigor principle:* Ask probing evaluation questions; think and engage evaluatively; question assumptions; apply evaluation logic; use appropriate methods; and stay empirically grounded—that is, rigorously gather, interpret, and report data.

3. *Utilization focus principle:* Focus on intended use by intended users from beginning to end, facilitating the evaluation process to ensure utility and actual use.

4. *Innovation niche principle:* Elucidate how the change processes and results being evaluated involve innovation and adaptation, the niche of developmental evaluation.

5. *Complexity perspective principle:* Understand and interpret development through the lens of complexity, and conduct the evaluation accordingly. This means using complexity premises and dynamics to make sense of the problems being addressed; to guide innovation, adaptation, and systems change strategies; to interpret what is developed; to adapt the evaluation design as needed; and to analyze emergent findings.

6. *Systems thinking principle:* Think systemically throughout, being attentive to interrelationships, perspectives, boundaries, and other key aspects of the social system and context within which the innovation is being developed and the evaluation is being conducted.

7. *Co-creation principle:* Develop the innovation and evaluation together—interwoven, interdependent, iterative, and co-created—such that the developmental evaluation becomes part of the change process.

8. *Timely feedback principle:* Time feedback to inform ongoing adaptation as needs, findings, and insights emerge, rather than only at predetermined times (e.g., quarterly, or at midterm and end of project).

(6) with timely feedback (8). Utilization-focused engagement involves collaborative co-creation (7) of both the innovation and the empirically based evaluation, making the developmental evaluation part of the intervention. Exhibit 15.5 depicts these interconnections.

In a developmental evaluation, all eight principles are addressed to some extent and in some way. This is not a pick-and-choose list; all are essential. This means that there is evidence in the developmental evaluation's processes and results that these principles have been addressed in some meaningful way (or, for specific contextual reasons, not incorporated explicitly). For example, let's imagine working with a social innovator and/or funder who hates the word *complexity* and thinks it is overused jargon—so the developmental evaluation process avoids explicitly using the term *complexity*, but does explicitly address *emergence, adaptation*, and perhaps even *nonlinearity*. Such negotiations are part of contextual sensitivity and adaptability, and part of the essential developmental evaluation learning process.

Bottom line: Incorporate and integrate all eight principles into DE.

EXHIBIT 15.5

Depiction of Interrelated, Mutually Reinforcing, Dynamic Connections among Developmental Evaluation Principles

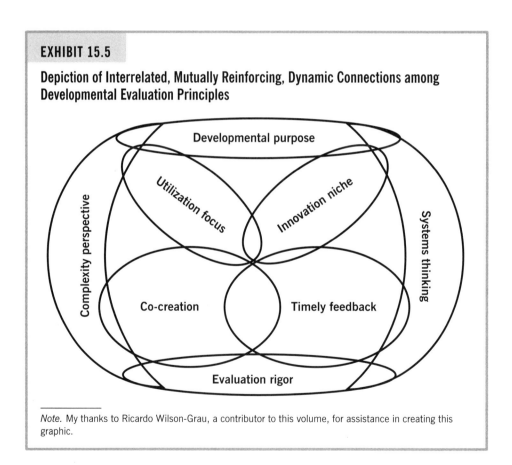

Note. My thanks to Ricardo Wilson-Grau, a contributor to this volume, for assistance in creating this graphic.

ACKNOWLEDGMENTS

Special thanks to Kate McKegg, Nora Murphy, Nan Wehipeihana, James Radner, and Ricardo Wilson-Grau, who suffered through several versions of this chapter and made many insightful suggestions. Other evaluation practitioners involved in developing and/or reviewing the eight guiding principles of developmental evaluation, and this chapter as a whole, include Mark Cabaj, Nathaniel Foote, Andrew Fyfe, Jamie Gamble, Meg Hargreaves, Mathias Kjaer, Chi Yan Lam, Zsuzsanna Lippai, Marah Moore, Lars Christian Oxe, Donna Podems, Hallie Preskill, Ricardo Ramirez, Lyn Shulha, Kelly Skeith, Sofia Avdeitchikova Söderquist, and Ryan Valois. Different views naturally emerged, so the final list of principles presented in this chapter (as well as their final labeling, wording, and explication) represents my own perspective informed by their feedback. My thanks to all of these colleagues.

REFERENCES

Cabaj, M. (2011). *Developmental evaluation: Experiences and reflections of 18 early adopters*. Unpublished master's thesis, University of Waterloo, Waterloo, Ontario, Canada.

Churchman, C. W. (1967). Wicked problems. *Management Science, 14*(4), 141–146.

Cousins, J. B., & Shulha, L. M. (2006). A comparative analysis of evaluation utilization and its cognate fields of inquiry: Current issues and trends. In I. Shaw, J. Greene, & M. Mark (Eds.), *The Sage handbook of evaluation: Policies, programs and practices* (pp. 266–291). Thousand Oaks, CA: Sage.

Gamble, J. A. (2008). *A developmental evaluation primer*. Montréal: J. W. McConnell Family Foundation.

Joint Committee on Standards for Educational Evaluation. (1994). *The Program Evaluation Standards*. Thousand Oaks, CA: Sage.

Lam, C. Y., & Shulha, L. M. (2014). Insights on using developmental evaluation for innovating: A case study on the cocreation of an innovative program. *American Journal of Evaluation* [published online before print]. Retrieved from *http://aje.sagepub.com/content/early/2014/08/08/1098214014542100*.

Mertens, D. M. (2015). Mixed methods and wicked problems. *Journal of Mixed Methods, 9*(1), 3–6.

Patton, M. Q. (2008). *Utilization-focused evaluation* (4th ed.). Thousand Oaks, CA: Sage.

Patton, M. Q. (2011). *Developmental evaluation: Applying complexity concepts to enhance innovation and use*. New York: Guilford Press.

Patton, M. Q. (2012). *Essentials of utilization-focused evaluation*. Thousand Oaks, CA: Sage.

Patton, M. Q. (2015). *Qualitative research and evaluation methods* (4th ed.). Thousand Oaks, CA: Sage.

Preskill, H., & Gopal, S. (2014). Evaluating complexity: Propositions for improving practice. Retrieved from *www.fsg.org/tabid/191/ArticleId/1204/Default.aspx?srpush=true*.

Rittel, H. W. J., & Webber, M. M. (1973). Dilemmas in a general theory of planning. *Policy Sciences, 4*(1), 155–169.

Senge, P., Hamilton, H., & Kania, J. (2015, Winter). The dawn of system leadership. *Stanford Social Innovation Review*. Retrieved from *www.ssireview.org/articles/entry/the_dawn_of_system_leadership*.

Westley, F. (2008). *The social innovation dynamic.* Waterloo, Ontario, Canada: Institute for Social Innovation and Resilience, University of Waterloo. Retrieved from *http://sig. uwaterloo.ca/sites/default/files/documents/TheSocialInnovationDynamic_001.pdf.*

Westley, F. (2013, Summer). Social innovation and resilience: How one enhances the other. *Stanford Innovation Review.* Retrieved from *www.ssireview.org/articles/entry/social_ innovation_and_resilience_how_one_enhances_the_other.*

Westley, F., Zimmerman, B., & Patton, M. Q. (2006). *Getting to maybe: How the world is changed.* Toronto: Random House Canada.

Williams, B., & van 't Hof, S. (2014*). Wicked solutions: A systems approach to complex problems.* Wellington, New Zealand: Bob Williams. Retrieved from *www.bobwil-liams.co.nz/wicked.pdf.*

Wilson-Grau, R., & Britt, H. (2012). *Outcome harvesting.* Cairo, Egypt: Ford Foundation Middle East and North Africa Office. Retrieved from *www.outcomemapping.ca/ resource/resource.php?id=374.*

Author Index

Subject Index

Page numbers followed by *f* indicate figure, *n* indicate note

About the Editors

Michael Quinn Patton, PhD, is an independent evaluation consultant with more than 40 years of experience. Based in Minnesota, he is a former president of the American Evaluation Association (AEA). Dr. Patton's six evaluation books include *Developmental Evaluation, Qualitative Research and Evaluation Methods* (now in its fourth edition), and *Essentials of Utilization-Focused Evaluation.* He is a recipient of the Alva and Gunnar Myrdal Award for outstanding contributions to evaluation use and practice and the Paul F. Lazarsfeld Evaluation Theory Award, both from the AEA.

Kate McKegg, MA, is an independent evaluation consultant with more than 20 years of experience. She is Director of The Knowledge Institute Ltd. and a member of the Kinnect Group in Hamilton, New Zealand. She is also the current president of the Aotearoa New Zealand Evaluation Association and a former board member of the Australasian Evaluation Society (AES). Ms. McKegg is coeditor of *Evaluating Policy and Practice: A New Zealand Reader.* With Nan Wehipeihana, Kataraina Pipi, and Veronica Thompson, she received the Best Evaluation Policy and Systems Award from the AES, for the He Oranga Poutama Developmental Evaluation.

Nan Wehipeihana, PostGradDip, is an independent evaluation consultant with more than 20 years of experience, based in Wellington, New Zealand. She specializes in evaluation and research with a focus on the Māori, the Indigenous people of New Zealand. She established Research Evaluation Consultancy in 1997 and is a member of the Kinnect Group. Ms. Wehipeihana is a board member of the Aotearoa New Zealand Evaluation Association and a former appointed executive member of the AES. Her tribal affiliations are to Ngāti Porou and Te Whānau-ā-Apanui, on the East Coast of New Zealand, and Ngāti Tukorehe and Ngāti Raukawa, north of Wellington.

322

Contributors

Susan H. Allen, PhD, School for Conflict Analysis and Resolution, George Mason University, Fairfax, Virginia

Julie Asher, MPP, Center on the Developing Child, Harvard University, Cambridge, Massachusetts

Deborah Askew, PhD, Southern Queensland Centre of Excellence in Aboriginal and Torres Strait Islander Primary Health Care, Queensland Health, Brisbane, Queensland, Australia

Moi Becroft, BSW, Foundation North, Newton, New Zealand

Megan Börner, MEd, Research, Evaluation and Capacity Building Branch, Student Achievement Division, Ontario Ministry of Education, Toronto, Ontario, Canada

Alex Brown, PhD, Aboriginal Research Programme, South Australian Health and Medical Research Institute, Adelaide, South Australia, Australia

Mark Cabaj, MA, Here to There Consulting, Inc., Edmonton, Alberta, Canada

Jane Maland Cady, PhD, International Programs, McKnight Foundation, Minneapolis, Minnesota

Alan Cass, PhD, Menzies School of Health Research, Darwin, Northern Territory, Australia

Sonya Egert, Southern Queensland Centre of Excellence in Aboriginal and Torres Strait Islander Primary Health Care, Queensland Health, Brisbane, Queensland, Australia

Nathaniel Foote, JD, MBA, TruePoint Center for Higher Ambition Leadership, Burlington, Massachusetts

Richard Franz, MEd, Research, Evaluation and Capacity Building Branch, Student Achievement Division, Ontario Ministry of Education, Toronto, Ontario, Canada

Mary Jean Gallagher, MEd, Student Achievement Division, Ontario Ministry of Education, Toronto, Ontario, Canada

Jamie Gamble, MM, Imprint Consulting, Hampton, New Brunswick, Canada

Jennifer Gill, BA, DipEd, Foundation North, Newton, New Zealand

Srik Gopal, MBA, FSG, Inc., San Francisco, California

Noel Hayman, MPH, Southern Queensland Centre of Excellence in Aboriginal and Torres Strait Islander Primary Health Care, Queensland Health, Brisbane, Queensland, Australia

David Hunsicker, MA, Office of Conflict Management and Mitigation, United States Agency for International Development (USAID), Washington, DC

Mathias Kjaer, MA, Social Impact, Inc., Arlington, Virginia

Paul Kosterink, MSc, Planning, Monitoring, Evaluation and Learning, Secretariat of the Global Partnership for the Prevention of Armed Conflict (GPPAC), The Hague, The Netherlands

Rebekah Krimmel, MPP, Office of Conflict Management and Mitigation, United States Agency for International Development (USAID), Washington, DC

Keiko Kuji-Shikatani, EdD, Research, Evaluation and Capacity Building Branch, Student Achievement Division, Ontario Ministry of Education, Toronto, Ontario, Canada

Cris Kutzli, BA, Grand Rapids Community Foundation, Grand Rapids, Michigan

Eric Leviten-Reid, MES, New Weave Community Consulting, Sydney, Nova Scotia, Canada

Katelyn Mack, ScM, FSG, Inc., San Francisco, California

Kate McKegg, MA, The Knowledge Institute and the Kinnect Group, Hamilton, New Zealand

Marah Moore, MCRP, i2i Institute, Taos, New Mexico

Nora F. Murphy, PhD, TerraLuna Collaborative, Minneapolis, Minnesota

Michael Quinn Patton, PhD, Utilization-Focused Evaluation, St. Paul, Minnesota

Kataraina Pipi, PG Dipl, Facilitation, Evaluation, Music (FEM), Auckland, New Zealand

Gabrielle Plotkin, MS, Social Impact, Inc., Arlington, Virginia

Nichola Potter, PostGradDip, Southern Queensland Centre of Excellence in Aboriginal and Torres Strait Islander Primary Health Care, Queensland Health, Brisbane, Queensland, Australia

James Radner, MPhil, School of Public Policy and Governance, University of Toronto, Toronto, Ontario, Canada; TruePoint Centre for Higher Ambition Leadership, Burlington, Massachusetts

Mabel Jean Rawlins, MSc, Community Social Planning Council of Greater Victoria, Victoria, British Columbia, Canada

Lynne Rogers, Dipl, Southern Queensland Centre of Excellence in Aboriginal and Torres Strait Islander Primary Health Care, Queensland Health, Brisbane, Queensland, Australia

Goele Scheers, MA, independent consultant, Ghent, Belgium

Kelly Skeith, MA, Social Impact, Inc., Arlington, Virginia

Veronica Thompson, BA, Sport and Recreation New Zealand, Wellington, New Zealand

Samantha Togni, MA, Indigenous Health Research, Baker IDI Heart & Diabetes Institute, and Menzies School of Health Research, Alice Springs, Northern Territory, Australia

Shawn Van Sluys, BFA, Musagetes, Guelph, Ontario, Canada

Dana Vocisano, BA, Human Systems Intervention, Concordia University, Montreal, Quebec, Canada

Tassy Warren, EdM, Center on the Developing Child, Harvard University, Cambridge, Massachusetts

Lisa Watson, PostGradDip, Strategies for Social Impact, Toronto, Ontario, Canada

Nan Wehipeihana, PostGradDip, Research Evaluation Consultancy and the Kinnect Group, Wellington, New Zealand

Ricardo Wilson-Grau, MA, Ricardo Wilson-Grau Consulting, Rio de Janeiro, Brazil